FAMILY LIFE IN
20TH-CENTURY AMERICA

FAMILY LIFE IN

20TH-CENTURY AMERICA

MARILYN COLEMAN, LAWRENCE H. GANONG, AND KELLY WARZINIK

Family Life through History

GREENWOOD PRESS
Westport, Connecticut • London

Library of Congress Cataloging-in-Publication Data

Coleman, Marilyn.
  Family life in 20th-century America / Marilyn Coleman, Lawrence H.
Ganong, and Kelly Warzinik.
      p. cm. — (Family life through history, ISSN 1558–6286)
  Includes index.
  ISBN–13: 978–0–313–33356–9 (alk. paper)
  ISBN–10: 0–313–33356–4 (alk. paper)
  1. Family—United States—History—20th century. I. Ganong, Lawrence H.
II. Warzinik, Kelly. III. Title. IV. Title: Family life in
twentieth-century America.
HQ536.C694   2007
306.850973'0904 — dc22   2007000546

British Library Cataloguing in Publication Data is available.

Library of Congress Catalog Card Number: 2007000546
ISBN–13: 978–0–313–33356–9
ISBN–10: 0–313–33356–4
ISSN: 1558–6286

First published in 2007

Greenwood Press, 88 Post Road West, Westport, CT 06881
An imprint of Greenwood Publishing Group, Inc.
www.greenwood.com

Printed in the United States of America

∞™

The paper used in this book complies with the
Permanent Paper Standard issued by the National
Information Standards Organization (Z39.48–1984).

10 9 8 7 6 5 4 3 2 1

Contents

Preface

The 100-year span from 1901 to 2000 was witness to massive changes in how families lived. At the start of the 20th century, the world was smaller for most individuals and their families. People worked near where they lived, they walked or rode horses to get around, and they did not travel far. Their social worlds formed a small network, mostly of family and friends. Unless they lived in a city, and most people did not, they probably knew nearly everyone they encountered in the course of a day, and they knew the family members of everyone they encountered. News of the "outside" world, if available, arrived via daily or weekly newspapers, and perhaps an occasional magazine. Most families at the beginning of the century ate two or three daily meals together, went to bed early, and rose early. What free time they had was likely to be spent together, at or near their home.

One hundred years later, the world had grown much wider for nearly all families. At the end of the 20th century, family members left their households for different destinations, sometimes traveling miles to work or school. People drove cars or took mass transit to get around because distances often were great. Most of the individuals they encountered in the course of a day were strangers. Social networks often were far-flung, not bound by geography, and not all daily contact with family and friends was face to face. News came from multiple sources—television, radio, newspapers, magazines, the Internet, and more. Families ate one meal together, if that, and they spent less free time together than families had a few generations earlier.

Technological advances and new inventions in the 20th century altered how U.S. families lived in profound ways. For instance, the widespread availability of electricity for household use enabled women to use appliances that lightened their workloads but also increased standards for cleanliness and order. The invention of the automobile dramatically changed courtship and contributed to the burgeoning of the suburbs. Air travel enabled family members to live hundreds, if not thousands, of miles apart yet still see each other on a regular basis. Many of the major inventions of the 20th century brought about sometimes sudden and sometimes massive transformations in how families lived. Looking back, the 20th century was an amazing period of innovation and change.

THE AMERICAN CENTURY

The 20th century was a remarkable period. The United States in the 20th century was witness to two world wars and countless smaller ones, a severe economic depression, and a population growth of 358 percent. Life spans increased dramatically, family sizes shrunk, increased, and then shrunk again. Divorce surpassed death as the way most marriages ended, and the proportion of family households headed by married couples diminished as other types of households rose in number—single person, cohabiting couples, same-sex couples, stepparent households. Over the century, more children had grandparents alive throughout their entire childhoods, and more children had stepgrandparents than ever before. More children also were being raised by grandparents.

During the 20th century, most children went from being income producers to being household costs, while wives and mothers went from generally not being employed outside of the home to generally being employed in the work force, even when they had young children. Even so, women's participation in the paid labor force continued to be organized around family considerations, with men's involvement in the world of work taking precedence. Nonetheless, many fathers went from being the primary or often sole breadwinners for their families to being co-breadwinners. Families generally became more affluent over the course of the century, and then earnings leveled off.

A higher proportion of children attended school over the course of the century, and for more years. Suburbs grew, small towns and farmers diminished, and cities gradually lost population as families moved away, leaving behind the impoverished. Commutes to work grew longer. Houses became smaller, and then bigger, and more houses were empty during the day as adults left for work and children attended school. Kitchens grew larger even as more meals were eaten away from home. Most family members got chubbier.

Families became more dependent on technology to meet their daily needs. Leisure time became less interactive with other family members;

board games were replaced by radio and television, which were replaced by computers and handheld devices. Middle-class families gained and lost leisure time because of labor-saving household appliances. Families spent less time together as the century progressed.

Despite the changes in daily living, Americans at both ends of the 20th century valued their families a great deal. Family life had changed significantly, but there were also constants—families were at the center of many Americans' daily lives. Even though immigrants were assimilated into the culture over the century, new immigrants continued to be viewed with fear and distrust. Class systems remained in place, and working-class and poor families had a more difficult time maintaining stability than did middle-class families. And even though the poor were probably better off at the end of the century than they were at the beginning, the gap between the living standards of the poor and the middle class was large. Gender roles were contentious throughout the century. Separate spheres remained despite much rhetoric to the contrary. Men were still expected to be the breadwinners, although greater responsibility for parenting was placed on them late in the century. Women were expected to continue their domestic responsibilities, but increasing expectations for second wage earners necessitated a "second shift" for many—they worked part- or full-time in the labor market while maintaining most responsibilities for running the household and taking care of the children. Finally, Americans remained concerned about the youth culture throughout the century. Moving from a highly supervised and structured adolescent upbringing and courtship system to one of rock and roll, high sexual involvement, drug use, and consumerism was a painful transition for many families, and yet most adolescents still became responsible adults.

We can document the changes and the constants in families in the 20th century easily enough, but interpreting what they mean is more challenging. Some social observers declared the family to be in a state of emergency and decline decades ago, while others declared, equally strongly, that families were never more vibrant. What both sides of these culture wars agree on is that families have been changing and continue to change. The pace of change in the 20th century was breathtaking at times, and individuals and families sometimes could not keep pace. Some felt threatened by the pace of change, and still do, while others embraced the changes as good for them and their loved ones.

THINKING HISTORICALLY

Americans sometimes tend to forget history and deny its importance in helping us understand current issues and problems. Instead, Americans like to look ahead and tend to project the present into the future, assuming that changes in how families have lived occur gradually and steadily over time and that such slowly evolving alterations will continue indefinitely into the future. But, as this book explains, family changes have not always been steady or predictable.

Many Americans, when looking back, compare current families to one particular historical period, as if that benchmark period was all of family history. When it comes to family life, the tendency of many critics of modern culture has been to use the time period from 1946 to 1964 (generally referred to as "the 1950s") as the comparison point from which to examine families of earlier and later decades. The problem in doing this is that this benchmark was in many ways an atypical time during the century.

This book attempts to present a balanced view of each of the major periods of the 20th century. We assess how families lived and related in each era, and we examine how families were affected by living in a particular sociohistorical context. We do not select a benchmark or standard period by which to compare all others, and we try not to project our own beliefs about how families should have been in our presentation of how they were.

This book looks at what transpired to families and within families over the course of the last century. In addition to describing how families lived, we also examine how the culture as a whole thought about how families *should* live. For some topics, we know more about the *shoulds* than we do about actual behaviors. The 20th century may have been the "century of the child," but it was also the "century of the expert," and there was no shortage of experts willing to advise mothers and fathers on how they should rear their children. Other experts and cultural pundits expounded on marriage, women's and men's appropriate work and family roles, and much more. Cultural beliefs affect families and individuals in families, and we describe these effects.

This book describes dimensions of the cultural and historical context in which families lived and also focuses on the major trends in American family experiences. We include the diversity of U.S. families when possible, but sometimes we fall short in this goal because much historical documentation is limited to white, middle-class families.

We start with an overview of family transitions in the century, emphasizing in chapter 1 broader social trends in courtship, marriage, childbearing, divorce, remarriage, cohabitation, and bereavement. We take a closer look at how families lived in chapter 2, focusing on housing, household duties, and leisure activities. One of the major stories in the history of 20th-century families was the change in work settings and the relation of paid labor to household labor, so chapter 3 focuses specifically on work and family issues. Before moving on to chapters about mothers (chapter 5), fathers (chapter 6), and childhood (chapter 7), in chapter 4 we examine a wide range of family rituals and celebrations and how they have changed over time. Following the three related chapters on the significant roles of parents and children, we describe family abuse and neglect and society's sporadic efforts to help family members who experienced the dark side of family life. Finally, we present a range of family variations to conventional, two-parent, nuclear families that became more visible in the 20th century.

The book attempts to capture the major trends affecting families, a task easier to state than to accomplish. We continued to think of important trends to include in this book right up to our deadline, and no doubt we have left out a family issue or phenomenon close to the hearts of some readers. We do think we have captured the heart of American family life in the 20th century, a heart that keeps beating into the 21st.

Acknowledgments

We needed the help of many people to write this book. Historian Steven Mintz was gracious and helpful whenever we asked him for guidance, and Greenwood editor Sarah Colwell was informative and collegial in our interactions with her. Several people allowed us to use family photographs when our extensive searches did not yield the images we wanted. We appreciate the generosity of these people in sharing their precious photos. We also want to thank Greenwood Press for giving us this opportunity. Finally, we are indebted to Jason Warzinik for lending us his computer skills to find pictures from the past and to Zoe Warzinik for sharing her mom.

Timeline of Major Events that Affected Families in the 20th Century

1870 through the 1920s	Progressive Era
1900	Average life expectancy was about 48 years for men and 51 years for women
1901	Vacuum cleaners invented; household models available in 1905
1903	Airplane invented
1908	Woodrow Wilson designated the second Sunday in May as Mother's Day
1909	First White House Conference on Child Welfare called by President Theodore Roosevelt
	NAACP founded by W.E.B. Du Bois
1912	Children's Bureau created
1914	Smith Lever Act enacted, establishing cooperative extension programs at land grant universities nationwide
1915	Alexander Graham Bell made first transcontinental telephone call from New York to San Francisco
1917–1919	United States in World War I
1916	Margaret Sanger opened first birth control clinic
	First zoning laws introduced in New York City

1920	19th Amendment adopted, guaranteeing women the right to vote
	First commercial radio broadcasts
1921	Margaret Sanger founded American Birth Control League
1927	Philo T. Farnsworth became first inventor to successfully transmit a television image; awarded a patent in 1930
1928	Alexander Fleming discovered penicillin; mass produced in 1943
1929	Frozen foods introduced by Clarence Birdseye
	Stock market crashed on October 29, leading to the Great Depression (1929–1939)
	Computer invented
1933	President Franklin D. Roosevelt launched the New Deal (programs designed to create jobs, provide relief, and stimulate the economy)
	Boeing introduced first commercial airliner
1935	Social Security Act passed, providing unemployment insurance, welfare grants, and a retirement fund
1936	Congress established Rural Electrification Administration
1941	First commercial television broadcast
1941–1945	United States in World War II
1945	Atomic bomb was dropped on Hiroshima, Japan, by the United States Air Force
1942	American Birth Control League became Planned Parenthood
1946	Dr. Spock's *The Common Sense Book of Baby and Child Care* published
1946–1964	Baby boom
1949	Congress passed Urban Renewal Act
	Opening of Levittown
1950	Credit cards invented
1950–1953	United States in Korean War
1951	Electrolux introduced washing machine
1954	*Brown v. Topeka Board of Education* case, banning racial segregation in public schools
	"Rock Around the Clock" became first rock and roll song
	Ray Kroc opened first McDonald's restaurant

1955	Jonas Salk produced polio vaccine
1956	President Dwight D. Eisenhower signed Interstate Highway Act
1960	Food and Drug Administration approved the birth control pill
1962	C. Henry Kempe and colleagues published *The Battered-Child Syndrome*
1963	Assassination of President John F. Kennedy
1964	Congress passed Civil Rights Act prohibiting discrimination based on race, sex, national origin, and religion
1965	Older Americans Act became law, establishing the Administration on Aging
	Medicare and Medicaid amendments were added to the Social Security Act as part of Johnson's Great Society
	Housing and Urban Development Act expanded public housing
	Project Head Start introduced as eight-week summer program by Office of Economic Opportunity
1965–1975	United States in the Vietnam War
1966	National Organization for Women founded
	President Lyndon B. Johnson declared Father's Day to be the third Sunday in June
	Kwanzaa invented by Dr. Maulana Karenga
1967	Microwave ovens introduced for household use
1968	Martin Luther King, Jr. and Robert Kennedy assassinated
1969	Neil Armstrong first person to walk on the moon
	California first state to adopt a no-fault divorce law
	Automated teller machine invented
1971	U.S. Supreme Court recognized custodial rights of unmarried fathers
	Videocassette recorder invented
1972	Congress passed Title IX legislation, Equal Employment Opportunity Act
1973	Supreme Court case *Roe v. Wade* legalized abortion
	Child Abuse Prevention and Treatment Act—first federal investigation of child maltreatment
1974	Divorce passed death as most common ending for marriage

1975	Congress established Office of Child Support Enforcement
1977	Personal computers widely available
1980	First divorced president elected (Ronald Reagan)
	Elizabeth Kane (pseud.) became the first U.S. surrogate mother
1981	IBM released first personal computer
	Doctors diagnosed first AIDS cases
1990	Americans with Disabilities Act extended protection from discrimination in employment and public accommodations to persons with disabilities
1991	World Wide Web became publicly available
1993	Congress passed the Family and Medical Leave Act
1994	President William Clinton signed the Violence Against Women Act into law
1995	Million Man March took place in Washington, DC
1996	Welfare reform—the Personal Responsibility and Work Opportunity Reconciliation Act implemented, limiting amount of time a person qualified for Aid to Families with Dependent Children
2000	Average life expectancy was about 74 years for men and 80 years for women

1

Courtship, Cohabitation, Marriage, Divorce, Remarriage, and Bereavement: Family Transitions in the 20th Century

Remarkable changes and happenings occur over the space of 100 years. Electricity, the automobile, the airplane, television, and personal computers are just a few of the 20th-century inventions that dramatically changed how Americans lived. Americans also experienced two world wars, economic booms, and a devastating economic depression before the century was half over. Changes also occurred on a more personal level—especially changes in families. This chapter describes the many transitions experienced by American families in the 20th century—courtship, cohabitation, marriage, divorce, remarriage, and stepfamily formation. This is not an exhaustive list, but these are the major transitions that changed how families were structured and how family life was perceived and experienced. Other types of family transitions are discussed in other chapters.

People commonly think about family relationships as specific social statuses held by individuals. For instance, you might describe a person you know as someone who is engaged, married, divorced, or single, or you might think of them as being a parent or childless. These terms suggest that such labels have shared meanings. If you tell your friend that someone is divorced or has a baby, you are conveying some important information about that person's life. These shared meanings about family statuses are useful because they are an easy and time-saving way to convey information about an individual or family. On the downside, thinking of family relationships in this overgeneralized way leads to viewing them as fixed and unchanging, while in reality families are ever-changing systems.

Family transitions are long-term *processes* that result in substantial changes in how individual family members think and feel about their families and significant modifications in how family members interact with each other. Family transitions are often thought of as events (e.g., getting married, having a baby), but they are really often the result of a series of choices that individuals make, either alone or with other people; and the experiences they have because of those choices result in changes in families and family members. Some transitions involve changes in family membership and household organization, and some consist of modifications in how individuals think about themselves as family members and/or how they regard their families. Family transitions may occur abruptly, or they may evolve so slowly and subtly that individuals are hard pressed to know they are experiencing a transition in their families.

American families changed substantially during the 20th century. Many of these changes resulted in more variability in patterns of family formation and modifications in how families were perceived by most Americans. Throughout the century, Americans married, had children, and ended their marriages, but the dynamic processes by which they formed and maintained their marriages, reared children, and transitioned into and out of family relationships was anything but constant.

Two family transitions that *increased* in frequency over the century were divorce and cohabitation. The 20th century saw a gradual, but steady, growth in the divorce rate until it leveled in the late 1980s. In the latter decades, there was a dramatic increase in the incidence of single adults living with members of the other sex (cohabitation). In addition, there were marked changes in the normative (expected) *sequence* or order of transitions and the *expected timing* of those transitions in an individual's life course. In any given historical time period and cultural context, people experience family transitions as either *on time*, in that the transitions take place when they are socially expected to take place, or *off time*, meaning that the transitions occur either sooner or later than expected, or they don't happen at all. People generally are aware of these timetables for family transitions such as marriage, parenthood, and widowhood, and when they are experienced *off time*, the transition is more stressful than it would have been otherwise. Over the 20th century, transitions increasingly occurred either out of normative sequence (e.g., parenthood before marriage) or too early or too late (e.g., motherhood in either early adolescence or late middle age) or not at all (e.g., married couples without children, single parents who never marry). Finally, because the life span of Americans increased at a steady rate over the century, so too did the number of family-related transitions encountered by individuals during their life times. As a result, more individuals and families faced multiple marital transitions (e.g., divorce, remarriage, redivorce, second remarriage) as the 20th century progressed. From the beginning of the century to the end, conservative social commentators voiced concern that the health and stability of the American family was in jeopardy, a situation which they thought threatened the very fabric of society.

COURTSHIP

The process of finding a mate has changed dramatically over the centuries. Marriage in the Middle Ages represented a contract between families; in wealthy families, the marriage contract was designed to expand land ownership and power. Courtship as we know it today was not a part of the process. Marriage contracts often were arranged when both members of the couple were infants. For poor people, marriage was more about survival than land and wealth acquisition, and courting a mate was brief and unromantic by contemporary standards. Much later, a process of letting couples get to know each other—labeled courtship by sociologists—emerged as a way to arrange marital matches.

In 1900, courtship among young adults—at least among wealthy and upper-middle-class Americans—was formal and supervised and consisted of activities such as making candy, playing the piano, and singing in the parlor of the home of the young woman being courted. The young women and their mothers were in charge of courtship in that they had the power to accept or decline offers by young men to make a social call and visit them in their home. The highly ritualized courting process began with a girl's mother suggesting to a few respectable (or at least suitable) young men that they call on her daughter. Young men who were not considered suitable yet tried to call would be told that the daughter was not at home or that she was otherwise engaged and could not receive them. These young men soon got the message that they were not suitable and should try their luck with someone else. As the daughter grew older, she was given more freedom in choosing who she wished to have call on her, but she by no means had free rein to choose her mate. The men that she encouraged to call had to have been previously properly introduced at some sort of carefully chaperoned social affair.

The social call itself was governed by very strict rules regarding how much time should elapse from meeting a suitable man to extending an invitation for him to call; what refreshments, if any, should be served; how long the visit should last; what were suitable topics of conversation; and how the young man should exit the home (it was not permissible for the young woman to accompany the caller to the door, for example). The entire process was governed by these various rituals, and upper-class men and women did not stray from them (Bailey, 1989).

Early in the 20th century, however, courtship began to move out of the home. In a story from *The American Husband and Other Alternatives*, a 1925 collection of magazine articles, a young man asked a young woman if he could pay her a call. He had in mind an evening in her home as was typical of courtship of that era, but realized that he had made an error when he arrived and she came to the door with her hat on—a signal that she expected to be taken out (cited in Bailey, 1989, and Rothman, 1984). This was a marked change in courtship, and, by 1920, going out had become the favorite activity of middle-class young people. This change in courtship rituals meant that the men were now in charge. Young women became dependent on young men to ask them out as opposed to men being dependent on young women allowing them to call. In a sense, however, the men had been in charge of the courtship process all along. Courtship and dating were based on the premise that men were going to be the breadwinners or providers. Young women could never have afforded to engage in courtship with men who could not support them; marital choices for women were highly dependent on men's financial prospects. Courting at the turn of the century, therefore, was very much about young women finding suitable husbands. That became somewhat less true as the century progressed, but it was a factor throughout the entire era.

It was from the working class that the concept of dating evolved. Working-class women did not have pianos or parlors available for receiving calls, so their courtship practices were much less ritualized than those of upper- and middle-class women. Working-class women often lived in boarding houses and could sometimes use the front room of the boarding house for courting a few evenings a week, but many did their courting on the streets. They frequently went to movies or to dance halls and met men there. Middle- and upper-class youth—especially those with a rebellious, adventurous streak—came to see the possibilities of this anonymous and unsupervised public courtship and began to gravitate toward it. As young women went to college and took jobs in the public arena by day, they began to seek courtship in the public arena by night. By the 1930s, public dating had become a universal custom of all social classes.

It was at some point between 1900 and 1910 that the word *date* began to be used in the context of courtship. In 1914, the popular magazine, *Ladies' Home Journal,* used the term several times, enclosing it in quotation marks and not defining its meaning, although it was reported that the term emerged from lower-class slang. The term *date* was originally associated with exchanging money for sex. Some social observers would wryly say that this exchange model of dating existed to an extent throughout the century. Men were expected to pay for dates, and what they were buying was female companionship, entertainment, and power. According to Bailey (1989), money spent on dates purchased obligation, inequality, and control of women. Although few would argue that this exchange constituted prostitution, dating certainly created an imbalance of resources and rewards.

During the first decade of the century, the ubiquitous *Ladies' Home Journal,* the arbitrator of social mores, advised young girls to not go out with or date young men until they had called at her home. Thus, the switch from calling to dating was somewhat gradual. But within a decade or two, dating had replaced calling as a universal custom. Although many attributed the rise of dating to the invention of the automobile, the process had long been underway. The freedom presented by the car greatly advanced the courtship process, however—especially in rural areas—and it increased the privacy of dating for all social classes. Dating thus quickly became a major part of the courtship process.

As courtship moved to public locations such as movie theaters, restaurants, and dance halls, the rituals associated with it increasingly became the focus of the newly emerging media "experts" and were no longer based on the norms determined by the girl's parents and her family's social network. Advice literature (such as magazines and self-help books) burgeoned in the early decades of the century, and young people began to establish their own courtship norms with the help of these national media sources. The growing peer culture of adolescents and young adults also had increasing influence on the courtship process.

By the 1920s, the new dating system that was regulated by the young people themselves had completely replaced calling, and dating and so-called petting (i.e., kissing and hugging, sexual touching above the waist with clothes on) were two rituals that would define the experience of courtship for the next half century. The dating that evolved in the 1920s, however, was not considered true courtship because the purpose was not necessarily to find a marriage partner. Sociologist Willard Waller concluded that dating on campus during the 1930s was a sort of rating system that rewarded thrill-seeking and exploitive behavior (of which he did not approve). He believed the goal of dating was prestige rather than mate selection, with personal popularity being the point. Men were rated according to the fraternity they belonged to, the car they drove, the clothes they wore, the money they spent on dates, their dancing ability, and their social skills. For women, it was important to have attractive clothes, to dance well, and to be popular. Of course, in the 1930s, less than 15 percent of young adults went to college, and, for those who didn't, "going together" was still the norm. Dating provided security to young people who wanted to have someone with whom to do things.

Just as public dating liberalized courtship, dating also liberalized sexual behaviors, although it remained the woman's role throughout most of the century to enforce the rules of sexual behavior. It was up to the woman to keep sexual behavior in check, and during the early decades of the 20th century, women were viewed by social observers as somewhat sexless, even though sexual fulfillment was seen as an important component to marital happiness. As sexual fulfillment became increasingly important to marriage, it also became more important to courtship. Opportunities for the middle class to experiment sexually increased with the advent of the automobile, movie theaters, and co-ed colleges. It was concluded from a

Dating at the dance hall, 1938. (Courtesy of the Library of Congress.)

study of adolescent girls at the end of World War I that the greatest influence of the war was in the field of sexual relationships (Rothman, 1984).
The war broke the conventionalities and outer restraints of women's
behavior; but, although sexual experimenting such as petting became
more common, "good girls" did not engage in intercourse.

One reaction to the increasingly youth-oriented courtship process,
conducted away from the prying eyes of parents and other older adults,
was the start of the scientific study of courtship and marriage during
the mid-1920s. The first marriage education course, offered in 1927 at
the University of North Carolina, was developed and taught by Ernest
Groves, a sociologist who helped found the *National Council on Family
Relations* and the *Groves Conference on Family,* named in his honor. Groves's
idea to educate young people about dating and mating rapidly caught
on, and 10 years later, 200 universities offered similar courses. By mid-
century, over 1,000 universities offered marriage courses, and, by the end
of the century, over 260 degree programs in family studies (bachelor's,
master's, and doctoral levels) existed in North America, most offering
multiple courses related to family issues, including courtship.

By the end of World War II, "going steady" was a common form of
dating, and sexual intercourse was more permissible when couples were

going steady. Changes in dating and sexual behavior took place as veterans flocked to college campuses after serving in the armed forces in World War II. Men returning from the battlefields were not interested in the competitive "games" that had previously accompanied dating. Gaining popularity by dating as many different men or women as possible was no longer in style. The war had made people feel insecure, and having a steady partner was seen as a means of establishing security. Courtship was taken much more seriously, the average age of marriage dropped to an all-time low, and couples started thinking about marriage after only a few dates.

Many courtship experts promoted early marriage following World War II because of societal concerns about upholding sexual mores. Early marriage allowed young couples to engage in sexual behaviors without the fear or stigma of unplanned pregnancy, thus upholding at least the appearance of maintaining sexual mores. It became the convention for teenagers to marry because other teenagers were marrying—teenage marriage led to more teenage marriage.

In many ways, dating may have peaked in the 1950s. Popular media were filled with advice to boys and girls about how to attract dating partners, and dating experts had plenty of advice about the etiquette of dating, particularly regarding sexual activities. Courtship experts thought that young people should marry young, but they also thought that it was necessary for couples to have experienced several relationships before choosing a marital partner. As a result, dating began at earlier and earlier ages after World War II. Going steady became a high school dating ritual, often accompanied by girls wearing their steady boyfriend's class ring or letter jacket or by exchanging inexpensive friendship rings. Going steady also allowed for greater sexual intimacy than was true of previous dating strategies, and even though most steady couples were monogamous, they usually did not intend to remain committed to their steadies forever. Couples who had sex had an understanding that if the girl got pregnant, they would get married. Although it would be difficult to determine how many weddings of the era were due to pregnancy, it was not a minor contributor to the incidences of early marriage in the years following World War II.

At the turn of the century, colleges and universities had strict rules about when male students could call upon female students in the dorms, and it was usually limited to certain times on weekends. These rather simple rules evolved into far more complex ones, and, by the 1950s, student handbooks were filled with information about curfews, lateness penalties, and other restrictions about male-female romantic relationships. Colleges were considered *parentis in loco,* and the behavior of students was carefully monitored by faculty and administrators. Rules also emerged on some campuses and in some communities about where couples could park to make out and talk, and local or campus police were responsible for patrolling the approved areas. The car was used as a source of privacy for courtship, and, although the rules regarding parking did not control the sexual behavior of the parked couples, they did regulate the times, places, and circumstances of this behavior by making it more difficult for couples to have access to complete privacy.

Dating and going steady with one person as practiced during the 1950s changed somewhat during the 1960s and the 1970s. Several events affected dating, courtship, and (eventually) early marriage during this period. First, Betty Friedan (1963), in an influential and widely read book, *The Feminine Mystique,* described marriage and childrearing in terms of the oppression and exploitation of women—a message that resonated with women who felt trapped and bored as suburban housewives and with younger women who saw their futures as being more restrictive than they would like. As women joined Friedan in protesting what they saw as power and privilege imbalances in conventional marriage (and all male-female relationships, for that matter), the age of marriage began to creep upward again as more young women listened to these feminist voices.

A second factor that changed dating and courtship was the widespread availability of the birth control pill beginning in the mid-1960s. Without the fear of unintended pregnancy, young couples were more likely to engage in premarital sex while going steady, and they also were less likely to have to marry because of unplanned pregnancy. In 1958, 10 percent of college co-eds had had sexual intercourse while dating, 15 percent while going steady, and 31 percent while engaged (Bell & Chaskes, 1970). Young women were in charge of setting the standards of sexual permissiveness, and most still did not admit to engaging in intercourse, although this changed somewhat in the 1960s. In 1968, 23 percent of women had sex during dating, 28 percent while going steady, and 39 percent while engaged. By 1979, 50 percent of urban teenagers had experienced premarital sex, and in 1982, 80 percent of male and 65 percent of female college students said that they had experienced premarital intercourse (Robinson & Jedlicka, 1982). Less is known about the sexual experiences of young people who did not go to college, but they were probably comparable.

Gradually, dating became less popular, and adolescents and young adults tended to socialize in groups rather than pair off on formal dates. When couples did go out, they did not necessarily have a specific date agenda, and men no longer always paid for dating activities. Adolescents in the 1970s dated less often than adolescents in the 1950s, and they also began dating at slightly older ages. Another dating practice that changed during the final decades of the century was a slight increase in girls asking boys on dates. It was still typically the boy, however, who initiated dates and made the first sexual advances.

In the 1970s and 1980s, as dating became more casual and less clearly tied to choosing a marital partner, new ideas entered the courtship process. Personal ads in newspapers surfaced as a way to meet people and establish relationships. Most of these ads consisted of a description of the person who had placed the ad, an indication of what sort of relationship was sought, and a description of the ideal respondent. For instance, a personal ad might read, "SWM [single white male], 6', 180, brown hair, blue eyes, 35, seeks a petite nonsmoker (25–35) who likes children, camping, and action movies. I am looking for someone to have fun with for now, but am open to an LTR [long-term relationship]." Women were more likely than men to be explicit in seeking financial security, sincerity, and an older partner. Men were more likely to be seeking attractiveness, marriage, and a younger partner while offering financial security in exchange. Divorced or never-married parents of young children submitted some of these ads, perhaps as a way to meet new people without going to bars, clubs, or other places where singles gathered. Gay, lesbian, and bisexual individuals also placed personal ads in newspapers and magazines for many of the same reasons that straight people did—convenience, discretion, and some control over the process.

Personal ads faded in popularity and were mostly replaced by online dating and chat rooms in the 1990s. Several online match services were launched, and one of them—Match.com, a publicly held operating business begun in 1995—quickly grew to more than 15 million members with profiles posted. Online dating had become so popular by the end of the century that online dating etiquette rules emerged. Virginia Shea earned the nickname Ms. Manners of the Internet with her 1994 book, *Netiquette*. Online etiquette was fairly straightforward for the most part—refrain from offensive language, refuse to defame any group of people, do not post sexually explicit material without permission, and do not type in capital letters.

Speed dating, also a product of the 1990s, was born in a Torah class in Los Angeles. Rabbi Yaacov Dego launched speed dating to help Jewish singles meet appropriate marital partners. As a sort of minidate musical chairs, speed dating rapidly spread in popularity. Speed dating essentially involved:

1. equal numbers of single men and women
2. seated couples, usually at tables
3. each couple talking for a certain number of minutes (a signal would sound when it was time to move to the next table, or "date")
4. each person marking a plus or minus for each "date" (a plus indicated a match)
5. the host providing contact information for matches

Speed dating was the antithesis of Internet dating in that a five-minute conversation allowed for little more than determining sexual attraction.

Another version of matchmaking at the end of the century included singles nights at supermarkets, arranged by stores to allow singles to meet while they shopped. Book stores in larger cities also sponsored singles nights.

Dating and Consumption   The consumption of goods and services played a major role in dating during the 20th century, just as it does in all of family life. When courtship went public, it meant that women had to be taken somewhere, and movies, dancing, and dinner cost men money. Women also spent a great deal of money on cosmetics, hairstyles, and clothing to look good and therefore enhance the possibility of future dates. The ultimate date in terms of consumption became the high school prom. By the end of the century, some couples were spending hundreds of dollars on prom. Among expenses for girls were designer dresses, jewelry, hairstyling, and manicures and pedicures. Boys spent vast sums on limousine rentals, tuxedos, flowers, and hotel rooms for after-prom parties. With this much consumption associated with a single event like a high school prom, it is not surprising that weddings became increasingly extravagant in the last decades of the 20th century—with some costing several thousand dollars. According to a 2000 *Brides* magazine survey, the average cost of a wedding that year was $19,000. The expenses of courtship rose to new heights as couples planned engagement and wedding activities.

Courtship at the End of the Century   For a variety of reasons, courtship and dating had become less formalized as a method to find a spouse. "Hooking up" (sexual involvement without commitment) became a common practice in the final decade of the century. Rather than courting or dating, young people would go to bars and clubs, meet someone, and leave with them to engage in sex with no strings attached. Courtship during the college years was far less popular than at any time during the century, and young people were postponing marriage to later and later ages.

Andrew Cherlin, a sociologist and demographer at Johns Hopkins University, was quoted in *USA Today* (see Peterson, 2000), as saying, "There is no courtship today" (p. 9D). Cherlin asserted that young Americans had lost the ability to slow down the process of becoming sexually intimate with someone and choosing a partner. In addition, because the mate selection process had become so private and individualized, Cherlin argued that young adults also had lost the assistance of parents and community members in helping them choose appropriate spouses. Other social observers were more positive about the new forms of courtship. For example, Bailey (1989) observed the similarity between online dating at the end of the century and the extensive letter writing of 19th-century courtship–both ways for potential couples to become better acquainted. Proponents of online relationships argued that getting well acquainted with someone via the Internet before meeting was a more logical way to make connections than more traditional ways of meeting people, such as dating, where sexual attraction complicates the process of getting acquainted.

Bridesmaids and bride, late 1960s Pennsylvania wedding. (Courtesy of Susan Troilo.)

Clearly, by the end of the century, dating and courtship had changed dramatically. Cherlin had proclaimed that there was no courtship, others thought that it had transformed in significant ways. Great concern about the future of marriage was voiced by conservative elements in society throughout the century. Without courtship, how could there be marriage? Yet, despite the changes in dating and courtship rituals, the forestalling of getting seriously involved at young ages, and the older average age of first marriages, most people in the United States, unlike those in many other industrialized countries, planned to marry at some point in their lives.

COHABITATION

One of the most significant demographic trends in the 20th century was the rise in the rate of cohabitation during the final three decades. Cohabiting, defined as a man and a woman living together as a couple without being married, had occurred before the 20th century. In earlier times, American slaves cohabited because slave owners did not allow them to marry, and the men and women who originally settled the American

West often lived together until a traveling preacher would reach the wilderness or prairie to officially marry them. However, such circumstances were typically exceptions rather than the rule, and, when the 20th century opened, cohabiting was considered by most Americans to be an immoral and unsavory practice—often referred to as "living in sin"—that was not to be engaged in by respectable people.

Although a few progressive scholars in the 1920s recommended that couples live together as a sort of trial marriage, for most of the century, young couples did not consider living with someone of the other sex without being married because of the social stigma of such an arrangement. This stigma was reflected in laws and social policy that restricted or banned heterosexual cohabitation. For example, cohabiting was grounds for being expelled from college until the early 1970s, and many cities and municipalities had ordinances banning unmarried couples from legally sharing a residence until the mid-1980s (and even later in some cities and states). Cohabiting started to become "legal" in the early 1970s, when statutory restraints such as not allowing unmarried couples to check into hotel rooms together began to be removed and common restrictions, such as landlords refusing to rent apartments and houses to unmarried couples, were no longer enforced as rigorously as they had been before.

The changes in legal and social policy and the gradual diminishment of social disapproval and stigma against cohabitation coincided with huge growth in the incidence of cohabitation. The number of cohabiting couples increased gradually during the 1960s and tripled in the decades after. In 1970, less than 1 percent of all households consisted of cohabiting couples; by 2000, almost 4 percent of all households were classified by the U.S. Census Bureau as unmarried couple households, but this is believed to be an underestimate. Some householders may have been unwilling to identify having live-in partners (despite being widespread, cohabiting was still a stigmatized status among some people for religious or moral reasons). Although cohabitation remained a small proportion of all households in the United States, the status of living together increased over 300 percent in the last decade of the 20th century alone. Younger adults were more accepting of cohabitation as a life-style and more willing to cohabit than older adults, but some older couples cohabited rather than remarried, especially when remarrying would have interfered with financial arrangements such as pensions and social security payments. In 2000, 25 percent of women and 16 percent of men under age 25 and 4 percent of adults older than 65 were cohabiting.

Cohabitation rates for blacks and whites escalated throughout the latter half of the century in sync with the falling rates of marriage. Growth in the numbers of cohabiting couples occurred among all strata of U.S. society, although the increases were greatest among individuals with a high school diploma or less education and among non–Latin American whites.

The reasons why couples lived together were diverse. For some there were economic reasons—two together **Why Couples** could live cheaper than two living apart, paying two **Cohabited** rents or mortgages and two sets of utility bills. For others, cohabiting became a step in the courtship process, and for still others, it was an alternative to marriage.

Financial motivations. Some cohabiters in the 20th century were individuals who were motivated financially to live together. Poor people who were socially marginalized from mainstream society because of their poverty or for other reasons were not subject to the social pressure to marry. Some of these couples did not perceive themselves as being able to afford to marry, and because they perceived little or no stigma about living together, there were fewer barriers to their cohabiting. Late in the century, when middle-class couples were openly cohabiting, those of the working class were still more likely to live together, although money was not the only motivation to do so.

Cohabitation as a prelude to marriage. In 1970, about 60 percent of cohabiting couples who were 25 or older eventually married. Although that figure had dropped to 35 percent by the early 1990s, cohabiting was still a significant stage of the mate selection process for many American couples. In fact, most couples cohabiting in the United States eventually planned to marry. In the 1980s, most cohabiting relationships either ended or the couple married within two years.

Changes in dating—the increased sexual activity made possible by the birth control pill and relaxed norms about sexuality, women exerting more control in the courting process, alterations in expectations for marriage— helped to make cohabiting part of the mate selection/courtship process. In the context of reduced social mores against premarital sex and greater freedom for women (and men, but the larger changes in cultural beliefs were about women) to express their sexuality without shame, cohabiting was seen by many as a step that couples took when the relationship was becoming more serious, but they were not yet ready for marriage.

Concerns in society about the growing rate of divorce made many young couples vigilant about making sure they chose the right person— one to whom they would stay married for the rest of their lives. Divorced adults, perhaps even more so than never-married individuals, were concerned about repeating mistakes that may have led to the demise of their marriages. Living together thus became a common way to determine whether a couple was compatible.

It was estimated at the end of the century that roughly 90 percent of Americans would marry at least once. This suggests that cohabitation was seen by most individuals as a step in the courtship process rather than as an alternative arrangement to marriage. That is, for some partnerships, especially among young couples, moving in together was seen as a way to continue advancing the relationship forward, with marriage either as a goal or a definite possibility. For some couples, living together became a means of evaluating compatibility with an eye toward a future long-term commitment, including marriage. By the end of the 20th century, about half of women ages 30 to 34 had cohabited before marriage. Over half of remarrying adults with children also lived together before they remarried. From supervised courtship calls in the parlor to sharing a home, cohabiting as a stage in courtship completed the changes in mate selection in the 20th century.

Cohabitation as an alternative to marriage. Early in the 20th century, cohabiting couples who lived together for a number of years and presented themselves as a married couple were considered to have a common law marriage, at least in slightly more than half of the states. These common law marriages were legal, with all the rights and responsibilities applied to married couples in those states. Common law marriages could only be ended by a legal divorce (there was no common law divorce process that differed from regular divorces). Gradually, most states did away with common law marriages, and, by the end of the century, only a dozen states recognized them. From 1960 on, most cohabiting individuals were not living together as a way to create a common law marriage; instead, they were choosing to live together without the legal complications of marriage.

Cohabitation as an alternative to marriage was particularly prevalent among formerly divorced people and individuals who were wary of long-term commitments. In addition, for some ethnic groups, cohabitation had become an acceptable alternative to marriage. For example, among Latin Americans, Puerto Ricans were far more likely to cohabit than to marry. A study of Puerto Rican women conducted near the end of the century found that, for nearly half of Puerto Rican women under the age of 29, their first union was cohabitation rather than marriage, and only about 12 percent of those cohabiting unions resulted in marriage. In fact, nearly 75 percent of Puerto Rican women who lived with a man considered cohabitation to be a form of marriage. In general, by the end of the 20th century, a growing number of individuals of all races and ethnicities viewed cohabitation as a marriage alternative. In a seemingly contradictory phenomenon, although they were more likely to cohabit than white Americans, blacks were more disapproving of cohabitation.

At the end of the century, as many as one-third of cohabiting couples had minor children sharing their households. Some of these were de facto stepfamily households; that is, they were comprised of a man and a woman and one or more children from prior unions of the adults. At least one of the adults was a parent to a child or children in the household and one was not, a de facto stepparent. Most cohabiting couples with children, however, lived with children of that union and were not de facto stepfamilies.

The trend toward cohabiting was a reversal of the normative sequence of family transitions that most Americans had observed for most of the century—marriage, then children was the normative order for these experiences. The reversed order of children first, then (possibly) marriage occurred more near the end of the century, at which time about 40 percent of children born outside of marriage were born to cohabiting couples. Poor people in the final decades of the century saw marriage as a huge step in their lives, much more serious than bearing and rearing children. Thus, they tended to live together until they were financially and emotionally ready to make the ultimate commitment to marry. People of color in particular did not feel compelled to marry before they bore children; in the 1990s, cohabiting white women who became pregnant were more likely to marry than were cohabiting black women.

In general, couples who lived together did not do so for long; about half of the couples who lived together did so for less than a year. These couples ended their cohabiting by either marrying or breaking up. There were differences between those cohabiting couples who eventually married and those who didn't, with the biggest difference being the availability of resources (i.e., personal incomes, assets and property, education). Cohabiting couples with more resources, white couples, and those who had children were more likely to marry. Unlike the burgeoning body of research on divorce that had accumulated by the end of the century, we knew almost nothing about the dissolution of cohabiting relationships.

Cohabitation had little legal recognition at the end of the century, so partners did not have the same rights that accompanied marriage. This may change in the future, especially as gay and lesbian partners press for marital rights. Cohabitation may continue to serve as an alternative to marriage for some couples, as a source of intimacy for couples who are not seriously committed to each other, and as a stage in courtship for others. All three of these types of cohabiting relationships existed at the end of the century. It remains to be seen how cohabitation will evolve in the future. We do know that the meaning of cohabitation has shifted over time, and it likely will continue to do so.

MARRIAGE

Marriage was a popular status for Americans in the 20th century. Throughout the era, most adult Americans married, and, at any given point in the century, over half of all adults in the United States were married and living with a spouse (May, 1999). Despite these signs of the widespread popularity of marriage, during the 20th century, U.S. marriages became increasingly fragile. The rate of marriage decreased, and the rate of divorce gradually increased (with the exception of the late 1940s and the 1950s, when there were slight drops in divorce rates). In 2000, 73 percent of all women in their early 20s had never married compared to

36 percent who had never married in 1970. The percentage of African Americans who were married declined from 62 percent in 1950 to 36 percent in 2000; whites who were married declined from 66 percent in 1950 to 57 percent in 2000 (Cantave & Harrison, 2003). Around the turn of the century, young black women were more likely than white women to be married, but, by the 1980s, the opposite was true. In fact, by the end of the century, it was estimated that 70–75 percent of black women could expect to marry during their lifetime, compared to 91 percent of white women (Ooms, 2002). At the end of the century, therefore, young adults were delaying marriage or claiming they had no intentions to ever marry, cohabitation was on the rise, and a greater proportion of American children were born to unmarried parents than ever before in U.S. history. What happened?

Companionate Marriages

Prior to the 20th century, marriage was a practical arrangement between a man and a woman. There might be love between them, but Victorians of the 19th century generally married for pragmatic reasons—to have help with farming and household work, to have a steady sexual partner, to bear and rear children, to achieve social status in the community, and for personal security. When households were primarily production units—making their own food, clothing, furniture, and even shelter—it made sense to marry so that there would be someone to help make ends meet. Companionship and romantic love were welcome, but these expectations for marriage were farther down the list in the 19th century than they were in the 20th.

As households became units of consumption more than production, and as Americans moved from small towns and farms into metropolitan areas, men and women began to search for different attributes in marriage partners because expectations for marriage were changing, at least among the wealthy and middle class. The Progressive Era (roughly 1870 through the 1920s) witnessed single men and women turning to each other for companionship as never before. This trend toward what was called *companionate marriage* was one that had started decades earlier in Europe (Coontz, 2005).

As love and intimacy increasingly became the focus of marriage, and as its presence increased people's satisfaction with marriage, the stability of marriage as an institution became endangered. People did not realize it at the time, but when marriage was no longer based on acquiring land, power, and the proper in-laws; when marriage no longer was a woman's means to financial security for herself and her potential children; and when marriage was no longer an informal way of organizing sexual companionship, childrearing, and the tasks of daily life, it became less stable. There were fewer reasons to stay married if love and companionship were not working out. As the century progressed and women gained greater rights and had access to jobs that could provide financial security, couples began to end unsatisfactory marriages that they could not have previously afforded to do.

Gender roles changed during the century as much or more so than did marriage expectations. The notion of *separate spheres*—that men's efforts should focus on matters outside the home and women's attention should be solely devoted to matters within the home—was dominant at the beginning of the century. Soon afterward, however, men and women began to treat each other more as equals than ever before. In fact, according to Coontz (2005), the changes that most affected marriage were the sexual revolution and the attack on separate spheres. Women gradually were less likely to be seen as property and more likely to be seen as humans with sexual urges, not unlike men. The Victorian era had been one of great sexual repression. Even chicken parts were referred to as white meat and dark meat because referring to legs and breasts was thought to be too overtly sexual and uncouth. Misunderstandings about sexuality and birth control were rampant. Coontz (2005) wrote about a man of the Victorian era who was so startled when his wife had an orgasm that he thought she was having a seizure. Victorian men idealized women to the point that they often sought out prostitutes for sexual activity rather than defile their wives' purity.

At the turn of the 20th century, although orgasms may have no longer been mistaken for seizures, many married couples still were not well informed about human sexuality. And, although information about sexuality was becoming more available, the misunderstandings about sexual issues that had been common during Victorian times were only slowly overturned. Widely circulated magazines such as the *Ladies' Home Journal* began giving advice to women about sex, and the popular media gradually became saturated with sex as advertisers determined that it helped sell products. The movies were influential as well. After going to the movies to find out how to kiss and be seductive like movie stars, couples would go home and practice what they had seen.

Early in the century, it was not uncommon for women to fear sex. Many died during childbirth and from infections that set in afterward, so having sex that led to pregnancy was a tremendous risk. In 1916, Margaret Sanger opened the first birth control clinic, where pamphlets explaining birth control were made available to the general public. The availability of birth control, albeit not always reliable until the advent of the birth control pill (often just called The Pill) in 1961, freed women to enjoy sex with less fear of pregnancy. This freedom, however, raised concerns among conservatives about the difficulty this would create for keeping women chaste. Some so-called experts, including psychologist John B. Watson (1924), predicted that if the fear of pregnancy was removed, in the near future marriage would cease to exist because women would no longer have to get married to have sex. Watson was quite wrong about this. In fact, during the first three decades of the century, the rate of marriage increased, and people married at younger ages. The median age at first marriage in 1900 was 21.9 for women and 25.9 for men. In 1940, the median ages were 21.5 for women and 24.3 for men. Two groups that had tended to postpone marriage in the 19th century, urban white men and college-educated women, began to marry at ever greater rates. Whereas less than one in four urban men had married by age 24 in 1910, by 1930, the rate had climbed to one in three. Half of college-educated women remained single in the 19th century, but, by the early 1920s, over 80 percent were married.

Although the rate of marriage dipped in the early 1930s due to the Great Depression, by 1939 it had returned to the 19th-century level. World War II brought a sudden interruption to this remarkable stability. The marriage rate rose and the median age at marriage fell, both dramatically. The uncertainty of life and questions about the future that existed before and during the war, and the euphoria and relief that followed victory, led many Americans to rush into marriages. In the late 1940s, more than half of all women were married by the age of 21. In 1956, the median age at first marriage reached an all-time low (20.1 years for women, 22.5 years for men), and a year later the birth rate reached its peak. Beginning in the mid-1960s, the median age at first marriage began a gradual rise, and, by the late 1970s, it had attained its prewar level. The median age of first marriage between 1980 and 2000 increased from 25 to 25.8 years for men and from 22 to 25.1 years for women (Cantave & Harrison, 2003).

The Eye of the Storm   The 1950s was a period of great marital stability, and, in many ways, it defined the U.S. cultural ideal of marriage. Demographic trends from 1946 until about 1964, however, did not conform to the rest of the century (either before or after). It was a time when most people saw marriage as the only avenue to adulthood and independence. To be an independent adult in the 1950s generally meant you got married, had kids, and settled down. Consequently, people married early and began having children shortly afterward. The fertility rate increased 50 percent from 1940 to 1957, and the rates for third and fourth births doubled and tripled. Almost half of white women became mothers before reaching age 20, and two-thirds of those who went to college dropped out before graduating.

As the century ended, many Americans looked back on the 1950s with great nostalgia as a simpler time when marriages were strong and stable and all was well with American families. The lowered rates of divorce certainly suggest that post–World War II marriages were stable, but were they happy and satisfying? There was considerable controversy about this. For instance, despite the positive demographic indicators of high marriage rates and low divorce rates, some scholars argued that the marriages of the 1950s resulted from a confluence of fortunate postwar economic conditions, relief from the stress of two world wars and a worldwide depression, and the historical culmination of 150 years of evolving norms about what marriage should be. These new norms resulted in a new marriage system based on love and companionship rather than on survival and financial gain.

During the 1950s, people seemed satisfied with the new marriage system and seldom sought an escape when love faded and the companionship did not work out. The stability of 1950s marriages, however, may have been an artifact of the overwhelming need for security and safety that Americans felt after the bleak years of two world wars and economic depression. Americans were ready to enjoy the fruits of their labors. People were primed to link marriage with consumerism, and getting married and beginning to accumulate goods were enticing goals for many young people.

Television began saturating the market in the 1950s, and TV shows and commercials touted marriage (and the accompanying consumerism) as part of the "good life." Marriage spurred the economy and provided people with the opportunity to buy homes, household appliances, and furniture, which they did with a vengeance. Interestingly, despite the spending spree that began after World War II and continued until the end of the century, married women were unable to get loans or credit cards in their own name (even if they worked full time) until the 1970s. Even without credit, however, married women learned to be excellent consumers. One of many unusual family aspects in the 1950s was the fact that it was the only time during the century that most families, even working-class families, could manage financially with a single breadwinner. At home during the day, women were expected to make their homes beautiful and comfortable—an expectation that fueled purchasing.

Despite marital stability, married life was not without problems in the 1950s. The new marriage system, an updated version of the companionate marriage ideal of earlier in the century, contained within it a new set of problems that economic growth and prosperity could only briefly conceal. Coontz (2005) described the 1950s as a period of calm before the storm.

Sex. One area of discontent was sex. Husbands and wives were no longer expected to have sexual relations just to bear children. Sex became a means of expressing mutual love and emotional closeness. Popular publications as diverse as *Ladies' Home Journal, Redbook,* and *Esquire* exhorted women and men to maximize their sexual fulfillment within marriage, and many marriage manuals were published that almost exclusively focused on sex. After being socialized to stifle their sexual urges during courtship, married women were expected to suddenly be able to fulfill their own and their husband's sexual desires. Sexual dissatisfaction was considered a major source of marital failure during the 1950s, and this failure was usually blamed on women. The height of sexual satisfaction was considered to be the mutual orgasm, and risqué novels of the period extolled its wonders. This remained an elusive goal until the work of Shere Hite (1976) provided evidence that a large number of women were unable to achieve orgasm at all with standard intercourse, never mind mutual orgasms. The *London Times* designated *The Hite Report* as one of the 100 key books of the 20th century. It is likely that many women faked orgasm during the 1950s to pretend that all was well within their marriages.

Marital roles. Another area of concern was gender roles in marriage. This concern revolved around at least three issues. One was that feminine and masculine roles were presumably converging. The second issue regarded the challenges of creating marriage as a partnership that included shared intimacy and companionship. The third major gender issue was concern about the overinvolvement of mothers in childrearing. Men left the house each day to commute to work, leaving women in charge of children. This left men out of the loop and feeling powerless, which had negative effects on marriage.

Anxiety about the converging of gender roles and how this might affect men, masculinity, and homosexuality somehow became linked with Senator Joseph McCarthy's crusade against communism, which in turn was linked with immoral and antimasculine behavior. This anxiety ultimately contributed to a fear of strong women. Media played into these fears, and television programs and cartoons such as *Dagwood and Blondie* portrayed men as weak and ineffectual. Sons who were not exposed to the influence of their fathers were considered at risk for inappropriate gender development, including homosexuality (concerns were exclusively about homosexuality in males, not in females). It is ironic that some of the most popular and acclaimed movie stars of the period such as Rock Hudson and Montgomery Cliff were deeply closeted homosexuals.

These fears of converging gender roles and strong women were misplaced, however, because gender roles were *not* converging. They were as specialized as ever, if not more so. The urgent goal of most women of the 1950s was to marry and have children, and they *expected* to be submissive to men. Those few women who went to college typically did not pursue professional careers, but rather enrolled in majors that would enhance their ability to be a good wife and mother (home economics) or that would provide them skills to work (nursing, education) if something happened to their husbands. Women whose greatest satisfaction was not from marriage and childrearing were considered to have serious psychological problems. Marriages that were childless by choice were virtually nonexistent, and women who chose to be childless were generally considered narcissistic at best, pathological at worst.

Media other than television also glorified the role of the submissive wife in the 1950s. Although the often-circulated "Good Wife's Guide" that appeared in the May 13, 1955, issue of *Housekeeping Monthly* is generally considered to have been intended as a spoof, the content did not greatly deviate from serious magazine articles and home economics textbooks of the era.

- Have dinner ready. Plan ahead, even the night before, to have a delicious meal ready, on time for his return. This is a way of letting him know that you have been thinking about him and are concerned about his needs. Most men are hungry when they come home and the prospect of a good meal (especially his favorite dish) is part of the warm welcome needed.
- Prepare yourself. Take 15 minutes to rest so you'll be refreshed when he arrives. Touch up your make-up, put a ribbon in your hair and be fresh looking. He has just been with a lot of work-weary people.
- Be a little gay and a little more interesting for him. His boring day may need a lift and one of your duties is to provide it.
- Clear away the clutter. Make one last trip through the main part of the house just before your husband arrives.
- Gather up schoolbooks, toys, paper, etc. and then run a dust cloth over the tables.
- Prepare the children. Take a few minutes to wash the children's hands and faces (if they are small), comb their hair and, if necessary, change their clothes. They are little treasures and he would like to see them playing the part. Minimize all noise. At the time of his arrival, eliminate all noise of the washer, dryer or vacuum. Try to encourage the children to be quiet.
- Be happy to see him. Greet him with a warm smile and show sincerity in your desire to please him.
- Listen to him. You may have a dozen important things to tell him, but the moment of his arrival is not the time. Let him talk first—remember, his topics of conversation are more important than yours.
- Your goal: To make sure your home is a place of peace, order, and tranquility where your husband can renew himself in body and spirit.
- Don't greet him with complaints and problems.
- Make him comfortable. Have him lean back in a comfortable chair or have him lie down in the bedroom. Have a cool or warm drink ready for him.
- Don't ask him questions about his actions or question his judgment or integrity. Remember, he is the master of the house and as such will always exercise his will with fairness and truthfulness. You have no right to question him.
- A good wife always knows her place.

The second gender concern was about companionate marriage, a status that reflected the thinking of sociologists, more so than the reality of modern marriages. The more intimate companionate marriage was fostered to an extent by corporations' frequent moves of their male employees (employees joked that IBM stood for I've Been Moved). Moving away from family and friends created greater interdependence in couples than ever before. For a time, this interdependence seemed to strengthen marriage, although it did not offset the submissiveness of women to their husbands.

Even though women remained submissive, the irrational fear of strong women was displayed in many ways. For example, mothers were blamed for their children's problems but were seldom given credit for their children's successes. Because mothers were home all day with the children, there was concern that they had too much influence on shaping their children's (especially their son's) behavior. Mothers also were castigated by the medical field. Schizophrenia in children, for example, was linked to professional women's cold and rejecting mothering, even though no evidence ever existed to support this notion. Popular literature of the time, such as Philip Wylie's (1942) *Generation of Vipers* blamed women for men's failures. He coined the term *momism*, which indicated that women were demasculinizing their sons by overprotective behaviors that prevented them from growing up to be competent men. Thus, mothers were both idealized and demonized during this decade.

After the Calm, the Storm Hits the Hardest

If the 1950s were the calm before the storm, the decades that followed were the peak of the tempest. As family historian Stephanie Coontz (2005) wrote, "It took more than 150 years to establish the love-based, male breadwinner marriage as the dominant model in North America and Western Europe. It took less than 25 years to dismantle it" (p. 247). Just as Americans became comfortable with the new version of companionate marriage, people began delaying marriage, divorcing at elevated rates, reducing the size of their families, and ignoring the strict division of labor with the husband as breadwinner and the wife as homemaker. The catalyst for these rapid changes in marriage is debatable, but what is not debatable is that marriage changed in profound ways shortly after the end of the 1950s decade. The 1960s and 1970s may have seen the rise of women's liberation, but even at the height of the feminist movement, most women still expected to be full-time homemakers and mothers.

According to Coontz (2005), the women's liberation rhetoric was greater than the actual changes, but there were changes nonetheless. She indicated that women tended to maintain their more conservative notions of family and work until they either went to work or experienced divorce. And, ironically, a 1962 Gallup poll reported that, although most women were highly satisfied with their lives, they wanted their daughters to get an education and postpone marriage, an attitude that somewhat belies their reported satisfaction.

It was not just women that were unhappy with companionate marriage, however. Many men were alienated by their breadwinner existence and the conformity required of them to maintain their workplace status. For instance, computer giant IBM had strict standards of proper workplace dress, including the color of suits and the amount of cuff that was allowed to show beneath the suit's sleeve. Not conforming to the dress code brought with it severe penalties, including being fired. Books about the punishing influence of corporate America on men, such as Sloan Wilson's *The Man in the Grey Flannel Suit*, published in 1955, and William H. Whyte's 1956 book, *The Organization Man*, were bestsellers. Whyte described the organization man as husbands who spiritually and physically left their homes to take the vows of organization (corporate) work life.

The social movements of the 1960s and 1970s changed society in general and marriage in particular. In 1973, *Roe v. Wade* legalized abortion. Legislation was passed in 1975 that allowed married women, without their husband's permission, to get credit cards and loans in their own names. Laws determining who you could and could not marry were overturned in most states (e.g., interracial marriage between whites and blacks, Native Americans, Asians, and people of other races previously had been widely banned), employers could no longer require women to stay single to maintain their jobs, and the legal distinction between legitimacy and illegitimacy was removed. According to Coontz (2005), previously, children born out of wedlock had no rights, nor did their mothers. For example, children could be removed from the mother's care and put up for adoption without her consent, a child could not sue if his or her mother was killed by negligence, and they could not inherit from either parent. However, removing the distinction between legitimate and illegitimate children, while humane, also removed some of the impetus for legal marriage.

Gender roles in marriage were greatly affected by inflation and the recession that occurred in the 1970s and 1980s. Women entered the workplace in increasing numbers to offset the effects of the downturned economy on family income. Real wages fell, and housing costs went up nearly 300 percent during those two decades. Women originally resisted work-force participation, but, by the end of the 1970s, nearly 75 percent indicated they would continue working regardless of whether their families needed the money, a percentage only slightly below that reported by men. By 1980, women had access to jobs, effective birth control, and abortion as well as other legal rights. They also began to have access to no-fault divorce. Perhaps as a result, many unhappily married women filed for divorce in the 1970s, and even more filed during the 1980s.

By the end of the century, unlike the beginning, it was highly educated women who were most likely to marry; poor women with little education continued to have children but their chances of marrying were slim. Concern about the lowered rate of marriage, especially among the poor and working class, seemed to spur the federal government to establish a *Marriage Initiative* in 1996. Funding was provided, with more promised, to promote marriage, and a welfare reform movement was launched that had marriage as a chief goal. Little evidence existed in 2000, however, that this legislation was increasing the rate of marriage among the poor and disenfranchised. Poor women were understandably reluctant to marry men who had little chance of stable employment—they could end up having to support the husband as well as their children. Even in cases of unmarried couples who had a child or children together and who had supportive attitudes toward marriage, trusted each other, and the father made favorable wages, only about 20 percent would marry.

Marriages became less stable but many became more satisfying over the course of the century. Despite the increased divorce rate and the fragility of marriage, couples still wanted to marry and most planned to do so. Although the high expectations for personal happiness were often unrealistic and led to high rates of divorce, these expectations also led to more personally satisfying marriages than could have been imagined at the beginning of the century.

Changes in Transition Sequences and Timing: The Disconnect between Marriage and Childbirth

For most of the 20th century, marriage preceded childbearing, and when this sequence was not followed (e.g., out-of-wedlock births), the individuals involved usually were heavily castigated as morally wrong. There were tangible sanctions as well, such as being fired from a job or being shunned by society. Violating the normative sequence of family events could be a source of enormous individual and family shame. For nearly the first three quarters of the 20th century, a young woman's life could be ruined if a nonmarital pregnancy were public knowledge, so women and their parents or partners often went to great lengths to hide this information.

This sequence of marriage first and childbirth later is still the normative expectation in most of U.S. society, but, in the final two or three decades of the century, there was a gradual disconnection between marriage and childbirth, especially among African American women.

Nonmarital births. In the 1930s, 82 percent of first births were conceived after marriage compared to 47 percent of first births in the 1990s. Trends in premarital childbearing between 1930 and the mid-1990s indicated that one in six births to women between ages 15 and 29 in the early 1930s were either conceived or born outside of marriage. Between that period and the 1960s, 50 to 60 percent of unmarried pregnant women were married before the birth of their first child, a number that dropped to 29 percent by the mid-1980s. By 1997, 26 percent of white infants were born to unmarried women. Among black women, the percentage of first births conceived or born before marriage doubled from 43 percent in the early 1930s to 86 percent in the mid-1990s. It should be noted that, although nonmarital births had always been more common among black women than white women, nearly 85 percent of black mothers were married and living with a husband as recently as 1950. Those figures had almost reversed by the end of the century, with approximately 70 percent of black mothers being unmarried at the time of giving birth.

Information from the National Center for Health Statistics indicated that nonmarital birth rates leveled off during the 1990s and stabilized at around 33 percent. This represented an increase of about 1 percent per year in nonmarital births through the 1990s compared to annual increases of 6 percent during the 1980s. Although the rates of increase had stabilized, it is obvious that a significant number of children in the

United States at the end of the 20th century were the result of nonmarital births, and there was little indication at the end of the century that this rate would soon drop.

Births to single mothers were referred to as illegitimate until around mid-century, and children born out of wedlock were often labeled bastards. Because of low tolerance and stigma among the white population, until the 1960s, single white women who became pregnant generally had the following choices: they married, had abortions (illegally until 1973, when abortions became a legal medical procedure), hid their pregnancy status, or stayed in institutions for unwed mothers until the baby was born and could be given up for adoption.

As the sanctions against unmarried parenthood decreased, single mothers were less prone to hide their pregnancies. They were less fearful that they would lose their jobs or be expelled from school. In fact, many public school districts established programs for adolescent mothers so they could stay in school while pregnant and after the delivery. Single mothers also became less likely to give up the baby for adoption, instead opting to raise the child alone or with the help of parents or the baby's father.

In fact, as noted earlier in this chapter, many unmarried mothers were cohabiting with the fathers of their children at the end of the century. Some of these women planned to marry the father once they become financially secure, but for low-income couples—particularly low-income and working-class African Americans—the long-established sequence of marriage before childbirth had been reversed by the end of the century. Instead of waiting to have children until they were married and financially able to afford the expenses of a child, many had children but waited to get married until they were financially able to make that commitment. Although poor women were reluctant to absorb the burden of financially supporting a man with limited earnings potential, this was not the complete story. Social scientists and pundits remained somewhat puzzled by the lowered rate of marriage among poor and working-class couples. Interestingly, polls at the end of the century reflected a destigmatization of unwed childbearing among Americans, but when it came to their own families, only 14 percent of women in general and only 28.5 percent of black adults thought it would be acceptable for their daughter to bear a child outside of marriage.

For reasons that were not entirely clear, even to working-class men and women, the relative importance of marriage and childrearing shifted during the century. Having a child became seen as a lesser commitment than marriage. It seemed that poor adults wanted to have enough money to pay for a nice wedding celebration, they wanted to be debt-free, and they wanted to afford their own dwelling and be able to furnish it before marriage. Speculation was that these priorities were the consequence of the cultural connection between consuming and marriage that started in the early 1950s. That is, poor Americans were saying by their words and actions that they would not marry until and unless they were able to purchase the *good life* for themselves and their children, just as do middle- and upper-class Americans.

One consequence of the disconnection between marriage and parenthood was the increase in the number of households headed by a single adult with children. Between the mid-19th century and 1970, about 10 percent of U.S. families were headed by a single mother or single father. By 1980, the proportion of households headed by single parents had doubled to over 21 percent and increased still further to 23.5 percent by 1994. There were 3 million single-mother households in 1970 and 10 million by 2000. Black women heading single-mother households were more likely to do so as a result of nonmarital childbearing, while white women did so as a result of divorce (Fields & Casper, 2001).

Because single women who had children were often poor, and poverty was related to lowered well-being of children, there was a strong push by policymakers at the end of the century to encourage them to marry. This push was stimulated by the interpretation of some research findings that marriage, or at least having two adults in the household, was related to lower poverty rates for women and children. Among the poor in 1998, the highest percentage of households (32.7 percent) who missed meals for economic reasons were single-parent households with no other adult present (Lerman, 2002). These households also were the least likely to be able to pay for utilities, rent, and mortgages. Critics of the social programs aimed to get poor parents to marry argued that relations between variables did not mean that there was a causal connection between marriage and children's outcomes; these critics argued that other factors, such as education and parental mental health and well-being, were causally related to both the probability of marrying and children's well-being. There was little evidence that the government efforts to facilitate marriage were working at the end of the century.

RISE IN DIVORCE

As the life span increased, widowhood became an increasingly less common reason for marital dissolution throughout the century, and divorce rates simultaneously rose. In 1900, divorce ended about 10 percent of marriages, and in 2000 the projected figure was 50 percent (Uhlenberg, 1996). The divorce rate gradually increased throughout the first 75 years of the century, although there was a decrease during the Depression. This decrease was artificial, however, because men who could not support their families during the Depression often deserted them (sometime called the poor man's divorce), and informal separations also were quite common because people could not afford the legal fees of divorce. The infamous hobo villages that sprung up near railroad tracks during the Depression were primarily inhabited by men who had deserted their families.

Partly because of difficulties in obtaining a divorce, the divorce rate was low at the beginning of the century. For a judge to declare that a marriage was over, one of the spouses had to be found guilty of a crime against the marriage or the marital partner. The guilty party was sometimes punished; for example, men who divorced because they were not financially supporting their families were not allowed to remarry. Even when a divorcing spouse was not the guilty party, divorce exacted severe costs. For example, at the beginning of the century even women who divorced because of physical abuse lost property and often access to their children.

Because divorcing was a difficult and complicated legal process, couples who wished to divorce sometimes moved to states that had fewer legal restrictions. This created animosity between the states, so the U.S. Supreme Court ruled that states had to honor divorces granted in other states.

Nineteen forty five was a peak year for divorce during the twentieth century. This spike in the divorce rate followed World War II, and a similar increase in divorce had occurred following World War I. These postwar peaks in the divorce rate are often explained in terms of the failure of rushed marriages of couples who had known each other only briefly before marrying, the result of couples being physically separated for long periods of time during the war, the subsequent loneliness and development of adulterous relationships, and the personal changes that resulted, especially in soldiers returning from the war. Certainly the divorce rate continued to rise, but the peak rate of 1945 was not again matched until the mid-1970s (Kain, 1990). Although only one in four marriages ended in divorce during the 1950s, the divorce rate doubled between 1960 and 1980. The year 1974 marked a watershed in that, for the first time in U.S. history, divorce rather than death became the most common ending for marriages. The divorce rate dropped a little in the 1980s and leveled off for the remainder of the century, but this change was more than offset by the rise in cohabitation and the decrease in the rate of marriage. At the end of the 20th century, the United States maintained the highest rate of divorce in the Western world (about 50 percent of all first marriages and 60 percent of remarriages were expected to end in divorce), and this had been true throughout the century.

It should be noted that, although African American families experienced the same trends in divorce as white and Latin American families, their rate of divorce was higher and their rate of marriage had dropped dramatically by the end of the century. In the 1990s, nearly 50 percent of African American married couples had separated within 15 years of the wedding, compared to 28 percent of European Americans. It was estimated that, in the near future, as many as 70 percent of African American women who married would be divorced before they had reached 25 years of marriage. The low rate of marriage and high rate of divorce was primarily attributed to the lack of employment opportunities for African American men and the lack of available marriageable partners for African American women. Studies also indicated that African Americans were more tolerant and accepting of divorce and less blaming than European Americans, thus reducing fear of social stigma as a reason for not divorcing. In general, however, there were few studies of African American divorce patterns that explained the differential rates of divorce between them and European Americans.

Even less was known about divorce among the Latin American population, although they were less likely to divorce than African Americans and European Americans. This did not necessarily mean their marriages were more stable, however; Latin Americans were more likely to end marital relationships by separating than either of the other two groups. Most of the investigations of Latin American divorce were based on census data, which categorized all Latin American groups together even though there were differences in rates of divorce among Mexican Americans, Cubans, and Puerto Ricans. Little was known about the process of divorce among Latin American couples, however, regardless of their origins.

Why the Rise in Divorce?

Three factors have been identified as major contributors to the shift from death to divorce as the most common ending to marriages. One was the increase in the life span. When the life span was shorter, marital longevity was likewise limited. For example, a 20-year-old in the early 20th century who married "till death do us part" faced an average of about 25 years of marriage. In contrast, a 20-year-old who married at the end of the 20th century could anticipate well over 50 years of marriage. Although it might be expected that the increase in life span would result in longer marriages, that did not prove to be the case; the duration of marriages did not significantly lengthen. Instead, the reasons why marriages ended shifted. More years together seemed to mean more opportunities to have problems and become unhappy—such prospects in the face of decades more of life together may have led some married individuals to divorce or separate.

A second factor identified as a contributor to the rising divorce rate was the changing biopsychosocial roles of women. Some economists estimated that the increase in divorce was related to decreased fertility brought about by the availability of modern contraceptive technology. In other words, having children reduced the likelihood that women would divorce. For example, demographers found that having one child reduced the divorce rate by about 30 percent and having two children reduced it another 30 percent. One economist estimated that the reduced fertility among women that was allowed by the advent of modern birth control accounted for as much as 50 percent of the variance in the rise in the divorce rate in the 1970s.

The third contributing factor to the rise of divorce was the increase in women's income. Both the freedom of choice of when or whether to become pregnant and the greater ability to support themselves made women less susceptible to either being forced to marry or having to remain in bad marriages to survive economically.

In the 1970s, states began adopting no-fault systems of divorce that removed the need to establish guilt on the part of one of the partners. By the mid-1980s, all 50 states had no-fault divorce laws in place. Some people have argued that the change in divorce laws from having to prove fault for the marriage's failure to allowing couples to decide the marriage should be ended (the no-fault grounds for divorce) increased the rate of divorce. However, the rate of divorce was increasing long before no-fault divorce laws were passed. Apparently, the legal system reacted to the culture and changes in people's behaviors, rather than the other way around.

In the mid-1990s, politicians and others proposed various policies to discourage divorce. In Louisiana and Arizona, state legislatures created covenant marriages in addition to conventional marriage licenses. Covenant marriage was an attempt to lower the divorce rate by returning to stricter standards for obtaining divorce, including required marriage counseling and a mandatory two-year waiting period between filing for marital dissolution and being granted the divorce, and other restrictions designed to keep married couples together. Other ideas included media campaigns against divorce and single parenting and outlawing divorce altogether for couples with children under age 18. Feminists in particular raised concerns that covenant marriage and other attempts to make divorce more difficult to obtain had the potential to trap abused women in marriages that were a danger to themselves as well as their children. Few couples opted for covenant marriages, however, and there is no evidence that covenant marriage laws lowered the divorce rate in the few states where it was available.

Perspectives on Divorce

Divorce has been described along a continuum from a normative transition (normative in the sense that half of all marriages are expected to end in divorce) to a cultural crisis. Some evolutionary scientists have suggested that the capacity to divorce comes from our evolutionary heritage. Humans needed to be flexible enough to find another partner if they lost theirs to war, famine, or disease; not being able to do so would have jeopardized the survival of the species. However, modern divorce, which is often followed by remarriage, not only *replaces* an original partner, but it *adds* an additional parenting figure to families, which increases family complexity and creates additional problems that are discussed later in this chapter.

Family sociologist Paul Amato (2004) identified three periods of social science research regarding divorce during the 20th century. These periods reflect cultural perspectives on divorce as well, because social scientists are members of society as well as scholars and researchers.

The first and longest period began at the start of the century and continued until approximately 1960. During this time, divorce was viewed as a *social problem* that was especially harmful to children. A *family deficit* perspective was taken, maintaining the assumption that deviations from the nuclear family result in negative outcomes for most children. In addition to stringent legal restrictions governing divorce that grew out of this family deficit view, Freudian psychoanalytic theory was widely accepted at the time, and one of Freud's basic tenets was that children needed two parents to develop normally. Therefore, many clinicians discouraged parents from divorcing, no matter how hostile their relationships. Investigations of the effects of divorce on children were somewhat meager during that time period, but most research indicated that children whose parents divorced were at a disadvantage compared to those in first marriage families. This was not that surprising considering the stigma associated with divorce at the time, the difficulty in negotiating the legal aspects of divorce, and the fact that children and their mothers often fell into poverty after divorce.

The views that were common during the divorce-as-social-problem era remained common throughout the century, but new ideas about divorce emerged between 1960 and 1980, a period that Amato labeled the *divorce revolution*. The rate of divorce increased dramatically during this time period, and laws governing divorce were changed to be more accommodating for divorcing couples. No-fault divorce was introduced and became the norm, supported by the widespread belief that, because fault divorce was so adversarial in nature, it was detrimental to children and families.

During the period of the divorce revolution, a view emerged that Amato termed a *family pluralism* perspective. This perspective suggested that divorce served a useful purpose in ending bad marriages, and that divorce did not have uniformly or universally negative effects on children. An underlying assumption was that unhappily married parents did not provide a good atmosphere for children, and that the key to children's adjustment was a competent, happy, and well-adjusted parent. This perspective reflected the period in which it evolved—the divorce rate was increasing rapidly, the legal system had changed dramatically regarding divorce regulation, and the general public was more tolerant, as evidenced by the election of a divorced man (Ronald Reagan) to the presidency in 1981. For the first time in U.S. history, divorce was not a relevant issue in considering the viability of a politician's candidacy for office. Prior to Reagan's election, divorce was the kiss of death to national political careers in the United States.

The period of the divorce revolution was followed by a backlash against divorce that was sustained throughout the remainder of the century. Amato referred to this as the *emergence of a middle ground*. The general public appeared to become more ambivalent about divorce, but, in general, attitudes toward divorce became more negative than they were during the *divorce revolution*. Divorce research became much more sophisticated during the middle ground period, and, although recent research refutes the earlier family deficit assumption that all or most children of divorced parents had problems, it did not necessarily support the family pluralism perspective either. Amato labeled this new understanding the *contingency perspective*. This perspective viewed divorce as a stressor and risk factor for children's well-being, but one that depended on family environmental factors before and after divorce and on other potentially protective factors. Rather than feeling comfortable with making sweeping conclusions about the effects of divorce on children, social scientists at the end of the century qualified their answers with "it depends." The contingency perspective, as did the family deficit perspective and the family pluralism perspective, seemed to reflect the more ambivalent, middle-ground view of divorce the general public held at the end of the century.

Regardless of the perspective taken, however, divorce had been and continued to be considered one of life's most stressful events. The American Psychiatric Association indicated in 1987 that divorce was a level four out of six levels in terms of stress (slightly less than the death of one or both parents). Although divorce carried less stigma than was true early in the 20th century, the stigma associated with divorce was still high, which adds to other stressors more typically thought to be associated with divorce (i.e., lost time spent between children and parents, lowered income, multiple changes such as moving to a different residence, stay-at-home mothers returning to work, etc.). Amato's contingency perspective regarding divorce shows promise for sustaining research that neither condones nor condemns divorce and perhaps represents a more balanced, somewhat less stigmatized view of the divorce process. However, at the end of the century, there remained strong currents in society that condemned divorce and bemoaned the rise in divorce.

INCREASES IN MULTIPLE TRANSITIONS ACROSS THE LIFE COURSE

Remarriage and Stepfamily Formation

Several demographic trends in the 20th century, combined with changes in beliefs about marriages and families, resulted in more and more family members experiencing multiple family transitions. As a result of the rising divorce rates, the increase in cohabitation, and the increased longevity of Americans, many families experienced the remarriage of at least one family member.

Although the incidence of remarriage did not change dramatically over the century, alarms were sounded in the early 1970s when remarriage began to follow parental divorce more often than parental bereavement. At the beginning of the 20th century, stepparents were considered necessary substitutions for parents who had died—although stepparents, especially stepmothers, had been vilified worldwide in fairy tales for centuries. The United States was mostly an agrarian society in the early decades of the 20th century; therefore, having a new spouse to replace a deceased one, at least in terms of economic activities and household maintenance tasks, was necessary for survival. It was not until the late 1970s that the general public and social scientists began to identify stepfamilies as a social problem. Remarriages formed after divorce created extra parents rather than providing necessary replacements for deceased parents. This phenomenon created much more complex stepfamilies than had existed earlier in the century, and this complexity was associated with stress for stepfamily members.

Just as the United States has the highest marriage and divorce rate in the Western world, it also had the highest remarriage rate. Americans remarry often, and quickly. Three out of four divorced persons remarried during the latter part of the 20th century, and about half of these remarriages occurred within three years of the divorce. At the end of the century, half of all marriages were a remarriage for at least one partner, and the projected redivorce rate for these remarriers was slightly higher than the divorce rate for first married couples. At the end of the century, over 10 percent of all marriages were a third, fourth, or higher order marriage for at least one of the partners. This means that many children transitioned through several different family configurations before becoming adults. Ironically, remarriage of a parent with minor-aged children, identified at the beginning of the century as the *solution to a social problem* (i.e., children having inadequate income or care due to the death of a parent) was viewed by many at the end of the century as a *social problem in need of a solution.* One social scientist late in the century went so far as to suggest that parents who remarried and created stepfamilies were engaging in child abuse.

The financial motivation to remarry was always greater for women than for men. Remarriage of mothers following bereavement early in the century kept widows and their children from extreme poverty. The most common way for divorced women to avoid poverty also was to remarry. Women who had more resources (i.e., education, income) were less likely to remarry than were those who were more impoverished, which provided some support for the notion of remarriage as a means of stabilizing family financial support.

Stepfamilies at the beginning of the century and stepfamilies at the end of the century differed in a number of ways. The major change, as noted, was the fact that stepfamilies in the last part of the century were formed post-divorce and typically added rather than replaced a parent. If both parents remarried, and perhaps remarried more than once, several replacement parents were added to the mix. This change in stepfamilies created a complexity that was nearly unimaginable to many people. For example, unlike postbereavement stepfamilies, in most postdivorce stepfamilies all members of the family did not share a household. Children were likely to go back and forth between two households— spending some time with their mother and stepfather and some time with their father and stepmother. This meant that, in stepfamilies, unlike first married families, households and families were not the same. This was a source of much confusion, even on the part of such institutions as the U.S. Census Bureau. In the 2000 census, stepfamily households were only identified if stepparents happened to be the ones filling out the census form. Stepparents filling out the census form would identify their relationship to the children in the home as a step-relationship. However, if the biological parent in the home filled out the census form, he or she would identify the relationship to the children as a biological relationship, which would preclude the family from being identified as a stepfamily. As a result, it is believed that the number of stepfamilies was greatly underrepresented in the 2000 census. To further complicate our understanding of the number and complexity of stepfamilies in the United States, many states no longer require people to indicate on their marriage license application form whether the impending marriage is a first, second, or a higher order marriage.

In addition to being complex, the norms regarding remarriage were ambiguous, and a seminal work by Andrew Cherlin (1978) referred to remarriage as an *incomplete institution.* By this, Cherlin meant that, unlike first marriages, there were few guidelines, norms, or laws surrounding remarriage and stepfamily formation. Simple matters such as how a child introduced family members (e.g., "these are my parents," "this is my mother and stepfather," "this is my mother and Jim," "this is my mother and her husband") could be stressful because there was no widely recognized way to do this. Additionally, in general, there was no legal relationship between stepparents and stepchildren. Even though in most states, stepparents were required to financially support stepchildren, if the parent and stepparent divorced, the divorce severed all legal ties between the stepparent and stepchild. The stepparent had no legal right to ever see the child again, even if they had raised the child from infancy. In fact, if the parent died, rather than be awarded to the stepparent who raised him or her, the child was most likely returned to the surviving parent, even if that parent had essentially abandoned the child.

Even more incompletely institutionalized was the growing number of cohabiting stepfamilies. These were couples that had not legally remarried but were bringing children from previous relationships to the household. Is a cohabiting partner considered a stepparent? These questions were emerging, at least among social scientists, at the end of the 20th century.

Just as there are arguments among social scientists regarding the effects of divorce on children, there are similar arguments about the effects of remarriage on children. Children whose parents have remarried seem to fare about the same as children whose parents have divorced—slightly less well than children in first married families. Whether that was true throughout the century is not known.

Widowhood   Average life expectancy changed considerably during the 20th century. Between 1900 and 2000, the average life expectancy for white men increased by 26 years and for women 29 years. For people of color, life expectancies increased 35 years for men and 40 years for women. In 1900, 39 percent of an initial birth cohort would survive to age 65, and 12 percent would survive to age 80. By the end of the 20th century, those rates had changed dramatically—86 percent would survive to age 65, and 58 percent would live to age 80, and one of the fastest rates of growth was among those reaching 100 years of age (Uhlenberg, 1996).

The change in mortality rates meant that extended families changed over the century as well. In 1900, 25 percent of newborn children had four living grandparents, and, by age 21, less than 25 percent had *any* living grandparents. By the end of the century, nearly two-thirds of newborn children had four living grandparents (and many no doubt had living stepgrandparents as well), and 75 percent still had at least one living grandparent when they were age 30. Many of these living grandparents were great-grandparents as well. A large majority of great-grandparents were women, although the difference in the life span between men and women was narrowing. In 2000, it was more likely that 20-year-olds would have a *living grandmother* than it was that 20-year-olds in 1900 would have a *living mother* (Uhlenberg, 1996).

In 1900, two-thirds of all marriages were ended within 40 years by the death of one spouse. By 1975, that number had been reduced to just over one-third of marriages, and, in 2000, the rate was reduced further. Marital stability prior to old age therefore increased over the century, even though the divorce rate went up. Because a large number of the people who divorced also remarried, the proportion of the elderly population who were married at the end of the century was almost exactly the proportion that was married at the beginning of the century (Uhlenberg, 1980).

In 1900, half of the men and a third of the women who lived to age 70 still had a living spouse. By 2000, 85 percent of the men and 61 percent of the women who lived to age 70 had a living spouse, and 67 percent of the men who lived to age 80 had a living spouse, a rate similar to that of 60-year-old men in 1900. Widowhood has always been a more common experience for women than men, but fewer persons at all ages became widowed as the century progressed.

Throughout the century, men whose wives died as young or middle-aged adults almost always remarried as soon as a suitable period of grieving had passed. Nearly all men were employed (or were looking for work), and they found it hard to manage household maintenance tasks—cooking, caring for children, house cleaning, laundry—and the demands of work. Consequently, the majority of widowers remarried, with the exception of very old men, who, for most of the century, went to live with children or remained in their own homes for as long as they could.

Because the divorce rate was low at the beginning of the 20th century and mortality rates were high, women and men who lived past midlife were likely to experience widowhood. Because support programs such as social security and pensions were not in place at the turn of the century, widowhood was a major traumatic transition for women. Widowhood for young women was relatively rare even at the beginning of the century, and it became even less common as the century progressed; but, because it was relatively uncommon, young widows had few models for coping with this unexpected transition. The standard method of adjusting chosen by the majority appeared to be remarriage, and, in 1910, it appeared that at least half of young widows remarried (Hareven & Uhlenberg, 1995).

Early in the century, young widows were much more likely to head their own household than were never-married women, who tended to live with their parents. By mid-century, more young widows were living with their parents than was true at the beginning of the century, but this could be attributed to the fact that increases in the life span meant they were more likely to have living parents with whom they could reside. The phenomenon of adult children living with their parents changed rather dramatically over time, however, as the norm of independent living began to hold sway. By the end of the century, despite the likelihood of having living parents, only 4 percent of young widows lived with them; 90 percent of those with two or more children headed their own households.

In the early 1900s, there was a strong norm against mothers of young children working, and about 5 percent of married women with children were in the work force as compared to over 60 percent of widows with children. By 1940, 40 percent of widows with children were in the work force, and, by 1970, when women were entering the work force in much higher numbers in general, the percentage of widows with young children working was lower than it had been in 1910. The major speculation for this low level of work-force participation by widows with young children was that it was difficult to find child care, and many of them received life insurance payments and social security.

Women who were widowed in mid-life had quite different experiences than young widows. Middle-aged women who became widows around the mid-point of the century were not all that different from those who were widowed in 1900 in terms of their living situations and their work-force participation. Most were not in the labor force and most headed their own households. This was to change rather dramatically, however. By 1970, the majority of middle-aged widows were in the work force, even more headed their own household, and far fewer were living with their parents. A partial explanation for this shift was the changing norm about independent living that began to prevail, the increasing acceptance of women in the work force, and the increase in various benefits such as welfare and social security.

Middle-aged widows in the 1970s often did not remarry, although there is little more than speculation about why this is so. Those who did remarry were certainly better off financially than those who did not. Middle-aged widows who were least likely to be household heads were those who were childless. They were also more likely to be in the work force. Interestingly, at the turn of the century, childless widows were twice as likely as never-married women to live as boarders in other people's households (keeping boarders was a common income-producing practice at that time), and they were much less likely to live with their parents or other kin. This was probably due to the common practice at that time of the oldest or youngest daughter not marrying and continuing to live in the family household to care for her aging parents and sometimes to care for younger siblings. Widows had already married and left the family household, and their return would add considerable financial burden to the family.

Becoming a widow or widower in old age has always been a normal family transition, although the transition was experienced differently depending on the older person's economic status and the support networks he or she had established. Many were able to maintain their previous status of living due to their own or a spouse's pensions, savings, and social security. Prior to the advent of social security, however, elderly adults were much more dependent on kinship ties for support. Interestingly, their chances of living with a child were the same if they had one child or if they had a dozen. By 1970, this pattern had changed, and 75 percent of elderly widows were household heads, the majority of whom lived alone. As they aged and became more incapacitated, these widows often moved into the home of one of their children. Older childless widows were more diverse in their living arrangements, but, by 1970, a quarter of childless elderly widows over the age of 80 were living in nursing homes, a much higher proportion than was true of elderly widows with children.

Nursing homes did not become an option for elderly widows and widowers until late in the century, and then only when the parent was senile or required constant care. About 5 percent of the elderly resided in nursing homes. Considerable stigma was attached to institutionalizing a parent, although, as women increasingly joined the work force, it became less and less practical for adult women to care for their aging widowed parents. If the children lived in another community, nursing home care often was the only option. White Americans were more likely to place an older family member in a nursing facility than were black Americans, Asian Americans, or Latin Americans.

The living arrangements of elderly widows and widowers were not dramatically different from those of elderly couples, but widows and widowers lacked the potential of being cared for by a spouse. Therefore, they had more need for family care or institutionalized care than a member of a couple who could count on care from the spouse.

The death of a spouse was always a difficult transition for American husbands and wives, but, as the century progressed, additional social supports were available to help ease some of the burdens faced by the bereaved. For young and middle-aged men, remarriage often followed bereavement, and this remained the case throughout the century. Women also remarried, but late in the 20th century, as their labor-force participation generally increased, widows were not as likely to remarry as they had been earlier. Children were the primary source of emotional, financial, and other types of support for bereaved parents throughout the century.

Concerns about social security were raised with considerable vigor as the century came to a close. As the elderly population outpaced the rise in workers paying part of their wages into the social security system, it became likely that this economic cushion might no longer be available to widows and widowers in the 21st century. The movement of family members away from where their parents lived meant that elders would experience another transition if they had to leave their community to live with a child. As the century ended, more problems than solutions had been identified and elderly widows and widowers remained a vulnerable population. Although their children continued to feel strong obligations to them, these obligations were contextual and far less obligation was felt for the rapidly increasing numbers of elderly divorced and remarried family members.

SUMMARY

From the beginning of the 20th century to the end, social critics and cultural commentators raised concerns that the American family was declining and the future of American families was in a state of crisis. Observers who were alarmed about family decline pointed to the reduced rate of marriage and the high divorce rate, the growth of cohabitation, the rise in childbirth outside of marriage, and the increasing numbers of mothers working outside of the home.

These observers were right in noting some of the demographic changes that occurred in U.S. families. During the 20th century, there were substantial alterations in family life, particularly in the normative, expected sequence and timing of family events. Compared to the start of the century, American families in 2000 were much more diverse. Although many Americans still lived what would have been considered a standard life course at the start of the century—courtship, marrying at a young age and remaining married until one spouse died, raising children, living to see grandchildren be born, widowhood, and death—by the close of the 20th century, a greater proportion of Americans lived out-of-sequence family lives (e.g., parenthood before marriage), or the timing of these events were different (e.g., having children in middle age), or they had missed some of the family experiences entirely (e.g., never-married single parents). Moreover, as the life span increased due to improved health care, better diets, and less risky work environments, many Americans lived long enough to experience multiple transitions in their family lives—divorcing and remarrying more than once, for instance. It is not surprising, perhaps, that the increased complexity of family life exhibited by these alterations in family transitions appeared to be family crises and decline to some observers.

Other cultural observers argued that these transitions did not mean that families were in trouble. Instead, they pointed to the variations to the normative life course expectations as instrumental in changing and challenging normative notions of what a family should be. These observers argued that it was a static cultural definition of family that was in trouble and not families themselves, who continued to exist in a variety of forms.

The picture of a family where couples married for life, their children were born within marriage, and the mother cared for the children in the home while the father worked outside the home to provide financial support was an idealized version of nuclear families, the norm in 1900 but only one of several family life courses experienced by American families a century later. Much study of the family during the 20th century focused on these demographic shifts. To better understand family change over time, we need more study of the internal organization and decision-making processes in families and how the demographic changes influenced family organization and roles.

2

How Families Lived

FAMILY HOUSEHOLDS

"Home Sweet Home! Be it ever so humble there's no place like home." What does this mean, and has home always been "sweet?" These song lyrics were written by John Howard Payne in 1823, and the song was extremely popular at the time. The concept of "home sweet home," or the family home as haven from a cruel world has changed over time. Housing for families in the United States has taken a number of forms (i.e., high-rise apartments, apartments over places of business, tenements, row houses, duplexes, single-family detached houses, co-operatives, condominiums), but when we think of family homes it is the single-family detached dwelling that is the most iconic, probably because it represents independence, a mainstay of American character and culture.

Family historians have found that nuclear family households (i.e., mom, dad, and their children) go back as far as the 12th century in England and Italy, but they were not always the private fortress against the world as they are often perceived to be today. The notion of home as the family's refuge began in the late 18th century, but only among the urban middle classes. Our idealized version of the family household—multiple generations sharing the family home—was a myth, what sociologist William Goode (1963) referred to as "Western nostalgia." Prior to the 20th century, dwellings were more places to live and conduct business than they were what we now think of as homes. Business was transacted in the house, and unrelated individuals such as servants, apprentices, and boarders lived with the family. Children sometimes shared beds with boarders, and people rotated beds, with some sleeping a night shift and some a day shift. Living quarters were cramped, and privacy was quite limited. Many immigrant families still lived this way to an extent in the early decades of the 20th century.

The idealization of the private family household and viewing the home as an escape or haven, according to historian Tamara Hareven (2000), came about partly as a reaction to changes in urban neighborhoods. The family household provided protection from the perceived dangers brought about by the increasing numbers of immigrants in the late 19th and early 20th centuries and the growing concentration of poor families in the cities.

Changes in family functions also contributed to the idealization of the home. More specifically, in the 20th century most family members' workplaces became physically separated from the home. Business was no longer conducted in the household. As men left the home for work, the household became women's sphere of influence. Children also began leaving the household during the day as their formal education switched from the home to the school. Because family members were increasingly separated from each other during the day, returning to the home in the evening and having dinner together became an important family ritual. These changes brought about an increasingly private family household and contributed to the glorifying of women's roles as homemakers and full-time mothers; at least this was the middle- and upper-class ideal. Sarah Josepha Hale, editor of the popular *Godey's Lady's Book* (a periodical aimed at the middle class), held a view of women as the more moral and purer sex; she argued frequently in the magazine that the only respectable occupations for women were wife and mother. In the Victorian era, owning a home was a status symbol, a sign of stability and respectability. For middle- and upper-class wives, maintaining a home was a high calling and one that greatly increased their work load. This was true because, after the turn of the century, the availability of domestic help dramatically decreased. As economic opportunities for poor women increased, the ratio of domestic servants to the general population fell by half between 1890 and 1920 (Mintz & Kellogg, 1988).

Although most work moved away from the family dwelling, working-class women were likely to maintain some sort of commerce within the home—sewing, piecework, or doing the laundry of others. Working-class families also continued to share their households with boarders and lodgers long after this practice had faded among the middle class. One motivation for doing this was to bring in enough income to pay the mortgage or rent. The elderly and widows also took in lodgers to maintain their independent living. Taking in boarders was not just an urban practice, however—small-town families also did this. Thomas Wolfe's classic novels, *Look Homeward, Angel* (1929) and *You Can't Go Home Again* (1934), were loosely based on his childhood experiences growing up in a boarding house run by his mother in Asheville, North Carolina. Such houses provided cheap lodgings for single adults and were an important source of family income. Although social reformers railed against this practice as a violation of family privacy and a source of immoral behavior (male boarders were seen as a threat to female family members—a potential source of corruption and seduction), the practice of taking in boarders was common and allowed many people to own homes who would not have been able to do so without the extra income.

For middle-class Americans, changes in the home, including the increasing lack of domestic help, were accompanied by a gradual migration to the suburbs. Moving from city neighborhoods to suburbs meant that women no longer had easy access to nearby services and shops within walking distance of their homes. An unintended consequence of suburban living was that women became somewhat isolated within their houses. Most did not own cars, and mass transportation in the suburbs was either poor or nonexistent. Thus, for middle-class families, women's household work was done in relative isolation within the home, and, although most tasks required no special skills, women increasingly had no hired help to complete them.

Moving to the Suburbs, Staying in the Cities

The move to the suburbs began with the wealthy and upper middle classes, who fled apartments and houses in the city to large Victorian style homes with big yards. Two factors influenced abandoning city centers for the suburbs. First, early in the century, a large influx of immigrants from southern Italy, Hungary, and Eastern Europe crowded into eastern U.S. cities. Combined with the steady relocation of African Americans from the rural South to northern urban areas that had begun after the Civil War, cities were becoming more racially, ethnically, and economically diverse. Feminists were also finding a voice in the cities. The middle-class movement to the suburbs was in reaction to what many Americans viewed as the danger to families of feminists, radicals, immigrants, and blacks. Margaret Marsh (1990) wrote in *Suburban Lives* that,

When these men and women took stock of urban society at the dawn of the 20th century, they saw filthy factory districts, crowded immigrant ghettos, reports of anarchist terrorism and socialist electoral encroachment, black migration from the rural to the urban South, and the beginnings of black migration to the North. In addition, there were visible and prominent urban feminists demanding opportunities identical to those of men. (p. 122)

Warnings against the dangers of urban living came from many sources, even children's literature. The popular children's book, *The Wizard of Oz*, was written in 1900 by Lyman Frank Baum to warn against urban life.

Dorothy follows the "yellow brick road," a symbol for gold and riches, to the urban Emerald City. The city turns out to be a fraud, and the moral of the story is to beware of the glitter and false promises of city living. As the book ends, Dorothy is happy to be back in her modest home on a Kansas farm. Baum's attempt to encourage families to stay on the farm, however, was not successful, and the exodus from farms to urban areas continued throughout the 20th century. Families from the cities converged with rural families in populating the suburbs.

The second factor that hastened the move to the suburbs was the development of reliable and inexpensive mass transit in the forms of streetcars and trains. Mass transit made it possible for families to move farther from urban employment centers, which meant that men could commute to work relatively easily, while keeping their wives and children safe from the allegedly deleterious influences in the cities.

Immigrant families, who were generally the poorest families, remained in the cities in cramped apartments and tiny houses. Nearly 10 million immigrants came to the United States between 1905 and 1914, and most of them settled in cities. The mass immigration that added about 10 percent to the U.S. population prior to 1916 greatly slowed after World War I, but immigration continued to have a huge influence on family life in cities.

Immigrant households tended to be crowded because settled immigrants often took in newly arriving family members and friends from the old country until they could find jobs and afford to rent their own apartments. Many of these immigrant families lived in substandard tenement houses that were threats to personal health and safety. Housing reform started in 1901 with the New York City Tenement House Law, which contained codes that would result in safer housing, and this law soon spread to cities throughout the country. The enactment of new building and housing codes, however, added to the expense of housing construction. Rather than providing better and safer housing for urban dwellers, housing codes sometimes resulted in landlords and owners of apartment buildings raising rents and pricing many low-income families out of the market. The first zoning law was enacted in 1916 in New York City; like housing laws, zoning laws also were passed in communities across the nation. Prior to 1916, large-scale housing discrimination was directed toward immigrants, Catholics, Jews, and people of color. Zoning laws did not stop discrimination against these groups, but they made it harder for landlords and property owners to refuse to do business with marginalized groups. Because these laws often did not extend outside of the city limits, suburbs continued to be relatively homogeneous communities dominated by white middle-class and wealthy Protestants.

In 1949, the U.S. Congress passed the Urban Renewal Act, which promised decent housing for all families, yet housing problems continued for many. One intention of urban renewal was to make affordable housing available to city residents who had not moved to the suburbs, particularly low-income Americans and people of color. Despite the U.S. Public Housing Administration no longer allowing housing discrimination based on political, religious, and other affiliations, discrimination based on race and color was still legal and widespread. It was not until the enactment of Title VIII of the Civil Rights Act of 1968 that discrimination based on race and color was prohibited in private as well as government-assisted housing.

The Civil Rights Act of 1968 did not, however, end housing discrimination (Freeman, 2006). Discrimination was due to a general desire by whites to keep blacks out of their neighborhoods and a belief by financial institutions that blacks were poor credit risks. If blacks wanted to buy and could afford to purchase homes in white neighborhoods, they were subjected to considerable hostility by their neighbors, a hostility that many blacks refused to impose on their families. The U.S. housing market, therefore, consisted of two streams—one for blacks and one for whites. Because blacks could only buy in certain neighborhoods and housing in those neighborhoods tended to be scarce, they ended up paying relatively more than did whites for comparable housing. During the 1990s, opportunities for blacks to become homeowners increased, partly due to policy reforms designed to increase access to houses and affordable home loans. Despite these policy reforms, however, at the end of the century, blacks still lagged behind whites in their likelihood of becoming homeowners.

Similar to African Americans, housing conditions of Asian Americans did not compare well to those of white European Americans. In 1990, according to *The Encyclopedia of Housing* (Van Vliet, 1998), 53 percent of Asian Americans and 62 percent of European Americans owned their own homes. Asian Americans also lived in smaller dwellings: 25 percent of their households had more than one person per room, whereas 3 percent of white European American households were that crowded.

Latin American families also fared less well with housing than did European Americans, but they had such a strong drive to own homes that even some poor Latin American families (21 percent) managed to purchase their own homes late in the century. This probably meant sacrificing other goods and services (e.g., health insurance, transportation) to be able to purchase a home. The homes owned by Latin Americans tended to be older, smaller, less well constructed, and in undesirable neighborhoods.

As more and more African Americans, Latin Americans, and other people of color began moving out of inner cities and into suburbs—helped by rising incomes, antidiscrimination housing laws, and changes in cultural attitudes about race and ethnicity—some white Americans responded by moving to privately owned and governed residential enclaves for the affluent. Many of these communities were gated and/or walled with restricted access, and they were the main form of new housing in the fastest growing cities and suburbs. They were supported by developers who built more housing on less land, local governments that wanted to increase property tax revenues without providing additional services (many of these communities funded their own parks, schools, police forces, road maintenance and repairs via dues charged to homeowners), and by middle- and upper-class families that wanted the perceived security of being protected from crime and what they saw as government mismanagement. McKenzie (2005) referred to this phenomenon as "privatopia" in his case study of Bonanza Village, a private gated community in Las Vegas, Nevada. Bonanza Village was created by developers who worked with city officials to legally force people out of their homes by the exercise of eminent domain, a procedure in which governments buy property from private owners, even if the owners do not want to sell. Once the homeowners were forced to sell their properties, developers razed the homes, built new ones, and gated the developments. City officials had been convinced to evoke eminent domain because they wanted to help developers create homes whose appearance would enhance the ambience of the redevelopment of downtown Las Vegas.

Not everybody thought the suburbs were the solution to middle-class family growth and safety. Charlotte Perkins Gilman, a prominent urban feminist in the early decades of the century, thought that the conventional family was anachronistic and suggested that women should maintain a separate identity from the family. She suggested building apartment buildings that were designed so that all cooking, cleaning, and child care could be done collectively by people trained for those jobs, thus freeing wives and mothers to pursue careers. This was a threatening idea to those who believed in the conventional family with well-defined gender roles for women and men, and such notions were suppressed until the 1960s, when the feminist movement revealed the bleakness some women felt toward their suburban isolation. It was not until the 1990s, however, that urban gentrification lured some middle-class Americans (mostly singles, but some young families moved as well) back to urban centers. The deterioration of the urban tax base that had begun decades earlier with the loss of the middle class and the subsequent deterioration of urban public school systems was a deterrent to many families with school-age children and adolescents moving back to central cities.

Home Ownership

The movement to the suburbs in the early decades of the century stimulated a boom in building outside the cities, although there was only a small increase in home ownership. Most of the newly built single-family homes went into the rental market. A large proportion of middle-class families in the first half of the century rented rather than owned their homes.

Prior to the Depression, in an attempt to entice middle-class families into home ownership, Sears, Roebuck, and Co. began selling kit houses by mail. The company's 1908 catalog included 22 styles of homes priced between $650 and $2,500, with the most popular model being a bungalow. These houses, which were shipped by rail and assembled either by the buyer or a contractor, varied in design and price, but were generally cheaper than comparable traditionally built homes. Sears sold about 100,000 of the kit houses between 1908 and 1940, but the Depression brought the operation to an end, and mail order housing never resumed again.

In the period from 1917 to 1956, the housing market fluctuated wildly. Housing fell to extremely low production levels during the two world wars and the Great Depression and boomed after each of these events. An important outcome of World War II was federal legislation and public policies (e.g., the Federal Housing Authority and the GI Bill) that expanded the opportunity for people to own homes. The 1949 U.S. Housing Act assured "a decent home and a suitable living environment for every American family," (preamble to the Housing Act of 1949. Cited in "Action Agenda," 2006) a mandate that was interpreted to mean owning a home. Home ownership was identified with autonomy and success, significant American values. Owning a home (and a car or two) symbolized that a family had achieved the American dream.

The Housing Act, federal tax policies that allowed home buyers to deduct the interest on their mortgage payments on their income tax returns, mortgage insurance provided by the Federal Housing Administration, and supplemental assistance provided by the Veterans Administration all favored home ownership and left renters, unable to take advantage of these programs, at a huge financial disadvantage. In 1950, the median income of renters was 85 percent of the median income of homeowners, a ratio that had dropped to 50 percent by 1990 (Doan, 1997).

People who stayed in the cities had difficulty finding decent, affordable rental housing. Efforts to revive the cities, which suffered tremendous blight due to the exodus to the suburbs, typically consisted of either gentrification (renovating older housing and selling the units at high prices) or tearing down poorly maintained housing. These strategies increased the burden on the salaries of poor people who could neither afford to move to the suburbs (and often were not welcome) nor could they afford to rent the newly gentrified units that they had previously occupied.

For a period in the 1960s and 1970s, publicly subsidized housing was built for poor people, condominiums were built for those with higher income, and the production of mobile homes peaked. Even so, the construction of single-family homes increased at a rate far greater than that of multiple-family dwellings or mobile homes. The lack of low-cost but decent rental property was reflected in the fact that, between 1960 and the end of the decade, renters were paying a higher and higher proportion of their incomes for rent. An additional problem was the age of the rental units available to families. For instance, in 2000 the median age of a rental unit in New York City, Chicago, Philadelphia, and Detroit was 50 years; in newer cities (such as Houston, Phoenix, San Diego, and Dallas), the median age of rentals was 25 years. Neither the private sector nor the government had addressed the problem of aging rentals at the century's end. The growth of real income, especially for those who rented, was not positive, which meant that renters were increasingly likely to be living in substandard housing and paying an increasingly higher proportion of their income for rent. Responsibility for subsidized housing had been passed from the federal level to the state and local level, and few states or local communities had budgets equal to the task.

In the 1980s, a new problem emerged—widespread homelessness. The homeless, some of whom were families, elicited public concern but little action. Shelters, which were often supported by private charities, provided most of the care for the homeless, and the problem seemed to be increasing at the end of the century.

HOUSING

The structural style of houses changed dramatically over the course of the 20th century. According to Clark (1986), housing styles in America changed from Victorian extravaganzas during the Gilded Age to rustic bungalows in the Progressive period to ranch houses in the 1950s and 1960s and then to very large and more eclectic styles in the later decades of the century. Architects, housing promoters, builders, trade associations, and family reformers did not always see eye to eye on housing design.

The Progressive Movement and Housing
Attempts to discredit Victorian beliefs as well as extravagant Victorian houses rose shortly after the turn of the century and following the initial flight to the suburbs. Large Victorian houses, the most popular style of homes at the end of the 19th century, were replaced by rustic bungalows and simple colonial home styles. This was not a matter of changing tastes as much as it was a matter of a general reorientation of U.S. culture.

Proponents of the Progressive movement (which spanned the early decades of the century) believed that science could be used to improve the well-being of individuals and society. They were reacting to the rapid industrialization and growth of U.S. society, and they sought ways to efficiently manage and solve problems. Some of the problems these efficiency experts tried to address had to do with housing.

Several societal changes that began in the 1870s and 1880s affected the way Americans did business. Commerce and industry rapidly expanded from ocean to ocean in tandem with the expansion of the railroad, the establishment of national telephone and telegraph networks, and the growth of newspapers and magazines. Large national companies such as U.S. Steel and General Electric began providing products and services for ordinary families, and these factory-made products affected the amount and type of space needed to manage the household.

These factory products also changed the way that families lived. Laundry and baking that had previously taken at least one day each per week no longer demanded that much time and effort. Servants were no longer needed, and advertisers began showing ordinary housewives, rather than servants, engaged in household labor. The new ideal home was designed to fit more informal life-styles, and the large entryways, multiple parlors, and servants' quarters of the typical Victorian mansion were replaced with living rooms and kitchens designed for efficient, sanitary food preparation. Sleeping porches became common as people grew increasingly concerned about fresh air and healthier living. By 1910, Victorian houses were seen as overly elaborate, inefficient, and gaudy, and they were attacked as architectural atrocities (Clark, 1986).

The style of housing that followed the Victorian was based on principles of simplicity. The clean lines of the new houses fit with the Progressive movement's goals to improve sanitation and health. Popular magazines and the newly formed home economics movement supported more healthful housing, and kitchens and bathrooms were designed to facilitate easier cleaning and more efficient use of space. The National (later American) Home Economics Association was founded in 1893 by Ellen Richards, and, by 1916, nearly 200 academic institutions were offering degrees in home economics. Much of the focus of these programs was on hygiene, household management, health, and nutrition. Household management was facilitated by smaller, better-designed homes. These bungalows, sometimes called prairie- or craftsman-style houses, were the first sign of modernism in housing (McAlester & McAlester, 1984).

While home design preferences were changing from the Victorian mansion to the simple bungalow, houses also changed to accommodate the growing importance of the automobile. Cars first became commonly available between 1910 and 1920, and they were housed as horses and carriages had been housed—in a separate structure, external to the family home, and usually designed to hold one car. Over time, cars were stored in garages attached to the family home, and the size of garages increased throughout the century. Two-car garages were typical, but three- and four-car garages that equaled the square footage of mid-century homes had become common by 2000. The single-car garage suited suburban families with one breadwinner, but, as women began to join the labor force in increasing numbers in the 1960s and 1970s, families often needed two cars.

According to Clark (1986), the standard floor plan of homes during the Progressive Era consisted of a first floor that included a small front porch, living room, dining room, and kitchen—all serving multiple purposes. The living room replaced the formal Victorian parlor that had been more for show rather than family use. Smaller furniture was designed to fit the more compact spaces, and built-in window seats, bookcases, and cabinets were fairly common. Less space was allotted for displaying bric-a-brac

than previously. Round tables became popular and were used for displaying family photographs or for playing cards and board games.

Dining rooms served multiple purposes, and built-in buffets were
common as replacements for large sideboards. The dining room often
served as a place to play the piano, read, or sew. Kitchens were designed
to replicate surgeries or laboratories with cleanliness and efficiency being
the chief guidelines for design. Kitchens had outside entrances to allow
service people (grocery, milk, and ice deliveries) to come and go without
disturbing the household, and Midwestern homes often had a bathroom
in the basement to accommodate the coal man and other workmen.

The upstairs of homes during this era included two or three bedrooms,
each much smaller than those in Victorian houses. Bedrooms were now
used primarily for sleeping and were not thought to need much space.
Built-in closets replaced the large and cumbersome wardrobes and
armoires that had been used in earlier times for clothing storage.

Two-bedroom bungalows sold for between $800 and $3,000 in 1910, a
time when the middle class earned approximately $1,000 per year, so this
new style of housing was affordable. In addition to promoting the suburbs
as safer places to live, bungalows were promoted as good for the needs of
children—instead of being cooped up in city apartments, children would
have yards in which to play and would get plenty of fresh air. The bungalow fit the less formal life-style that incorporated outdoor living as well
as simplicity, and it was viewed as the ideal American home. It remained
popular into the 1920s and 1930s.

The expansion and contraction of the housing market paralleled major
events in history. Housing slowed considerably during World War I but
boomed during the prosperous Roaring Twenties. The Depression further
slowed building, and, just as the Depression ended and housing construction was underway again, the Second World War shut it down—housing
materials were needed for the war effort. Housing construction began to
accelerate again immediately following World War II.

**Housing after
World War II**
There was an enormous need for housing as military
men returned from the war and began civilian life—
going to college, working, or starting families. The high
employment following the war coupled with optimism
about the economy resulted in an unprecedented population growth—the
baby boom—and increased consumerism.

These new, larger American families needed new and larger homes and
a new housing style. The ranch house and various versions of the ranch
(e.g., split-level, tri-level) replaced the bungalow and became the new
ideal American family home. The bungalow had represented a rejection
of the excesses of the Victorian style; the modern ranch house, rather than
rejecting the simplicity of the bungalow, changed primarily to incorporate
outdoor living. Captivated by the California life-style, ranch-style houses
featured large picture windows, sliding glass doors leading to patios, and

substantial lawns. Kitchens were no longer sanitary surgeries hidden at the back of houses, but were built conveniently next to the garage (so groceries could be efficiently moved from the car to the kitchen), or at the front of the house. Family rooms became popular as places for children to play and for adults to watch television so that those who wished to read or engage in quiet activities could use the living room and not be bothered. Family rooms were often in the basement or were built as additions to ranch homes when the family income was sufficient. Families on television and in advertisements were shown radiating joy in their new ranch homes surrounded by the products of the new consumerism. Some social critics deemed the suburban ranch house developments as tasteless and boring. Despite the criticism, owning a single-family dwelling was the hallmark of middle-class status and the public in general remained satisfied with suburban living.

Because of the rising cost of building supplies, the cost of housing increased rapidly during this period. By the end of the 1940s, the median price of a home was close to $8,000 and builders searched for ways to keep costs down. A partial solution to this dilemma was prefabrication and mass production. The classic prefabricated subdivision was developed by William Levitt. His Levittown was a planned development that included recreational areas, shopping, and meeting places. The small houses (800 square feet) came in two styles—Cape Cod or ranch—had open floor plans, a picture window, living room, kitchen (built at the back of the house so mothers could supervise their children playing while they worked), bathroom, and two bedrooms on the first floor with the capability of adding two more bedrooms in an attic expansion. The houses did not have basements. By mass producing these houses, Levitt could keep costs down and allow returning veterans and their young families to become homeowners for about the same as rent would cost for much smaller apartments in the city. Levittown became the target of social critics who thought that these mass-produced housing areas fostered conformity and ultimately despair. A popular early 1960s folk song referred to the houses as "little boxes on the hillside . . . and they're all made out of ticky-tacky and they all look just the same" (Reynolds, 1962). Some of the housing developments encouraged conformist behavior by having clear rules about when laundry could be hung outdoors and how often lawns must be mowed. Families tried to create differences among their identical houses by painting them different colors, adding plantings, and sometimes customizing them by adding a room or a porch.

Families were not especially pleased with the small size of these mass-produced houses—they wanted more rooms, larger rooms, and two rather than one bathroom, among other things. Yet they bought them because they were affordable. Most young families considered them starter homes and planned to move to more spacious quarters when they began earning higher salaries. Others had saved enough money before buying a house to be able to add rooms and other amenities as soon as they moved in. This sparked the beginning of the do-it-yourself movement as many of the home improvements were done by family members.

Housing at the End of the Century The ranch-style home became less popular during the 1970s and 1980s. Once again, a modern style was followed by a return to adapted period styles. Faux Victorians, Tudor-style houses, and mock Colonials began to appear in suburban America.

Over the last few decades of the century, houses became larger. According to the Census Bureau, between 1982 and the end of the century, the median house size increased from 1,520 square feet to 2,114 square feet. This increase in size has been attributed to a combination of factors. First, low mortgage rates enabled people to buy larger homes. Second, Americans sought houses large enough to hold all of their consumer goods. Overscaled furniture such as king-sized beds, restaurant-quality kitchen appliances, large-screen televisions and home entertainment centers, sports equipment, large numbers of children's toys, vast wardrobes of clothing, and other possessions characteristic of "the good life" required display and storage space. American homes became status symbols that represented the rewards of hard work and success, even when those living in them sometimes could not afford such large and expensive homes. Architects argued that houses were designed to impress others more than they were designed to support the quality of the lives of those who lived in them (Gauer, 2004). According to critics, design and workmanship was sacrificed for size and show. Gauer argued, just as critics in the first decades of the century had argued, that such large homes added to life's complexity and stress rather than served as havens from a cruel world. Critics at the beginning and at the end of the century were dismayed at the use of large houses to show the homeowners' wealth and status. American homeowners had come full circle.

TECHNOLOGY AND LABOR IN HOUSEHOLDS

Technology and the invention of labor-saving products affected all family members in the 20th century, but perhaps none were affected more than middle- and upper-class women. From the beginning of the century, technology was brought to bear on women's new responsibilities within the family household, and new household appliances were designed to improve women's work efficiency. One such appliance was the vacuum cleaner, which became available in 1905. Although vacuum cleaners quickly became middle-class status symbols, they tended to add to women's burdens rather than alleviating them. Previously, rugs had been hung on a clothesline, where they were beaten with whisks or rug beaters to remove dust and dirt. This was heavy labor and was usually done by the husband or a male servant. The notion of spring cleaning meant just that—some cleaning was done only once a year, and carpet cleaning was one of those annual tasks. The advent of the vacuum cleaner meant that carpets and rugs could be cleaned daily, if one wished. Other so-called labor-saving devices resulted in more complex homemaking chores, which took considerably more time and also distanced men and children from housekeeping chores. Lugging a heavy rug from the house to the clothesline might require more strength than some women had, but most women could run a vacuum cleaner without difficulty. Also, standards for cleanliness began to increase—because it was easy for women to run the vacuum sweeper, husbands, neighbors, and friends expected rugs to be cleaner; women exchanged a difficult annual task that they supervised for a daily or weekly task that they were expected to do themselves.

Some machines—such as automatic washing machines and dryers—did reduce women's household labor. Prior to the availability of automatic washing machines and dryers, neither of which were available in even half of all households after World War II, laundry was went out to a laundress or was done by hand in large tubs with the help of children, husbands, and servants. Water had to be hauled and heated via a wood stove, a task requiring either muscle (often supplied by the husband) or numerous trips (made by children or a servant). The clothes were washed and rinsed by someone bent over the tub, and then the heavy, water-laden clothes were run through a hand-operated wringer to remove the excess water. The clothes were then carried outdoors and hung on a line to dry. Even with many people working together, washing a family's laundry took the better part of a day. Once dry, the clothes were brought in, starched, and dampened to prepare them for ironing, a task simplified by the electric iron, which was readily available in most households by 1941 (Cowan, 1983). Doing the laundry was an extremely time-consuming and arduous task, and it is little wonder that those who could afford it either hired a laundress or sent the laundry out. Once automatic washing machines and dryers were widely available, women began to do the family laundry on their own. By 1960, about 75 percent of homes had electric washing machines.

Another technological change that reduced women's household labor was the commercial sewing machine. Early in the 20th century, clothing construction became a chore that was increasingly relegated to outside the home. By 1910, machine-made clothing was affordable for everyone (Cowan, 1983). As late as 1894, the Sears Roebuck catalogue displayed no women's attire, but, by 1920, it offered 90 illustrated pages of women's clothing. Although women still sewed some family clothing, it was done more as a hobby than as a necessity, except for a brief period during the Depression.

The technological changes in household labor meant that women were now expected to do all of the household work—men had work responsibilities outside of the home in the factories and offices, and children's work was at school. Women still had responsibility for seeing that the same household chores were done as before these technological advances—laundry, cooking, cleaning, nursing the sick, and caring for small children and the elderly—even though they generally no longer had help with these tasks.

COOKING

Cooking was another area of domestic life that changed significantly in the 20th century. In 1900, the typical woman spent 44 hours a week preparing meals and cleaning up after them. This was much more time consuming than either cleaning or doing laundry. Wood and coal stoves were used to prepare food, so wood and coal had to be hauled from an outdoor shed or cellar. Most food was prepared from scratch, so cooking was extremely labor intensive. Baking bread took the better part of a day each week. Canning and preserving fresh fruits and vegetables in the summer—a hot, arduous task—was the only means of having fruits and vegetables to eat throughout the year.

Prepared foods increased in number and variety over the century and gradually cut down on cooking time. Dry cereals that were ready to eat out of the box were introduced in the late 1890s and began to replace cooked breakfasts. By the 1920s, the time spent on food preparation and cleanup averaged 30 hours per week, a significant reduction from the time spent 20 years earlier. Nutritionists cautioned people to cut back on the heavy lunches that were common at the turn of the century, which somewhat lifted women's food preparation workload. Widespread ownership of refrigerators (by 1950, 80 percent of households had them) combined with the availability of frozen foods, made a huge difference in how American families were fed in the middle of the century. The first frozen pot pies became available in 1951. Time spent cooking in the 1950s dropped to 20 hours a week, including cleanup. Fast food restaurants started the trend of eating out, which increased throughout the latter part of the century, as did pizza delivery and other takeout foods. By 1975, household food preparation and cleanup had dropped to 10 hours per week, and, by the end of the century, some women spent no time at all on food preparation. By 1998, 47 percent of the food dollar was spent on food eaten away from home. Ironically, at the same time that food preparation time for the average woman was dropping, there was a growing interest in gourmet cooking, and large, expensively equipped kitchens became standard in some new houses.

Cooking and Immigrants: The Real Melting Pot Was in the Kitchen

Cooking and eating are important activities for families in the United States, as they are in all cultures. The large influx of immigrants at the beginning of the 20th century slowly changed American eating habits and the food that was eaten. Immigrant-owned restaurants and cafés became gathering places where immigrants could socialize and speak in their native tongues as well as share food from their homelands. These restaurants and the bakeries and grocery stores that supported them began to attract native-born Americans by the 1920s, and Americans' tastes in food began to expand.

Seeing little hope for economic improvement in their own country, some Italian men tried their luck in the United States and left their wives and children behind. One consequence was that immigrant Italian men became far more involved in cooking in the United States than they had been in their home country (Schenone, 2003). After their wives and families joined them in the United States, Italian men maintained their interest in food preparation, although daily cooking was quickly turned over to the women. Although many poor Italian immigrants had never tasted the rich food that Italy was famous for (olive oil, wine, ricotta cheese), they often helped prepare and harvest it so they knew what the upper-class Italians ate, which influenced the foods that they prepared in the United States. Italian American cuisine became increasingly popular over the course of the century, and fusion cooking that mixed the distinctive cuisines of the various regions of Italy and adapted them to the abundance of American foodstuffs became popular. For example, Americans' love of meat and cheese was integrated into an Italian American cuisine.

Immigrant Chinese men also knew their way around the kitchen. Chinese men who came to the United States to help build the railroads were not allowed to bring their wives with them—policymakers hoped that this restriction would discourage Chinese families from settling in the United States. By 1900, there were about 4 Chinese women for every 85 Chinese men in the United States, so men learned to cook and shop for food. Chinese men opened restaurants where they served traditional Chinese food as well as fusion dishes such as chop suey and chow mein. When Chinese women arrived in large numbers later in the century, they had no idea how to cook in an American kitchen and had to be taught by their husbands. Even after Chinese women became adept at cooking in the United States, Chinese men often continued to cook for their families.

Not all immigrants were men, of course. Irish women sought jobs in American kitchens as cooks and domestic servants, and because they tended to marry late and remain relatively independent of men, they were able to work and buy land and homes with their earnings. Unlike other immigrant cultures, the Irish did not have a long tradition of exemplary cuisine. Potatoes were the central feature of Irish cuisine, and they were typically eaten plain and boiled. Many American women complained about their Irish cooks because the food they prepared was simple and somewhat bland, but, because American women were desperate for household help, Irish women had no difficulty finding jobs.

To many immigrant men and women, food was about preserving their culture. Jewish women organized their labor around Jewish dietary laws, and in kosher kitchens they carefully separated meat and dairy foods, never served shellfish, and only used meat that had been butchered according to Jewish traditions. They followed these rules because that is what they believed God wished them to do; cooking was about religion and culture as much as it was about eating. Mexican and Italian women's cooking also was related to religious observation in that specific foods were prepared for certain religious holidays.

Immigrant women's cooking was especially fervent and emotional during holiday times. The Chinese prepared special cakes for New Year's Day and remembered the dead by placing special food at shrines or burial grounds. Many Chinese women also made great efforts to prepare dishes that followed the Taoist notion of yin and yang on a daily basis. Their cooking was about balance—the right relationship between sweet and salty, grains and meats, rich and spicy. Japanese New Year's customs required the labor of both men and women to pound rice in mortar and pestle to prepare a sweet rice dish. Although more recent immigrants from Asian countries other than China, as well as immigrants from the Middle East, gradually influenced American cooking, at the end of the century, their impact on cuisine was still comparatively minor.

Mainstream American Cooking   The experiences of immigrant families with cooking were quite different from those of middle-class American families at the start of the century. The Progressive Era in America saw the application of scientific principles to cooking, using labor-saving devices, and attempting to be efficient. The beloved foods of immigrants could take a long time and a great deal of effort to cook, and the preparation was anything but scientific.

Home economics. Ellen Swallow Richards, founder of home economics and the first woman to receive a degree from the Massachusetts Institute of Technology, set up a café to demonstrate scientific and sanitary cooking at the 1893 World's Fair in Chicago. The practice of home economics began with cooking clubs and expanded into schools and universities. Professional home economists organized to improve public health, sanitation, and food standards; developed the school lunch program; and encouraged better diets containing more fruits and vegetables. They also encouraged the use of convenience foods and created a bland diet lacking the flair of most immigrants' cooking.

Although her book, *The Chemistry of Cooking and Cleaning* (Richards, 1882), was popular for three decades, Richards became frustrated with the domestic science movement and with housewives in general. She thought that, because women never became scientific in their understanding of household labor, men and technology took over and women were left with only cooking and cleaning within their control. Home economics, however, provided career opportunities for women who wanted careers but did not want to stray too far from the domestic environment of the home. Most women in the field of home economics became teachers; a few managed cafeterias in schools, businesses, and other institutions. In 1914, the federal Smith Lever Act required all state agricultural or land

Housewife preparing dinner using 1940s time-saving electric appliances. (Courtesy of the Library of Congress.)

grant schools to extend their knowledge of home economics to local citizens of the state. The Department of Agriculture hired home economists to write books and pamphlets about household issues and sent home economists out across the states to help women develop more scientific and efficient ways of running their homes. Their focus was on nutrition rather than preparing women to be good cooks.

Scientific cooking. Although focus on nutrition was paramount, another goal of the home economics movement was to establish an American cuisine. Concerns were expressed about how an American culture could develop with such a variety of foreign dishes. The logic was that if Italian immigrants continued to prepare Italian dishes, and immigrants from other countries continued to prepare dishes from their native lands, the United States would be a nation divided by food preferences and would not form a strong homogeneous society.

Cooking schools were established in cities on the East Coast to promote an American diet to immigrant women to Americanize them. The cooking taught by home economists was more scientific than artful, and white sauces, boiled roasts, gelatin concoctions, and overcooked vegetables were promoted as traditional American fare. The same New England cooking school techniques were used with Native American girls in the

Indian Boarding Schools discussed later in this book. They were taught domestic science and Americanized cooking, in hopes that learning the habits and cooking techniques of the white middle class would enable them to assimilate into white society.

At the famous Boston Cooking School courses lasted approximately six months and included psychology, physiology and hygiene, bacteriology, foods, laundry work, and the chemistry of soap, bluing, and starch. The most renowned name associated with this school was one-time director Fannie Farmer, whose name lives on today in the cookbook that bears her name (Farmer, 1918). Farmer was noted for what we might now consider rather bizarre combinations of food. For instance, in a 1905 issue of *Woman's Home Companion,* Farmer shared a favorite recipe for a salad made of Brazil nuts mixed with grapes, pineapple, celery, and mayonnaise, each serving stationed in a little fence made of four saltine crackers (Shapiro, 2001). Even though measuring cups and spoons had been in use for some time, Farmer sought to standardize expressions such as a "pinch," "heaping" teaspoons, and "rounded" cups, which commonly appeared in early cookbooks as well as in recipes handed down in families. Farmer was interested in using level measurements so that measures would be more exact and cooking failures would be minimized.

Commercialization of cooking. Most companies that sold food products or kitchen appliances set up test kitchens to help promote their products. Women responded well to these efforts, and free pamphlets and cookbooks provided recipes using new products and appliances. During the 1920s, home economists became corporate shills rather than professionals trying to revolutionize household labor in the kitchen, as it became obvious that the principles of scientific home economics that relied on chemistry, physics, and other basic scientific skills would not be adopted by housewives. Housewives would instead spend their intellectual efforts on determining what products to buy—they would become consumers rather than scientists.

Once advertisers became involved in American cooking, the concern for nutrition lessened and this continued throughout the century. According to Schenone (2003), the advertisers sold beauty, guilt, and boundless longings for perfection. Although the new food products such as boxed cereal, gelatin, and cake mixes saved time spent cooking, women spent more time on household labor related to feeding their families: They cooked less, but shopped more. Because most women lived considerable distances from grocery stores, they had to drive to buy food, a phenomenon that changed food buying in a way that negatively affected nutrition. Women no longer either raised their own food in gardens or shopped frequently in fresh food markets. Fewer fresh fruits and vegetables were purchased and eaten, because food could be canned or stored in refrigerators and freezers, thus requiring fewer trips to the store. Corporate food producers had also convinced homemakers that frozen, canned, and other processed foods were healthier than fresh foods. Processed foods were untouched by people and consumers could not determine who might have touched fresh foods. Home economists had helped develop a national phobia about bacteria and germs, and the corporate world capitalized on it.

At various times during the century, women increased their work outside the home, and, by the end of the century, a significant majority of women were employed in paid labor. During World War II, ads about Rosie the Riveter were popular, but little thought was given to helping Rosie with her cooking responsibilities. Instead, women's magazines resorted to the earlier domestic science notions of greater efficiency—take fewer steps, plan to bake for the week ahead on the weekends, do everything you ever did but do it faster. Processed cheese products, whipped cream in aerosol cans, instant mashed potatoes, and other food-like items that provided a quick fix became popular. Other products aimed at improving efficiency simultaneously became popular—dishwashing detergent that cut through grease, potato peelers that were speedier than paring knives, plastic food storage containers, automatic toasters, and many others. In fact, the advertising industry promoted time-saving products aimed at increasing homemaking efficiency throughout most of the century. One consumer advocate noted that the ultimate triumph of the advertising business was baking soda. Having found that adding baking soda to certain dishes (such as green beans) removed vitamins, new uses for the product needed to be discovered. Baking soda was then touted as a cleaning product that removed odors. Consumers were encouraged to buy the product and pour it down the drain.

During these periods of efficiency in the kitchen, creativity in food preparation was lost, unless one counted squiggles of whipped cream sprayed from a can on gelatin concoctions as creative. Anxiety among middle-class cooks was reflected in the prologue to Laura Shapiro's (2001) book, *Perfection Salad: Women and Cooking at the Turn of the Century*. She opened the book with a question posed to a popular food magazine in 1923.

> Q: *Are vegetables ever served at a buffet luncheon?*
> A: Yes indeed . . . provided they appear in a form which will not look messy on the plate. . . . Even the plebian baked bean, in dainty individual ramekins with a garnish of . . . toasted marshmallows, stuffed with raisins. (p. 3)

Cooking changed significantly during the 20th century. At the beginning of the century, nearly all meals were cooked and eaten at home. The food came from the family garden or from local farmers, and, although the cooking techniques often resulted in a great reduction of the food's vitamin and mineral content, the food was primarily fresh. In many homes at the turn of the century, hired help assisted with the cooking. By the end of the century, nearly half of all meals were eaten outside the home, and there was national concern about the American diet of high-fat, high-sodium, fast foods that have low nutritional content. In 2000, two-thirds of American adults and 16 percent of children were overweight or obese.

Cooking gradually became less central to women's lives over the course of the 20th century. Sylvia Lovegren's 1995 book *Fashionable Food* noted that tremendous shifts occurred over the 20th century in how Americans live and eat. She cited the vanishing of household servants, including cooks, the rise of the giant food-processing industries, the influence of the home economics movement, the invention and widespread use of electric refrigerators and gas or electric stoves and microwave ovens, and the entry of increasing numbers of women into the work force as potent stimuli that created sea changes in what Americans ate and how the food was prepared.

FAMILY FUN AND GAMES

Family Entertaining   Family entertaining in the 20th century often involved food. Church suppers were common family-oriented events at the turn of the century, and people joined clubs and civic organizations in record numbers. Americans liked to gather in groups, and organizations for children such as Boy Scouts and Girl Scouts became popular.

Small towns as well as urban communities often had civic bands made up of volunteer musicians, and families could attend free musical events. Parades and public parties, especially those celebrating holidays such as the Fourth of July, were mainstays of leisure life in the early part of the century. Schools also hosted social family events such as athletic contests and spelling bees. Informal social gatherings spontaneously happened, at least on the main streets and in the general stores of rural America, especially on Saturday nights. "Going to town" on Saturday nights was looked forward to each weekend, a community-wide social event for rural Americans that was partly replaced later in the century by driving to the local shopping mall.

The economic problems that beset most families during the Depression moved family gatherings from restaurant meals back into the home. Nonetheless, even though budgets were tight, family entertaining during the Depression involved food, and the Sunday night supper became a central feature of entertaining. Because money was limited and food was scarce, meals for company typically consisted of inexpensive recipes such as creamed chicken on waffles and toasted cheese on bread. Cream sauce and canned soups were recipe essentials. Women entertained each other with tea, tiny sandwiches, and cookies, and tea rooms that served dainty salads and sandwiches were popular among women. Dutch treat, or pot-luck, parties—to which guests would bring a dish to contribute—became more common as the Depression deepened and budgets became tighter. Families gathered in public parks for picnics, and buffet and potluck dinners were popular.

Because eating and drinking have always been associated with socializing, neighborhood bars, drug stores (which nearly all maintained soda fountains), ice cream shops, and diners became popular family gathering places from early in the century until the 1950s and 1960s. The gradual demise of the soda fountain, the ice cream shop, and the diner was due to a number of factors. First, smaller fountains were manufactured that enabled restaurants to offer soda drinks, and grocers realized that they could make money selling soft drinks in bottles and, eventually, in cans. Second, ice cream had been considered a luxury, and going out for ice cream was a special family treat. As family incomes increased, people felt less guilty about their indulgences, and grocers again determined they could profit by selling ice cream just as they had by selling sodas. The near-universal availability of refrigerators with freezing compartments also made it easier for families to store ice cream at home, so there was less incentive to leave the house to indulge. Third, diners, and to an extent soda fountains, were replaced in the 1960s by fast food franchises. The food from drive-in restaurants and other fast food places could be accessed more quickly than eating at a diner, and it was cheaper. Concerns about the high levels of fat in fast food were of little concern in the 1950s and 1960s, so families quickly availed themselves to this cheap but filling food. Finally, television watching began to take up an enormous amount of family time. Families no longer saw the need to leave their home to socialize—they stayed home and watched TV instead.

Leisure activities that were not accompanied by food included gardening, which became quite popular with men **Gardening** during the Depression when they raised fruits and vegetables to feed their families and among middle-class women, especially after World War I. Cultivating plants and flowers was considered to be appropriately ladylike as well as morally uplifting and healthy (Braden, 1988). Fathers' attention gradually turned from the garden to the lawn, and growing a healthy stand of grass became a status symbol and source of leisure for middle-class men. Yards were also maintained to provide safe places for children to play, which was important because children had more and more leisure time as the century wore on.

Sports have always been popular family diversions, but, over the course of the 20th century, some notions about **Sports and** sports changed; Americans participated less in sports and **Games** instead tended to be spectators. Early in the century, town football and baseball teams drew the participation of men of all ages, and these contests were attended by most residents of the community. Women were relegated to sports such as tennis, croquet, and swimming.

Later, football, basketball, and baseball largely became spectator sports, especially after the advent of television at mid-century. By the end of the century, large numbers of people were participating in sports and fitness activities (while many others were getting no exercise at all), and public and private sports facilities were available to families in even the smallest communities.

For children, sports changed from informal sandlot baseball and other loosely organized games to highly structured experiences such as Little League baseball and other sports leagues for children as young as pre-school age. The number of public parks and playgrounds expanded over the years, and large sports facilities became sources of pride in nearly all urban areas. Sports were supported as appropriate family activities by social groups, and churches often sponsored various sports leagues.

During the first half of the century, children played games in special areas of the home (such as a third floor, an attic, or basement) and on porches, in backyards, and in streets and vacant lots. Children's play activities were informal and rarely supervised or planned by adults; children's play did not become highly organized until around mid-century. Games children enjoyed playing outdoors included tag, jumping rope, leapfrog, walking on stilts, and flying kites, all activities that were brought to the United States by immigrants from other countries. Children also played various ball games outdoors. Girls were more likely to jump rope and play jacks, and boys were more likely to play marbles. Girls also played with dolls and had tea parties, activities considered appropriate socialization for their future roles as wives and mothers. Many toys early in the century were meant to prepare children for their lives as adults. Boys were offered toy rifles and hobby horses (when horseback riding was still common) to socialize them toward military service.

Parents were encouraged throughout the century to play games with their children as a way to teach values while having fun. Board games that the whole family could play were popular and many reached fad proportions—Monopoly in the 1930s and again after World War II, Scrabble in the 1950s. Card games were popular in most families, and, although some conservative religious groups opposed card playing, the disapproval was not widespread. Jigsaw puzzles became prevalent during the Depression because they were inexpensive entertainment for the entire family.

After World War I, work weeks became shorter, which allowed for more leisure time for families. This added leisure time led to widespread partic-ipation in various hobbies, a term derived from the name of the children's toy, *hobby horse*. Indeed, hobbies were first meant for children, although they later spread to all age groups. Popular hobbies could be divided into four categories—making things (e.g., needlework such as quilting, knit-ting), collecting things (e.g., stamps, coins, comic books), learning things (e.g., languages, musical instruments), and doing things (e.g., photogra-phy, gardening, sports) (Calkins, 1934). By the end of the century, hobbies were widespread among family members of all ages, and both general and specialized hobby stores could be found in most shopping malls. Hobbies continued to be somewhat faddish, with decoupage being the rage during the 1970s and scrapbooking during the 1990s. Hobbies had become big business by the end of the century.

By the turn of the century, middle-class families generally were able to afford pianos, and singing and playing the **Home Media** piano became common leisure-time activities. Once the phonograph and radio became available, however, the sheet music industry was almost wiped out along with playing the piano and singing in the home. The phonograph reached peak popularity in the 1920s, but record sales dropped sharply during the 1930s, when radios became widespread. As records improved in quality, their acceptance returned and radio disk jockeys contributed to record sales by promoting songs and albums. The delivery of music continued to improve throughout the century, and downloading music from computers was the choice of young people by the mid-1990s. The ready availability of musical choices (small transistor radios in the 1960s and 1970s, portable personal radio/tape players in the 1980s, and MP3 digital audio players at the turn of the century) meant that listening to recorded music became less a family activity and more an individual one

Family members gathering around the piano. (Courtesy of the Library of Congress.)

Listening to the radio in the 1920s. (Courtesy of the Library of Congress.)

Radio. Before television, families listened to favorite shows on the radio. Soap operas (named for the soap manufacturers who sponsored them) were well-liked dramas broadcast during the day to housewives. Children's programming was primarily on the weekends when children were not in school, although adventure shows that appealed to older children were broadcast after school. Evening programs often consisted of dramatic plays, quiz shows, and comedies that the family would enjoy listening to as a group. Radio probably reached its peak during the Great Depression. Because many families could no longer afford to go to movies, listening to the radio became a major source of family entertainment.

Television. By mid-century, television had replaced radio as the source of in-home family entertainment, and television's influence and the amount of time families spent watching it steadily increased. In 1950, 9 percent of families owned a television set; 10 years later, 87 percent had them. In 1950, people watched television about 33 hours per week, and this increased to around 50 hours per week by 2000. Families became so addicted to television and spent such a large portion of their leisure time watching it that floor plans for homes began to include space for television sets. In fact, the television set replaced the fireplace as the focus of many family living spaces. Products were invented that would help families enjoy their televisions even more. For instance, during the 1950s and early 1960s, the evening meal was often frozen TV dinners eaten on folding TV trays in front of the television so that families would not miss their favorite shows. Critics raised concerns in the early years of television that family communication would be drastically reduced if families spent a great amount of time watching TV together. To offset these concerns, advertisements for television sets stressed that television would revive domestic life by keeping children off the streets and families in the home. There was also a strong message that children who did not have access to television would fall behind intellectually, a strategy that was later used to promote the sale of computers to families. Thus, fear motivated some of these purchases.

Although the number of family conversations may have been affected negatively by television in the early days, this became much more evident in the last quarter of the century. In 2000, the average number of sets per household was 2.5, which meant that family members could simultaneously watch different programs in different parts of the home. Cable and satellite TV brought almost endless viewing choices, unlike the two or three network channels that were available at mid-century, and television programming increasingly was targeted to specific audiences. Adolescents, for example, were no longer likely to watch or appreciate programs that appealed to their parents.

As cable and satellite expanded viewing choices, and the widely available videocassette recorder (VCR), digital video disk (DVD), and pay-per-view channels expanded choices even more, family members could record and watch television whenever they wished. Consequently, it was unlikely that entire families would gather around the television set eating frozen dinners on TV trays. Although viewing rates remained high, family members increasingly were not watching the same programs or renting the same movies, so there was less and less for them to talk about. It was much more likely that family members' leisure time in the 1990s, more than at any point during the century, was spent being entertained alone or with friends rather than engaging in activities together as a family.

Personal computers. Similar to the influence of television, the personal desktop computer altered family life in the 20th century. Computers supplemented rather than displaced television. The percentage of households with children that had personal computers increased from 15 percent in 1996 to 41 percent in 1999, although there were demographic gaps in who had them and who did not. For example, single parents, African Americans, Latin Americans, and households with incomes below $40,000 were less likely to have computers than two-parent, white, higher-income families. In a study of reports from parents released in 2000, it was found that 48 percent of 9- to 12-year-olds were online, and 71 percent of 13- to 17-year-olds were using the Internet. Children reported that they were primarily using the computer for entertainment purposes. The average total time that children and adolescents spent in front of a television screen or computer monitor in the spring of 1999 was 4.35 hours per day (Stranger & Gridina, 1999). These were not hours spent with family.

Going Out   Not all family entertainment during the 20th century was conducted in the home. Movies provided popular family entertainment, as did carnivals and circuses. From 1915 to 1955, movies were arguably Americans' favorite form of narrative entertainment. The advent of television, however, seriously affected the movie business, and many theaters went bankrupt in the 1950s. Gimmicks such as 3-D movies and larger screens were used to attract families back to the movies, but they were only moderately successful. In the 1970s, some movie studios tried to ban home ownership of VCRs on the basis of copyright violations, but they lost their case. In the 1980s and 1990s, the studios changed how they marketed movies and focused heavily on blockbuster movies that opened nationwide, as opposed to the limited showing of premiers that had previously been the norm. Large multiplex cinema structures were built in the suburbs to be more conveniently located for the population base, but movies never fully recovered from the effect of television.

Carnivals traveled the country, setting up wherever people gathered, such as county and state fairs—and, later in the century, shopping center parking lots. Circuses traveled similarly during the first half of the century, using mammoth tents as the venue, but, by mid-century, most were performed in urban areas in permanent indoor arenas. In 1919, Barnum & Bailey and Ringling Brothers merged and became the largest circus in the country—and remained so for the rest of the century. Circuses continued to be somewhat popular, but traveling circuses were primarily solicited for purposes of charity fundraising, and they would not likely have remained profitable without such sponsorship. A modest revival of interest in circuses was brought about by circuses on television.

Amusement parks were another source of family entertainment, with Coney Island in New York being the first such park established in the 1890s. Amusement parks continued to gain in popularity for family vacations, but the Depression and movies dampened people's enthusiasm for them and many closed. In 1919, there were nearly 1,500 amusement parks in the United States, a number that had dwindled to less than 100 by the end of the century. People became bored with amusement park rides over time, and, to stay competitive, amusement parks had to keep upgrading and adding new rides to keep customers coming through the gate—an expensive and not always profitable enterprise. Some early amusement parks discouraged attendance by African Americans, a stance that was economically unfeasible and difficult to maintain in the late 1950s and early 1960s. As urban amusement parks became less lucrative for the owners, they also became seedier, and families perceived them as somewhat unsafe. Adolescents and young adults often had access to amusement parks via the subway, and their quite visible presence made some families uncomfortable. The 1955 opening of the first theme park, Disneyland in California followed by Disney World in Florida, established theme parks as family vacation destinations that were unparalleled in U.S. history. These theme parks fit well with the growing popularity of family vacations and were thriving at century's end.

By the end of the 20th century, unlike the beginning, family vacations had become part of the cultural ideal as an essential element of the good life in America, and many families from all economic backgrounds expected to take family vacations. **Family Vacations** Originally, family vacations were enjoyed only by middle-class and wealthy Americans. Few companies offered paid time off to employees, so few workers could afford vacations. Moreover, many Americans in the early century had concerns about the value of vacations—they thought that too much leisure time was potentially dangerous, leading workers astray with opportunities for sloth and laziness. Although there was a general cultural uneasiness about leisure time in particular and vacations specifically, the sentiment began to shift, at least among middle-class workers, to a belief that vacations were beneficial to those engaged in mental work, if done in moderation and if appropriately wholesome activities were involved.

In contrast, having too much free time, particularly in the form of a week or two of leisure time spent away from the demands of the workplace, was seen by many middle-class Americans as possibly harmful to men and women who worked in physical labor, such as factory workers. For physical laborers, a day or two of rest on the weekend was seen as an adequate amount of relaxation.

Many families went to destination resorts and spent their entire vacations there. Swimming, bathing in the ocean or the Great Lakes, or "taking the waters" at thermal hot springs were popular family destinations. The thermal waters were seen as possessing curative powers for individuals who had arthritis, gout, and polio, and for mental problems as well (e.g., "nerves," depression). Rigorous physical activities such as swimming, hiking, and camping were seen as character-building and physically rejuvenating.

Touring via train, bus, or car to national and state parks also was a popular vacation choice; such trips were seen as educational for the whole family and could be combined with other outdoor activities. The National Park system, originally accessible only by railroad, eventually became accessible by car, and families began to flock to the hotels and motels that grew up around the parks. Park service reports indicated that 1 in 300 Americans had visited a national park in 1916, a number that had increased to 1 in 3 by 1954, and those figures continued to increase steadily throughout the century.

Despite concerns about the working classes wasting time on vacations, from 1900 to 1940, a growing number of working-class white, African

American, and immigrant families also began to enjoy vacations. Factory owners and managers tried to restrict the amount of vacation time available to them, and before World War II most vacation time was unpaid. Consequently, camping and short outings to fish and picnic at nearby lakes and public parks were popular vacation choices for poor families, as were visits to family members. As cars became more affordable, short road trips became part of working families' vacation plans. The annual vacation was slow in coming as a worker benefit, however; in 1927, only about 5 percent of American wage earners worked in factories that had vacation plans.

During the first three decades of the century, more and more middle-class black Americans took annual vacations. Because they were not usually allowed to go to the same resorts as whites, enterprising black American entrepreneurs built resorts specifically for African Americans, often near popular vacation spots for affluent white Americans, such as Atlantic City, New Jersey, and Newport, Rhode Island. Many of these destination resorts thrived because they provided middle-class African Americans a chance to relax with their families and not have to deal with separate but equal policies and outright racial discrimination. Jewish families also were banned in some popular resorts, so resorts for middle-class Jewish families also were built in the early part of the century.

During the Depression, the idea of a family vacation seemed frivolous to many Americans. Although vacationing remained popular even during this period of economic hardship, far fewer families could afford them, and, for many families, a vacation made little sense when the breadwinner was unemployed. Middle-class and wealthy individuals and their families continued to take vacations in the 1930s, however, if it was financially feasible for them to do so.

In 1940, about 25 percent of union members and a smaller number of all workers received annual paid vacations, usually one week. World War II reduced the opportunities for families to travel. Young and middle-aged men were at war overseas, older men and women of all ages were engaged in the war effort in the United States, and gas and other commodities were rationed. Vacations were taken, but it was more patriotic to stay on the job and to spend free time doing something to help win the war.

After World War II, Americans were more than ready to enjoy the fruits of victory and peace, and hitting the road on a family vacation was one way that Americans celebrated their newfound prosperity. Perhaps the historical distrust of time off from work and the possible pitfalls that awaited people with too much free time were reduced after years of economic difficulties and war. Thousands of Americans had sacrificed, suffered, and risked everything they had, including their lives, so that the American way of life could prevail. Americans seemed to think collectively that they had earned some recreational time. Paid vacations more often became part of the benefit packages that companies offered laborers and skilled workers and these paid vacations sometimes were two weeks rather than one.

A growing recreation and leisure industry was eager to help working Americans and their families discover ways to have fun on vacation. New amusement parks sprang up, and cheap gasoline and interstate highways built in the late 1950s and 1960s made it easier than ever before for moms and dads to pile the kids in the car and hit the road. A popular advertisement from this era encouraged Americans to "See the USA in your Chevrolet. America is inviting you to call." Antidiscrimination laws, first passed in the northern United States and later in the South, opened up vacation venues to African Americans, Jews, and other groups that had been discriminated against.

The motel industry expanded rapidly near mid-century, making traveling vacations appealing to families who were not interested in spending their nights in camping tents or holed up in tiny remote cabins. But some families *were* interested in camping for pleasure, and the popularity of family camping trips spawned a major industry developing and selling innovative and lightweight camping equipment.

In the late 1950s, concerns that the Russians and other potential enemies of the American way of life were doing a better job of educating their children led to many educational changes that extended to family vacations. Reminiscent of the early years of the century, parents included trips to Washington, DC, to the Smithsonian and other federal buildings, to Civil War battlefields, and to cities rich in U.S. history such as Boston and Philadelphia, so that family leisure could be combined with enrichment for children and adults.

Gradually, in the last quarter of the century, vacations became more about fun and relaxation and less about enrichment and self-development. Of course, there were still plenty of parents who used vacations to expose their children to new ideas, help them learn new skills, and develop themselves in some ways. However, vacations in the last few decades of the century were increasingly seen as opportunities to bond as a family, to get away from the hassles of daily life for a while, and to focus on relaxation and fun.

SUMMARY

At the beginning of the century, many middle-class and wealthy families lived in Victorian homes in the suburbs, poor immigrant families typically were crowded into tenement settlements in cities, and most of the population lived on farms. Few families owned their own homes. Cooking and cleaning was laborious work that required participation of the entire family, including children, plus sometimes paid helpers. Leisure time was rare, even for children. As the century progressed, many farm families and middle-class urban dwellers moved to the suburbs. The poor were left behind, often in urban ghettos. The American dream of home ownership and the possession of cars and household goods became a possibility for large numbers of families following World War II, but one-wage-earner families among the working class were a brief mid-century artifact. By 2000, home ownership was common, most wives and mothers worked, and meals were increasingly eaten out of the home. Although most jobs allotted at least a few days of vacation (few did in 1900), many families were on such a financial treadmill that they often did not take them, or at least they did not use all of their vacation days.

If a family from 1901 could be transported in a time machine to the end of the 20th century, they would be amazed at the differences in how family members spent their days. Technological advances made house-work easier, but some of the ease was offset by increased standards. Technology made more leisure time available for families, but electronic-based entertainment tended to separate family members from each other as each person pursued his or her own leisure activities. Household chores were sometimes outsourced to professionals, which provided family members with both more time for leisure and more time for paid work outside the home.

It is likely that visitors from the year 1901 would quickly learn to like the ease of modern life, but they might also wonder why family members spent so little time together and why they felt so stressed. Home may still have been sweet, but, in 2000, homes were more likely to be empty much of the time.

3

Work and Family Life

Work is a term that can be used in many ways. You can work for a living, work out at the gym, work on a relationship, or work on improving your math skills. As we discuss work and family in this chapter, we define work as activities that either produce goods or services for the family or as activities in exchange for pay or support. Work can be categorized as *market work*—which is paid—and *nonmarket work*—which is not paid. Family survival is dependent on both kinds of work.

This chapter gives much attention to the market work of wives and mothers throughout the 20th century. The employment of women outside the family home was a controversial social issue, partly because cultural norms and ideologies about the roles and duties of wives and mothers placed their lives within the boundaries of home and family life. In contrast, men were expected to work outside of the home to support their families, so *not* being employed was the issue for family men. With the exceptions of farm families, turn-of-the-century poor and immigrant families, and the Depression years, children were not generally expected to work, and when they did, the purpose usually was not to help support the family. Consequently, this chapter focuses more on the employment of wives and mothers than on other family members' market work.

WORK AND FAMILY BEFORE 1900

In preindustrial societies, almost every family member, including children, worked in order to survive. Work was such an integral part of everyday life that the notion of a weekend did not exist. Until the early 1900s, Sundays and holidays were considered days of rest, but Saturdays were working days.

Prior to the 20th century, most American families worked in agriculture, but they also engaged in carpentry (e.g., making furniture) and they made other goods for use in their homes such as candles, cloth, and clothing. Families had to be self-sufficient, and what they could not grow or make they obtained by bartering. Men, women, and often children shared home-maintenance activities, although cooking, cleaning, and sewing were nearly always done by women. In fact, work in most societies has been assigned to people on the basis of sex, although which sex has been assigned to what jobs has changed over time and varies among cultures.

In 1700, parents taught their children how to make a living raising crops and livestock or, in some cases, parents had special crafts or skills (e.g., shoemaking, saddlemaking) that they taught their children to enable them to make a living as adults. Families were self-sufficient, but they usually raised enough food only for themselves and did not sell produce or crops to others. By the late 1800s, this style of life had markedly changed. Farmers began to raise cash crops, meaning they grew more than their families could consume, and they used the money from selling crops to purchase household goods rather than producing everything themselves. At first made by individual craftsmen, increasingly household goods were manufactured in factories. As a result, factories became a source of employment, attracting men from rural areas who had struggled to make a living as farmers or were too poor to farm. Because small farms in the 1800s usually could not support large families, many children at very early ages left the farm to work in the factories where many of the household goods they had previously helped produce were now being made.

As this transformation of the economy took place, many tasks that children had performed to help their families survive were now bartered or purchased and, thus, children in many families changed from being an economic asset to an economic liability. In earlier years, children helped provide for the family, but now parents needed to provide for them and invest in their education. When children were no longer economic assets, families began to have fewer of them, which generally enabled parents to invest more emotionally and financially in each child.

Industrialization brought about many changes, and throughout the 19th century the paid labor force became increasingly dominated by men, which left women in charge of the unpaid labor of running the household. In fact, in 1840 women and children made up nearly half of the industrial labor force. As labor force positions became scarcer due to an economic depression in the mid-19th century, unions decided that women and children were threats to take jobs from male workers, and they organized to drive them out of the factories and mines. The unions' efforts were joined by those of middle-class social reformers who were concerned about the safety of women and children in the paid work environment. Working together, the unions and the reformers managed to ban women and children from certain jobs considered dangerous or immoral.

First they succeeded in passing laws that reduced the hours that women and children could work and the types of jobs they could perform. Risky positions such as working in steel mills and in mines were outlawed, but women also were banned from relatively safe jobs such as practicing law, tending bar, delivering telegrams, and serving as streetcar conductors (Padavic & Reskin, 1990). Although the efforts to protect women and children from certain job-related dangers were successful, in the process they also were prevented from earning the higher wages that accompanied some jobs, and eventually they were prohibited from working for wages at all. This joint movement of the unions and the reformers succeeded in identifying the paid labor market as primarily an adult male enterprise.

Industrialization led to men working away from home, which greatly reduced fathers' contact with their children. They no longer, except in rural areas, worked side by side with their children, teaching them skills and guiding their moral development. Children became the responsibility of their mothers, and wives became almost totally dependent on their husbands for financial support. Thus, 19th-century industrialization resulted in a gendered work force that brought about the ideology of *separate spheres*—the notion that men's natural environment was outside the home and that women's natural environment was within the home. This ideology weakened but did not abate over the course of the 20th century, at least among white middle-class Americans. By the end of the 20th century, the labor market was shared by both men and women, but wage discrepancies remained, even for men and women holding the same jobs.

THE PROGRESSIVE ERA

For urban families, the work lives of men and women became increasingly separate in the early decades of the 20th century, as did nearly all aspects of married life. Marriage and childbearing were the socially expected goals for women, material success in the outside world the goal for men. When married women worked, it was a sign of the husband's failure to support his family. Public policies and popular sentiment worked consistently toward the goal of ensuring that, as six-term Congressman Joe Eagle of Texas put it in the first quarter of the century, a woman's work was making one good man a good wife and properly rearing a family of children (Chafe, 1991, p. 75). In 1900, the societal value that mothers should stay home with their children was so strong that some states passed legislation providing funding to support single mothers whose husbands had died, were disabled, or were in prison. Only in extreme cases was it considered appropriate for a mother to work outside the home.

In 1924, Lynd and Lynd (1929) did a sociological study of family life in a town in Indiana that, for privacy's sake, they referred to as *Middletown*. They concluded that most husbands and wives in Middletown had little in common as a result of a sharply gendered division of responsibilities and interests. Middle-class and wealthy couples in particular lived in separate subcultures.

The separate spheres ideology, although seemingly functional for middle-class families, was an impossible arrangement for most working-class families. Most working-class families also supported the cultural value that "a woman's place is in the home," but few could get by on one paycheck. Consequently, in the first two decades of the 20th century, the division of labor between work and family life for couples in middle-class white families differed markedly from the division of labor in black, Latin American, and white working-class families. Although men from all racial, ethnic, and social class backgrounds were expected to earn money to support their families, and women, regardless of background, were expected to manage their households and children, primarily it was only middle-class white women who were completely out of the paid labor force. When they did work, their expectations were quite different from those of working-class women. To financially help their families, yet maintain the cultural standard that women should not work outside the home, working-class women and women of color sometimes took in laundry, did piecework, or engaged in other paid activities that they could do in the home. They usually were very poorly paid for this work, and social reformers, intending to challenge the inequity of the pay, removed these meager opportunities to earn money, leaving the families in even worse financial shape.

For immigrant families, work evolved a bit differently. Beliefs regarding women working outside the home varied among immigrant groups. Many Slavs, Italians, and Irish removed children from school and sent them to work because they considered it unseemly for women to work outside the home. In many immigrant families, because the welfare of the group was more important than the welfare of the individual, children's education fell by the wayside if the family needed them to earn money (Mintz & Kellogg, 1988). Some immigrant families required their daughters to leave school and work so that their sons could continue their educations. Jewish immigrants and black Americans were more likely to keep their children in school, even if it meant lost family income.

"Getting a living." At the start of the 20th century, workplaces in cities tended to be fairly close to home, so nearly everyone walked to work. Change in work-home proximity was starting to be evident by the First World War, and, although men still walked to work when they could, by the middle of the 1920s, some had commutes that required use of public transport (e.g., trolleys, trains). In Middletown, 45 percent of men lived more than a mile from where they worked, and 20 percent lived more

than three miles from work (Caplow, Bahr, Chadwick, Hill, & Williamson, 1982). Because men often left their homes early in the morning for work and did not return until late in the day, people began to see disconnections between "living" and what was sometimes known then as "getting a living."

Getting a living generally was easier for middle-class men than it was for working-class men. Middle-class men started their workdays an average of two hours later than working-class men, had more flexible work schedules, and they could take an hour for lunch away from the work site. In contrast, working-class men typically arose at six A.M., walked to work, worked for 10 hours every day except Sundays (Saturdays were half-days), ate lunch hurriedly near their work stations, and left at five P.M. (Caplow et al., 1982). The work in factories was dirty and exhausting, and the conditions often were stressful (loud, smelly, hot) and unhealthy. Pay was low, the work was grueling, and the hours were long. According to Mintz and Kellogg (1988), typical industrial workers earned 22 cents an hour and worked an average of 59 hours a week. Coal miners worked an average of 52 hours a week for 20 cents an hour. Working conditions were dangerous, accidents were common, and mortality rates were high. There was no disability insurance or workers' compensation. When accidents occurred, the victims' working life was often over. Accidents or not, the working lives of individuals tended to be short because people could not keep up with the hard physical labor much past the age of 40.

Even when working-class individuals had jobs, the work usually was sporadic. Few could count on continuous work throughout the year, and the threat of layoffs was constant, even when the economy was booming. Most working-class families could not afford for the primary wage earner to be laid off for any length of time. Shift work in factories meant that some men had to work at night, which further created distance between these husbands/fathers and their families; they slept while the family was awake and worked when the family slept, leaving little time together. Working-class families sometimes had to relocate to find better work opportunities. In some cases, moves contributed to family instability and, in others, strengthened kinship ties. Family members had to depend on each other for support, and this was especially true of immigrant families who had no one but kin to turn to for help.

Working-class laborers typically had shorter working lives than white-collar workers—a factory worker was considered old at age 40 to 45. Men in their 40s were often let go by employers because they were no longer productive—they were too tired and beat up to do the demanding work. Middle-class men generally were considered to be productive for slightly longer—they might work into their 50s before being thought of as too old to keep pace with the work's demands.

Unemployment. Working-class men were frequently out of work. The average immigrant factory worker in the first decade of the 20th century was unemployed three months of the year. Even though the U.S. economy flourished after World War I, about 25 percent of American families in the 1920s experienced a work disruption of their primary wage earner due to layoffs or being fired.

Few community support services were available to help families who had financial problems, and the loss of the primary family wage was a crisis. Working-class families generally lived from paycheck to paycheck, so unemployed fathers hustled to make money any way they could. Finding work could be a discouraging proposition because layoffs frequently were industry-wide and involved hundreds of men, so there was a lot of competition for any local job openings. Most poor fathers had a relatively small geographic area in which to search for work because they did not have cars or access to other reliable means of transportation. Unemployment became a family affair in poor families—everybody in the family was expected to help earn money if he or she could.

Middle-class families tended to face different challenges than did working-class families. It was not socially acceptable for middle-class wives or children to work, so middle-class fathers had to find work quickly or borrow money from family and friends until they were able to find work. Wives were expected to help by economizing on household purchases and creatively stretching grocery budgets, but rarely did they seek jobs—even when their husbands were unemployed. The children were more likely than the women to find jobs outside the home to help out the family.

For both working-class and middle-class men, loss of employment was a source of shame and embarrassment. It meant they had failed at their main family-related responsibility: to be the breadwinner. Marital quality suffered when men were out of work, and family life in general was stressful when fathers were unemployed and money was tight.

Even when fully employed, working-class men seldom made enough to financially support large families. At the turn of the 20th century, a family of five needed about $500 per year to pay for essentials (food, rent, coal and gas, clothing, and a few extras such as $7 a year for recreation)—more than a factory worker typically made. Nearly three decades later, the average family needed about $1,500 annually to make ends meet—again, more than working-class men typically earned. It was not unusual, therefore, for wives and children also to earn money however they could. Earning a living was hard and demanded long hours from nearly everyone in the family who could contribute.

Wives and mothers at work. Low-income women were more likely than middle-class women to work—nearly half of working-class women were employed in Middletown in the 1920s. Working-class wives worked out of necessity, to supplement their husbands' earnings, to compensate when men were laid off, and to help pay off debts. They made money by working in factories when they could and working as domestics in the households of wealthier women. Women's wages were low; factory workers earned about half of what men did for comparable labor. Neither wives nor husbands were pleased when women had to work.

In contrast, most middle-class women stayed at home, caring for children and tending to household duties, sometimes with the help of servants (if they could afford them). In Middletown, 2.5 percent of middle-class wives worked in 1924 (Caplow et al., 1982), most were employed in "semi-artistic" jobs (e.g., artists, private music teachers) that were not intended to supplement the family income as much as they were to provide the women with a creative outlet. For most middle-class married women, working outside the home was thought to be demeaning and unladylike.

Even if a middle-class married woman was interested in having a job, there were few opportunities. With the exception of small mom-and-pop business operators, employment prospects for married women were restricted. Single women could teach school, wait on tables, or be secretaries or nurses, but once married they were usually required to resign from their jobs. In some communities, married women could work until they became pregnant, but then they either had to quit or were fired.

Children as workers. Working-class families in general and immigrant families in particular relied heavily on their children for income. Most second incomes in families came from employed children rather than from wives. Because few jobs were open to women and they were expected to run the households, children had to bring in money for families to survive (West, 1996).

Although labor reformers tried to spare children from doing factory work or mining, working-class children often still worked in such jobs. They also found jobs as newsboys, messengers, or they helped shopkeepers by doing odd jobs. Working-class parents generally were opposed to child labor reforms designed to restrict the employment of children. Although they wanted a better life for their children, they also needed their children's wages for survival.

Middle-class children usually did not work for wages, but when they did (e.g., delivering newspapers, cutting the neighbor's lawn, babysitting), it was more likely because their parents wanted them to develop strong character than for economic gain. School was compulsory until age 14 in most states, and most middle-class children attended past the compulsory age. When they worked, it usually was after school and on Saturdays.

Farm families and work. Farm families early in the 20th century worked and lived as farmers had lived for decades—everybody pitched in. Farming was labor intensive, and all hands were needed to run a farm. On the farms and ranches of America, some work responsibilities were divided by gender (wives did the cooking and laundry, husbands did the heaviest physical labor, such as stacking hay bales), and other duties were done by whoever was available and old enough. That is, everybody

Some of Newark's small newsboys. (Courtesy of the Library of Congress.)

helped harvest crops, pull weeds, and tend livestock. Hours were sunrise to sundown in the growing season, and family life activities were dictated by what needed to be done to keep the farm operating smoothly. As late as 1935, 6 million of 6.8 million farm families did not have electricity (Mintz & Kellogg, 1988), so even family members who had enough energy to engage in family activities after dark were limited to what could be done by the dim light of kerosene lamps.

Very young children were able to aid in many farm tasks, including working in the fields. After men and older boys plowed and created large furrows, younger children helped flatten the soil so it would be ready for planting. Some used knives or hoes to break up the clods of dirt while others used a horse or mule to pull a log or a harrow made of wood with iron hooks. Young boys and girls also helped plant crops, weed fields, and keep hungry livestock and birds away from the crops. Other chores included milking cows, gathering eggs, and herding cattle. Rural boys and girls were often responsible for providing food for their families by hunting small animals and birds, fishing, and gathering wild greens, berries, and fruits. Family members of all ages had to work to harvest the crops. It was not unusual for children in rural areas to spend 14 hours each day helping their parents with a variety of tasks.

Farming was so labor intensive and so demanding of the resources of the whole family that Progressive Era child labor reformers were careful in drafting child labor restrictions to distinguish "good" laboring experiences that taught children skills and built character from exploitative child labor. Most legislatures considered family farm work to be a good child labor experience (Zelizer, 1985). In fact, the reason that schools in the United States do not meet during the summer months was originally to enable farm children to help with various agricultural tasks. Southern schools also dismissed students during the cotton harvest in the fall. At the end of the 20th century, the anachronism of dismissing students during the summer months created child care problems for many dual-earner families.

Paid work and fringe benefits. World War I had a considerable effect on the economy; employment opportunities increased, especially in manufacturing. Workers received wages, but benefits such as health care and pensions were not provided and were not considered critical. If someone was ill, too old to work, or had expenses beyond what they could manage, other family members were expected to step in and help. Unions and employers agreed that families should be responsible for helping in this way, and unions focused their efforts on increasing wages and workplace safety. Samuel Gompers, president of the American Federation of Labor, argued in 1917 that providing other kinds of benefits "weakens the spirit" and breaks down individual freedom. Unions did, however, provide lump sum survivor benefits after the death of an employee, and payments were also made to workers who became disabled on the job. Retirement benefits were uncommon, but the average life expectancy for men in 1915 was 52.5 years, so this was likely of little concern.

THE GREAT DEPRESSION

Millions of people's lives were changed by the Great Depression. Many men and women were laid off, and wide-scale factory and business closings meant that there were few places where an unemployed man could find work. The competition for jobs was fierce, which meant that employers did not have to pay high wages to hire good people. Those who were lucky enough to have a job usually made less money than they had a decade earlier. Almost no sector of society was spared from the effects of the Depression. Even seasonal farm workers and ranch hands lost jobs because of years of drought in the Midwest and western United States in the 1930s. Many farm workers and their families, especially those from the South and Midwest, headed west to California looking for better economic opportunities. John Steinbeck's 1939 classic novel, *The Grapes of Wrath,* was a powerful portrayal of the plight of these migrants.

Although about 6 percent of married women worked at the turn of the century, 15 percent were working in the paid labor force during the Depression and many others worked "off the books"—that is, the employers paid them cash, which was not reported to the state and federal

Depression-era rural Midwest dust storm. (Courtesy of the Library of Congress.)

governments for tax purposes (Coontz, 2005). In addition to taking on paid work, women's unpaid work within the home increased. Because of scarce resources, women had to return to making clothes for the family, canning and preserving food, and cooking from scratch rather than using more expensive prepared foods.

The economic pressures placed on nearly all families during the Depression were harsh and affected family relationships and family stability. Many people avoided marriage, believing that they could not afford the responsibilities—the marriage rate fell to an all-time low in the early 1930s and stayed low until 1940. The birth rate also fell, as couples were reluctant to add another mouth to feed. The strain of trying to make ends meet was too much for many married couples to bear—marital conflicts increased in the 1930s, and there were many permanent separations (never filed as divorces to avoid the legal expenses).

The Depression shaped family structures—tearing some couples and families apart, preventing others from coming together, reducing the size of families and households as childbearing was postponed and family members left home looking for work, and increasing the size of other households as adult offspring delayed establishing their own homes by remaining with their parents. The Depression also shaped how couples and families functioned. Not surprisingly, given the financial straits that families encountered, issues involving work and money were paramount. Some families became more cohesive, and board games such as Monopoly became popular as families spent more time at home together because there was no money for outside entertainment. Financial stress over paying bills, however, was more likely to pull families apart than bring them together.

In addition to its immediate effects, the Depression had many long-term effects on families and individuals. Many of those who experienced deprivation feared being poor again and were reluctant to invest money or to purchase anything—including houses—without having the cash to do so. Some older Americans at the end of the century, the remaining survivors of the Great Depression, were frugal beyond common sense. They sometimes refused to operate their air conditioning during the hot summer because of the expense, even though they could afford to pay their bills. Some would not turn on lights in order to minimize electric bills and would fall in their homes because they could not see. It was not uncommon for some of these ultra-frugal Depression-era survivors to suffer from heat stroke and sustain injury as a result of preventable falls. Although frustrating to the children of these Depression survivors, the influence that decade had on those who lived through it generally marked their psyches forever. Many could not be convinced that they would not end up destitute if they gave up their frugal ways. Children who grew up during the Depression remembered the family tension created by their mothers working during that time. They associated their mother working with the failure of their fathers to adequately provide, and, as adults, this generation was particularly averse to mothers working outside the home.

Women and work. A 1936 Gallup poll indicated that 82 percent of those surveyed thought that wives of employed husbands should not work. By 1939, 90 percent of men believed that women should not hold a job after marriage, and 75 percent of women agreed. The breadwinner-helpmate model of marriage—which reflected social, cultural, and religious beliefs about the proper role of men and women—continued to be a popular cultural ideal, even though most families could not afford to live on one income.

Although media of the era—movies, radio, magazines, and newspapers—praised the plucky single girl who could hold her own and was not easily pushed around, they did not depict these young women continuing their autonomous ways once they married. The ideal model was not that of a marriage between equals (May, 1999). Instead, media portrayals of autonomous women in egalitarian marriages tended to show marriages in trouble until the woman allowed herself to be "domesticated," either by having children and settling down or by subordinating herself to the wishes of a strong husband (e.g., *Blonde Venus,* 1932, starring Marlene Dietrich or *His Girl Friday,* 1940, with Rosalind Russell and Cary Grant).

A wife prepares breakfast for her husband before he leaves for work. (Courtesy of the Library of Congress.)

At the start of the Great Depression, few white married women were employed—70 percent of single white women aged 20 to 44 were working in 1930, compared to less than 12 percent of married white women. Marital status, however, did not affect the working status of black women; married black women were three times more likely to be employed than were married white women. In 1930, nearly 60 percent of the employed women in the United States were blacks or immigrants. Most of these women worked in low-paying jobs as domestics or apparel factory workers. Domestics typically worked between 10 and 12 hours per day for as little as a dollar per day in some cities. Live-in housekeepers for rich people made more, but they had to leave their own families during the week to do these jobs and went home to their families only on weekends.

Their mothers or a relative usually filled in for them by taking care of their households and children while they were gone.

Even though the Depression served as an impetus for married women to seek outside employment, they faced pressure not to do so by their husbands, society as a whole, and government at all levels. Hostility toward working women was common. The American Federation of Labor resolved that married women whose husbands had permanent positions should be discriminated against in the hiring of employees.

Governmental policies. President Franklin Roosevelt's New Deal plan to get America back to work was radically different from previous government policies, but little in the New Deal encouraged employment equality between husbands and wives. Instead, policies supported jobs for unemployed men and discouraged married women from working. For instance, the Economy Act of 1932 mandated that only one spouse could be employed by the executive branch of government, if personnel reductions were necessary. As a result, 1,600 married women lost their jobs. State governments followed this lead, prohibiting married women from holding state jobs. Many local governments would not allow married women to teach. A 1930–1931 study showed that, of 1,500 school systems surveyed, 77 percent refused to hire married women, and 63 percent fired female teachers if they married. City councils across the country asked local employers to refuse employment to married women, and federal laws were passed that comparatively overtaxed single male workers and all female workers as a means of increasing men's incentive to marry and women's incentive to not work outside the home.

Although it was understandable at a time when some families had no breadwinners for there to be resentment against families that had two, for the most part, the jobs held by women were not ones that men would have taken. Most married women were employed in low-paying "pink collar" jobs or in service jobs. When married women had to leave a position, their jobs were not taken by men; instead, they were taken by single women, who often were contributing breadwinners to their parents' households. Thus, governments at all levels—local, state, and federal—encouraged married men to assume the primary responsibility for their families' financial well-being and encouraged married women to stay at home.

The Social Security Act of 1935 provided for unemployment compensation and retirement benefits for workers as well as aid to single mothers (Aid to Dependent Children). Single mothers at this time, as was true at the turn of the century, were primarily widows, and the federal aid was intended to enable them to stay home with their children rather than having to work outside the home. Unlike earlier decades of the century, unions during the Depression sought better hours for employees, better pay, safer working conditions, unemployment compensation, and retirement and health benefits. The unions' goal was to push for a high enough wage for men that their wives and children would not have to work.

Despite the governmental and institutional support for male breadwinners, some married women found work to help support their families. By 1940, slightly over 15 percent of married women were employed. Rates of employment for married women increased five times faster in the 1930s than for other women, mostly because married women were working for the first time. They did not take jobs away from men for the most part, but from other women. Some white women took more menial jobs than they would have otherwise because they needed to work. They took jobs as domestics that had been held by black women—36 percent of married women worked as domestics or in personal service jobs, with another 20 percent working in canning and apparel factories. Working wives during the Depression were not working for pin money or fulfillment; they were working for family survival. In 1940, less than 6 percent of married women worked if their husbands made over $3,000 a year, but 24 percent worked if he made less than $400.

Most single mothers, of course, worked out of necessity, and there were more of them in the Depression years because of desertions, separations, and divorces brought on by financial strain. Family dissolution was common because many men felt they had failed and could not face their families and because marital hostilities were greater when money was tight (or nonexistent). For some mothers, unemployed husbands were financial burdens, and they were better off without them, even if this meant struggling to make ends meet on her wages alone.

WORLD WAR II

In 1940, although about 30 percent of all women were working, the percentage of married women working outside the home was only slightly higher than it had been in 1910 (Chafe, 1991). The Japanese bombing of Pearl Harbor, Hawaii, and the subsequent U. S. declaration of war in 1941 began a period of dramatic change in the U.S. work force. By the end of World War II (1945), the size of the female labor force in the United States had increased by 50 percent. The proportion of all married women who were employed increased from 15 percent in 1940 to more than 24 percent by the end of 1945—by the end of the war nearly half of all female workers were married; 75 percent of the women involved in war industries were still working in 1946, but most (90 percent) were earning less.

Work also changed dramatically for men during World War II. Hundreds of thousands of men enlisted or were drafted into the military, and, in a matter of months, U.S. soldiers, sailors, and airmen were spread across the globe. Men too old to serve in the military and those who had physical characteristics that prevented them from serving had many job opportunities as the country geared up its industries for the war effort. Shortly after war was declared, thousands of men and their families relocated to work in factories that made weapons, planes, and other military gear. The war galvanized the country, and nearly everyone did something to help the cause.

For women, the war suddenly made it acceptable for them to be employed outside the home. As the war continued and more and more men were needed to fight, women began to replace them in jobs that were previously not seen as feminine and, therefore, not appropriate. Chafe (1991) quotes a newsreel in which the skills of female factory workers are likened to a homemaker's skills:

Instead of cutting a cake, this woman [factory worker] cuts the pattern of airplane parts. Instead of baking a cake, this woman is cooking gears to reduce the tension in the gears after use. . . . [Women] are taking to welding as if the rod were a needle and the metal a length of cloth to be sewn. (p. 83)

Although the newsreel was a form of propaganda, the facts were that women generally were good workers in all kinds of jobs.

Although job opportunities grew for all women during the war, black women may have benefited the most. Before World War II, black women

Women welders on the way to their job at the Todd Erie Basin dry dock during World War II. (Courtesy of the Library of Congress.)

were twice as likely as white women to be working, but their jobs were primarily in low-wage sectors such as domestic and farm work. The war created better paying factory jobs, and hundreds of thousands of black women quit their jobs as domestics. Although these women still faced racial discrimination in hiring and were often assigned to the lowest paying jobs in factories, many of these jobs paid more than being a household maid.

The war changed a number of issues regarding work and family in America. During the war, companies were restricted by the National War Labor Board from providing salary increases (to reduce the costs of the war effort), so many of them began offering incentives such as time off with pay, limited medical care, and company-sponsored pensions—incentives that were of great help to families (Wallen, 2002).

After the war, women were encouraged to leave the factories and other places where they had worked as part of the war effort and return to their homes to once again prepare a haven for their husbands and children. However, 75 percent of women who had worked during the war wanted to continue working, including 69 percent of wives. Although huge numbers of women worked during the war, attitudes about women and work had not really changed. In fact, some critics of working mothers complained that their higher rates of absenteeism and more frequent job changes during the war showed that women were ill-suited for the world of work.

The reasons women missed work more often and more frequently changed jobs than men were identified as a case of the *DTs*—mothers usually faced domestic and transportation difficulties. For the first time in the country's history, large numbers of mothers had to juggle outside employment and child care duties, and there were few backup supports for them—fathers also were at work or were deployed in the military overseas. Many women had moved for jobs, so their siblings and parents were not close, and even if they were, they also were probably employed. If children were sick, mothers had to stay home. Transportation problems occurred because businesses and factory employers were not well-suited for working mothers. For instance, stores, shops, and banks closed too early for working mothers to do their grocery or other shopping. Many war-related factories had been built outside of urban areas, and factory buses taking workers to and from the cities did not allow for the needs of parents to leave work early enough to shop, take children to doctor's appointments, or perform other parenting tasks.

Concerns about who would care for the children of working parents arose during World War II, and controversy about state-supported day care raged. To enable women to work, the federal government provided some support for child care centers, but most day care was financed by employers. Some critics were opposed to subsidized day care; they argued that child care was only available because industries could charge the expense to manufacturing costs, and thus the government was indirectly financing child care centers. Other critics asserted that day care was damaging to families. The belief that women should be home was such a firmly entrenched societal value, at least for white middle-class women, that there was little political will to support mothers to work, even when there was a war and women were badly needed to help win it. Some working mothers were ambivalent about someone else caring for their children in day care, so instead they left children alone, made piecemeal arrangements, and were absent from work when they had to be. Federal and industry support for child care ended after World War II, and women were again expected to stay home with their children. Some, but not all, did exactly that.

POST–WORLD WAR II DECADES

The television icons of 1950s family life, such as Beaver Cleaver's family (*Leave It to Beaver,* 1957–1963) and the Nelsons in *The Adventures of Ozzie and Harriet* (1952–1966), did not have working wives, although Donna Reed played a wife who helped out in her husband's doctor's office in the *Donna Reed Show* (1958–1966). College women typically were prepared through their curricula to become wives and mothers, not business leaders or professionals. Their degrees would be put to use as they helped their husbands entertain business associates, served as interesting companions to their husbands, and raised intelligent, secure children. Women in the 1950s joked about going to college to earn their MRS degree, and, in fact, many college women married and got pregnant before they finished school. Many returning GIs and Korean War veterans were in a hurry to make up for lost time, so delaying marriage and parenthood was not an attractive option.

Stay-at-home wives were encouraged by magazines and television programs to make their homes a beautiful, restful, welcoming place for their husbands and children. Homemaking was a woman's highest vocation, according to many social observers, and girls were socialized from young ages to fulfill this calling.

Men continued to be expected to serve as the primary, if not sole, breadwinner in the 1950s. In a survey of middle-class women, two-thirds saw this as husbands' most important role (May, 1999). Although many men found this stressful, most would not have traded it for anything—with the responsibilities of paying for his family, a man also got to be the head of the household, the chief decision-maker, and the one with the final say and most power. For most men of the post–World War II period, this seemed to be a fair tradeoff—or at least one with which they were satisfied.

Employed mothers. Although at the end of the century the 1950s were nostalgically seen as the heyday of the "traditional" American family—with a stay-at-home mother, a breadwinner father, and several happy children—the number of mothers who were employed outside of the household after World War II continued to grow. The number of working mothers increased four times during the decade of the 1950s, although they usually worked part-time. Three times the number of wives worked in 1952 as had worked in 1940, and the number of working wives doubled between 1950 and 1960. For the first time, the majority of employed women were married (52.4 percent in 1950). World War II and the attendant changes in wives' employment served as an impetus for more middle-class women to seek jobs.

The phenomenon of working mothers contributed to the strains some men felt about their family roles. Many men whose wives worked felt uneasy—what did this say about their breadwinning abilities and their own success? If earning money was the father's primary contribution to family life, what did it mean for them as men and fathers when their wives had to help?

Media images that reinforced long-standing cultural values did little to ease men's fears. Magazines articles expressed worry about problems with the American family, and working mothers were often seen as the culprits behind juvenile delinquency, marital tensions, and divorce. Hollywood did its part by portraying strong working women in a generally negative light, as seducers who ruined good men through their sexual wiles; happiness for both men and women was found in conventional marriages in which the compliant woman found peace and contentment being guided by a protective husband (see any Doris Day/Rock Hudson movie, for instance).

The cultural climate against working mothers was so negative that Dr. Benjamin Spock in his best-selling 1960s version of *Baby and Child Care* discussed working mothers in the chapter on "Special Problems." Spock's neo-Freudian book stressed the importance of full-time mothering and portrayed the father primarily as an emotional supporter of the mother who helped her with child care on occasion. Few day care centers had survived the end of the war, and most new employee benefits programs supported conventional one-earner families: time off with pay and medical care protection against loss of income. Unions continued to promote better wages, shorter working hours, safer working environments, and retirement benefits, but they generally were not interested in supporting policies such as day care (Wallen, 2002).

Employers also did their part to discourage working women. Advocates of women's equal rights accused employers of creating "glass ceilings" that limited the career promotions of women and placed quotas on women at higher levels. Women made up 25 percent of all government workers but held 3 percent of the high-level positions, and medical schools put a quota of 5 percent on female admissions (Chafe, 1991). Job discrimination was widespread—women bank tellers who held identical jobs with the same duties as men were called junior tellers. Men's titles were senior tellers, and they were paid about twice what women were paid for the same duties.

Given the cultural climate regarding working wives, and the likelihood that her husband would be less than thrilled, why did any middle-class married woman work? For the most part, the answer could be found in American consumer culture. Yes, some women worked because they found having a job was more fulfilling than being a housewife, particularly when children were grown and on their own. But most middle-class wives worked because their families could not afford what was considered "the good life" without an added income. Family size grew in the 1950s, demanding that family homes be larger to accommodate the third, fourth, and fifth children that many families had. The U.S. economy was robust because essentially the North American societies were the only industrialized nations in the world that were still intact after World War II, and American industry was helping Europe and Japan rebuild. Men were able to find well-paying jobs, and a grateful nation had instituted a number of policies to help returning GIs be able to afford to go to school and get loans to start small businesses. This resulted in more college-educated men and women than ever before, and they were anxious to get on with their lives after the war. Factories that had been relegated to producing war weapons began to produce household appliances, television sets, and other luxury items. Even in the positive economic environment, however, men's wages did not keep pace with all of the new products that were available. Notions of what constituted the necessities of life had expanded.

Even though men worked longer hours after the war than they had before and made more money, the increased expectations for a middle-class standard of living, coupled with growing inflation, led some wives to seek work, and some men to "let" them. Maintaining social status and the pursuit of the American way of life resulted in more middle-class women working to help their families get ahead than ever before. By 1960, in more than 10 million households both the husband and wife worked—an increase of 333 percent from 1940. Almost one-third of women workers were mothers of minor-age children in 1960.

Working-class women, of course, continued to work outside the home in the 1950s, just as they had before and during the war. In poor families and middle-class black families, women worked as much as, if not more than, their husbands.

THE BABY BOOM GENERATION GOES TO WORK

The 1960s was a time of great social and political conflict and change. The economy was prospering, and middle-class families were doing well. The free education provided by the GI Bill and Federal Housing Authority low-cost loans allowed large number of the families of working-class veterans to move into the ranks of the middle class. Because the economy was thriving, the federal government was able to spend a great deal of money on social programs meant to help low-income families. Under President Lyndon Johnson, the Great Society or War on Poverty brought about funding for Head Start, a model for early childhood education designed to help low-income children succeed when they entered public school. There was also a reversal of the federal government's position on mothers working outside the home, at least for low-income women. The new approach required that mothers receiving welfare should be trained for employment if their children were six years of age or older. This work incentive program provided training for single mothers as well as day care for their children, but the program was never well funded, so relatively few single mothers were served by it. Women who received training found few jobs, especially jobs that paid enough to support the day care expenses that they were responsible for once they completed their job training.

During the 1970s, the economy began to slow, just as the "baby boomers" (children born in the years following the Second World War) were graduating from school and looking for jobs. For the first time since the Depression, real incomes stopped rising during the early 1970s, a condition that endured through the end of the century. Wage increases did not keep pace with the increases in the costs of goods and services. In order to get ahead, to improve one's standard of living beyond what earlier generations had achieved, U.S. workers had to work longer hours than they had in the past.

Women went to work at accelerated rates, and they worked mainly for the reasons women had worked in earlier decades: to help financially support their families. Some women, however, worked because they enjoyed it, and they wanted to put their skills and education to use in the world outside the boundaries of home and family. The world of paid labor was still geared toward the one-wage-earner family, however. Day care facilities were seldom provided, parental leave usually was not an option, and, for the most part, neither were flexible work hours. Families with two working parents were challenged with dilemmas about child care—how to find good, safe, affordable day care was a major issue. Federal legislation was passed in the mid-1970s that provided income tax deductions for child care, but this helped only middle-class families—poor people paid few income taxes, so earning a tax deduction was not a realistic probability for most of them. Middle-class parents, if they were fortunate, found affordable quality day care near their homes or work; most parents settled for a good baby-sitter or they put their preschool children in home day care. Older children often became latchkey kids, a label attached to school-aged children and adolescents who stayed home alone after school until their parents got home from work.

In the 1970s, as more and more mothers moved into the paid work force—a trend that appeared to be ongoing rather than a reaction to something specific such as the Depression or World War II—critics raised concerns about the negative effects of working mothers on their husbands' and children's well-being and on their family's functioning. Social scientists, however, found no differences between the happiness and personal well-being of working mothers' family members and the family members of mothers who were not employed. Mothers in the paid labor force essentially added work to the household tasks they had fulfilled throughout most of the century. Although some studies reported that husbands of employed wives did more household work and child care than did husbands of wives who were not employed outside the household, they did not do much more. The overwhelming evidence was that women in the labor force still did approximately the same amount of household labor as they did when they were not employed.

These findings led social scientists to investigate how holding multiple roles affected working women. In some studies, women reported that they did not have enough time to spend with their families, and they complained of fatigue, irritability, and feeling torn between work and family demands. This was labeled the *scarcity hypothesis*—the central idea was that having multiple roles as wife, mother, and wage earner created role overload because women had too many responsibilities and not enough time and energy to do them all well. The husbands and children of these women did not do much more of the household work than in families where the wives and mothers stayed at home. The additional duties mothers took on when they got jobs generally were hard on them, both physically and psychologically. Sociologist Arlie Hochschild (1997) contended that working women were tired and hassled because of their *second shift*, referring to the fact that women were working a shift of paid labor followed by another long shift of unpaid household labor.

In contrast, research support also was found for another perspective, the *enhancement hypothesis*. Some researchers found that married women who worked outside the home had fewer psychological problems than those who were not employed. They hypothesized that, instead of being a problem to working mothers, multiple roles had a buffering effect. That is, they found that if a mother had a negative experience in one role, those negative experiences were offset by positive experiences in other roles. For example, if a mother had a problem at work, she could feel better about her life by focusing her energies on her family, or if she had arguments with her spouse, she could feel reassured by her successful relationships with coworkers. Not surprisingly, the effects on mothers of being employed outside of the home was related to a complex set of factors, not the least of which was whether she was doing what she wanted to do. The happiest women were working women who wanted to be in the paid labor force and homemakers who did not want to be in the paid labor force.

LAST QUARTER OF THE CENTURY

In the last quarter of the century, Americans worked hard. Compared to citizens of other industrialized nations, Americans worked more hours per week, worked more weeks of the year, and had fewer days off. Although the basis for the economy had shifted from industry and manufacturing to information and services, Americans still spent a great deal of time and energy making a living. For families, this meant that a higher proportion of family members—including fathers, mothers, and adolescent children—were employed than ever before in the century.

The trend of mothers working outside the home that had begun during the Second World War was a widely accepted part of American family life by the 1980s. Slightly over 42 percent of the nation's workers were women. The ideology that married women, especially mothers, should not work for wages outside the home was still alive and well, however, and mothers who worked were often castigated for doing so by social conservatives. They continued to blame children's problems on the fact that their mothers were working. To avoid this criticism, some women became entrepreneurs. They avoided the label of working mother by becoming somewhat independent agents for organizations such as Avon and Mary Kay (cosmetics) and Tupperware (plastic storage containers). Avon was founded in 1886 and appealed to women by promoting the idea that selling cosmetics to friends was more like sharing than work, although the earned income was what attracted most women to the business. Tupperware was founded in 1951, and holding Tupperware parties for friends became an extremely popular way for women to earn money. The final major player in the "working but not working" category was Mary Kay Cosmetics, which employed 1.2 million women in 2000. Again, the idea was that women could earn money, not by working, but by introducing products to their friends. By the end of the century, women were selling everything from candles to underwear via home parties.

A schism developed late in the century between women who worked and did not work outside the home, and popular magazine articles and television talk show hosts discussed whether working women could be good mothers. To maintain her self-image of being a good mother, a nurse who worked nights might describe herself as not a working mother if she was home when her child got home from school and she did everything that any other mother did (Garey, 1995). Despite this controversy, the most rapidly growing segment of the work force by the end of the century was mothers.

In 2000, 64 percent of black women were in the labor force, and 56 percent of Latin American women were in the labor force (slightly higher and lower percentages, respectively, than white women in the work force). Nearly 80 percent of Latin American men were in the labor force, compared to 74 percent of white men and 66 percent of black men

(U.S. Census Bureau, 2000). As was true throughout the century, black women worked at higher rates than did white women likely out of necessity. Latin American women were probably less likely to work than other women because of conservative cultural values related to family and motherhood. By the end of the century, approximately 75 percent of all men and 60 percent of all women were in the paid labor force, and families with a breadwinner father and a stay-at-home mother had dropped from 67 percent in 1940 to 19 percent of all families by 2000.

It should be noted, however, that only 35 percent of married women with children under six were working full-time year-round in 2000. Many women with infants and toddlers dropped out of the work force and re-entered it when the children started school. This employment pattern, often called the *mommy track,* was used by some corporations as a reason to limit mothers' access to positions of high authority and high pay. As a result, women who wanted to advance in demanding careers were increasingly delaying childbearing until they were well established in their professions. At the end of the century, mothers in the work force made 70 percent of men's earnings; women who were not mothers did better—they earned 90 percent of men's earnings.

The issue of women's, and perhaps especially mothers', pay is important for a number of reasons other than the fairness of equal pay for equal work. Although men engaged in more household labor at the end of the century than they did at the beginning, and young fathers as a rule engaged in more household labor than was true of their fathers and grandfathers, women still did twice as much housework as men. School-aged children, especially daughters, performed almost as much house-work as fathers. This pattern was somewhat different, however, for wives who earned as much or more than their husbands. When work outside the home was equally compensated, or when wives earned more money than their husbands, work in the home was shared more equally. A more equitable distribution of household tasks was shown to improve marital satisfaction, at least for women; wives' sense of being treated fairly was increased and their likelihood of depression was lowered (Reskin & Padavic, 1990).

As the economy became more based on information and technology, the demand by employers for education and skilled workers grew. Thus, in some sectors of society, more years were spent in school or other types of training. For some occupations, a college degree was not enough. Parents went into debt to help pay for their children's education, and young adults delayed their entry into full-fledged adulthood until their mid- or late 20s, postponing marriage and having children. Young people increasingly worked part-time while they attended college, so higher education took more time to acquire—it was not unusual for a college student to spend five or six years getting a baccalaureate degree, and then to be in debt and living with his or her parents after graduation.

Manufacturing jobs increasingly went overseas, so many working-class families found it harder to find well-paying jobs. Parents in working-class families trying to get ahead might work two jobs (or at least one parent would), which meant longer hours away from home and less time spent together as a family. Working-class youth also were more likely to be employed, except in urban areas where there were few jobs.

In the last two decades of the century, many social observers decried what they saw as the relentless treadmill on which Americans were running. Concerns rose about the challenges in finding balance between work and family life—critics complained that Americans lacked balance because work (and getting to work in increasingly longer commutes) consumed so much time and energy. Parents complained about the stress in trying to have it all—a satisfying home life and success on the job. Social scientists studying work and family balance concluded that how well family and work stress was managed depended on a number of factors: the number of parents in the family; the number and ages of children; how much family members, including children, participated in household labor; the availability of quality child care; the values of the family (did family members expect mothers to work or stay at home, did they expect fathers to be the breadwinners); and the extent to which family members valued time together and material success.

Juliet Schor, in her 1991 book *The Overworked American,* blamed the culture of consumerism that seemed to start in the 1980s for the tension in families. It was her view that American families had become trapped in a "work-and-spend-cycle" and that the thrift and saving values associated with the so-called Protestant work ethic of earlier U.S. generations were no longer operating. Obtaining material possessions became an obsession with families, and family members worked long hours to make enough money to be able to consume at high rates. The Protestant work ethic, a set of values originally promoted by European religious leaders John Calvin and Martin Luther, taught that a good person was one who worked hard, was financially successful, made a profit but did not enjoy the wealth by making a show of it, was thrifty, accumulated savings, earned interest, and invested. According to Schor, this work ethic was gradually replaced over the century by an ethic of consumerism that emphasized beliefs that: having material possessions made people happy, earning money was better than having more leisure time, owning luxuries was necessary for the good life, spending was valued over saving, obtaining credit was easy, and shopping was a leisure-time activity in its own right. According to Schor, the culture of consumerism, coupled with wages remaining stagnant against inflation, was the reason married women went to work in record numbers. It was also why more adolescents began working: they worked so they could afford to buy cars; pay for car-related expenses; and purchase clothes, video games, compact disks, and other "necessities." Americans on average worked harder (more hours) than did citizens of other Western cultures, but U.S. families lived in larger homes than those in other countries, owned more and larger vehicles, and had more possessions. They also were deeper in debt.

Consumerism (and the resulting debt for some) meant that many Americans needed to continue to work past the standard retirement age of 65. During the Depression, President Franklin Roosevelt's New Deal legislation had included social security as a safety net for older adults and individuals who were not able to work for a variety of reasons (children and widowed individuals also were covered in social security). During the 1930s, as a way to encourage older adults to give up jobs so that younger men with families could have them, age 65 was set as the legal retirement age to be eligible for social security payments. By the last decade of the century, many older adults found that they had not saved enough to retire at age 65, or they could not afford to live on social security alone. Many of these individuals remained in the work force, often in part-time positions, even after retiring from their regular jobs.

Some older workers had to stay in the labor market because their companies had defaulted on retirement pensions promised to them. Critics contended that corporations were abusing their pension funds and their retirees because unions had lost bargaining power. During the last part of the century, many companies moved their operations from states with strong unions to nonunion states or to foreign countries. In the 1960s, one-third of workers belonged to unions, a figure that dropped to less than 17 percent in the late 1980s. Whatever the reason, some pension funds managed by large corporations for their retirees' benefits, and into which workers paid monthly sums, either lost money or defaulted, necessitating a return to the labor force for many retired individuals.

Starting in the mid-1980s and continuing for the rest of the century, there was a trend toward corporate downsizing at the middle management level. This trend squeezed middle-class families economically, and also resulted in workers remaining employed longer—enforced unemployment in what would have been a person's peak earning years in middle age forced many workers into staying with new jobs longer than they would have otherwise.

Another factor that affected the employment of workers of all ages was the need to be employed to be eligible for health care benefits. Fringe benefits offered by employers, beginning in the 1940s, proved to be costly for employers, yet were an integral resource for American families. The rising costs of employee benefits brought about changes in their availability and how they were administered. Employees paid a higher and higher percentage of the costs of such benefits as health care and pensions. By the latter part of the century, workers sought and stayed in jobs sometimes mostly for the health care benefits offered. Without a job, health care was prohibitively expensive—an overnight stay in a hospital or minor surgery could financially ruin the average American family without health insurance Health care costs were so expensive that few families could afford to pay the bills without insurance.

Older adults (through Medicare, a Great Society program of the 1960s) and poor families (through Medicaid, a program focused mostly on children) had health care insured by the federal government. Political efforts to make health care a right for all citizens rather than a benefit tied to employment failed in the early 1990s, so health care benefits remained a major motivation for employment.

One indication that the participation of mothers in the paid labor force was becoming more widely accepted was a shift in welfare policies. The Family Support Act of 1988 required that most low-income families receiving government financial support had to take part in education, training, and employment programs unless they had children younger than age three. The goal was to get both mothers and fathers off welfare and into jobs. Welfare reforms in the 1990s went further, mandating that poor mothers work outside the home. In 1996, the Personal Responsibility and Work Opportunities Reconciliation Act, which placed limits on how long welfare recipients could receive benefits, was passed by Congress and signed into law by President Bill Clinton.

The federal government in 1993 also attempted to relieve stress on middle-class families with more than one earner by implementing the Family and Medical Leave Act. This legislation required employers with 50 or more employees on the payroll for 20 or more weeks to grant unpaid family leave of up to 12 weeks during any 12-month period for a variety of personal or family reasons—birth or adoption; care for a seriously ill parent, spouse, or child; or for medical treatment of a serious nature. Eligibility for this benefit was dependent on having worked for at least 12 months for at least 25 hours per week. Employers had to return the employee to the same or an equivalent job when they returned from the leave. Although this law provided relief to some higher-income families, low-income families could seldom afford unpaid leaves; thus, the act tended to most benefit those who least needed it. It also applied to a small number of U.S. workers.

SUMMARY

American families worked hard throughout the 20th century—perhaps harder than families in any other country in the world—but the nature of work changed from producing goods on farms and factories to exchanging information and services in office businesses. Consequently, the American family shifted from being a unit of producers of goods to a unit of consumers. Middle-class children went from being financial assets to their families to needing financial support to spend years in school or in training before they could join the world of work. Women's paid labor outside the home—a contentious issue in U.S. society throughout the 20th century—remained controversial, but at the end of the century the United States' economic vitality depended on there being many working mothers in the labor force. In fact, societal messages to mothers about working changed dramatically from time to time, with attitudes being more favorable toward them working during World War II and at the end of the century when the culture of consumerism was predicated on two-earner families. Women were strongly discouraged from working anytime their working had the potential to interfere with men's wage-earning ability, such as during the Great Depression.

Industrialization brought about separate spheres for men and women, with men being assigned to the paid labor force and women being responsible for unpaid household labor. Separate spheres worked reasonably well for most middle-class families throughout much of the century, but it was never an especially functional concept for working-class families, who were only able to survive on the salary of one wage earner for a brief time at mid-century. The importance of work to family survival was especially notable during the Depression, when large numbers of families were plunged into poverty with disastrous results in many cases.

As the century ended, critics of American employers and the effect of work on families identified a number of problem areas. Among them was the need for more formal support for working parents, such as flexible work hours; a continued movement toward equal pay for equal work; a strong job economy that incorporates black men as well as other unemployed, underemployed, and poorly paid Americans; and excellent child care at reasonable prices.

4

Rituals: How Families Developed and Maintained Shared Meanings

Rituals have always been a central feature of family life. Family rituals are activities that involve one or more family members, are meaningful to them, and have a formal structure. Although families probably spend little energy and time thinking about rituals, their importance to family life is evident in many ways. Newly married couples often struggle to blend and adapt rituals learned in their families of origin, a process that may lead to conflicts (e.g., he wants to open presents on Christmas Eve, and she wants to open presents on Christmas day). The death of a family member may heighten awareness of certain rituals, because some rituals involve specific family members fulfilling specific tasks. If Thanksgiving is always at Grandma's house and she cooks the turkey, her death changes holiday observance in profound ways. Another indication of rituals' importance is the amount of money Americans spend on various ritual observances (e.g., Thanksgiving, birthdays).

Rituals are so important that some therapists and researchers contend that family units cannot exist without them. Late in the century, therapists advised newly formed stepfamilies to develop new rituals as a way to build "family-ness" and avoid battles over whose rituals will be observed in the stepfamily.

Family rituals potentially serve a number of purposes; they:

- Make changes manageable. For example, wedding rituals signify daughters and sons leaving families of origin and beginning new families. Bar and bat mitzvahs signal coming of age.

- Provide family members with a sense of belonging and identity—"We are the Smiths and this is how the Smiths do things."
- Clarify family membership when new family members are added (e.g., marriage) or lost (e.g., death).
- Help family members cope during times of loss. Mourning rituals, for example, are often linked to sharing food and companionship with the bereaved, which helps reduce their feelings of loneliness and isolation.
- Celebrate family and individual milestones.
- Give voice to important beliefs held by family members. Religious and cultural meanings are passed on to younger generations through rituals.
- Build morale among kin. Coming together to celebrate helps build a sense of mutual belonging and family esteem. (Imber-Black & Roberts, 1998)

Rituals celebrated by families, such as Thanksgiving, also serve functions for society. They build national pride and identity, foster consumption of goods and services, and encourage citizens to enjoy a break from daily work responsibilities. On a broader scale, national holidays and the surrounding rituals serve society in ways similar to how family rituals fulfill families' needs—to celebrate, to create bonds, to foster relaxation, and to instruct.

Rituals range from daily activities engaged in by family members to special events that occur once a year or less. Family rituals can be mundane and performed with little thought or planning (e.g., calling mom on Mother's Day or sending her a card) or they can be intensely important and demand extensive preparation (e.g., weddings). Family rituals such as Thanksgiving are shared by most households and families in the country, although each observes societal celebrations in their own ways. Other rituals are exclusive to a specific family, such as an immigrant family who ritually observes their anniversary of moving to the United States by gathering to share a feast.

Four kinds of rituals have been identified that involve families: daily rituals, family traditions, life cycle events, and holiday celebrations.

Daily rituals such as bedtime and mealtimes are sometimes called *family routines* by social scientists. Families differ widely in their daily rituals and routines. Some families are highly structured and follow clear, unalterable routines; others are more flexible.

Family traditions are rituals that involve specific events, such as birthdays. These traditions vary across families as much as daily rituals do. For instance, in the Lee household children are allowed to stay home from school and choose their favorite foods on their birthdays. The Kim family eats at a nice restaurant when someone has a birthday, and in the Johnston-King family the birthday child goes on a shopping trip to pick out gifts, regardless of his or her age.

Rituals that mark *life cycle events* include births, transitions from childhood to adulthood, weddings, and deaths. Many life cycle events are connected to religious beliefs. Although life cycle rituals are based on individuals' transitions that involve changes in status, they almost always consist of public observances that include non-family members as well as extended kin networks. In some cases, such as in bar and bat mitzvahs, the entire religious community may be involved in the ritual.

Finally, *holiday celebrations* are rituals based on civic celebrations (e.g., the Fourth of July, Thanksgiving), religious observations (e.g., Easter, Ramadan, Yom Kippur), or commercial activities (e.g., Halloween, Valentine's Day). Holiday rituals vary from family to family, yet they also include widespread practices because they are celebrated or observed by many families.

How did family rituals change over the course of the 20th century? Some historians have argued that holidays and other rituals celebrated by families have changed little since the Victorian era (Gillis, 1996), while others assert that rituals are ever-changing and are being modified by both family members and outsiders (Pleck, 2000). Both positions may have elements of truth.

FAMILY TRADITIONS

Children's birthday parties began as early as the 18th century in the United States. The fundamentals—a cake **Birthdays** decorated with candles, the birthday boy or girl making a wish while blowing out the candles, guests bringing presents—originated with the English upper class and Germans.

At the start of the 20th century, children's birthday parties were relatively simple—a few friends were invited to the child's home to share a meal, have cake and ice cream, and give presents to the birthday boy or girl. In middle-class and wealthy families, the children attending the birthday party dressed up in their best clothes, and the birthday party meal was a test by the parents to see how well the children had learned the rules of etiquette. These parties, closely supervised by parents, were, by modern standards, pretty dull affairs. In addition to the birthday party, most families also celebrated the birthday in a private family gathering.

Although mothers generally were responsible for organizing children's birthday parties throughout the century, early on parent-controlled birthday parties gradually gave way to more peer-oriented parties. Changes in societal views of children (from *child as innocent* in the Victorian era prior to 1900 to *child as consumer* in the 20th century) were evident in how peer-culture birthday parties were celebrated. Childrearing experts in the 1920s advised parents that letting them lead the planning or their own birthday parties helped children learn management and organizational skills. Emily Post, an etiquette expert, advised parents that putting the birthday child in charge of the guest list taught the child about social obligations. During this period, parties became smaller—experts recommended one guest for every year of the birthday child's age. These smaller parties coincided with the decline in middle-class households that hired servants, but the main reason for recommending fewer guests was concern that the birthday boy or girl would be overwhelmed and overstimulated if too many attended the party.

The rise in child-planned parties coincided with the growth of an age-graded peer culture in the United States. Increasingly, children in America spent more and more time in peer groups. Schools and clubs such as Boy Scouts and Brownies were organized according to age, and, in the first quarter of the 20th century, the increase in junior and senior high schools made it easier for adolescents to spend less time with adults or older and younger children and more time with peers. As the century continued, children's input into birthday parties expanded—children planned not only the guest list but suggested new formats (e.g., slumber parties, a trip to the movies after cake and ice cream at home). By the 1950s, the age-appropriate birthday party in the home was the ideal. Inspired in part by psychologist Arnold Gesell's (1925) work on children's physical, social, emotional, and intellectual development from birth through adolescence, experts advised parents to plan party games and activities that

Typical family birthday celebration. (Corbis)

fit children's developmental stage. The Gesell Institute at Yale University published a set of manuals suggesting décor, refreshments, games, and activities for birthday parties appropriate for children ages 3 to 15.

In the 1960s through the 1980s, as mothers increasingly were employed outside the home, it was popular to hold birthday parties at commercial establishments that catered to such entertainments (e.g., restaurants such as Chuck E. Cheese and McDonald's, skating rinks, bowling alleys, party centers). Parties were hosted by paid employees of these establishments, with mother, and perhaps father, as supervisors. The number of children was no longer restricted to the child's age in years; in fact, parties grew in size as middle- and upper-class parents competed to see who could throw the most unusual and elaborate celebration. By the end of the century, it was no longer enough that the birthday child got presents—it generally was expected that the host would give party favors to all the guests. Some parents competed to provide the best (and most expensive) gift bags for the party guests. Although holding birthday parties in commercial establishments reduced the work, it certainly did not reduce the cost. Of course, many families continued to have private, family-only birthday celebrations, usually with a special meal—more likely eaten at a restaurant rather than at home,.

Throughout the century, many poor and working-class families tried to emulate middle- and upper-class birthday parties, but on a less costly scale. Their parties were often limited to immediate and extended family members, and gifts were likely to be more modest. For poor families, birthday parties were almost always held at home, and some families were too poor for even that. Parents had to work long hours to make ends meet, and there was not enough money for parties or presents.

Immigrant families sometimes incorporated traditions from their home cultures into children's birthday parties, although they often readily adopted such American birthday elements as cake, the "Happy Birthday" song, and presents at their children's urging. Immigrants also tended to wear traditional costumes from their homelands, to prepare traditional foods and beverages, and to invite adult friends and relatives to the party, along with the children's friends. As they became more acculturated, immigrants gradually dropped practices from their home cultures and often retained only traditional foods as the last reminders of their cultural roots. For instance, over the course of the 20th century, Chinese American families' birthday celebrations became gradually shorter, simpler, and more egalitarian. In the late 19th century, immigrant Chinese typically celebrated a son's, but not a daughter's, birth for a month after he was born with rituals conducted at home and at the Chinese temple and with a banquet. By the 1980s, both sons and daughters' births were recognized as worthy of celebration, but the ceremonies might be limited to a banquet. Traditional birthday-month rituals of the Chinese, such as the cutting of the infant's hair, also were usually shortened and simplified.

A greater proportion of American parents than ever before held birthday celebrations for their children as the 20th century ended. Birthday parties were an expected part of a normal American childhood. Given the widespread expectation that children deserved a birthday celebration, it is likely that some poor children and their parents suffered disappointment, guilt, and regret if they could not have some kind of birthday party.

The birthdays of adult family members also were celebrated in the 20th century, but these tended to be quiet, family-only dinners. In the last quarter of the century, as with children's parties, these family meals for adult birthday celebrants were more frequently eaten in restaurants.

Wedding Anniversaries Wedding anniversaries tended to be rather low-key affairs throughout the 20th century, unless the anniversary was a milestone. The societal ideal was a quiet dinner for two, during which the couple reminisced about their years of marriage. Although the societal ideal excluded children, some families turned wedding anniversaries into family celebrations. In most families, spouses exchanged small gifts and/or anniversary cards.

In contrast to the private nature of most anniversaries, milestone silver (25 years) or golden (50 years) wedding anniversaries were celebrated with extended families, friends, and sometimes entire neighborhoods, church congregations, and communities. These events usually were planned by the couple's children and grandchildren. Attendees were not necessarily expected to bring gifts, although greeting cards were common, particularly in the latter decades of the century, and it was not unusual for children of the couple to pool money to buy something special for their parents—for example, a big screen television, matching recliner chairs, or a trip to Hawaii.

Wedding anniversaries were not heavily commercialized in the 20th century, although leisure industries such as cruise lines, travel agencies, and businesses such as jewelers and greeting card companies made efforts to promote them. But, for the most part, wedding anniversaries were among the most noncommercial of family-related rituals. Perhaps the growing divorce rates in the latter third of the century reduced the number of couples celebrating milestone anniversaries and thus reduced commercial interests in promoting these ritual celebrations. The high divorce rate, though, would have been offset by the increased longevity over the century, which resulted in more partners living to reach a milestone wedding anniversary. For whatever reasons, milestone anniversary rituals changed relatively little over the century.

Family Reunions Gatherings of extended kin networks, or family reunions, are rituals that many families consider important activities at which they reaffirm their identity as a family and maintain extended kin relationships. As with wedding anniversaries, family reunions in the 20th century were primarily privately observed and noncommercialized celebrations. They occurred mostly in summer to allow families to attend without removing children from school and to use vacation time to travel to the reunion site.

There is little historical or folkloric research on family reunions. Such gatherings have occurred for generations, but there is speculation that families reunite more often during times of stress; reconnecting with extended kin and loved ones provides a sense of comfort and security. As Americans became more mobile, often moving hundreds or thousands of miles from family members, maintaining connections became more challenging. In the early years of the century, before the widespread use of telephones, individuals who lived far away from kin wrote letters and visited when they could. It was in this context that family reunions became meaningful rituals for many families. Particularly for African Americans and rural Americans of all racial and ethnic backgrounds, annual or periodic gatherings of far-flung relatives were significant. Many African Americans had left the rural South in large numbers early in the century to seek factory employment in cities like Detroit, Cleveland, Chicago, and New York. For generations after this migration, "home" for many black citizens of northern cities remained the small towns and rural areas of the South. Attending a family reunion was going home, the highlight of the summer for some individuals. Similarly, rural Americans from European backgrounds began to migrate to suburban and urban areas during the 1960s—a migration stimulated by economic hardships that hit rural areas and farmers in the 1970s and 1980s. These individuals also celebrated family reunions, often back in the home community.

Reunions ranged from casual gatherings sharing potluck meals to highly organized affairs with a wide variety of scheduled activities such as games, contests, sing-alongs, picnics, barbecues, trips, and tours. Family reunions' popularity probably peaked in the 1950s and 1960s. Since then, long-distance communication has become easier, reducing the need for face-to-face get-togethers. In addition, because more women were employed outside the home, fewer people were available to organize family reunions; women tended to be the kin keepers, the ones who maintained communication and saw that disparate family members were contacted and included.

LIFE-CYCLE EVENTS

Life-cycle events are rituals commemorating significant transitions in status for individuals and their families. In addition to involving individual family members and their kin networks, these life-cycle rituals almost always include friends and members of the community. The most significant of these rituals in 20th century American families were weddings and funerals. Other family life-cycle rituals included religious rites of passage (e.g., christenings, bar and bat mitzvahs). Families also may participate in rites of passage, such as retirements or graduations, but these rituals focus on the individual, and are not family life-cycle events as much as they are celebrations of individual transitions of status in which families participate as supporters.

Childbirth   Some readers may be surprised to see childbirth mentioned as a family ritual. Childbirth was once a major life transition firmly rooted within family and household boundaries. It went from being a family function to a medical procedure or property of the medical establishment in the 20th century.

In 1905, only 5 percent of U.S. births took place in hospitals. Instead, women gave birth at home, usually attended only by other women. Middle- and upper-class urban women may have had a physician's attendance at some point in their labor, but this was not the norm for rural and low-income women. Home births were, in some ways, communal events involving rituals associated with the serious business of delivering infants under less than ideal conditions with the anticipatory celebration of adding a new family member. When women gave birth at home, a community of women gathered to assist. Some of the helpers were midwives, women who specialized in assisting mothers in labor and childbirth. Others prepared food for the helpers of the mother-to-be as they waited and worked on her delivery (and afterward, when there was some kind of celebration). The gathering of community women to help with childbirth ended when the majority of births moved into hospitals.

Medicalization of childbirth. Within one generation, childbirth changed dramatically. By 1930, 50 percent of all births and 75 percent of urban births took place in hospitals. Prior to the 20th century, hospitals were considered to be extremely dangerous, full of disease. For most people who entered hospitals as patients, death was expected. However, once medical staff understood germs and sterilization practices, mortality rates declined substantially, and hospitals became middle-class women's location of choice for childbirth. In addition, the 19th-century invention of anesthetics made it possible for childbirth to be less painful, a step that modern women welcomed but Victorians had not taken (because suffering was associated with the status of motherhood).

The medicalization of childbirth, which made labor and delivery safer and less painful, was greeted eagerly by feminists who wanted women to have more control over their bodies. Ironically, hospital births had the opposite effect—control of childbirth shifted from women and midwives to male doctors who tended to view birth as potentially pathogenic and dangerous. Middle-class pregnant women thus sought more prenatal care from doctors, resulting in healthy pregnant women gradually becoming "patients" and pregnancy treated as an illness. In general, middle-class women in the first decades of the 20th century accepted the scientific and medical models of childbirth and, by doing so, turned over control of the process to men. Working-class women followed suit when they could afford to go to the hospital.

When the medical profession took over, births were no longer the family events they once were—most fathers and other kin were excluded from the labor and delivery room Mothers were anesthetized as though they were having surgery, and access to newborns was controlled to prevent infections. From the 1920s onward, mothers' behavior was governed by ideas borne in the era of "scientific motherhood"—experts promoted scheduled feedings and sleeping for infants and advised feeding babies formula rather than breast milk.

By the 1940s, some women were questioning anesthetized births. A natural childbirth movement grew among middle-class women who wanted more control over the process and who objected to the factory-like atmosphere of labor and delivery in hospitals.

From the 1960s on, pregnant women, regardless of whether they planned to have anesthetic-free childbirth, often chose to deliver using some form of natural childbirth, such as the Lamaze technique. Expectant fathers were encouraged and then expected to attend childbirth education classes and function as their partner's coach and supporter. During the 1970s, hospitals began allowing fathers in delivery rooms, but they were assigned to observer roles only. Gradually, over the last three decades of the century, fathers began to assume the role of childbirth coach.

By the 1980s, some women were advocating a return to home births, and there was a rise of birthing centers, home-like hospital rooms where women could experience labor and delivery surrounded by family and friends. Some women's groups promoted midwives as an alternative to doctor-run deliveries, but laws in most states limited their ability to practice.

By the end of the 20th century, 85 percent of U.S. births took place in hospitals; only 1 percent occurred in homes. Although the presence of fathers during labor and delivery might suggest a return to childbirth as a family ritual—albeit one under the control of health care professionals—in some ways childbirth was more of an individual rite of passage for women only, rather than a family ritual. The medicalization of childbirth resulted in procedures that emphasized mother-child bonds and the health and well-being of mothers and their infants. Fathers were brought into the system near the end of pregnancy to support mothers during labor and delivery, and, although some fathers were given the option of cutting the umbilical cord, their involvement was limited by hospital rules and procedures.

Baby showers. A prebirth ritual invented in the 1930s was the baby shower. Previously, it had been thought that giving pregnant women gifts before a child was born was bad luck. Baby showers accompanied the change of childbirth from an experience fraught with danger and possible death for the mother and the baby to one of hope and celebration, with low expectations for mortality or injury.

Emily Post first offered rules for baby showers in the 1937 edition of her guidebook, *Etiquette.* Baby showers were modeled after wedding showers—a gathering of women hosted by friends or relatives ate cake, played games, and gave gifts to the honoree. It was a rite to initiate a woman into her maternal role in the company of other women. As the mother-to-be unwrapped each present, the gift giver might explain how it was used—providing a brief introduction to the consumerism of modern motherhood. Although started by middle-class women, working-class and immigrant women also quickly adopted this ritual. As pregnant women began to be employed in greater numbers, showers sometimes were held in workplaces or at restaurants as well as in homes. Men were invited to some baby showers.

Certain immigrant groups (e.g., Greek Orthodox, Russian, Episcopalian, and Irish Catholics) also had a "churching" ceremony that welcomed new mothers back into the church (usually a few weeks after the birth). Churching had disappeared by the 1960s.

Religious Rites of Passage

Christenings. Baptisms had somewhat different purposes depending on the faiths. Among Catholics, christening was the event at which godparents were formally given to the child. In the first half of the century, many Americans of German descent (Lutherans as well as Catholics), Italian Americans, and Latin American parents hosted parties after christenings, sometimes for hundreds of guests. Most working-class christening parties were held in homes but also might have been held in social halls and saloons. Guests and godparents were expected to bestow gifts of coins and praise on the infants. Christenings were so important that poor people borrowed money to have such parties. Over time, these gatherings became smaller, more private, and less expensive. By 1960, christening parties were usually gatherings at home of family and close friends.

In addition to christenings, Catholics had extensive rituals related to godparents. Latin Americans had the most elaborate godparent system; in fact, they had separate sets of godparents for birth, first communion, confirmation, weddings, and graduations. Godparents were generally charged with overseeing the spiritual life of the child, but Latin American godparents sometimes were asked to help pay for children's expenses throughout childhood, including, sometimes, weddings. In the 20th century, responsibilities for godparents gradually lessened. The Depression made some reluctant to accept godparent responsibilities if they involved monetary support. In the last 60 years of the century, it became more common to name kin rather than nonkin to be godparents, and godparents became more symbolic with fewer expectations that they would assume any financial responsibilities for children.

Bar mitzvahs and bat mitzvahs. In the Jewish tradition, the child in transition to adulthood takes on a different status within his or her family, religion, and community following the bar mitzvah (for boys) or bat mitzvah (for girls). During the ritual, the child has to demonstrate competency

A Jewish mother and father with their son at his bar mitzvah. (Courtesy of Jean Ispa.)

in reading Hebrew (the sacred language) and lead the congregation in a short period of religious exercises. Family members and friends give gifts to acknowledge the child's new status. The entire religious community is involved in the ritual, and the symbolic activities of the ritual link families from the past, present, and future.

Probably few family events involve as many rituals as weddings. Prior to the mid-19th century, weddings were **Weddings** generally small events that were held in homes or in a nearby park or garden. Many of the familiar trappings of the modern "white" wedding ceremony—with bridal gowns, veils, and bouquets— were introduced prior to the 20th century in the Victorian era. The focus of these early weddings was clearly on the bride, with grooms increasingly becoming bystanders at their own weddings.

Early 20th-century middle-class wedding rituals continued from Victorian times, and not following the earlier rituals would create an impression that one's means were insufficient. Church weddings, popular well before 1900, were the norm. Engraved invitations were sent to guests who were escorted by formally dressed ushers to pews draped with satin ribbons. The bride, dressed now almost invariably in white, was attended by numerous bridesmaids. Courtship autonomy disappeared after the engagement, and the bride and her family took over the planning of the wedding. For lower-middle- and working-class couples, weddings were more modest affairs, often conducted at home with a small meal as a post-wedding celebration.

Wedding presents were universal by 1900, and suitable gifts were frivolous—silver, cut glass bowls, toothpick holders, opera glasses—nothing you could furnish a house with; the couple was expected to supply the basics themselves. Wedding receptions also were invented prior to the 20th century, about the time of the Civil War. Another popular ritual of the time was the wedding trip, or honeymoon. The location was kept secret and was a time for consummating (literally) the marriage. Most advisors suggested choosing wedding dates to coincide with the least fertile part of a woman's menstrual cycle. However, until the beginning of the 20th century, most lay and medical writers misunderstood the timing of ovulation and thought the most fertile part of the cycle was the safe period.

At the start of the 20th century, weddings began to surpass funerals as family gathering times for middle-class families. For the working class, weddings tended to remain small, rather quiet affairs. Women typically married in their best dresses rather than white gowns, and weddings were held more often on weekdays than on weekends. Honeymoons were rare, and receptions, if any, were small. There began a trend, however, at least among the middle class, toward larger ceremonies and more elaborate receptions. To accommodate more guests, weddings were shifted from weekdays (60 percent in the 1920s) to weekends (80 percent by 1970). Also expanded were the number of named functions—ushers, guest book attendants, punch pourers, candle lighters, etc.

Following World War II, a huge industry, often called the bridal industry, was launched to help brides-to-be and their mothers plan the grand spectacle weddings were becoming. Although many weddings between returning GIs and the fiancées who had waited for the war to end were small affairs attended by family and friends, the 1950s witnessed the return of the formal white wedding that was as much show as solemn ceremony. By 1960, the average wedding cost $3,300 (average annual income was $4,970). In the 1980s, 85 percent of brides had formal weddings.

During the 1950s, weddings were variations on a common theme, depending on the amount of money available. For many middle-class and wealthy American couples, weddings were major affairs requiring months to plan and costing thousands of dollars. Weddings often were preceded by women-only bridal showers held in honor of the future bride, usually hosted by the maid or matron of honor. Gifts were given to help the newlyweds set up housekeeping together. For most middle- and upper-class couples, living together before marriage in the 1950s and 1960s was rare. Most young adults lived with their parents or roommates before marrying, so bridal showers helped young couples prepare to establish a household.

Although the wedding ceremonies themselves did not change greatly—with the exception of more attendants and fancier, more costly wedding dresses—the related trappings of weddings became much more elaborate.

Rehearsal dinners, usually held the night before the wedding following the wedding party's practice for the big day, started out as small gatherings of immediate family members and attendants of the bride and groom. If the wedding was held in a church, the rehearsal dinner likely was held in the church basement. Over time, these dinners sometimes evolved into multiple-course meals at restaurants attended by out-of-town guests as well as the wedding ensemble. Wedding receptions also became more elaborate, growing from gatherings in church basements or church halls in which mints, nuts, fruit punch, and wedding cake were served to catered formal dinners followed by dances with hired bands or disc jockeys in rented halls. The wedding industry fueled profits for florists, caterers, musicians, and created a new career: wedding consultant.

Beginning in the 1960s and continuing throughout the rest of the century, weddings became more varied and sometimes served as a way for couples to convey a message about their personal styles. Although large formal weddings were still popular in the 1960s, in the mid-1960s members of the counterculture began to view marriage and weddings as an individual choice rather than as predictable and inevitable. They wanted to differentiate themselves and their weddings from those of their peers and also from the weddings of their parents' generation. Couples might take their vows on a beach or in a mountain meadow rather than in a church or a city hall. Rather than follow more traditional wedding scripts, some brides and grooms wrote their own vows or borrowed ideas for their wedding ceremonies from favorite poets and songwriters. White formal wedding gowns were exchanged for more casual dresses or pantsuits. Some brides were barefoot and wore flowers in their hair. Tuxedos or dark suits were still the order of the day for most American grooms, but men's formalwear came to include pale blues, bright colors, patterns, and textures. Gradually, weddings began to be less formal and more like extended parties.

Grand, formal weddings got a boost on July 29, 1981, when 750 million people around the world watched the televised wedding of Lady Diana Spencer and Charles, Prince of Wales. Inspired by this display of pomp and circumstance, many young women, particularly middle-class white Americans, turned to large, elaborate fairy-tale ceremonies, and for the remainder of the century, elegant weddings were the dream of many young women.

With close to 2.5 million couples marrying annually and spending an average of $19,000 on their weddings, the wedding industry was a lucrative business at the close of the century. The wedding industry brought in total revenues of $32 billion per year and included businesses that offered rings, flowers, bridal wear, photographs, invitations, hairstyling, cakes, gifts, and so forth. Several magazines were devoted solely to wedding planning, with names like *Bride, Modern Bride, Elegant Bride,* and *Martha Stewart Weddings.*

The wedding industry focused primarily on nuptials between individuals who had not been married before, but 15 percent of brides and grooms in the 1990s had been married previously, and these individuals were not ignored by the wedding industry. Remarriage ceremonies, particularly among couples with children from previous unions, tended to be smaller affairs than most first marriage ceremonies, and many were performed by justices of the peace or judges in civil ceremonies; yet the lure of formal weddings was great. Books and magazines told experienced brides how to conduct formal weddings with newly created rituals that would celebrate their remarriage vows. A minister in Kansas City created a family medallion that was designed to be worn by children as well as the adult couple in a symbolic union of families. Another remarriage ceremony ritual involved having children from the couple's prior relationships, along with their parents, light a family candle, and it was not unusual in the 1990s for children to serve as best man or maid of honor for their remarrying parents. Social norms and etiquette rules about conducting second or third weddings were rapidly being created in response to the growing number of remarrying individuals who wanted to mark their union with a special ceremony. Etiquette books also were published to provide guidance to stepchildren who were marrying. Many of the traditional rituals such as family and wedding-party receiving lines were uncomfortable for everyone. Even the tradition of the father of the bride walking his daughter down the aisle created stressful decisions for young women who primarily may have been raised by their stepfathers and may have had a more distant relationship with their biological fathers.

Although in the past it was typical for the bride's parents to foot the majority of the bill, it became increasingly common in the last two decades of the century for the bride and groom to pay at least a portion of wedding costs. Men and women were marrying later after establishing careers, which put them in a better financial position. At end of the century, the average age of brides was 25.1 years and 26.8 years for grooms; 83 percent of brides and 89 percent of grooms were in the work force. Many couples owned homes prior to their marriages, which required a shift in gift-giving as well. While blenders, crock pots, and toasters may have been practical gifts for previous generations of wedding couples, sports equipment and house and garden tools became popular gifts at the end of the century.

A number of traditions surrounded weddings. The bride's wearing of "something old, something new, something borrowed, something blue" was adopted by many brides, and most still tossed their wedding bouquets to a group of young women eager to catch it and be the next bride. The tradition of the white wedding dress originally signified that the bride was a virgin, but, by the end of the century, women who were mothers, cohabiting women, and those who had been married before were wearing white; the tradition survived but not the meaning behind it. Because couples at the end of the century were older and often living together, some began to see weddings as long parties (extending over two to three days) for their friends and families.

Everyone appeared to enjoy the rituals and traditions of weddings. During the 1990s, weddings were commonly featured on both television and in the movies (e.g., *Four Weddings and a Funeral*, 1994). TV comedies staged weddings to boost ratings (e.g., *Frasier* [1993–2004], *Friends* [1994–2004], *Will and Grace* [1998–2006]), and it was common for television series to end a season with a much-anticipated wedding. Weddings also were commonly included in "bloopers" TV shows, and reality television shows like The Learning Channel's *A Wedding Story* (1996) featured couples preparing for their big day.

Another phenomenon of the 1990s was the *destination wedding*. Couples invited small groups of family and friends to help them celebrate their union at a glamorous location away from home. The Caribbean, Hawaii, and Disney World were among the most popular locations for these events. After the wedding, guests usually returned home while the couple remained for their honeymoon.

Honeymoons. The term honeymoon has not always referred to a bride and groom's post-wedding vacation. It originated in northern Europe from a tradition of drinking wine made from mead and honey to bring good luck. Newlywed couples drank the sweet wine for a month (a "moon") after getting married, so this post-wedding ritual came to be known as the honeymoon.

The private wedding trip as we know it today was a 20th-century phenomenon. During much of the 19th century, honeymoons were limited to upper-class couples who often took friends and family along on their wedding trips. By the 1870s, it became an event reserved for the couple only, reflecting the increasing emphasis on romantic love as the basis for marriage.

With the advent of automobiles and more affordable accommodations, elaborate wedding trips became feasible for a greater number of couples, and in the early 20th century, middle-class couples joined their upper-class counterparts in taking wedding trips. Natural outdoor settings tended to be the most popular honeymoon sites, including destinations such as Niagara Falls and the Pocono Mountains.

By the late 1930s, honeymooners began discovering more modern and exotic destinations, seeking locales with amenities that nature alone could not provide. Honeymooners sought vacation spots that offered both natural beauty and luxurious accommodations. This trend continued through the end of the century for many couples, but gradually destinations became more varied. During the 1990s, Niagara Falls remained a popular location for romantic couples who sought a nostalgic wedding trip. Others saw their honeymoon as an opportunity to take a once-in-a-lifetime trip abroad to Europe, Australia, and other far-flung destinations.

Another 1990s trend was the packaged resort or cruise honeymoons. Although marketed honeymoon tours were available prior to the 1950s, they were not widespread until later in the century. Recreational opportunities abounded on these packaged tours, ranging from engaging in rigorous sports and exercise to having relaxing massages. Packages often included all meals, snacks, and drinks, including alcoholic beverages.

Although exotic honeymoons became increasingly popular, so too did staying closer to home. Work and family commitments limited honeymoon options for some newlyweds. In some cases, both spouses had hectic work schedules; in other cases, children at home required care. For these couples, a few days at a nearby bed and breakfast may have served as their honeymoon. The very end of the century also witnessed the introduction of the "family moon," in which children accompanied parents and stepparents on the wedding trip or destination wedding.

The honeymoon once served as a couple's initiation into sexual intimacy; however, between 1970 and the end of the century, it became increasingly less common for couples to reserve their first experience of sexual intimacy for the wedding night. Despite the fact that, for many, honeymoons no longer served this function, they remained a significant event for many newlyweds, although some couples took honeymoon trips before the wedding rather than afterward, if it was more convenient.

Divorces Although divorces became, over the century, if not normative, at least relatively common, there were no cultural rituals or ceremonies to mark the passage of status from being married to being divorced. In fact, in the last quarter of the century, following the passage of no-fault divorce laws, divorcing couples did not even need to appear in court when their marriage was dissolved legally. In sharp contrast to the major public celebratory event that weddings had become, divorce was observed in private, and the final divorce decree was received via certified mail.

Until the last decade or two of the 20th century, divorce was a stigmatized status that people tended to hide out of shame or embarrassment, and divorce never lost its stigmatized status among some subgroups of society (e.g., conservative religious faiths). In general, divorce was still associated with negative connotations, so it is little wonder that there were few efforts to create rituals to help people adjust to their new single status, much less to celebrate such a status change. People who divorced were still widely seen as failures at one of life's most important relationships.

However, 1990s entrepreneurs began selling divorce greeting cards, divorce announcements to send to friends and family to let them know of the change in marital status, and divorce party kits. Therapists sometimes advised people to celebrate their divorce and denote it with a ritual or ceremony, usually a gathering of close friends. Web sites were developed with advice on how divorced people could mark the event publicly.

Despite these efforts, at the end of the 20th century, divorce was far from being a life experience observed by ritualized and/or public ceremonies.

In the 19th century, Victorian Americans created the modern funeral—which tended to be far more elaborate than funerals **Funerals** of earlier times—and much of what was created then about this family ritual continued throughout the 20th century. For instance, gleaming caskets surrounded by huge banks of flowers replaced simple pine coffins; embalming and cosmetizing the dead person replaced simple washing of the body with soap and water; displaying pictures and mementos representing the deceased replaced viewing the body in the home for days before the funeral service; and dressing the dead in their best clothes replaced burying them in a linen shroud. Despite these enduring Victorian legacies, funerals also changed profoundly over the course of the century.

The Victorians had transformed funerals from mainly a family experience to a professionally managed event. In the early 19th century, the dead family member's body was cleaned at home, usually by female family members, and the deceased then lay in the parlor of the home for viewing. Friends and family members came by to look at the body, mourn with other survivors, and celebrate the life of the deceased. Wakes were often held in the home, with mourners eating, drinking, laughing, and crying around the body of the departed.

Many of the behaviors emphasizing death as a normal part of everyday life changed when embalming became widespread late in the 19th century.

Horse-drawn hearses at mass burial in a cemetery in North Collingwood, Ohio, near the turn of the century. (Courtesy of the Library of Congress.)

The practice of embalming, along with other modern funeral practices, helped foster a denial of death that continued throughout the 20th century. Prior to World War I, experiencing the death of others was inescapable because most people died at home, but, by 1937, 37 percent of deaths in the United States occurred in a hospital or convalescent home. This number had increased by 1949 to about half of deaths, and, by 1992, 77 percent of all deaths occurred in hospitals or nursing homes. By the end of the century, it was common for Americans to have never seen anyone die. Death had become medicalized and institutionalized, even more so than birth. In fact, funeral home directors began taking custody of the body from hospitals and nursing homes, and, increasingly, family members were not in control of their loved ones' remains.

Embalming allowed funeral directors to make a corpse appear to be sleeping rather than dead. Caskets became increasingly elaborate and sometimes contained box springs and mattresses to replicate the appearance of a bed and sleep rather than a coffin and death. The language used reflected avoidance of death as well. Terms such as *passed away* replaced *died,* and *loved one* replaced *body* and *corpse.*

Funeral professionals. By 1900, preparing the body for burial and organizing the mourners had largely been taken over by funeral home directors, at least for middle- and upper-class white Americans. Rather than being mourned in their own parlors in their own homes, the dead loved ones were mourned in funeral parlors situated in funeral homes and in churches where the final ceremony was typically held. Black Americans, rural immigrants, and poor whites in the South, however, continued to have home-based funerals well into the 1940s.

Middle- and upper-class families prior to the First World War generally carried on the Victorian traditions of large, expensive funerals. They thought deceased loved ones deserved lavish funerals, and, by employing professional morticians to handle the preparations, middle-class Americans could somewhat distance themselves from the experience of death and dying.

A shift in attitudes about funerals took place after World War I. The ostentatious funerals of the Victorian period were seen as gaudy, and Americans began to prefer simple ceremonies. In the 1930s, funerals cost almost as much as weddings, and many people established savings accounts to help pay for their funeral arrangements. By the 1950s, the average cost of funerals had fallen to 17 percent of the average wedding cost, and that ratio was still true in 2000.

As Americans' denial of death grew, wakes evolved into visitations that took place in funeral homes' viewing rooms, were of limited hours during the early evenings, and food and drink were not included. After World War II, funeral services increasingly took place in mortuaries rather than houses of worship, although some were still held in churches throughout the century. Earlier funeral customs such as kissing the dead in the casket and taking pictures of the deceased gradually diminished; these customs eventually stopped among middle-class and upper-class white Americans. Certain immigrant groups (Asians, Poles, Russians, Italians, and Celts), working-class families, and African Americans continued some of these customs well into the 20th century.

As the mortuary business grew into an industry run by professional morticians, clergy in the middle of the 20th century became louder critics of the expenses associated with funerals. They urged simple services and honoring the deceased by donating money to the poor or to the dead person's favorite charity in lieu of expensive floral tributes. Nonreligious people also argued for simple ceremonies.

In the 1960s, social critics of funeral home practices, such as Jessica Mitford, led to policy changes and greater controls over funeral professionals. These new ideas, coupled with Elizabeth Kubler-Ross's influential 1969 work, *On Death and Dying,* and that of other scholars, led to changes in the norm for American funeral practices. In the 1970s, Kubler-Ross and other academics and health care professionals stimulated the development of the hospice movement in the United States. This was part of an overall attempt to demedicalize death and give dying people and their families more control over the dying process. More people chose to die at home, either in hospice programs or on their own, and living wills and advanced directives became more popular as Americans searched for ways to die on their own terms.

Cremations became more frequent near the end of the century. In 1975 only 7 percent of dead bodies were cremated; this had increased to nearly 25 percent by 2000. Once forbidden for religious reasons, the Catholic Church declared cremations to be acceptable in the late 1970s, which cleared the way for more Americans to choose this option. Cremations tended to be accompanied by simple ceremonies; sometimes, rather than funerals, memorial services or small private gatherings of family and friends celebrated the life of the deceased. Cremations allowed families to plan memorial services relatively free of the time restraints of a typical funeral. Cremated remains were buried, scattered at sea or in other favorite spots, or kept by members of the family. Near the end of the century, a new choice was to create a gem (and a piece of jewelry) out of the loved one's remains.

The century was marked by changing rituals for mourning the death of family members and changing practices related to death and dying. In many ways, Americans came full circle—from dying and being prepared for burial in one's home to turning the process over to professionals—first doctors in hospitals and then morticians in funeral parlors—to the hospice movement, which again reflected people's preference to die at home surrounded by family followed by intimate memorial services controlled by family and friends.

Race, social class, and funerals. Most of the described changes in funerals were experienced by white middle-class Americans. Working-class families, immigrants, and African Americans engaged in somewhat different funeral rituals, and funeral observance changes these families experienced reflected somewhat different patterns.

For instance, poor families, in general, and black Americans of all socioeconomic backgrounds tended to abandon lavish funerals much later than white middle-class families did. Not until the 1960s did African Americans' funeral observances converge with that of whites, mostly because there were more middle-class African Americans who shared their white counterparts' views. Poverty and historical/cultural traditions had contributed to racial differences in funeral ceremonies. For example, black funerals typically were more openly emotional and entire communities participated. Sometimes, particularly among African Americans in the South, a second funeral attended only by extended family was held a few weeks after the community observance. Blacks generally spent a greater proportion of their household incomes on funerals than did whites, and the lavish displays of the Victorian era persisted among rural African Americans well into the second half of the century. Burial associations and funeral insurance were among the ways blacks financed elaborate funerals that often lasted hours and were accompanied by energetic emotional displays by the deceased persons' loved ones, eloquent sermons, and exuberant singing. In New Orleans, in the 1990s, mourners began wearing T-shirts bearing pictures of the deceased, and jazz funerals remained a common practice there.

Immigrant families tended to continue religious and cultural practices from their countries of origin, although acculturation and assimilation over time helped to homogenize funeral observances across immigrant groups.

Family transitions and funerals. Complicating funeral rituals in the final decades of the century was the growing structural diversity of families. Instead of only genetic (or adoptive) kin to mourn a loved one's passing, there were former spouses, stepfamilies, and other individuals not legally or biologically related to the deceased, but who held family-member status. Deciding how to deal with these quasi-kin mourners sometimes added stress to already stressful experiences for families, and conflicts were not uncommon when former spouses and others attempted to join family mourners. Many individuals stayed home and mourned privately rather than participate in public funeral rituals that could add discomfort and disagreements to their grief and that of other family members.

HOLIDAY CELEBRATIONS

Holiday celebrations, whether sacred, secular, or both, are generally important times for families to gather together. Many holiday celebrations Americans view as traditional were either invented or their trappings were created in the 19th-century Victorian era. Thanksgiving became a national holiday in 1863 when President Abraham Lincoln passed a proclamation establishing the last Thursday in November as an annual day of giving thanks.. It was later changed to the fourth Thursday in November by President Franklin Delano Roosevelt. Many typically American Christmas traditions, such as the exchange of gifts and cards, tree decoration, and jolly Santa Claus also began with the Victorians. Prior to the 19th century, Santa Claus was more often portrayed as dour Father Christmas, a figure related more to death (Father Time) than to gifts for obedient children.

Victorian middle-class Americans were major advocates of family traditions and rituals because, according to historian John Gillis (1996), they felt the quality of family life was eroding. New traditions were invented or old ones modified to evoke nostalgia for an imagined past when families had been closer, more loving, and more satisfying. The Victorians hoped that such celebrations would somehow transfer to families. People in the 20th century inherited this legacy and, with the help of merchants, maintained it.

The United States enjoys many secular national holidays— Thanksgiving, New Year's Day, Independence Day, Labor Day, and Memorial Day are the major ones. These holidays influence families' behaviors in various ways. Other holidays that many families celebrate, albeit without official national holiday status, include Valentine's Day, Mother's Day, Father's Day, and Halloween. **National Holidays**

Thanksgiving. Thanksgiving did not originate with the Pilgrims and Native Americans in the 1600s, as legend has it, but by a mid-1800s journalist and author, Sarah Josepha Hale. In a popular middle-class women's magazine that she edited, Hale wrote annual editorials encouraging the establishment of a national day of thanksgiving and celebration of unity. Over several years, Hale created Thanksgiving traditions in her magazine, including what to serve for the Thanksgiving Day meal. Much of what we now know as Thanksgiving traditions and the sentimental tale of the first Thanksgiving (the grateful Pilgrims sharing their bounty with the Indians) were created by Hale. For over a decade, she sought support from governors and federal politicians to make Thanksgiving an official holiday, and eventually found an ally in President Abraham Lincoln, who saw this created festivity as an opportunity to help heal a nation at war with itself. Once Lincoln declared Thanksgiving a national holiday, it quickly became extremely popular, first in the North and later throughout the country.

By the start of the 20th century, Thanksgiving was topped in the North and Northeast only by Christmas as a family day of observance. Although nationally celebrated, regional, religious, and racial differences in daily activities related to Thanksgiving (and other holidays) had evolved early in the century. For instance, African Americans often went to church services on Thanksgiving, and some rural men and boys went hunting while the women and girls prepared the feast. In New York and Philadelphia, some lower-income men conducted raucous, often drunken, parades wearing costumes, and in some urban areas, costumed children went door to door seeking treats. Southerners considered Thanksgiving a Yankee holiday and generally did not observe it. Catholics thought of the holiday celebration as something that Protestants did, so they, too, did not celebrate it.

The new European immigrants flooding into the United States early in the century were unsure about celebrating Thanksgiving. This distinctively North American holiday (Canada's Thanksgiving occurs in October) was unfamiliar to most immigrants—it was not a religious holiday, yet it had trappings of religion—public and private prayers of thanks, frequent references by clergy and public officials to bountiful blessings, and rituals that centered on family. Hale's creation of Thanksgiving as a day to return to the family homestead quickly became a primary feature of the holiday, a tradition that continues. Joined with the theme of homecoming were notions of solidarity and societal unity, notions that felt strange to most immigrants early in the century—they did not, in general, yet feel like Americans.

In an effort to assimilate immigrants, educators seized upon Thanksgiving's values and social messages (family, love of country, gratitude) as a way to socialize young immigrants to think like Americans. School Thanksgiving pageants portrayed friendly Pilgrims and Indians enjoying traditional foods, and Pilgrims were extolled as examples of American virtues. Children, in turn, socialized their immigrant parents into observing the rituals of Thanksgiving. Although the traditional Thanksgiving foods were from Sarah Josepha Hale's recipes, not the Pilgrims, her menu of turkey, dressing, and a variety of pies (including chicken pot pie as a main course), had taken hold by the early 20th century and were considered historically accurate and integral to the holiday. Many immigrants added their own cultural foods to the menu.

Educators in the early decades were intent on ending the practice of drunken parades and children begging for treats, practices inconsistent with a national day of thanksgiving. By 1924, the parades had become the Macy's Thanksgiving Day parade, and, by the 1930s, going door to door for treats had moved from Thanksgiving to Halloween. Although reformers and educators had eliminated some nonfamily focused aspects of Thanksgiving, the Macy's parade was designed to signal the start of the Christmas shopping season, and other commercial interests were simultaneously attempting to commercialize the day. From the middle of the century to the end, retail sales on the day after Thanksgiving were reported as the highest of the year, illustrating the success of these commercial interests.

Although religious and national leaders originally decried Thanksgiving Day parades that both commercialized the holiday and interfered with morning religious services, the parades stayed in fashion. The parade was held in the morning because Thanksgiving afternoon, from the 1870s

A traditional family Thanksgiving dinner. (© Royalty-Free/Corbis)

on, increasingly belonged to football. By the 1930s, it was common for families to listen to football games on the radio as they ate or digested their Thanksgiving dinners. By the late 1950s, watching televised football games had become a Thanksgiving tradition for many families, at least among the men and boys. Football was often criticized as separating men and women on this day of supposed family unity. Women typically spent all day (or days before) preparing the meal and cleaning up afterward, while men enjoyed leisure pursuits, both in the home (watching football) and outside (hunting, playing touch football on the lawn, drinking at bars with friends). Interestingly, Thanksgiving Day football games helped overcome some Southerners' distrust of this Yankee celebration and made it more accepted in Southern homes.

In the last decades of the century, changes in Thanksgiving rituals began to occur. More families ate Thanksgiving dinner in restaurants (10 percent did so in 1995 according to one survey), more dinners were prepared from frozen and prepackaged foods, and men as well as women participated in the cleanup (cooking continued to be mostly women's work). People continued to travel great distances to visit kin, but individuals also celebrated Thanksgiving dinner with friends rather than far-flung family members. Traditional foods remained popular, but the Pilgrims were less often portrayed as kindly benefactors and possessors of ideal American values and more were seen as exploiters of Native Americans and archetypes of European domination of North America and its inhabitants. Nonetheless,

Thanksgiving was more popular at the end of the century than it was at the start. More Americans of all backgrounds and social classes celebrated it, but less sentimentally than they had done earlier. Movies such as *Home for the Holidays* (1995) and *Avalon* (1990) portrayed Thanksgiving as a time of mixed family conflict and unity.

Memorial Day, Independence Day, and Labor Day. Over the course of the 20th century, Memorial Day and Labor Day became the unofficial markers of the start and end of summer, respectively. Both days were created to honor ordinary people. Memorial Day, started in 1868, originally honored those who died in the Civil War. By the late 1800s, communities across the country celebrated Memorial Day, honoring those who had died in all wars. In 1971, Congress declared Memorial Day a national holiday to be celebrated on the last Monday in May.

Memorial Day was known throughout most of the century as Decoration Day because it was the day that families decorated graves of deceased relatives with wreaths and flowers. Family members returned to home communities to decorate family graves, visit with relatives and friends, and perhaps share a picnic. Gradually, the focus shifted to honoring the military dead, and parades, military shows, and public ceremonies in which war veterans were honored became common.

Labor Day was first enacted September 5, 1882, in New York City to honor American workers. Over the next 12 years, states gradually passed legislation to honor workers, and, on June 28, 1894, Congress passed an act designating the first Monday in September a legal holiday. Independence Day was established in 1870 to celebrate the signing of the Declaration of Independence from England. Neither of these holidays originally were particularly family oriented, although families took advantage of time off from work to enjoy recreational activities together (e.g., swimming, shopping, picnicking, attending ball games). Following World War II and the advent of inexpensive gasoline and the new interstate highway system, Labor Day weekend became a time for families to take short vacation trips—one last fling before children returned to school. Independence Day, celebrated on the fourth day of July, typically included community celebrations (parades, picnics, fireworks displays), which became family outings. As Americans' lives became increasingly busy over the course of the 20th century, holidays such as these summer celebrations were savored as opportunities for families to be together. Politicians, clergy, and members of the media encouraged family members to use the holidays to strengthen family bonds even as the holidays were designed to strengthen the societal bonds of all Americans.

New Year's Day. For most of the century, New Year's Day was primarily celebrated by adults only. However, in 1976, a Boston group discouraged excess alcohol consumption by promoting a family-friendly celebration known as First Night to replace traditional New Year's celebrations. Families attended concerts, art shows, and a variety of other activities on New Year's Eve. First Night celebrations eventually attracted over a million revelers each year in Boston alone. Interest in the concept soon spread to other communities, and, by 1999, the event was emulated in more than 100 cities.

Mother's Day. The first official Mother's Day celebration was held in 1908. Mother's Day was designed as a national holiday to honor mothers' piety in Protestant churches across the country. Its existence is almost solely due to the efforts of Anna Jarvis, a young woman from rural West Virginia who settled in Philadelphia as an adult. Started as a memorial to her own mother in her hometown Methodist church, Jarvis encouraged other churches and religious organizations to also celebrate this holiday. Politicians quickly jumped on the bandwagon, and, in 1914, President Woodrow Wilson issued a presidential proclamation declaring the second Sunday in May to be Mother's Day.

In the beginning, Mother's Day was centered on religion, particularly fundamental Protestantism, and the home. Jarvis's image for Mother's Day was a somber, holy celebration of mothers' contributions to home, family, church, and community. Churches originally held special services and awarded roses and other small gifts to the oldest mother, the mother with the most children, the mother who traveled the farthest to be in attendance, etc. Families attended these services together, followed by a quiet day at home. If the mother was deceased, a trip to the cemetery or time spent in solitude appreciating the gifts she had provided was Jarvis's ideal for how Mother's Day would be spent.

Soon, however, the sober and religious tone of Mother's Day had competition from commercial interests who saw the opportunity to make money. The florist and greeting card industries linked the celebration of mothers with the giving of cut flowers and cards. Although Jarvis fought the intrusion of commercial interests throughout her life, florists were extremely successful in making this holiday conspicuously celebrated by the giving of flowers (churches also were heavily adorned with flowers for the occasion). The greeting card industry and other retailers also made inroads into commercializing the celebration of Mother's Day prior to the 1920s. This commercialization that began with flowers and greeting cards was followed by taking mothers to dinner or brunch after church, and giving her (usually small) gifts. Later in the century, department stores and malls began advertising Mother's Day sales.

By the 1970s, Mother's Day ritual observances no longer necessarily included attending church, and in the latter decades of the century, for many Americans, Mother's Day had evolved into a holiday on which such religious traditions were secondary. Far more Americans engaged in the commercially inspired rituals of giving cards, flowers, and gifts and going out to eat with their mothers than attended religious services.

Father's Day. Father's Day seemed to be a natural extension of the extremely popular Mother's Day, and credit for its creation goes to two sources. First, early in the century, Sonora Dodd, a young woman from Spokane, Washington, lobbied for such a day with local Protestant churches and civic organizations. In 1910, she engineered a petition to make the third Sunday in June a day to honor the father's place in the home, the training of children, the safeguarding of the marriage tie, and the protection of womanhood and childhood. Her inspiration was her own widowed father, who had raised Sonora and her five siblings alone (Pleck, 2000).

This new holiday struggled for years for recognition and might have quickly died as a minor local Spokane celebration, except that Dodd would not drop the idea. Although she was a tireless advocate of Father's Day, people did not take it seriously. Humorists such as Will Rogers and Groucho Marx ridiculed it, and others mocked Father's Day by suggesting that there might as well be a Maiden Aunty's Day, Household Pet Day, Mother-in-Law Day, and the like. Some of this ridicule was rooted in gender differences—people thought Mother's Day was appropriately sentimental and sweet, but fathers were too manly to enjoy being celebrated and adored in the same way as mothers, which was how early Father's Days were celebrated.

Sonora Dodd's efforts finally received support from the National Council for the Promotion of Father's Day, an organization started in 1938 by the New York City Associated Men's Wear Retailers trade association. This organization likely promoted Father's Day as a national holiday because they wanted to sell a few hats, ties, and suspenders as presents. They influenced their retailer members to promote the national observance of Father's Day, efforts that were gradually successful. Father's Day thus became a national family holiday of sorts, although it never reached the popularity of Mother's Day.

Valentine's Day. The greeting card industry adopted St. Valentine's Day as their favorite holiday long before the 20th century. In fact, the popularity of valentine cards in the mid-1800s helped stimulate the growth of the original greeting card industry. By the 1920s, Valentine's Day cards were a $60 million business, and, by the end of the century, over a billion dollars were spent every year on Valentine's Day cards. Similarly, candy and flower sales were huge on Valentine's Day. Rivaled only by Christmas, Valentine's Day is an example of how consumer culture and commercial enterprises have shaped national family holidays in the United States.

Although Valentine's Day was not initially a family holiday, helped along by several commercial industries (e.g., greeting card companies, candy makers, florists), observances gradually shifted from exchanges of inexpensive cards between sweethearts, to a day in which cards and gifts were exchanged between all kinds of loved ones—spouses, parents and children, grandparents and grandchildren—as well as sweethearts and lovers. By the end of the century, husbands and wives were expected to join boyfriends and girlfriends in celebrating the day with cards, gifts, and romantic dinners.

Stepfamily Day. Stepfamily Day was started as Stepparents' Day in the early 1980s to show appreciation to stepmothers and stepfathers. Those who supported the idea of celebrating stepparents' contribu-

tions to their stepchildren believed that Mother's Day and Father's Day should continue to celebrate parents, but that stepparents deserved their own day, one that would not interfere with the previously established days for moms and dads. Of course, many stepchildren considered their stepparents their functional mothers or fathers and honored them on Mother's or Father's Day, but the idea behind Stepparents' Day was to honor stepparents, recognize that they are different from parents in some ways, and destigmatize the label of stepparent. The founders of Stepparents' Day were stepparents and active members of the Stepfamily Association of America, a self-help organization that promoted stepfamily well-being though education and support. In 1997, President Clinton proclaimed September 16 as Stepparents' Day, a few companies produced Stepparents' Day cards, and the Stepfamily Association of America made annual announcements to make the public aware of Stepparents' Day—however, the holiday never received widespread recognition.

Grandparents Day. Grandparents Day was created by legislation signed by President Carter in 1978. Atlantan Michael Goldgar was the driving force behind this day, and he spent several thousand dollars and many hours traveling to Washington, DC, to lobby legislators for a bill honoring grandparents for their contributions to families. Like Stepparents' Day, Grandparents Day was not widely accepted and celebrated. It is not clear why—unlike stepmothers and stepfathers, who were often stigmatized and negatively stereotyped, grandmothers and grandfathers were nearly always viewed positively, at least in the abstract. It was somewhat surprising, therefore, that Grandparents' Day, the first Sunday after Labor Day, did not become a major commercial success, although greeting card makers and florists encouraged its observance.

Many religious holidays either centered primarily on families or involved family members in celebratory rituals. This section highlights the major religious holidays in the United States, paying

particular attention to the family-related aspects of these holidays.

Christmas. The Christmas traditions that Americans observed in 1900 were mostly products of 19th-century Victorians who combined English, German, and northern European traditions into a distinctly American holiday. From the Germans came Christmas trees, from England came cards and the tale of Scrooge being redeemed on Christmas morning, from the Dutch came Christmas stockings and the name (Sinter Class) of the jolly old elf (Santa Claus) who filled the stockings and brought presents, and from both English and American writers came a nostalgic view of Christmas as a time for families to bond and for parents to make the season a special delight for their children.

Although Christmas presents and commercial interests in Christmas long predated the 20th century, in this century Christmas clearly became "a sacred season within a consumer festival" (Pleck, 2000, p. 44), much to the discomfort of many Christians. Starting early in the century, the Christmas season had two faces that had quite diverse effects on families. The religious face of Christmas presented a sentimental season focusing on commemorating Jesus' birth, idealized notions of family life, and nostalgia for a simpler time when caring, sharing, and love for others supposedly ruled human interactions. The commercial face of Christmas was a secular season in which the emphasis was on gifts and a kind of generalized good will and celebration of the end of another year. The baby Jesus was the symbol of the religious Christmas celebration; Santa Claus was the icon for the consumer festival of Christmas.

Throughout the first 60 years of the 20th century, these two views of Christmas coexisted, albeit with increasing discomfort. Community and national leaders started putting up public Christmas trees as early as 1912 (in New York City) and holding Christmas pageants as a way of promoting civic involvement and unity. These activities were likely seen as religious in nature by most Americans, but the singing of Christmas carols and presenting public displays of various symbols of Christmas (decorated trees, crèches) began to blur the line between religious and secular holidays and may have served secular aspects of Christmas more than the religious.

Similarly, Christmas movies such as *A Christmas Carol* (1938), *Miracle on 34th Street* (1947), *It's a Wonderful Life* (1947), *Holiday Inn* (1942), and *White Christmas* (1954) conveyed messages about the need for love, hope, and sharing with others, but these morality tales were not based on religious ideologies as much as on some generalized sense of good will thought to pervade the Christmas holiday season. Although not everyone believed in Jesus, every child could believe in Santa Claus or the ghost of Christmas past. Popular television Christmas specials that started in the 1950s and continued throughout the 20th century (such as *A Charlie Brown Christmas*, a series of *Frosty the Snowman* cartoons, and countless made-for-TV movies) also helped secularize Christmas. The lessons of these entertainments, such as keeping Christmas in one's heart and caring for the poor and less fortunate, were applicable to all, regardless of religion. At the end of the 20th century, cable channels ran humorist Gene Shepherd's classic childhood recollections, *A Christmas Story*, for 24 hours continuously on Christmas Day. This amusing story about the child of working-class parents in the middle of the century made no mention of religious themes, not-so-subtly suggesting that all can enjoy Christmas, regardless of individual beliefs.

The business community promoted the commercial and economic Christmas holiday by capitalizing, some would say exploiting, the emotional and sentimental aspects of Christmas to stimulate sales. For instance, the story of Rudolph the Red-Nosed Reindeer was created in 1939 by an advertiser for Montgomery Ward, a department store chain, as a booklet to be given as a store souvenir. There was a moral to the tale of the outcast reindeer that used his talents to help Santa Claus save Christmas for children around the world ("everyone can use their talents for the greater good"). Rudolph's rapid popularity among children grew as a song recorded by well-known cowboy actor and singer Gene Autry and a cartoon movie made Rudolph an instant symbol of Christmas. His image was placed on many commercial products, making Rudolph a financial success as well as a beloved icon.

Many black Americans saw the secular celebration of Christmas as excluding them—they had difficulty participating fully in the gift-giving aspects of Christmas when they could not shop where they wanted in all parts of the country (prior to the Civil Rights movement in the 1960s) and when discriminatory practices excluded them from Christmas festivities in a variety of ways. This discontent led to the creation of Kwanzaa, a celebration for Black Americans that coincided with the Christmas season.

Many low-income Americans also felt on the fringe of commercialized holiday festivities because they could not afford to buy the latest, most-wanted toys for their children. Starting early in the century, middle- and upper-class parents bought their children's presents from retailers—poor and working-class parents either made gifts for their children and/or bought food that was generally unavailable to them at other times of the year, such as oranges and apples. As Christmas became more commercial, and increasingly emphasized showering children with toys and other gifts, the celebration became a painful reminder to low-income parents that they could not provide for their children in the way they were expected to provide. The establishment of Christmas clubs, bank savings accounts that parents contributed to during the year in order to finance a lavish Christmas for their children, were popular starting in the 1950s. Even though these savings accounts provided no interest income to parents and the banks were able to utilize the money at no cost to the banks, many parents liked the discipline of making regular deposits. As credit cards became more widely available, Christmas clubs became less popular and many parents annually went into debt to buy Christmas presents for their children.

By the last quarter of the century, many Americans expressed ambivalence about the Christmas holiday. This "most joyous of seasons" was also characterized by depression, alienation, and anxiety. Conservative Christians were angry that Christmas had become too secular, non-Christians and poor people felt left out, mothers and fathers became anxious about creating the perfect holiday for their families (especially

Gifts piled up under a Christmas tree, 1980s. (Courtesy of
the authors.)

children), and post-divorce families struggled with trying to negotiate
where and when children would be celebrating Christmas among their
assortment of parents, stepparents, and extended kin. Women's magazines instructed readers about how to create ideal Christmas holidays via
homemade decorations and cooking the perfect Christmas feast next to
articles about coping with depression during the holidays. Christmas had
become both a grand holiday that brought families together and a source
of family stress and anxiety. Regardless of this ambivalence, what had
begun as a holiday for Christians became a huge economic engine that
represented a large percentage of the annual earnings for many retailers
and in which nearly all Americans participated to some extent.

  Chanukah. Chanukah, the Festival of Lights, begins on the 25th day of
the month of Kislev in the Jewish calendar (November/December) and
continues for eight days. It celebrates the victory of Judah Maccabee over

the Syrians. About 2,300 years ago, a Syrian king, Antiochus, ordered all Jewish people to reject their religion and its customs and instead worship Greek gods. Many refused to follow his orders, including Judah, who along with his brothers formed an army, and succeeded at driving the Syrians out of Israel. After reclaiming the Temple in Jerusalem, they began clearing it of Greek symbols and statues, a task that was completed on the 25th day of Kislev. After finishing, they rededicated the Temple by lighting the eternal light, but found only enough oil for one day. A miracle occurred, however, and the light remained lit for eight days. In honor of this miracle, Jews light a menorah, a candelabrum that holds nine candles; eight represent the eight nights that the small flask of oil remained lit in the Temple, and the ninth is used to light the others. On the evening before each one of the days, the corresponding number of candles is lit on the menorah.

Although not generally considered an important religious holiday, numerous public opinion polls of American Jews since World War II indicated Chanukah was the most popular Jewish holiday in the United States. This was primarily because Chanukah provided Jews with an alternative holiday to Christmas, complete with toys for the children, songs, and family dinners. As Christmas became more commercialized, Chanukah correspondingly increased in importance and popularity.

Easter. The peripheral aspects of the Easter holiday—chocolate bunnies, Easter egg hunts, new clothes, giving flowers as gifts, and exchanging greeting cards—were Victorian inventions that greeted the start of the 20th century. During the first six decades of the century, families celebrated Easter by going to church, where they showed off new spring clothing, returned home for a large breakfast or lunch and Easter egg hunts for the children. Pastel colors and floral arrangements were the rage, especially for middle-class and upper-class women and their families. Church attendance diminished somewhat in the 1960s and 1970s, as did the tradition of parading in new clothes. The improved financial conditions of most post-Depression, post–World War II families meant that new clothes were purchased year round, not just at Easter. Ironically, some clergy, who in earlier decades had chastised parishioners for ignoring the solemn reason for the holiday (the death of Jesus) in favor of showing off their wealth and new finery, complained that their casually attired congregants were not dressed up enough to show the proper respect for the occasion.

Despite the best efforts of business leaders, Easter never became a commercial success in the same way that Christmas did. Whereas the Christmas shopping season kicked into full gear the day after Thanksgiving, the changing dates of Easter made it harder for merchants to exploit an Easter season. The founder of Kodak, George Eastman, and other business leaders in the 1920s tried to get a fixed date for Easter but failed. The serious religious nature of Easter (death and resurrection) helped tone down commercial interests a bit as well. However,

Easter parades were popular fashion shows that encouraged middle- and upper-class Americans to buy new outfits, and gift giving, albeit much more restricted in price, were commercial aspects of Easter that made it an important day for candy and toy makers, florists, and clothiers. As the century ended, it was not unusual to see all kinds of products—even washers and dryers and cars—offered in Easter sales.

Although Easter never rivaled Christmas as a secular celebration, the broader culture adopted some aspects of Easter. President Rutherford B. Hayes started the first White House Easter egg hunt and egg roll in the 1880s, public schools held Easter pageants early in the century, and children made Easter gifts for their parents at school. For most of the century, secular celebrations of Easter—such as community-sponsored Easter egg hunts, public school dismissals for Good Friday (and often the Monday after Easter)—went unprotested by non-Christians. In the latter two decades, however, there were enough protests that Easter breaks were renamed spring breaks, and school events became spring festivals rather than Easter celebrations. Spring breaks gradually evolved away from celebrations of Easter, and most were scheduled midway through the spring semester regardless of when Easter occurred. Easter was never the family homecoming holiday that Thanksgiving and Christmas were, and the focus on family observance of Easter lessened considerably as the century came to a close. In the latter decades of the century, however, Easter egg hunting and Easter baskets for children began to mimic Christmas morning. Commercial interests seemed to be winning the hearts and minds of young Americans, and the Easter bunny became the counterpart to Santa Claus.

Passover. This Jewish religious observance is second to Chanukah in popularity among American Jews, and, because it falls approximately at the same time of the year as Easter, it provided an alternative holiday for Jewish families. Passover, or *Pesach,* begins on the evening of the 15th day of the Jewish month of Nissan. It is an eight-day holiday that recalls the exodus and freedom of the Israelites from ancient Egypt about 3,500 years ago, as told in the Book of Exodus. When the Pharaoh freed the Jews, they were not given time to bake their bread. Therefore, they prepared raw, unleavened dough that they could cook in the hot desert sun during their journey.

The highlight of Passover is the observance of the Seder, celebrated on the first two nights of Passover. It is a highly structured and educational ceremony that focuses on the story of the Israelites' departure from Egypt. One of the most significant observances of Passover is the removal of *chametz,* or leavened products, from households. The primary symbol of Passover is the matzo or matzah, flat unleavened bread that represents the bread Israelites ate following their hasty departure from Egypt. According to Jewish religious law, matzo may be made from flour derived from one of the five primary grains: wheat, oats, rye, barley, and spelt.

To make dough, water is added to the flour and is not allowed to rise for more than 18 minutes.

Over the course of the 20th century, Passover generally became shorter and more simplified by American Jews, and came to represent a time to celebrate freedom, hope, and family solidarity. Older family members used the holiday as an opportunity to instruct children about their Jewish identity in a culture in which they were a small minority to a sometimes hostile majority. The Passover Seder became an important ritual for the Jewish community—who, by the middle of the century, were mostly assimilated and middle class—to reaffirm their identity as Jews.

Ramadan. This is a Muslim holiday that most Americans had not heard of until late in the 20th century. Muslims, who are followers of Islam, believe that one can only find peace by submitting to Almighty God (Allah) in heart, soul, and deed. Muslims observe two major religious holidays each year, one of which is Ramadan.

Ramadan is the ninth month in the 12-month Islamic lunar calendar. Unlike fixed months of a Gregorian calendar based on the movements of the sun, a lunar month depends on the appearance of a crescent moon. As a result, the specific date of Ramadan is not known until the night before it starts, when the crescent moon is sighted. The lunar year is 11 to 13 days shorter than the Gregorian year, so over time Ramadan cycles backward through the year, eventually falling in each season. At the end of Ramadan, when the next crescent moon appears, Muslims around the world observe a three-day celebration called Eid al-Fitr (the festival of fast-breaking).

For Muslims, Ramadan is believed to be the month in which the first verses of the Holy Qur'an (the divine scripture) were revealed by God to the Prophet Muhammad. It is a time when Muslims practice self-restraint, cleanse their bodies and souls of impurities, and refocus attention on helping those in need and worshiping God. During Ramadan, emphasis is on learning self-control, and Muslims spend each day in a complete fast, taking in no food or water during daylight hours. The fast also includes refraining from evil actions, thoughts, and words. Therefore, fasting is not merely physical, but is a way of facing hunger, developing sympathy for those who are less fortunate, and appreciating all of God's bounties.

Not all family members must participate in the fasting rituals of Ramadan—pregnant women and mothers who are breast-feeding are exempt, as are very old adults, people in poor health, and young children. Older children are encouraged to participate in partial fasting to help them feel part of the observance and to socialize them into adult Muslim responsibilities.

Ramadan as a holiday entered the U.S. mainstream as a result of the immigration of thousands of Muslims over the course of the century, mostly individuals from the Middle East and Asia. In addition, about one-third of the 3 million Muslims in the United States at the end of the 20th century were African Americans or their descendants who had converted to Islam. Because they are one of the most rapidly growing religious groups in the United States, Muslims and their holidays, such as Ramadan, are likely to become increasingly familiar to all Americans in the 21st century.

Invented Traditions
Kwanzaa. This holiday festival was invented in 1966 by Ron Karenga, a black Nationalist who created Kwanzaa in part as a reaction to what he saw as African Americans' marginalization in the increasingly commercialized Christmas holiday season and in part to encourage pride among blacks in their African roots. Kwanzaa is an example of an *invented ritual* or tradition—defined as a tradition created to evoke a sense of continuity with the past, although that continuity was largely fictitious. Karenga, who had never been to Africa, created the rituals of Kwanzaa on his own, and there were only loose connections between this African American harvest celebration and any known African traditions.

Kwanzaa begins on December 26, continues for seven days, and was originally planned to be a quiet holiday celebrated mostly at home among family and friends. Each evening a candle was lit and a different principle of African heritage—unity, self-determination, collective work and responsibility, cooperative economics, purpose, creativity, and faith—was honored. As envisioned by Karenga, this celebration was not about gifts being exchanged; instead, it was an opportunity for blacks to be together and honor his version of their shared African culture and heritage.

Kwanzaa was not widely observed until the 1980s, when middle-class blacks began to reshape the holiday to make it more acceptable to black Christians and others who saw themselves as more mainstream Americans than the black separatists who initially championed the holiday. Articles about how to celebrate Kwanzaa began to appear in the early 1980s in magazines such as *Jet* and *Essence*. Middle-class blacks promoted the notion that Kwanzaa was a time to celebrate and honor family, and some families began to exchange gifts. Commercial interests started selling Kwanzaa cookbooks, cards, and gift wrap, and churches, day care centers, and schools began to spread the traditions of Kwanzaa.

By the end of the century, Kwanzaa had been accepted as a holiday by a large number of people, although only about 15 percent of African Americans celebrated it in 1997. President Clinton issued a proclamation that year sending good wishes to Americans celebrating this holiday, and the postal service released a Kwanzaa stamp. In 2000, Kwanzaa was still dwarfed by Christmas.

SUMMARY

Rituals are important activities in families. Most of the basic trappings of the major national rituals in the 20th century were begun in the previous century. However, as the century advanced, many family rituals became more elaborate, more expensive, and more commercial, as businesses found ways to make money from them. Everything from children's birthday parties and weddings and funerals to Thanksgiving and Halloween became simultaneously more sentimentalized, more commercialized, and more important to individuals and families. Even intentional reactions to these trends, such as the rituals of Kwanzaa, were at risk of falling prey to the same forces that commercialized Christmas, Chanukah, and other family-related celebrations.

New rituals such as Mother's Day, Father's Day, and Kwanzaa were created during the century. Some became quite successful, but newer celebrations such as Stepfamily Day and Grandparents Day have yet to catch on. It is clear that ritualized activities serve important functions in families, and, as the pace of family life quickens, rituals appear to take on even greater importance.

5
Mothers and Motherhood

The 20th century marked the coming of age of motherhood as a vocation in America. Prior to that, although mothers were largely responsible for the physical care of children (e.g., diapering, feeding, bathing), fathers were seen as responsible for children's character and moral development, leading them in prayers and disciplining them when they misbehaved. Consequently, 19th-century parenting advice was aimed at fathers, and the emphasis was on children's moral education. Legally, fathers were the primary parents.

In the latter half of the 19th century, however, childhood came to be seen as a distinct life stage, a view accompanied by the belief that responsibility for childrearing should be placed mainly on mothers. Children, no longer seen as immature adults in need of moral instruction and job skills training (fathers' expertise), came to be viewed as vulnerable, dependent, and in need of extensive maternal care. As the 19th century ended and the 20th century began, clergymen, doctors, and child experts directed their advice specifically to mothers, emphasizing children's needs for nurturance.

PREGNANCY AND CHILDBIRTH

When the century opened, motherhood was dangerous—there were over 60 maternal deaths for every 10,000 births in 1915, a percentage similar to the preceding 50 years. Women tried to control their pregnancies, but birth control methods were unreliable and abortion was illegal, so women commonly had more children than they wanted. Over time, the availability of dependable birth control and legalized abortions, medical advances that reduced infant and maternal mortality during labor and delivery, and improved understanding of maternal nutrition and fetal development gave women more control over whether and when they became pregnant and reduced risks when they decided to have children. Medical and technological advances, such as the invention of antibiotics and the use of blood transfusions (beginning in 1935) helped drastically diminish maternal deaths. The maternal mortality rate at the end of the century was 65 times lower than it was at the beginning (Mintz & Kellogg, 1988).

Birth Control and Abortion   Although many women were interested in birth control, there were substantive barriers to gaining access to or knowledge about it. Margaret Sanger caused great controversy by distributing to women sex education pamphlets that contained information about birth control, and she was arrested in 1915 for violating postal obscenity laws under the 1873 Comstock Act by mailing contraceptive information. This law was amended in 1923, allowing doctors to distribute information about contraceptives, but legal restrictions on disseminating this material existed into the 1950s. Sanger opened the first birth control clinic in the United States in 1916 in Brooklyn, New York. She was arrested nine days later, charged with maintaining a public nuisance, and the birth control information, diaphragms, and condoms the clinic distributed were confiscated. Nonetheless, she founded the American Birth Control League in 1921; the organization was renamed Planned Parenthood in 1942.

In the 1920s, about two-thirds of married couples used some method of birth control, but it was often coitus interruptus or the douche rather than a contraceptive. Not until the 1950s were more reliable devices such as diaphragms and condoms widely available. By then, 81 percent of white wives were using some form of birth control (May, 1994), but the major breakthrough came in 1960 with the invention of birth control pills. With the "Pill," women were able to control their fertility. They could decide whether and when they would become pregnant, which made them less fearful of sexual intercourse—marital or nonmarital. Consequently, the sexual double standard regarding premarital sex, which had been maintained partly by women's fear of pregnancy, began to fade (Collins, 2003). Other birth control methods became available later in the century, but none were as widely used as the Pill.

Another major event affecting women's fertility control occurred in 1973, when the U.S. Supreme Court decided in *Roe v. Wade* that it was unlawful to deny women abortions because of their right to privacy. Before this decision, many women had illegal abortions, and, although some (mostly middle- and upper-class) women were able to locate doctors who performed abortions, hospital boards and physicians were reluctant to approve them, which left most women with unwanted pregnancies seeking "back-alley" abortions performed by untrained people in often unsanitary conditions that posed great risks for infections or death. During the 1940s and 1950s, illegal abortions were responsible for 40 percent of all deaths of pregnant women (May, 1994).

After *Roe v. Wade*, the abortion rate rose for a decade, peaking at nearly 30 abortions per 1,000 women in the early 1980s. This rate remained constant before declining during the 1990s, reaching the lowest rate since 1974 in 2000 at slightly over 21 abortions per 1,000 women (Wind, 2003). Among adolescents, there were 28 abortions per 1,000 women in 1997, a 33 percent decrease since the late 1980s (Boonstra, 2002).

Safer labor and delivery did not lead to more pregnancies. Instead, better birth control methods and a desire to have fewer children lowered the fertility rate dramatically. Even without adequate birth control **Childbirth and Fertility Rates** methods, births to white women had dropped 50 percent during the 19th century—in 1800, mothers had an average of seven children; by 1900 this had fallen to between three and four children per mother. Between 1900 and 1936, the fertility rate dropped another 41 percent (Degler, 1980), and, during the Depression, there were about three million fewer births annually than there had been prior to the stock market crash in 1929 (Collins, 2003). During the Depression, many couples who wanted larger families simply could not afford more mouths to feed.

Between 1940 and 1957, the fertility rate rose 50 percent, partially because couples delayed having children until the Depression and World War II ended. After World War II, women of all ages and backgrounds had more children—one million more babies were born *each year* during the 1950s than had been born during the *entire decade* of the 1930s (Mintz & Kellogg, 1988). During the 1950s, couples had an average of 3.2 children and had them within a relatively short amount of time; families were usually complete by a mother's 30th birthday (Collins, 2003).

The postwar "baby boom" reached its peak in 1957, with 123 births per 1,000 women, and then the birth rate began to drop (Van Horn, 1988). The trend in having fewer children was accelerated by the Pill, and eventually birth rates fell below replacement—American women were not bearing enough children to replace themselves and their partners. By the end of the century, women had an average of 2.1 children, a slight increase over the previous 30 years. Birth rates varied by race and ethnicity, with Latinas having the most children on average (2.5), followed by blacks (2.1), and whites (1.8) (U.S. Census Bureau, 2000).

Multiple births. During the last two decades of the century, there was unprecedented growth in the birth rate of twins, triplets, and higher-order multiple births. Between 1980 and 1997, there were 52 percent more twin births and 404 percent more triplets and other higher-order births. An increased number of women age 45 and older gave birth to multiples—in 1997 alone, women 45 and older gave birth to more twins than had women of that age during the entire 1980s decade (444 vs. 174). Although twin births to older women comprised only a small portion of twin births, the increase of older women giving birth to multiples raised public health concerns about the mothers' and infants' physical health (Martin & Park, 1999). The increase was a result of women waiting longer to have children (older women were more likely to have multiples), and women using reproductive technologies and fertility treatments, which often resulted in multiple births.

Technology and Surrogate Mothers   Because women's socialization to become mothers was so strong, some went to great lengths to bear a child. Infant adoption had become increasingly difficult in the final decades of the century because adolescents were generally keeping their infants rather than placing them for adoption. Many couples were reluctant to adopt older children because of perceived health and behavior problems among these children. Some women had delayed childbearing long enough that infertility was an issue. The "biological clock" was ticking loudly for these women regardless of whether they were married, and they turned to technology for help.

There were major advances in assisted reproduction for infertile couples during the last three decades of the century, and single women and couples had a number of treatments available to them—many were enormously expensive. In some procedures, eggs and sperm were combined in laboratories; other times, eggs were fertilized in vitro. The first child conceived via in vitro fertilization was born in the late 1970s in England.

Technology sometimes led to complex arrangements. For example, women unable to carry a pregnancy had the option of using surrogate mothers. In some cases, mothers' eggs were fertilized by the fathers' sperm in a laboratory before placement in the uterus of the surrogate mother, who then carried the baby to term. Other times, when intended mothers were unable to provide eggs, the surrogate mothers' eggs were fertilized by the intended fathers' sperm. Because the surrogate was the child's biological mother, couples choosing this arrangement faced legal and ethical issues, and several complicated legal cases made headlines in the 1980s. One high-profile case involved Baby M, a child born to surrogate mother Mary Beth Whitehead, who became pregnant through artificial insemination of her egg with the intended father's sperm (Chesler, 1988). Whitehead refused to give up custody of Baby M to the father and his infertile wife. The New Jersey Supreme Court ultimately awarded custody to the father and visitation rights to Whitehead. That case led many states to either ban surrogacy or regulate it.

Conservatives were concerned about the ethics of the technologies involved in fertility and reproduction treatments, and other critics wondered about the ethics of "designer children"—couples or single women choosing sperm and/or eggs from donors who had desired characteristics (e.g., eye color, height, intelligence). Despite legal and ethical issues and the procedures' expenses, many women pursued any available methods to have a child. At the end of the century, celebrities older than 50 were heralded for giving birth using various fertility treatments or other technologies, and in England a psychiatrist older than 60 made headlines giving birth using technological assistance. Despite a steadily decreasing birth rate, motherhood had not waned in status among some women, and they would spend whatever it cost to attain it.

"If you bungle raising your children, I don't think whatever else you do matters very much" (Jacqueline Kennedy, widow of President John F. Kennedy, in 1965, in Lewis, 2006). This quote conveys a cultural message about the expectations of

Intensive Mothering and the Myth of Motherhood

motherhood that prevailed in the 20th century—mothers were responsible for raising their children, and if the children did not turn out well, it was her fault, and her life was worthless. This sentiment became deeply embedded in U.S. culture. It combined the ideology of *intensive mothering* (i.e., mothers are the ideal, preferred caretakers of children; expert-guided, emotionally absorbing, and labor-intensive childrearing is best; and children are sacred, their worth immeasurable) and the *myth of motherhood* (i.e., a belief that motherhood was instinctual, that having children fulfilled women in ways that nothing else could, and that mothers were children's best care providers). These ideologies defined how Americans thought about motherhood as well as how mothers thought about themselves, and they represented a huge change from 19th-century childrearing ideology that championed harsh, punitive childrearing methods. In both centuries, however, it was strongly believed that women, especially birth mothers, were most qualified for children's daily caregiving.

The ideology of intensive mothering and the motherhood myth began evolving when the Industrial Revolution changed family work and brought about the establishment of separate spheres for men and women—women's sphere or place was in the home, which included control of the children, and men belonged in the work force.

American culture placed mothers on pedestals, but held them responsible for producing children who would become capable adults. Although the motherhood myth implied that mothers' parenting skills were instinctual and mothers

The Rise of the Experts

were their children's best caregiver, some members of society believed that mothers were unqualified or at least unprepared for childrearing. The rise of the ideology of intensive mothering was accompanied by the elevation of childrearing experts—givers of grand, glorious, and often contradictory advice to mothers about raising children. Nearly all of these experts, many of whom gained fame and wealth advising mothers, were men (and some were not all that successful at raising their own children).

The child experts often replaced older female relatives, neighbors, and friends as the primary source of mothers' childrearing information, partially because the nation's families became more mobile, and kin increasingly lived too far away to be regularly consulted by new mothers. Into this gap came a variety of experts spreading the message that raising children was difficult and could only be achieved if mothers followed specific rules they identified. The experts implied that if mothers depended on instinct alone (and not experts' advice), their children could be at risk and the future of society in jeopardy.

Early in the century, Americans had a great trust that science could improve daily living. They looked to scientists to help resolve social problems, including childrearing. The world was changing rapidly, becoming more urban and industrialized, and no longer were traditional methods of doing things seen as relevant or functional. Progressive Era reformers wanted to use scientific principles to help mothers raise the next generation. Motherhood was too important to be left to amateurs.

In the 20th century, there were five major, highly publicized conferences that, "early on became a trademark of that 'new conception of the vocation of motherhood'" (Hulbert, 2003, p. 8). These conferences revealed "shifting social concerns and aspirations of science" and provided a platform for the childrearing sages of the time. The experts speaking at these conferences, if not already famous and influential, became major forces of their respective eras. They promoted their advice fervently because they believed they had scientific answers about how to successfully raise children. Mothers were sometimes confused, however, because these experts were notable for proposing conflicting advice. Only Benjamin Spock, during the middle of the century, reigned relatively unopposed in his time as the guru of childrearing advice.

Holt and Hall. The first national conference that influenced the nation's mothers took place in 1899. The National Congress of Mothers challenged women to prepare children physically for the new urban, industrialized world. The two leading experts presenting at the conference were L. Emmett Holt, one of the nation's first pediatricians, and G. Stanley Hall, the first psychology Ph.D. in America.

Holt studied the effects of nutrients on growth, especially in babies. His research on safer formulas for infant nutrition was credited with saving thousands of lives, and his 1894 book, *The Care and Feeding of Children,* went through 12 editions and 75 printings. Holt's book inspired a series of five free bulletins issued by the federal Children's Bureau between 1914 and 1921: *Prenatal Care, Infant Care, Your Child from One to Six, Your Child from Six to Twelve,* and *Guiding the Adolescent.* The Bureau estimated that the care of half of all babies born between 1915 and 1930 was influenced by advice in these pamphlets, regardless of their race, class, or geographic region (Rosenberg, 1992).

Dr. L. Emmett Holt, child development guru of the Progressive Era. (Courtesy of the Library of Congress.)

Holt advised mothers to follow scientific mothering practices rather than instinct; he admonished mothers who responded to babies' cries for being overly indulgent (he believed that crying was a necessary form of exercise for babies). Among his recommendations was that mothers restrain their children's arms to prevent them from sucking their thumbs, and he believed that infants should be toilet trained beginning at three months. He also recommended weighing babies before and after feedings to determine whether they had been adequately nourished. His book contained numerous charts and schedules for mothers to follow to keep infants and children well fed and safe from germs.

Hall, the other Progressive Era child expert, was concerned with puberty and adolescence. His 1904 book, *Adolescence*, was the first on the topic. Hall's views of childrearing were less rigid than Holt's, but, because both men welcomed attention to the scientific study of childhood, they endorsed each other's ideas. In the Progressive Era some mothers who previously had relied on their own sense of what was right, the guidance of their mothers, and religious dogma, now consulted empirical data from scientists to support their parenting decisions.

This scientific approach to motherhood served two purposes. It fit with the Progressive Era's emphasis on applying scientific principles to the home and family, and it was a method for dealing with the dilemma of what to do with increasing numbers of female college graduates. These women were prepared to do more than follow in the (usually) uneducated footsteps of their mothers, yet the thought of a middle-class mother working outside the home was unseemly. To solve the dilemma, intensive mothering using scientific principles became a substitute for a postgraduate degree. Just as kitchens were being designed to replicate sterile surgeries and scientific principles of chemistry were being applied to cooking, parenting became a science of sorts, complete with the guidance of textbooks written by experts. Mothering had truly arrived as a vocation. These early parenting experts basically ignored fathers. If motherhood was a vocation for women, fathers were breadwinners only and parenting bystanders.

This period of the 20th century was a transition for mothers, many of whom were torn between applying childrearing philosophies and methods of their childhood and the new scientific approaches touted in popular media and governmental bulletins. Fathers were gone most of the day, so childrearing increasingly was left to mothers. The advice they received was sometimes both contradictory and hard to follow. Societal messages were confusing, too—if motherhood was instinctual, then why did they need so much help?

Watson and Gesell. The second major conference that influenced motherhood was the 1925 Conference on Modern Parenthood sponsored by the Child Study Association of America (Hulbert, 2003). This conference celebrated a growth in the child study movement that had been headed by Hall and Holt. The new parenting gurus who presided at the 1925 conference were John B. Watson, a behaviorist, and Arnold Gesell of the Yale Psychological Clinic.

Watson, like Holt, was parent-centered and had established himself in the public eye with his book, *Behaviorism* (1925). In this book he claimed that he could take any randomly selected infant and make the child grow up to become any kind of person he wanted—doctor, lawyer, merchant, chief—by using rewards and punishments to shape behavior.

Gesell, child-centered like his predecessor Hall, also became well known as a result of a 1925 book, *The Mental Growth of the Pre-School Child*. Gesell's work, unlike Watson's, encouraged conformity by focusing on typical child development. He presented developmental guidelines, based on intensive observations of middle-class white children, denoting at what ages children should accomplish certain tasks. Mothers should have been assured that their children were thriving if they accomplished the tasks within the guidelines, but, instead, many mothers worried if their children were not accomplishing tasks *before* Gesell said they should. On the other hand, some mothers whose children accomplished tasks prior to the expected age bragged about their children and believed they had scientific evidence they were good mothers.

Gesell coined the terms *toddler* and *preschooler* during the 1920s, which led to the beginning of serious scientific scrutiny of young children. Prior to this time, most scientific observations had been limited to either babies or adolescents, the focus of Holt's and Hall's attention. Almost as soon as the label preschooler was coined, nursery schools were created, although fewer in number before World War II than nursery school proponents hoped. Children's enrichment in nursery school was important, according to child experts, because adequately caring for a preschooler required more knowledge of children's developmental needs than they believed most mothers possessed.

The 1920s, when Watson and Gesell were most well known, marked the height of restrictive, directive (but conflicting) advice to mothers. In addition to ensuring that their children stayed physically healthy, mothers were charged with looking after their children's mental and emotional health. They were urged to be vigilant, but at the same time to avoid "emotional bondage" of their children (making them too attached to their mothers) because it could cripple the children's psychological development (Hulbert, 2003, p. 114). According to Hulbert, "revising its earlier verdict that the literature of child psychology is so muddled and contains so much twaddle that the average American mother should be warned against it," (p. 99) the federal government supplied mothers with the latest psychological wisdom in *Child Management,* a widely distributed pamphlet. Child welfare reformers pressed for an expanded role of government in educating mothers, and local, county, and state departments of health, university extension services, and other services were made available to mothers. Parenting classes for mothers were offered in schools, women's clubs, and social agencies. Magazines and newspapers introduced advice columns and articles to help inform mothers about baby care. *Parents Magazine,* founded in 1926, was thriving to such an extent in the 1930s and 1940s that it was called the most successful educational magazine in the world (it was still published in 2000).

As the 1920s progressed, parenting advice was dominated by behaviorists such as Watson, who recommended strict scheduling in eating, sleeping, and toilet training, and he taught that holding, hugging, and kissing young children would spoil them. He advised mothers to never hug, kiss, or let children sit on their laps. He eventually relented to allow mothers to give children a kiss good night on the forehead and a handshake in the morning.

Scientific methods of childrearing placed an enormous psychological burden on mothers. Many of them believed that not following experts' advice would result in neglect, and if they implemented the advice incorrectly they would be liable for every shortcoming of their children's personality. Although many mothers tried to follow Watson's suggestions, others ignored them. For example, results from the Berkeley Growth Study, a longitudinal investigation of the development of "normal" children born in 1928 and 1929, indicated that mothers were not following the strict schedules that Watson and others recommended. The mothers in the Berkeley Study—mostly middle-class or upper-middle-class women—were more permissive and significantly warmer than behaviorists had advised, and there was little evidence that they followed Gesell's prescriptive advice about how to interact with children at specific ages, either. Watson and Gesell had claimed that their science held the secrets of prediction and control of children's behavior, if mothers would master it. Ironically, their advice generally had little effect on the mothers who were the most likely to read or hear their recommendations—the well-educated.

Early in the Depression, public concerns arose about experts' emphases on the negative features of families. During the 1930 White House Conference on Child Health and Protection, President Herbert Hoover encouraged childrearing professionals to more positively support mothers rather than cause panic among them. Rigid directives about childrearing were gradually replaced by advice about using more permissive, indulgent techniques. Watson's theories about strict toileting, sleeping, and feeding were still considered a good way to condition those behaviors, but other experts maintained that childrearing should result in secure, well-adjusted personalities, and Watson's behavioral conditioning was not always appropriate. Mothers were encouraged to reason with their children rather than be too authoritarian. Gesell, for example, advised mothers to observe their children's preferences to determine when they should eat or nap rather than following strict schedules. According to one estimate, by 1940, nearly two-thirds of childrearing advice articles recommended a more permissive style over rigid scheduling (Mechling, 1975).

Family life was hard in the 1930s. Fathers were either doing everything they could to keep their jobs or taking desperate measures to find work; mothers had to make sure that children's misbehaviors did not add to family stress. Childrearing experts may have shifted their advice toward more relaxed scheduling as a way to help reduce the daily tensions families faced during the Depression—if a mother was concerned about being able to feed her children, keeping them on a strict feeding schedule hardly made sense.

The 1940s brought still another shift in experts' recommendations for mothers. Childrearing professionals, who were growing increasingly concerned about children's emotional and psychological well-being, emphasized how childrearing shaped mental health. These experts were concerned that mothers were directing their hostilities and frustrations toward their children, negatively affecting children's well-being. To lessen these negative outcomes, experts encouraged parents to be warm and affectionate when interacting with their children.

Mothers in the 1940s often were heading their households while fathers served in the military or worked away from home in war-related industries. This meant that in addition to being told that their children's emotional well-being was at risk if they were not warm enough, mothers had extra household management duties. Some also had jobs for the first time since they married, so they were busy.

Following the war, medical advances in finding cures resulted in accidents replacing diseases as the leading causes of children's deaths. Mothers could relax about some health threats to their children, but they still had to be vigilant about cars, toys, playground equipment, and other sources of children's accidents.

Expert and public concern about emotional attachments between mothers and infants grew, based on the research of psychiatrist John Bowlby, who studied the behaviors of English children who had lost parents in World War II. By 1946, every American child had known only extremely stressful world conditions during their entire lives—the Depression, which started in 1929, and then a world war. Given this context, it is not surprising that the official topic of the 1950 Mid-Century White House Conference on Children and Youth was the healthy personality. Childrearing experts worried about children's psychological well-being and advised mothers to be equally concerned. This put a great deal of stress on mothers to do the right thing, but what was the right thing when it came to childrearing? Pediatrician Benjamin Spock provided the answers in a best-selling self-help book, *The Common Sense Book of Baby and Child Care,* first published in 1946 *Dr. Spock and commonsense parenting.* Spock's book quickly became one of the top-selling parenting books of all time. Published in paperback for 25 cents, it was affordable to nearly all parents. Spock took Freudian psychoanalytic ideas and communicated them in a clear and down-to-earth way to nervous first-time parents. He encouraged mothers to trust their own instincts, to shower their children with love and affection, and not to be too worried about adhering to rigid schedules for feeding and toilet training. Spock advised parents to watch for signs of toilet training readiness; most clinicians of this period generally agreed that children were ready to begin toilet training around 18 months, to complete the process by two or three years, and by age four, most children were expected to close the bathroom door, flush, and wash their hands. Spock and other parenting experts encouraged the goal of raising cooperative, mentally healthy children that were sociable and could get along with others.

Many mothers embraced Spock's advice. His child-centered approach differed greatly from the behaviorists' ideas earlier in the century. Unlike his more demanding and dogmatic predecessors, Spock reassured parents that they could handle children's problems and knew more about raising children than they thought they did. His advice, however, proved problematic for some. Behaviorists' recommendations tended to be applicable to all parents, but Spock's advice had a middle-class bias. He assumed that women would have unlimited time to watch their children, which made some working mothers feel guilty and anxious.

In the late 1960s, Spock's childrearing methods were heavily criticized for encouraging parents to be too permissive. Critics blamed him for the growing number of young adults who wore their hair long, dressed in ragged jeans, experimented with drugs, dropped out of school, and lived in communes—in short, some people accused Spock of creating the hippie movement. Another 1960s criticism of Spock's work was his sexism. Not until the 1976 revision of his book did he refer to children as "they" instead of "he" and to "parents" instead of "mothers" (Hulbert, 2003, p. 272). In that edition, Spock began to assign fathers some responsibility for looking after their children. His final edition (Spock & Rothenberg, 1992) contained additional information for fathers and new or expanded information on timely issues such as divorce, stepfamilies, open adoptions, and AIDS.

By the 1960s, there was pressure on experts to revise their views of mothering. Some medical experts and child professionals came to see mothers as knowledgeable participants in their children's welfare rather than passive recipients of experts' wisdom. However, old notions sometimes prevailed. In 1965, the Parents' Institute published the *Mother's Encyclopedia: Expert Advice on Child Care and Family Living*, in which the authors again told mothers they were mostly responsible for children's upbringing and that they could not keep up with late-breaking ideas without relying on the advice of experts. This widely available book thus perpetuated the turn-of-the-century view that mothers could not raise their children without expert help.

Mothers continued to shoulder a great deal of blame for children's problems. In clinical psychology journals in the 1970s and early 1980s, mothers were identified as either directly or indirectly responsible for causing 72 different children's problems, including schizophrenia, bedwetting, poor coping with color blindness, and aggressive behaviors (Garey & Arendell, 2001). Some children's problems were linked to mothers' social situations (i.e., being poor, unmarried, divorced, and employed).

The White House Conference on Families convened by President Jimmy Carter in 1980 was partly in response to the Carnegie Corporation's Council on Children's highly publicized 1977 report, *All Our Children*. The report raised concerns that parents had no guidelines or supports for raising children and were not feeling in control. The report argued that parents felt embattled. In response, conference planners invited parents to articulate their needs. Previous conferences had featured experts chastising parents to follow their rules—the 1980 conference provided parents a chance to chastise the experts. Partly as a result, a kinder, gentler expert became popular.

Brazelton and Dobson. One of the most prominent child development experts beginning in the late 1960s was T. Berry Brazelton. His 1969 book, *Infants and Mothers,* launched him as a neo-Spock parenting expert. He emphasized that parents who knew how to read their babies' cues would be better equipped to raise children without guilt. He advised mothers that infants could withstand their parenting mistakes and would even let mothers know when they were on the wrong track. Brazelton tried to alleviate parents' feelings of childrearing incompetence and he frequently appeared on national television, encouraging parents to be observant but relaxed.

Brazelton's inclusion of fathers reflected changes in societal attitudes about the roles of mothers and fathers. Starting in the 1960s, more mothers were employed, and a few couples were trying to equally share daily caregiving of children. Mothers in most families still were responsible for managing households and overseeing children's development, but there were more expectations for fathers' involvement. At the same time, divorce and unmarried motherhood meant that more mothers were solely responsible for their children.

During the 1980s and 1990s, child development research went in new directions once again. In the 1980s, questions were raised about how much influence on children parents really had, including a nature-versus-nurture debate about the varying influences of heredity and one's environment. In the 1990s, questions were raised about brain research and the importance of children's first three years of life on brain development. In the 1990s, parenting advice was increasingly splintered between parent-centered traditionalists who followed religious teachings on the one hand and child-centered experts (including Brazelton) who relied on research findings. Among the traditionalist group was James Dobson—a psychologist, evangelical Christian, and founder of Focus on the Family—who promoted conservative family values. Dobson widely influenced conservative religious parents via his radio programs and many books. Child psychologists and child development experts objected to Dobson's use of spanking and harsh discipline and his exhorting of parents to use what these experts believed were unproven religious principles to guide their children's development. These criticisms echoed those earlier in the century when scientific experts challenged ministers as the providers of parenting information—the century closed in much the same way. Although they disagreed with each other, both the scientific parent mentors and the religiously oriented childrearing experts conceptualized mothers as needing guidance and being unable to do an adequate job on their own.

Thus, the two opposing positions of experts that had faced mothers at the beginning of the century also were still present at the end. Hulbert (2003) identified the issues as, "How much power and control do, and should, parents wield over a child's journey from dependence to independence? How much freedom and intimacy do children need, or want, along the way? What do the answers imply about mothers' rights and responsibilities?" (p. 365). Despite the conflicting advice given to mothers, what the experts continued to agree upon was that women should engage in the pursuit of the intensive mothering ideal.

Throughout the century, experts focused their attentions mostly on white middle- and upper-class mothers. Although racial and ethnic minority mothers and low-income white mothers were aware of the intensive mothering ideology and the guidelines put forth by childrearing gurus, their marginalized status in society meant they got attention mostly when they were defined as contributing to social problems.

MOTHERS AND LABOR FORCE PARTICIPATION

In a 1905 speech to the National Congress of Mothers, President Theodore Roosevelt said,

[T]he primary duty of the woman is to be the helpmate, the housewife, and mother. The woman should have ample educational advantages; but save in exceptional cases the man must be, and she need not be, and generally ought not to be, trained for a lifelong career as the family breadwinner; and, therefore, after a certain point, the training of the two must normally be different because the duties of the two are normally different. (Roosevelt 1905, par. 4)

Roosevelt's emphasis on motherhood and housework over labor force participation reflected popular opinions throughout most of the 20th century. Although most white, middle-class mothers stayed at home early in the era, this was not realistic for many immigrant and working-class families. Men in these families rarely earned enough to support their families, so wives and children supplemented the family income. During the final four decades of the century, middle-class families also found it increasingly difficult to get by on one income.

During World War II, as growing numbers of men and women left the civilian labor force to enter the armed forces, the federal government campaigned to convince women—including mothers of young children—that it was patriotic to work outside the home. Most mothers ignored the barrage of information encouraging them to enter the labor force. Minimal child care was available, so some working mothers resorted to leaving their children home alone or locking them in their cars while they worked during the day. The government also sent contradictory messages—telling women they needed to work to help support the war effort, while also telling them a mother's primary duty was to stay home and care for her children. Women may have decided that being considered unpatriotic trumped being viewed as unfit mothers, although many mothers did enter the labor force.

In fact, between 1940 and 1944, mothers of young children in the labor force increased by 76 percent. The federal government opened over 3,000 day care centers between 1942 and 1946, which helped but was far fewer than needed (Mintz & Kellogg, 1988). Following the war, many of these centers closed, partially because of a change in the public's view of working women. Postwar propaganda primarily targeted at the white middle class, urged women not to work. Poor women, however, especially those of color, were expected to be employed.

During the 1950s, most black women continued to engage in paid work just as had their mothers and grandmothers, and the black press generally portrayed them in a positive light, praising their efforts to help support their families. Mainstream media, on the other hand, tended to exhort white women to stay home and helped reinforce an emphasis on family life by picturing career women as neurotic, unhappy, and dissatisfied. Women's magazines also described how children were negatively affected by their mothers' employment.

By 1960, however, studies began to suggest that maternal employment was not to blame for children's problems. Instead, a combination of factors—including mothers' satisfaction with work, fathers' work habits, family size, and family income—affected children's reactions to mothers working. Media messages began depicting housewives as bored and discontent. As women came to see the benefits of paid labor, a growing number of white, middle-class mothers sought employment; a much larger proportions of low-income and racial and ethnic minority mothers were employed, as had been true in previous decades. In 1960, for example, 31 percent of married black mothers of preschool-aged children were in the labor force compared to 18 percent of married white mothers.

A combination of inflationary costs of goods and low rising wages (termed *stagflation*) in the 1970s resulted in another labor force influx in working mothers. By 1975, more than 36 percent of married U.S. women with children younger than six were employed compared to 10 percent in 1940. By the end of the 1980s, just over half of mothers of children under age six were in the labor force (Collins, 2003). It had also become less common for mothers to drop out of the work force after the birth of a child, and many returned to work within a few weeks of childbirth.

Maternal employment was more socially acceptable at the end of the century than it was at the beginning, although conservative social critics continued to condemn working mothers because they believed that maternal employment weakened mother-child bonds, ultimately resulting in societal problems. Others worried that working mothers neglected their children by spending less time caring for them; however, researchers determined that the hours white married mothers spent doing primary care tasks (e.g., feeding, bathing) for individual children *nearly doubled* between the 1920s and 1980s. When families were larger earlier in the century, mothers had less time to interact with children individually than did mothers later on who were in the paid labor force but had fewer children.

Near the end of the century, women who wanted to work and also be wives and mothers found it challenging to balance the roles, often more challenging than they anticipated. They were still expected to engage in intensive mothering, but some were in work environments that required at least 40 hours of paid labor per week, and those in competitive fields worked even more hours. By some estimates, working mothers at the end of the century spent an average of 80 hours a week engaged in parenting and paid employment (Crittenden, 2001). To allow time for their children, working mothers often cut back on housework and leisure pursuits, despite cultural messages that, in addition to being the perfect worker and ideal parent, mothers should also pursue self-improvement (e.g., join book clubs, engage in important volunteer work), keep a nice home, and maintain their looks and sex appeal. Despite the challenges, some studies suggested that having multiple roles was beneficial. For some women, multiple roles gave them a greater sense of purpose and meaning in life and enhanced their psychological functioning.

As societal acceptance of working mothers increased, stay-at-home mothers began to feel a need to justify not being in the paid labor force. They felt their contributions at home were devalued, and, as a result, many stay-at-home moms resented working mothers for what they perceived to be an abandonment of their roles as housewives and mothers. In fact, mothers who preferred one role over the other were often pitted against each other through what the media called the Mommy Wars. For example, television talk show hosts would engage working mothers and stay-at-home mothers in bitter verbal battles over the proper way to be a modern mother, much to the delight of studio audiences.

Despite greater acceptance of women working outside the home, women continued to be challenged with the demands of work and family and were harshly judged by conservative critics for not meeting the expectations of intensive mothering. Whereas men throughout the century experienced home as a refuge from work, demands placed on working mothers prohibited similar feelings. These societal arguments about whether mothers should work continued to apply only to middle-class mothers—the conservative critics who castigated middle-class mothers for joining the paid labor force castigated poor mothers on welfare for not working outside the home and for their dependence on government subsidies.

SINGLE MOTHERS

Single motherhood was defined as a social problem throughout the century. In the early decades, single mothers were usually either widowed or abandoned by their husbands. Later, as the divorce rate grew and more women chose to have children without being married, the proportion of families headed by single mothers increased considerably, peaking in 1996 at nearly 27 percent of all families with children (Huang & Pouncy, 2005). Single mothers throughout the century often found themselves raising children alone, without much outside help.

During the Progressive Era, social reformers identified single mothers as victims of the harsh realities of the world, and attempts to help them were aimed at protecting them and keeping their virtue intact. They were provided a pension of sorts, which social workers referred to as "wages" for taking care of their children. These so-called wages were meant to keep mothers from becoming involved with another man, which might lead to immoral behavior, and to allow them to remain home caring for their children. Prior to the establishment of this pension, which later became Aid to Dependent Children (ADC), single mothers often had to place their children in day care or orphanages so they could work to support themselves. Mothers who sought day care for their children so they could work were more stigmatized than mothers who lived on ADC.

During the Depression, welfare and social security helped poor single mothers, many of whom were unable to find work, even if they wanted it. World War II and its aftermath offered more employment opportunities for single mothers, but the lack of suitable day care restricted their work options. Working single mothers struggled with work and childrearing demands, and single mothers on welfare, while not juggling competing demands, generally lived in poverty.

Adolescent Mothers

Throughout the century, adolescent childbearing was not unusual, but most teen mothers married before the baby was born, so it was not seen as a social problem, as was the case later. In fact, there were nearly twice as many births to teenagers in 1957 as there were in the 1990s, but about 85 percent of those teen mothers were married.

In the Progressive Era, reformers saw unmarried adolescent pregnancy as a moral—rather than a health—issue, and they established group homes for unmarried pregnant girls with the expectation that they would put their children up for adoption after birth. For decades, this was the solution—pregnant unmarried teenagers left home, gave birth, and gave children up for adoption. This typically was a cause for personal shame but not societal concern.

Beginning in the early 1960s, the country witnessed what was considered by many to be an alarming rise in the number of pregnancies and births among unmarried teenagers. The average age of adolescent mothers was getting younger, and adolescents were no longer considered mature enough to assume the responsibilities of motherhood. Additionally, by the last decades of the century, among middle class and upwardly mobile working-class families, higher education was considered critical to future career prospects, and childbirth was an obstacle to receiving an education and achieving those prospects. Few adolescent parents attended college, and more than 25 percent of white, half of Latina, and more than 60 percent of African American teen mothers were still living in poverty by their late 20s.

It was not until the late 1970s, however, that adolescent pregnancy was identified as a public health concern and a social problem requiring immediate attention. The Alan Guttmacher Institute's 1976 report, *11 Million Teenagers: What Can Be Done About the Epidemic of Adolescent Pregnancies in the United States*, emphasized that adolescent childbearing was harmful regardless of whether it occurred within the confines of marriage. For example, adolescent mothers had higher mortality rates, and their children were more likely to be born prematurely and be underweight at birth—two conditions that often led to later health and development problems. Children born to teen mothers also were more likely than children of older mothers to be abused and neglected, and their chances of surviving their first year of life were lower. Young age, lack of prenatal care, and cigarette and alcohol use contributed to pregnancy complications for adolescents and their babies.

Despite such concerns, teen pregnancy rates rose through the 1980s and early 1990s before hitting a plateau and then dropping through the end of the century. During the late 1980s and early 1990s, over one million adolescents became pregnant every year; 50 percent gave birth and kept their babies, 40 percent had abortions, and 10 percent either had miscarriages or gave their babies up for adoption. Nearly 80 percent of these pregnancies were unintended (Coley & Chase-Lansdale, 1998). The lower adolescent pregnancy rate in the last decade of the century likely reflected an increase in contraceptive use rather than a reduction in teen sexual activity, although the application of birth control methods was often sporadic and ineffective. Many adolescents remained uninformed about reproduction and contraception, lacked access to family planning services or contraceptives, or considered themselves immune to pregnancy.

During the 1990s, researchers identified several risk factors related to adolescent pregnancy. Teenage girls who became mothers were more likely than their peers to have been raised in single-parent families living in poverty, to have had parents who had not finished high school, and to have had low educational goals for themselves. In fact, in the mid-1990s, one-third of adolescent mothers had dropped out of school *before* they became pregnant.

Racial and ethnic differences. Black adolescents have historically had higher pregnancy and childbearing rates than whites and Latinas, and, by 1977, the rate was six times that for whites. During the early 1990s, about 19 percent of all black teenage girls 15 and older became pregnant every year compared to 13 percent of Latinas and 8 percent of whites (East & Felice, 1996). Black teenagers were more sexually active than whites and did not use contraceptives as consistently, but other pervasive sociocultural factors contributed to pregnancy among unmarried black adolescents, including poverty, social isolation, cultural attitudes toward sexuality and childbearing, and peer influences.

Similar to whites, childbearing rates among black adolescents declined substantially through the 1990s, but birth rates among Latin American teens rose steadily. Latina adolescents were not more likely to have early sexual experiences, but they were less likely to use contraception and were less likely to have abortions if they became pregnant. At the end of the century, black teenagers were considerably less likely than their white and Latina counterparts to be married when they gave birth; whites and Latinas had comparable likelihoods of being married.

The number of births to unmarried women increased significantly during the 20th century, and by 2000 accounted for 31 percent of all births (U.S. Census Bureau, 2000). Although far more white women had children **Never-Married Mothers** outside of marriage, most Americans thought that unwed mothers were more likely to be black women, perhaps because the proportion of black women having nonmarital births was higher.

Early in the century, single motherhood presented great difficulties for unmarried women who could not or chose not to have an abortion. Most young couples opted to marry rather than face the stigma surrounding unwed pregnancy, but this became less likely over time. In the 1930s, 15 percent of white women 15 to 29 years old conceived or had a child prior to marriage. In the early 1990s, the percentage had increased to 45 percent. Among black women, the percentage of first births conceived or born before marriage doubled from 43 percent in the early 1930s to 86 percent in the early 1990s (Bachu, 1999). Late in the century, some births were to unmarried women who were cohabiting, but most were not.

Until the 1940s, single motherhood was identified as a problem exclusively among lower-class women, immigrants, and those with little education; however, social workers and others began reevaluating their views, in part because growing numbers of single white middle-class women sought aid from social agencies that served single mothers. Racial stereotypes remained, however. Out-of-wedlock pregnancies among white women were attributed to individual psychiatric problems; out-of-wedlock births among black women were seen as a major societal problem. Some suggested that the matriarchal structure of black families was to blame for out-of-wedlock pregnancy among black women, and the "welfare queen" label was widely attached to unmarried black mothers.

One of the first references to increased birth rates among black unmarried mothers was in Swedish economist Gunnar Myrdal's 1944 classic, *An American Dilemma.* He noted that, in 1936, the rate of unmarried childbearing among whites was 2 percent compared to about 16 percent among African Americans, a difference that continued through the 1950s.

Between 1960 and 1984, the number of black families headed by women nearly doubled, and social policymakers pointed to black males' higher mortality rate, incarceration, and homelessness as reasons. In a controversial 1965 report to President Lyndon Johnson, sociologist Daniel Moynihan wrote that welfare dependency, illegitimacy, delinquency, unemployment, and educational problems among blacks were due to the breakdown of black families. The absence of two-parent households were among the indicators of "the tangle of pathology" (Moynihan, 1965, p. 30) of black families he mentioned, and he identified unwed childbearing as one of the primary reasons for economic differences between whites and blacks. Moynihan called for the federal government to use its resources to change the situation. Although he was attacked by black civil rights leaders and feminists, his themes were echoed by other social critics and sociologists during this period.

The feminization of poverty near the end of the century was one outcome of the growing number of female-headed households. Never-married mothers often faced great difficulty supporting their families. In 1999, over 36 percent of households headed by single women lived below the poverty level compared with 6 percent of married couples with dependent children. Although unmarried mothers of all races and eth-nicities experienced hardships, Latinas and black women tended to have higher poverty rates than their white counterparts. Nearly half of black and Latina households headed by single women were below the poverty level (46 percent and 47 percent, respectively), compared to 25 percent of white female-headed households (Fields & Casper, 2001).

Older Unmarried Mothers

Although out-of-wedlock childbearing was always more prevalent among the less educated and the poor, late in the century it became less unusual for middle-class single adult women to bear children. This trend, although never large, was seen by social conservatives as a threat to the institution of marriage and a problem for the well-being of children raised without a father. In 1992, Vice President Dan Quayle took issue with the single parenthood of a television sitcom character, Murphy Brown, played by Candace Bergen. Although he appeared to be confusing real life with the actions of a fictional character (for which he was ridiculed), Quayle's comments were taken seriously by many who decried what they saw as single women purposefully depriving their children of fathers.

Quayle's comments and the debate that followed illustrated what became known as the "culture wars," disagreements between social conservatives and progressives who predicted different outcomes for a variety of family trends. In this case, progressives countered that most dire effects on children were due to living in poverty rather than living with a single mother, and that most children of single mothers had many male role models in their lives—such as grandfathers, uncles, youth leaders, and even their fathers—who more often than in the past were involved in some ways with their children. Critics of single motherhood by choice countered that researchers generally found that, compared to children who grew up in two-parent, first marriage families, children who lived with mothers who had never married tended to complete fewer years of education, earn less as adult workers, have lower occupational status, engage in delinquent activities more often, and have more troubled marriages. Researchers did not always attribute such outcomes to the children's family structure, however, instead pointing to the effects of growing up in poverty, experiencing higher levels of stress, the relative lack of parental supervision and control, and the peer-like nature of parent-child relationships that were common in many single-parent families.

Annual divorce rates for women at the beginning of the century were 4 out of 1,000, double the rate of 1865, but still miniscule by modern standards. Divorce was not a viable possibility for most mothers until mid-century. Mothers seldom worked outside the home and, if they **Single Mothers following Divorce** did, generally made extremely low wages, which made them dependent on their husbands for financial support. Although legally possible in the 19th century, divorce was rare, and laws relating to it maintained a strong double standard in favor of men. Granting mothers custody after divorce had become more common at the turn of the century, but maternal custody could be revoked at any time if a judge determined the mother was not meeting his (all judges at the time were men) standards for maternal behavior. Fear of losing custody of their children kept many mothers in unhappy marriages.

Reasons for divorcing were originally limited primarily to desertion and adultery. Two-thirds of divorces granted to women early in the century were because they had been abandoned. Even in cases of abandonment, there tended to be considerable shame and stigma associated with divorce, but at least a legal divorce provided a woman with a chance to remarry. Most divorces granted to men early in the century were attributed to the wife's adultery, and women accused of adultery often lost custody of their children. It was not that women were more likely than were men to engage in adultery, but it was viewed as more forgivable in men.

Beginning in the 1980s and continuing through the end of the century, about 50 percent of first marriages were expected to end in divorce. Despite the relatively high incidence and increased acceptance of divorce, individuals who experienced it had higher rates of emotional and physical health problems than did their continuously married counterparts. Single divorced mothers faced many challenges as they raised their children, chief among them were economic problems. The financial status of women and children worsened considerably following divorce, unlike that of men, whose economic status was more likely to slightly improve.

Considering that most early divorces were granted to women on the basis of desertion, they were left to financially fend for themselves and their children with no help from the children's father. Although that later

Single mother and her son in the late 1970s. (Courtesy of the authors.)

changed, the U.S. Census Bureau did not begin collecting data on child support and alimony until 1980, so little was known about how much divorced women and their children previously received in the way of support. Once data were kept and stricter laws forced parents to be financially responsible for their children, compliance with court-ordered child support increased, but still barely over 50 percent of women who were supposed to receive child support received all of the amount the courts had awarded.

There was no question that mothers had fewer financial resources after divorce, but, as the century ended, there was considerable debate about which group—mothers or fathers—was more financially strained after divorce. The lack of financial stability probably led some mothers to rapidly remarry in order to adequately support their children. Some women expressed relief that, although there was less household income than when they were married, they were now in charge of the income—the increase in financial control offset the decrease in total finances for these mothers.

Welfare Dependency and Single Mothers

Welfare programs originally emerged out of the long-held belief that children fared best in their mothers' care, and aid was designed to help poor widows and mothers whose husbands abandoned them stay home with their children. Although most states passed legislation between 1911 and 1920 to institute mothers' pensions, due to a lack of funds, these pensions were distributed first to widows of English descent and last to unmarried African American and immigrant mothers. Against reformers' wishes, administrators believed that women who were able to earn money should find employment, and even women who received pensions often had to work to supplement the meager funds the government provided. Some argued that the primary result of the pensions was a welfare system that heightened class differences, and, by the 1920s, support for mothers' pensions had diminished.

Among President Franklin Roosevelt's New Deal initiatives designed to move the country out of the Great Depression was Aid to Dependent Children for needy children. States were given discretion to distribute funds as they saw fit, which meant that they could (and sometimes did) limit or deny programs for poor black children. Similar to mothers' pensions, ADC originally primarily served white widows who were in need through no fault of their own, so few people complained about the practices.

After World War II, wartime employment declined, and the number of people needing welfare increased, although the percentage who were widows diminished from 43 percent in 1937 to less than 8 percent in 1961 (Reese, 2005). This increased need for welfare was due partly to increased childbearing among unmarried women and partly to decreases in workplace accidents causing male disability or death. When ADC expanded to provide aid to single mothers who were not widows and to racial minorities, opposition to welfare programs began to grow.

During the 1950s, states adopted various rules to limit welfare eligibility. Some adopted rules requiring employable mothers to work if suitable child care was available; others denied aid to unwed mothers because their homes were considered unsuitable for children; and still others denied mothers welfare if they lived with a man who could serve as the family breadwinner. Because unmarried childbearing and its related poverty was thought to occur more among black than white women, there were efforts to limit women's access to welfare. "Suitable home" policies were direct attacks against black women on welfare (Reese, 2005).

Prior to the 1960s, much of the backlash against welfare was limited to state-level concerns, but the number of families receiving welfare had tripled from 787,000 to over 2.2 million by the 1960s, and concerns spread to the national level. An even greater backlash against the welfare system occurred in the 1980s and 1990s, particularly among conservatives. Policymakers decried the cycle of poverty in which most unmarried parents and their children found themselves. Children of unwed mothers often became unwed parents themselves. Many single mothers were on welfare, leading to public discontent with the welfare system. Critics complained that the only mothers who could afford to stay at home raising their children were the wealthy and mothers on welfare—everyone in between had to work outside the home.

Some critics believed that welfare encouraged unwed motherhood and should be abolished for moral reasons. Many conservatives blamed welfare dependency on low-income families' lack of a strong work ethic and avoidance of traditional family values. Politicians and others also urged implementation of strict work requirements, reflecting widespread beliefs that many welfare recipients were lazy rather than the product of structural obstacles of unemployment and poverty. The concept *culture of poverty* was coined, which suggested that the combination of early parenthood, non-marital unions, and welfare dependency was a self-perpetuating fact of life. Between 1988 and 1994, welfare caseloads increased from 10.9 million to more than 14 million, and, in 1995, 57 percent of cases were unmarried mothers and another 25 percent were divorced or separated mothers. As a result, the long-held view that mothers should not work was replaced by the view that it was better for mothers to work than to be on welfare.

In 1996, Congress passed the Personal Responsibility and Work Opportunity Reconciliation Act (PRWORA), which significantly limited poor families' access to income and social services. As part of the act, Aid to Families with Dependent Children was replaced with Temporary Aid to Needy Families. A central goal of the new law was to end welfare dependency and help promote the self-sufficiency of low-income mothers by increasing employment. Work requirements were problematic for many; minimal training, inflexible scheduling, low wages, and problems with child care were among women's top complaints. Many mothers and their children continued to live in poverty. At the end of the century, some critics recommended new solutions, including renewed support for public orphanages—the same system used to take care of poor children in 1900.

Despite the PRWORA's attempts to reduce welfare dependence by creating incentives for poor single mothers to work, in 1997, female-headed households with dependent children had a poverty rate of 32 percent, compared to 5 percent among married couple families. There were significant racial and ethnic group differences in these rates. White female-headed households had a poverty rate of 28 percent, compared to 40 percent among blacks and 48 percent among Latinas (Arendell, 2000). Despite long-held stereotypes that the vast majority of welfare recipients were inner-city black mothers, in 2000, 31 percent were white, 25 percent were Latin American, and 39 percent were black.

Mothers who lived in poverty, especially those who were single, experienced multiple stressors and obstacles to childrearing, including the underpayment of child support by children's fathers, a low minimum wage that was inadequate to live on, and limitations of the availability of welfare. By the end of the century, the fastest growing group among the homeless was families with children, especially families with very young children headed by women.

NONCUSTODIAL (NONRESIDENTIAL) MOTHERS

Noncustodial or nonresidential mothers are those who live apart from their children most of the time. The Census Bureau and other national surveys have not gathered data on the number of noncustodial mothers, and, because it was relatively rare, few studies of nonresidential mothers had been conducted by the end of the century. Mothers became noncustodial for a wide variety of reasons; some willingly sought this status, others had it imposed. Among those who voluntarily gave up custody, financial problems were one of the most common reasons. Other reasons included mothers' desire to have time to pursue their own interests, which often meant time to engage in higher education so they could eventually adequately support themselves; mothers' emotional inability to care for their children; career demands; the threat of a costly legal battle with their former husbands over physical custody; mothers' drug or alcohol abuse; children's desire to live with their father; and paternal abduction.

Before the 20th century, mothers rarely were given custody of their children following divorce, but divorce was so uncommon that the number of noncustodial mothers was quite small. However, by the turn of the century, children were no longer considered their fathers' property, mothers' influence on child development was considered paramount, and it was extremely rare for fathers to gain custody. This pattern remained until the 1970s, when mothers' position as primary caregiver began to be questioned. The higher divorce rate, women's improved economic standing, some fathers' growing interest in parenting, and changes in the legal system reduced the traditional bias toward awarding custody to mothers, but they nearly always were granted it. Near the century's end, the courts had moved toward awarding joint legal and sometimes shared physical custody to both parents. This still often meant that children spent most of their time living with their mothers.

Noncustodial mothers often experienced a variety of negative feelings, including guilt, depression, loneliness, shame, anxiety, life dissatisfaction, and lowered self-esteem. Some noncustodial mothers were in split custody arrangements, meaning at least one child lived with them. These women generally had more positive feelings than those with no children in their homes. The role of noncustodial mothers is highly stigmatized, and many people treated them with disdain, which likely influenced how they felt about themselves.

STEPMOTHERS

Stepmothers and stepfamilies were common early in the century when the mortality rate associated with childbirth was high. Nearly all American families probably have a stepmother somewhere on their family tree. Although stepmothers have been important family figures raising children of mothers who passed away, they have been maligned throughout history. Stories of wicked stepmothers go back hundreds of years, and the stigma remained prevalent throughout the 20th century. Although fairy tales did not depict real behaviors of stepmothers, the portrayed images of wicked stepmothers may have helped shape children's views of stepmothers and stepfamilies in general. For example, stepchildren who expected their stepmother to be wicked and mean to them may have regarded any discipline as an illustration of her inherent wickedness.

In the early 1900s, most stepmothers replaced deceased mothers, who often had died in childbirth. Fathers were not equipped to take on heavy childrearing responsibilities while also making a living, so, unless there was a daughter old enough to shoulder the child care duties, the fathers tended to quickly remarry. These stepmother-family households typically were invisible to the public as such because women usually took their husbands' last names. In rural areas, people were aware of deaths and remarriages of neighbors, but cities were generally more impersonal. If the family next door all shared the same last name, it was probably assumed that the family was a conventional first marriage union.

Little is known about the early stepmother families other than what has been shared through diaries, novels, and short stories. These offerings present a mixed picture, with some stepmothers fitting the cruel image of stepmotherhood (e.g., *The Robber Bridegroom* by Eudora Welty, 1946) and others being depicted as warm and loving substitutes for their stepchildren's mother (e.g., *Sarah Plain and Tall,* a novel by Patricia MacLachlan [1985] set in the 19th century).

Perhaps because remarriage was considered almost a necessity after a mother died, social scientists paid little attention to stepmothers. It was not until the late 1970s and early 1980s when divorce began to be considered a major social problem that stepfamilies (and stepmothers) received attention. By then, mothers typically received physical custody of children following divorce, so most stepfamily households contained a stepfather rather than a stepmother. In the mid-1990s, just over one million children lived with their father and stepmother; nearly 4 million lived with their mother and stepfather. Thus, during the final decades of the century, most stepmothers were nonresidential; that is, they had married men who had children who lived most of the time with their mothers. Although some nonresidential stepchildren spent no time with their fathers, others lived half of their time with their fathers and stepmother, a situation that created stress for some stepmothers. Because of the ideology of *intensive mothering,* some stepmothers had difficulty overcoming their socialization to want to intensely "mother" their stepchildren, yet not usurp the biological mother. Stepmothers also were fully aware of the stereotypes of the mean, wicked stepmother, having grown up hearing the same fairy tales as their stepchildren. Most wished to avoid the stereotype, yet they did not want their stepchildren to be in charge of the household. Some stepmothers resented that family income, including their own earnings in some cases, went to support their husbands' nonresidential children. And because stepchildren were not always appreciative of their stepmothers' efforts or financial support, there was tension in many nonresidential stepmother-stepchild relationships.

Fairy tales for children were not the only places portraying stepmothers. Modern media also played a part in how stepmothers were perceived. In a review of movies produced during the 1990s, it was noted that, of the few films depicting stepfamilies, none portrayed only positive aspects of stepfamilies. Stepmothers tended to be shown as mean, money-grubbing, and unwanted intruders (Leon & Angst, 2005). Stepfamilies in television shows were generally shown in a more positive light; however, only a limited number of shows included them. Early stepfamily shows, such as the popular sitcom *The Brady Bunch* (1969–1979), were unrealistic in their lack of complexity (both spouses of the parents in the Brady household had evidently died and were rarely mentioned), and the family dynamics reflected few real-life stepfamily challenges identified by social scientists. In 1999, the more realistic stepfamily television drama, *Once and Again*, debuted to critical acclaim, perhaps signaling that stepfamilies and stepmothers in particular were finally being viewed more complexly and more realistically.

SUMMARY

Motherhood changed vastly in importance over the 20th century. Beginning as a risky proposition due to high mortality rates during childbirth brought about by infections and unsanitary conditions, the safety of childbearing was greatly improved by the discovery of antibiotics, greater knowledge of sanitation, and greater skill on the part of doctors. As women had fewer children and more time to spend with each one, the ideology of intensive mothering evolved. Being a mother was seen as an innate drive, and the societal view was that motherhood would "complete" a woman—it was her ultimate destiny. As women moved into the work force in large numbers, intensive mothering became more difficult and many women felt guilty because their work schedules would not allow them the time to mother intensely. The century ended with ever-increasing numbers of mothers entering the work force, including those with newborn infants. Chief social worries were the lack of adequate day care for these children and the fact that 17 percent of children in America, regardless of whether their mothers worked, remained in poverty.

Many mothers at the end of the century who attempted to engage in intensive mothering, felt intense guilt when they left their children in the care of others, and their sense of pride and accomplishment in other spheres of their lives (such as the workplace) was often undermined by ambivalence about their choices and the adequacy of their mothering. Feminist philosopher Sara Ruddick (1980) advanced a theory of maternal thinking near the end of the century and argued that specific activities associated with the work of mothering can—and should—be shared by men. Her position was that mothers, fathers, and children would benefit if society would demystify the mothering ideology in a way that would include fathers as caregivers and nurturers.

6

Men in Families

FATHERHOOD AND FATHERS

As historian John Demos (1986) noted, "Fatherhood has a very long history, but virtually no historians" (p. 42). Despite being important to the functioning and well-being of families, fathers had been relatively ignored by historians—at least until toward the end of the 20th century. Historians, social scientists, and policymakers began to acknowledge and examine the role of fathers as the century came to a close, but, nonetheless, considerably more is known about mothers and children as family members than about fathers.

In addition to the lack of written history about fathers and fatherhood, most historical accounts focused primarily on white middle-class fathers. Although knowing the history of white middle-class fathers is important, their experiences were different from those of immigrant fathers, poor fathers, and fathers from ethnic minority groups.

The historical study of fathers consisted of two related but distinct elements: the *culture of fatherhood* (e.g., cultural norms, beliefs, values about what fathers *should* do) and the *conduct of fathers* (i.e., what they actually did). That is, some history has been about what fathers were expected to do at various points in time (i.e., cultural ideals) rather than what they actually did. These expectations were found in popular periodicals, self-help books, and other mass media reports that reflected the culturally shared scripts about what fathers were supposed to be doing. The other strand of historical work revealed what fathers actually did—information that came from men's diaries, letters, memoirs, interviews and other sources of self-reports, including surveys, and observations of fathers with their children.

What fathers were expected to do at different time periods was some-times quite different than what they did, and, of course, at least part of what fathers did in families was affected by the cultural images to which they aspired; thus, these two aspects of fathering—the cultural ideal and the real—did not always differ. However, it would be a mistake to assume that cultural beliefs and values about fatherhood always were translated into daily practices of fathers.

American Fathers in the 1700s and 1800s
In sharp contrast to modern fathers, fathers in Colonial America were the primary parents in families. Men were seen as morally superior to women, which made fathers more suitable to the demands of guiding children. Fathers' primary responsibility was to assure that children developed strong moral character. In addition to teaching children a set of ethical and religious values, fathers were expected to set examples for principled and honorable behavior, especially for their sons. Fathers had ample opportunities to influence their children's behaviors because they were with them a lot; their place of work generally was also their home. This frequent contact also provided opportunities for fathers to teach sons how to make a living as either a farmer or craftsman, the major career choices for men in the 1700s in America.

Eighteenth-century fathers had considerable control over their chil-dren, primarily because they controlled the access to wealth—virtually all men made their living from farming, so holding title to the land and owning the animals, farming tools, and, in the South, slaves, gave fathers tremendous power. They also owned their children in a sense—fathers "gave" their daughters away in marriage, and they always were granted physical custody of the children in the rare cases of divorce. Wives had more power than children, but were not their husbands' equals—women could not own property, so wives could not inherit, for instance. The identity of married women was so tied to their husbands that they were known publicly by their husbands' names and were addressed that way (e.g., she was Mrs. George Washington, not Martha Washington). Given a father's power to bequeath resources to his children upon his death, fathers cast tremendous influence over their children's behaviors. This power extended to such major life issues as who children married and where they lived, as well as over more minor daily issues such as how children conducted themselves in public. Fathers could exert control over children's behaviors well into the children's adult years.

During the 1800s, there were profound shifts in how Americans viewed fathers, mothers, and children. These changes led to substantive altera-tions in how family members interacted with and perceived each other. For example, children's needs for moral instruction, seen as paramount at the start of the 1800s, were replaced with the need for emotional support, a necessity that women were believed to be more capable than men of providing. In particular, infants and young children were thought to need the kind of nurturing that only women could provide. Gradually, the education of children also was seen as the purview of women, and the prevailing theories of children's development late in the 19th century (e.g., early Freudian psychoanalytic theory) began to attribute primary importance to mothers rather than fathers as parents.

Changes in how fathers made a living also contributed to changes in cultural norms about fathers' roles. It was easier for 18th- and early 19th-century fathers to be responsible for their children's moral instruction and to guide their behavior because most men's work was done at home in the presence of their children. Industrialization took fathers out of the household and into factories, businesses, and other workplaces away from their children. This made it difficult for fathers to be as involved with their children and facilitated the shift to the primacy of mothers as parents.

As the 20th century began, a number of societal factors contributed to a new vision of fatherhood: changes in beliefs about the natural roles of men and women in families and about the nature of children, the gradual transformation of the economy from farm and households as production units to households as consuming units in a market economy, and a move to the suburbs for the growing number of middle-class families. One thing that didn't change, however, was that fathers still were expected to be the primary family breadwinners.

Fathers in the First Half of the Century

Companionate families and masculine domesticity. For middle-class men and their families, the early decades of the century were a time of increasing economic stability. As middle-class men became more financially secure, their interest in becoming more involved in their families grew. Prior to World War I—as work for urban fathers became increasingly bureaucratic and segmented, as cities grew and daily living involved more and more impersonal encounters with strangers—family life took on special importance for middle-class fathers. Home was where their emotional needs were met and where they could assert their masculinity in ways they could not as white-collar professionals. Men sought to find new meaning in their family roles, including fatherhood.

The old ideal of fathers wielding power as strong authority figures gradually gave way to an ideal in which fathers displayed what has been called *masculine domesticity* (LaRossa, 1997). This new ideal did not involve equal sharing of household tasks by mothers and fathers, nor did it represent interest among fathers in engaging in child care activities. Masculine domesticity was an ideal that was based on fathers (when they were at home) showing greater interest in helping out with the children, teaching them skills, and playing with them.

New groups of helping professionals (e.g., social workers, psychologists, home economists, psychiatrists, sociologists) emerged early in the century, and they helped fathers become more involved. There was evidence that these childrearing experts had a sizable audience of middle-class men in the 1920s and 1930s who sought advice through reading, listening to instructive radio shows, and attending classes about child-rearing (LaRossa, 1997). These professionals advised fathers to be role models for their sons and daughters so that the children could develop appropriate gender role identities. To accomplish this, men were advised not to be distant authority figures, to spend time with their children, have fun, and be a guide and companion. Fathers were expected to engage in hobbies and sports with children, to guide them and help shape their developing personalities. Men were urged to take emotional interest in their families and spend more time at home when they were not working. Mothers were still expected to be in charge of household duties, including child care, but fathers were expected to help with the children more than their fathers had. Fathers were still expected to be the family provider, but they were no longer seen as the sole authority and lone decision maker in the family. Instead, a more democratic model was emphasized in which adults, and sometimes children, shared decision making.

Masculine domesticity fit the new model of family life promoted by psychologists, psychiatrists, and childrearing experts—the *companionate family* ideal—which took root among middle-class urban and suburban families in the years before and during the Depression (1921–1939). Fathers in companionate families were supposed to be kind and understanding and spend time with their children to help build their characters. These ideals or cultural beliefs were those of childrearing experts, doctors, and psychiatrists—it is not known how well fathers managed these expectations.

For many fathers, work demands increasingly kept them away from home, and children's lives increasingly also were lived away from home—at school, in clubs, and in sports activities. This was especially challenging for suburban fathers, who added sometimes lengthy commutes to their workdays—for these men, active involvement in family life was relegated to weekends.

Of course, fathers were still expected to be disciplinarians and authority figures, and some men found it difficult to abandon old styles of fatherhood to become companionate fathers. In addition, some fathers actively rejected masculine domesticity sentiments, partly because this view of fatherhood was at odds with a focus on manliness in leisure pursuits (e.g., hunting, boxing, playing football, socializing in bars) that was popular during this era.

The experts focused their advice on urban and suburban middle-class fathers. Immigrant fathers and men in working-class families were less influenced by the ideals of companionate marriages and masculine domesticity. It is also likely that farmers continued to see their children more as unpaid employees and coworkers than chums.

Fatherhood for working-class men probably changed little in the early decades of the century. Although there are few records about immigrant fathers and poor urban factory workers, such fathers likely had little free time to spend having fun with their children. Many immigrants came from Italy, Germany, and eastern European countries—cultures in which families were patriarchal systems, meaning that fathers were family heads who had authority over their children and their wives. It is unlikely that the suburban middle-class masculine domesticity movement affected these working-class immigrant fathers. The major role of working-class fathers was primary breadwinner, and they also were likely to be disciplinarians and authority figures. Their main struggle as fathers—in addition to earning enough money to feed, clothe, and house their families—was to maintain their place as patriarch. In some ethnic immigrant groups, children earned as much as 46 percent of their family's income by working in factories, and it was rare among any ethnic groups for fathers to be the lone family wage earners. This may have presented a challenge to fathers' authority, but a bigger challenge was immigrant children's more rapid acculturation into American society. Children learned English and adapted to American society and customs more quickly than their parents did. This placed fathers in situations in which they needed their children to serve as interpreters, or *language brokers,* for them (e.g., with landlords, doctors), which gave children a certain power. The phenomenon of children as language brokers was not isolated to the early immigrants, but was a common immigrant experience throughout the century for immigrant families from non–English-speaking countries. Little is known about how early immigrant fathers handled this power imbalance, but it created stress and conflicts between Latino and Asian immigrant fathers and their children in the latter half of the century.

Fathers and children apart. A cruel blow came to fathers and their families during the 1930s, when many men lost their jobs during the Great Depression. For these men, their primary family role as breadwinner was taken from them, with few prospects for regaining their main way of contributing to family life. Out of shame from their failure to provide for their families, some fathers simply disappeared; they felt they had nothing to offer and could not bear watching their families suffer. Desertion in the 1930s was known as a "poor man's divorce."

When the Depression hit, families lost homes and farms, possessions were taken by creditors because of defaults on payments, and extended families moved in together (adult children and their offspring sometimes moved in with grandparents, and sometimes the older generation moved in with younger kin) to save money. Most fathers, rather than abandoning their families, left to find work, with the idea of sending money home once they got a job, and to return home when financial times improved.

Leaving a family behind was not unique to the 1930s in the United States. Starting during World War I and continuing through the Second

World War, some African American fathers moved from the rural South to the cities of the North and Northeast, sometimes leaving their families behind until they could find work and earn enough to bring them North. A few of these men, however, started new families once they settled in the North and left their previous wives and children in the South.

The theme of fathers leaving their families to fulfill financial obligations to their children and wives was repeated for many groups of fathers throughout the century. Immigrant fathers typically came to the United States alone, leaving wives and children behind—sometimes temporarily and sometimes permanently. Individuals from various European countries (e.g., Italians, Poles, and Irish) were among those who came to the United States in the early part of the 20th century hoping to find a better life for themselves and their families. Many found work and paid for their family's passage across the Atlantic when they were financially able. Some fathers, however, ended up deserting their families and started new lives and new families in the United States. Mintz (2004) estimated that, early in the 20th century, 25 percent of Jewish immigrant fathers abandoned their children. It is likely that the stress of migration to a new land, adapting to new language and strange customs, and the challenges of making ends meet were overwhelming to many immigrant fathers. Some managed their problems by disappearing into a new life that did not include a wife and children back in the old country.

Some immigrant fathers came to the United States for a short period of time, maybe just a few years, before returning to their families. For instance, in the early part of the 20th century, 73 percent of Italian fathers returned to their home villages after earning enough money to establish some economic security for their families. Most Chinese immigrants, with the exception of a few middle-class merchants, considered themselves temporary workers well into the 1940s. They had to return to China if they wanted to see their families because restrictive immigration laws made it nearly impossible for Chinese women to immigrate; in 1930 20 percent of the Chinese population in the United States were female. Single Chinese men had to return to China if they wanted to marry and have children. They were legally barred from interracial marriages in 15 states, so their options for becoming fathers were few unless they returned to China. Immigration bans against the Chinese—based on racist fears and prejudice—prohibited Chinese immigrants from becoming American citizens until 1943, when China became a U.S. ally in the Second World War. Later in the century, Latino fathers—particularly Mexican fathers—typically came alone to the United States as farm workers for months or years at a time with the intentions of sending money home as well as saving enough money to return home to start anew. Other Latino immigrant fathers came to the United States without their families because they could not afford to bring all of them at once. Some were undocumented, and it was easier for one man to cross the Mexico–United States border without being detected than for a whole family to do so.

World War II and fathers. The Second World War brought more separation for fathers and their families. Many were drafted or joined the armed forces and were deployed for long periods of time. Even fathers who were not in the military were sometimes separated from their children for a time during the war, following work in industries supporting the war effort. For the most part, unlike during the Depression, most men sent for their families once they were settled into their new employment. Between 1941 and 1945, approximately 20 percent of Americans moved at least once, representing the largest migration in U.S. history.

Following World War II, jobs remained abundant, the economy was booming, and most fathers were able to meet cultural expectations about being the breadwinners for their families. Europe and Japan were in shambles as a result of the war, and postwar economic opportunities for Americans were enormous—the country was shifting its attention from World War II and its attendant financial sacrifices to new building projects and economic expansion. Politicians and other public opinion makers exhorted men to finish the job they had started during the war of making the United States the most powerful nation on earth—but this time the goals were economic rather than military.

Cultural expectations about gender that prevailed after World War II pushed men and women into increasingly divergent family activities. During the 15 years or so following the Second World War, the ideology of male breadwinning was emphasized perhaps more than before the war, and men and women began to be seen as living in separate worlds in many ways. The companionate family ideal that flourished among the middle-class between the two world wars was obliterated by a combination of economic challenges men faced during the Depression, the extraordinary demands placed on men and their families during World War II, and the abundant economic opportunities available after the war.

Fathers in the Latter Half of the Century

By the 1950s, the separate spheres of men and women in families meant that mothers were almost solely responsible for childrearing and fathers for family income production. Fathers were still seen as the ultimate household authority and chief disciplinarian (a common refrain heard from mothers of the era to disobedient children was, "Wait until your father gets home"), but this was more image than reality—mothers did the heavy lifting of childrearing, including most of the discipline.

In the *separate spheres* era, popular sentiment was that men did not want to be bothered with the daily demands of taking care of children, but that women relished such tasks. Fathers were not expected to change diapers, prepare meals, dress children, and do the many other activities that are necessary in childrearing—these responsibilities were seen as women's work. It was also a normative belief that fathers were not capable of adequately taking care of children on their own—they lacked the necessary temperament and the presumably inborn skills needed to meet children's needs on an ongoing basis. Despite widespread cultural support for this separate spheres model of parenting, mothers sometimes felt they were stuck with the dirty work of raising children, which led to some frustration by mothers with fathers and their involvement in only the fun aspects of childrearing.

Ideals of fatherhood in the 1950s were embodied in TV portrayals of middle-class men such as Ward Cleaver (*Leave It to Beaver* [1957–1963]), Jim Anderson (*Father Knows Best* [1954–1960]), Dr. Alex Stone (*The Donna Reed Show* [1958–1966]), and Ozzie Nelson (*The Adventures of Ozzie and Harriet* [1952–1966]). Stable, financially secure, good natured, and a source of wisdom and understanding, these warm and wise men were the ultimate arbiters of rules and discipline for children while their wives ran the households. These fathers were in control, their children were happy and cared for, and the fathers had the last word in their households, even though they ruled with loving cooperation with their wives. They listened to their kids, but, ultimately, as the title of the popular TV show indicated, father knew best. These idealized images of fathers were tough for real men to emulate.

In contrast, media images of working-class men typically portrayed fathers as clownish and inept (e.g., in the *Life of Riley* [1949–1950, 1953–1958], nice-guy airplane riveter Chester Riley never could get ahead, in his life or in his family). Poor fathers in these media images apparently had less right and less ability to head their households. They were often the butt of jokes and were easily manipulated by their wives and children. Such media portrayals underscored the importance of men being capable breadwinners if they wanted to be viewed as accomplished fathers.

Another general media theme was that fathers were heads of the family in name only—many fathers portrayed in radio series and television shows were easy to fool and control; they were the family heads only because mothers and children allowed them to think they were. Popular culture was gentler to middle-class fathers than working-class dads, but all fathers received some harsh treatment.

Despite economic demands on fathers and the amount of time "getting ahead" financially required, fatherhood experts in the 1950s encouraged fathers to be actively engaged with their children. Men were expected to play with and have fun with children and to be emotionally available to them. The most noted parenting expert of the day, Benjamin Spock, advised fathers to be warm, friendly guides to their sons, to share secrets with them, and to sometimes take them alone on excursions—daughters also needed dad's warm approval and attention, but got less mention by Spock and other experts than did sons.

Men increasingly found it difficult to meet expectations of childrearing experts and be the primary earners for their families, especially with the growing material needs and wants of families. Families desired newer and larger homes in the suburbs, more household appliances, and cars. Because families were relatively large, fathers usually had to feed and clothe several children. During this time, family members' lives became more segmented. Fathers tended to spend more time commuting, children got more involved in organized activities outside the home, and women sometimes felt trapped in the suburbs. This era saw the development of a separate youth culture, distinct from adult society.

Some childrearing experts worried about fathers' roles in childrearing. Because men were gone most of the day working and commuting and childrearing was mostly the duty of mothers, there was growing unease that children would be too heavily influenced by women. Without dad's presence, children were in danger of being *overmothered*, which many scholars in the 1940s and 1950s thought led to homosexuality, juvenile delinquency, and antisocial behaviors, particularly for boys. Philip Wylie (1942) coined a term for this phenomenon, *momism.*

The concern about overmothering was summed up by Kenneth Keniston in 1960, who wrote,

American boys are increasingly brought up by women—mothers and school teachers—who have the greatest power and authority over them. This matriarchal situation tends to encourage identification with women, their functions, and activities. Yet as adults, the same boys must have a relatively firm sense of their own maleness. (p. 305)

Concerns about girls not being exposed to fathers and being overmothered were relatively minor. Mostly, childrearing experts worried that girls would not know how to be good wives and mothers if they grew up without their fathers being around much.

Psychiatrists, psychologists, and other childrearing professionals argued that fathers needed to function as models for appropriate gender roles so that children could learn what culturally expected masculine and feminine behaviors were anticipated from them as adults. Thus, the renewed interest in fathers focused on their absence and its presumed effects as much as on fathers' presence and their interactions with children. Although mothers were cautioned by experts of this era not to be inappropriately masculine in their behaviors, the brunt of the responsibility to model culturally prescribed gender role behaviors for children (primarily boys) belonged to fathers. They were the antidotes to momism.

These cultural beliefs about how boys learned to be men created tensions for fathers because succeeding at breadwinning often was at odds with the demands on them to be available to children. Some experts recognized the strain that these competing demands placed on fathers—at home they were supposed to be warm, funny, and playful, but at work men were expected to be cool, competent, competitive, and practical.

A father and son play baseball. (© Royalty-Free/Corbis)

Sometimes known as the *John Wayne syndrome* because of the hyper-masculine roles played by actor John Wayne, a leading mid-century action and western movie star, the ideal American man was supposed to be tough, independent, unemotional (except when driven to justifiable anger over an injustice), violent, and aloof. None of these qualities served men especially well as fathers; the John Wayne syndrome referred to the difficulty that some men had in turning off their competitive personas when they were home.

Black fathers and matriarchal families. A number of scholars, both black and white, studied black families after World War II and reported a growing number of fatherless households among African Americans—a situation they decried. From 1949 to 1964, between 19 percent and 23 percent of African American households with children were headed by mothers. By the mid-1960s, about 25 percent of marriages between African Americans ended in divorce and about one-quarter of all black births were to unmarried mothers. In Daniel Moynihan's controversial 1965 report about black families, one set of solutions to reduce the matriarchal nature of black families was for the government to help black men economically, which would encourage them to marry and take their "rightful" place as household heads. Whites had *momism,* blacks had *pathological matriarchy*—both were widely voiced social concerns about the importance of fathers and their relative absence from the lives of their children.

Despite the public interest in fatherhood, there is evidence in the 1950s that many fathers were content to let their wives raise the children. This may have been truer for working-class than for middle-class fathers. From studies of working- and middle-class parents, sociologist Melvin Kohn concluded that "Working class fathers seem to play neither the directive role their wives would have them play, nor a highly supportive role. Rather, they seem to see childrearing as more completely their wives' responsibility" (Kohn & Carroll, 1960, pp. 391–392). Most middle- and working-class mothers wanted their husbands to be more involved in childrearing, setting limits and showing affection to children. Neither group was entirely satisfied with what their husbands did as fathers.

The Rise of the "New Fathers"

By the latter quarter of the century, fathers and children were spending even less time at home together than they had earlier. This was due to a combination of factors: longer commutes and longer working days for fathers, more after-school activities for children, and a higher proportion of adolescents who were employed after school and on the weekends. In addition, the divorce rate continued to increase, resulting in even less time with children for many separated and divorced fathers. Finally, it became more common for single women to give birth and raise their children without assistance or involvement of the children's fathers.

Experts responded to these changes in family life by telling fathers to get more involved in their children's lives in order to meet their children's emotional needs. This advice, in some ways, extended the concerns raised about father absence following World War II. In the late 1960s and 1970s, however, the worries about absent fathers were broader than apprehension that the effects of too-little-fathering would contribute to boys' homosexuality, that children's gender identity would be affected in negative ways, and that delinquency would increase. Instead, experts began to encourage father involvement to enhance the general well-being of children rather than to offset problems in development. Experts continued advising fathers to be present, but they also began suggesting ways in which fathers and children should interact.

By the final quarter of the century, a *new father* image emerged to offset fears about the effects of father absence on children's well-being. The new father was supposed to be nurturing and sensitive, yet masculine. These new fathers were described by childrearing experts and

Egalitarian parenting in the 1960s meant fathers were
more involved. (Courtesy of the authors.)

fatherhood advocates as *wanting* to be actively engaged in raising their
children—wanting to do the hard work of caregiving, such as changing
diapers, feeding, and bathing children. They also wanted to be in charge
of the fun areas of parenting, such as taking the children to ball games
and picnics. Movies from the late 1970s and 1980s (e.g., *Kramer vs. Kramer*
[1979], *Three Men and a Baby* [1987]) and television series from that time
(e.g., *Full House*, [1987–1995], *Who's the Boss* [1984–1992]) portrayed men
being active, loving parents—albeit often comically incompetent at doing
simple household chores and child care tasks. Advertisements in magazines and on television showed fathers pushing strollers, playing with
children, and being actively involved in their children's lives.

Prior to the 1970s, fathers generally were not allowed to be in the labor
and delivery rooms. Images of expectant fathers portrayed in the media

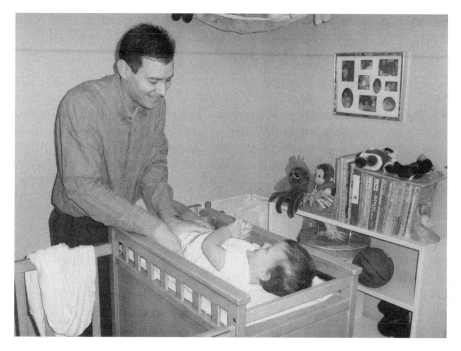

A "new father" and his daughter near the end of the century. (Courtesy of the authors.)

were of frazzled, anxious men, pacing in the waiting room with other expectant dads, waiting to be told of the birth of their child so they could celebrate by distributing cigars. New fathers were expected to take child-birth classes with their partners and be in attendance during labor and delivery. They also were expected to be loving, involved parents, even to infants and toddlers. Sociologist Scott Coltrane (1988) identified the new father as a phenomenon of white, middle-class America; working-class and ethnic minority fathers still tended to be macho family men who left childrearing to their partners.

The image of the new father and the reality of fathering did not always match, however, even among the middle class. Social scientists reported that, in the last two decades of the 20th century, fathers were more involved in raising their children, but they were far less involved than the new fatherhood image and mass media suggested they were. In fact, findings from most studies of men's behaviors did not support the belief that men were fulfilling the new father image, although a few researchers found limited evidence that more men were providing care and becoming emotionally engaged with their children than was true of earlier decades. For instance, husbands' proportion of child care increased from 20 percent to 30 percent between 1965 and 1981; the amount of time fathers were either accessible or directly engaged with children under the age of 13 increased from 2.64 hours per day in 1981 to 3.25 hours per day in 1997; and fathers increased the amount of time they spent each day interacting with their children from 24 minutes in 1965 to one hour in 1998. Fathers' levels of engagement with and accessibility to their children increased more when mothers were employed outside of the home, although the difference was small. In fact, fathers with working wives spent only 4.8 minutes per day more with their children than did fathers whose wives were not in the labor force. So, although fathers were more actively interacting with their children than they had been—and more so than their fathers had with them—the time involved was still brief, and it was not clear how meaningful it was.

In all the studies comparing fathers to mothers, mothers spent substantially more time with children, regardless of whether the mothers were in the labor force. Mothers remained the parent who was primarily and constantly responsible for children. Fathers interacted with children episodically—providing backup child care, taking their children to the park or to soccer and baseball practices, helping with homework, and teaching them specific skills. Fathers joked more, played more, and did specific tasks (e.g., helping children with homework or scouting projects) more than did mothers. Most fathers saw themselves as being there for their children, supporting them, and generally setting limits. Mothers, on the other hand, tended to do everything else, including making plans for what the father and children would do. Mothers not only prepared meals, for example, they planned what and how much to get at the store. Fathers may have taken the grocery list to the store, but late-century commercials for cell phones showed clueless fathers calling their wives from the grocery store asking questions about what to buy.

As children became older, fathers did more with them, particularly sons; however, mothers were still the parenting executives. It was, therefore, not surprising that researchers consistently found that children felt emotionally closer to their mothers than they did to their fathers.

Title IX and father involvement with daughters. In 1972, the U.S. Congress passed civil rights legislation, known popularly as Title IX, which inadvertently increased fathers' involvement with their daughters over the last decades of the century. Title IX stated that "No person in the United States shall on the basis of sex be excluded from participation in, be denied the benefits of, or be subject to discrimination under any educational program or activity receiving federal financial assistance." This legislation was controversial at the time, and it took three years for Congress to pass an amendment that unequivocally declared that Title IX applied to school athletic programs. This meant that Title IX required schools to provide equal access to athletic teams and scholarships for girls. As a result of this law, which came about after a great deal of lobbying by feminists and other individuals interested in equal rights, institutions from middle schools through college began creating sports programs for girls. Developmental leagues designed to teach athletic skills to girls in grade school soon followed. The explosion of new athletic teams for girls provided many opportunities for fathers to engage with their daughters over mutual interests in softball, volleyball, basketball, soccer, tennis, track and field, golf, and other sports. Fathers volunteered to coach or be assistant coaches for their daughters' teams, just as they had over the years for their sons. Sports was an area of life familiar to many men, and so fathers who might have spent less time with their daughters prior to Title IX now found many good reasons to spend time with daughters, bonding with them during practices and games. By the end of the century, girls' athletics had become widely accepted, and young fathers who had come of age after this legislation assumed they would spend as much time with their daughters' sporting activities as with their sons'.

Stay-at-home fathers. One phenomenon that reflected the new father was stay-at-home dads (SAHDs). The emergence of SAHDs—men who voluntarily left the labor force to engage in childrearing, usually of young children—was facilitated by changes in attitudes about men's and women's roles in families and the increase in mothers entering the labor force. Couples who were trying to create egalitarian households in which duties were shared equitably often believed that children should be raised by both parents, but that the parent with the better temperament for raising young children should be the one primarily responsible for childrearing. In some families this was the father. Although salary inequities between men and women persisted, by the 1970s, more women had moved into well-paying professions and a few wives made more money than their husbands; thus, for some couples, a combination of temperamental suitability for childrearing and salary differentials that favored mothers led to the decision that dad should stay home with the children.

SAHDs became visible in the 1970s. A popular movie starring Michael Keaton, *Mr. Mom* (1983), humorously portrayed a stay-at-home dad of that era, and some people began calling men who stayed home to raise children "Mr. Mom" The 1990s witnessed an increase in the proportion of households in which men were the full-time parents, but by the end of the century there were not quite 100,000 stay-at-home dads, less than 1 percent of fathers.

Men who opted to be full-time parents tended to be white, married to women who made enough money to support a family, middle-class, and college educated. Although they often lived in metropolitan areas, stay-at-home fathers sometimes described themselves as lonely because they did not fit in with either full-time mothers or working fathers. Although by most anecdotal accounts, stay-at-home dads and their wives (generally) were content with their choices, couples with SAHDs were people willing to ignore social norms about men's and women's primary family responsibilities to do what they thought was right for their children and their families. Fathers willing to be SAHDs had to leave career paths, at least temporarily, just as women did, with the attendant risks to future advancement that leaving work entailed. It is likely that many men who decided to be SAHDs received some pressure from male friends not to do so. Given the strength of the breadwinning expectation for men in families, it is not surprising that more men have not opted for full-time fathering.

The greater availability of high-speed home computers and the Internet in the 1990s made it possible for more parents, both mothers and fathers, to work at home while raising their children. It is likely that at least some of the increase in fathers staying at home was due to men who could run their businesses or work for an employer from their homes while their children were napping or playing with friends.

Fatherhood Movements

Late in the 20th century, several social movements encouraged father involvement. These movements affected some fathers' behaviors as well as cultural norms about fathers.

The increase in divorce and the tendency of courts to award physical and legal custody of children to mothers led to the development of *fathers' rights* groups in the 1970s. These organizations, also sometimes called children's rights groups, were joined by a diverse collection of fathers. Some men were involved primarily because of their desire to be more engaged in their children's lives after divorce; others were motivated by anger toward their former wives and perceived biases within the legal system toward protecting women's rights in general and divorced and separated mothers in particular. The fathers' rights groups effectively promoted legal preferences for shared legal and physical custody, so both parents now had legal decision-making rights over children after divorce, which was seldom true in the 1970s, and children were more likely to reside part-time in each parents' household after divorce. Although the fathers' rights movement was not the only influence on the legal system, greater sharing of postdivorce childrearing responsibilities was certainly a major part of their agenda.

Divorced fathers also were assisted inadvertently in their efforts by feminists, who had long argued that women should have equal legal rights to men. Although these feminist arguments were made about the general legal status of men and women, when applied to child custody issues, fathers benefited by getting more access to their children than they had before such gender-neutral laws were passed. By the end of the 20th century, most states had either a preference for joint custody arrangements after divorce or judges presumed that such arrangements would be best unless one of the parents contested it.

Other fatherhood movements included fundamentalist Christian groups like the Promise Keepers, who encouraged fathers to be actively involved in protecting their children and teaching them moral beliefs. This organization, started in 1990 by University of Colorado football coach Bill McCartney, encouraged men to become more active leaders in their families. Within a few years, the Promise Keepers were holding rallies for thousands of men in football stadiums across the country, and, by 2000, this movement had spread to several other nations and become a full-time organization ministering to men.

Another movement was led by black Muslim leader Louis Farrakhan specifically for African American men; like the Promise Keepers, the Million Man March started as a large public gathering. In Washington, DC, on October 16, 1995, celebrities, politicians, and other leaders of the African American community exhorted black men to become more active in their communities and families. The Million Man March did not lead to an ongoing organization like the Promise Keepers, but there were follow-up activities (e.g., voter registration of black men). Although both the Promise Keepers and the Million Man movements had broader goals than promoting father involvement, central to both of their missions was the goal of encouraging men to be concerned and significant fathers.

Another fatherhood movement which included a number of social science scholars, was formed out of alarm about never-married fathers, especially young men and adolescents who had fathered children with adolescent mothers and divorced fathers who did not reside with and were not part of their children's daily caregiving. The federal government and some state and local governments became involved in what became known as the *Responsible Fatherhood* movement. Government officials were motivated by an interest in reducing child welfare spending by encouraging fathers to be financially responsible for their children. Some religious organizations (e.g., Promise Keepers) also were involved, but they were less worried about child financial support and more concerned with moral aspects of father involvement. A number of programs established by this movement's adherents were designed to encourage young men to assume a variety of obligations for their children, whether they lived with them or not. The more diverse Responsible Fatherhood movement was never as organized as the Promise Keepers, but nonetheless was growing in strength as the century ended.

Divorced Fathers

The numbers of divorced fathers grew throughout the century. Prior to the 20th century, legal presumptions that reflected societal beliefs about children's needs and mothers' and fathers' relative abilities to meet those needs meant that in most divorce cases mothers were given physical custody of children. Consequently, for most of the 20th century, divorce meant that fathers no longer lived with their children and, in many cases, gradually lost contact with their children.

Notions such as shared physical custody and children residing part of the time with both parents after divorce were extremely rare for most of the 20th century. Because one spouse had to sue the other for committing a violation against the marriage, divorces were often hostile litigations.

Because divorce was uncommon, even in unhappy marriages, when a spouse filed, it usually meant that the marriage was seriously flawed. In such contexts, it was not unusual for men to start their lives anew, severing ties with former spouses and their children. Fathers who remarried either had children with their new wife or raised her children, acting as a substitute father. Well into the 1980s, sociologists found that many divorced and remarried men engaged in this sort of child substitution—ending contact with children from a first marriage and "replacing" them with another set of children with whom they lived in subsequent partnership households. For at least the first half of the century, the model of marriage applied in legal circles was the husband-as-breadwinner and wife-as-homemaker model. When the marriage ended, judges expected wives/mothers to continue their childrearing responsibilities and husbands/fathers to continue their financial obligations; beyond that, there were few expectations and even fewer social supports for nonresidential divorced fathers to maintain contact and involvement with their children.

In 1973, a New York court ruled that "The simple fact of being a mother does not, by itself, indicate a capacity or willingness to render a quality of care different from those which the father can provide" (*State ex rel. Watts v. Watts*). This ruling opposed nearly a century of rulings favoring maternal custody. Although most courts still clung to the belief that mothers were better suited to raise young children, between 1960 and 1990, nearly every state abandoned the presumption of preference for mothers over fathers in child custody after divorce. These legal rulings led to more shared custody and to more father-only custody decisions after divorce—although these remained relatively unusual throughout the century, at least for school-age children and preschoolers.

From the early 1970s to the end of the century, changes in grounds for divorce, the rise of the new father ideal, and an emphasis on gender equality in legal judgments contributed to gradual shifts in the experiences of divorced fathers. Compared to earlier in the century, more fathers shared decision-making duties with their former wives, more fathers saw their children and spent time with them, and more children spent some of their growing-up years living alternately with fathers as well as mothers. Older children and adolescents sometimes resented having to do this because it meant leaving their social lives and friends behind when they went to the other parent's household, but many younger children grew up not knowing any other life except one in which they went back and forth between their parents' residences. It was not unusual in the last quarter of the century for adolescents, particularly boys, to shift their primary residence from mom's house to dad's house, often without going to court to make these changes legal. Likewise, it was not unusual for children to make the shift back to mom's house.

Despite greater involvement of some divorced fathers in the last part of the century, almost half of divorced fathers lost contact with their children and an even greater proportion did not financially support them. These so-called deadbeat dads became an increasingly recognized social problem, and legal efforts to get them to accept financial responsibility for children increased. In 1975, Congress established the Office of Child Support Enforcement and created incentives for states to set up similar units. Additional federal laws were passed that set guidelines for child support award levels (1984 Child Support Enforcement amendment) and made income withholding from nonresidential parents automatic (1988 Family Support Act). Finally, in sweeping reform legislation designed to change nearly every aspect of welfare, the 1996 Personal Responsibility and Work Opportunity Reconciliation Act set up additional enforcement mechanisms to get child support—wage and income tax withholding mechanisms were expanded, and states were allowed to revoke many kinds of licenses (e.g., driver's licenses, business licenses, fishing permits) and to deny food stamps to obligators who were behind on payments. Despite these efforts, the proportion of children receiving child support did not change much—30 percent received some support in 1976, and 31 percent received support in 1997 (Sorensen & Halpern, 1999). Although these laws helped increase the levels of child support being paid for some children, particularly following parental divorce, other factors—such as increases in nonmarital childrearing and inflation—meant that some children benefited less from legislative changes. Paternity testing, part of the 1988 bill, helped unmarried mothers receive more child support because fatherhood could be genetically established, but many never-married mothers had no child support awards because they had not sought them. As the century ended, nonresidential fathers' financial responsibility for children remained a serious and unresolved social issue.

For most of the century, unmarried fathers were largely invisible. Children born outside of wedlock **Unmarried Fathers** were stigmatized as illegitimate. In the last 30 years of the 20th century, however, the number of children born to single mothers increased, first among black women and then among whites, and the stigma against unmarried parenthood diminished somewhat. In fact, among some low-income African Americans, becoming a parent was an indicator of adulthood, and, for some men, having children by several women was seen as a sign of manliness.

One indication that unwed fatherhood was becoming more acceptable was that the courts began to recognize the rights and responsibilities of unwed fathers. In 1971, the U.S. Supreme Court first recognized the custodial rights of unmarried fathers. In later decisions by the Supreme Court, it was affirmed that unwed fathers who helped raise their children were eligible to claim paternal rights. By 1990, most states had granted unmarried fathers comparable rights to married fathers, but the federal government and every state government also tried to enforce financial responsibilities of fathers who had never been married to their children's mothers.

Reasons for Father Absence A paradox of the last quarter of the 20th century was that, as some fathers became more involved in raising their children, a growing number never saw their children at all. One challenge in addressing the social problems of absent fathers was the multiple reasons why fathers were not involved with their children. Poverty, cultural beliefs about the primary role of fathers as breadwinners, gender socialization and fathers' beliefs about gender and parenting, fathers' self-confidence and personal skills, interpersonal constraints, and institutional policies and practices (particularly workplace rules that served as barriers to participation) all contributed. In fact, many of these same factors were at work in the lives of all fathers to varying degrees.

Poverty. Impoverished fathers, regardless of whether they resided with their children, found it difficult throughout the 20th century to spend a lot of time with their children because they had to work long hours to make ends meet. Working-class and low-income fathers typically earned hourly wages and were not paid if they were not working. This meant they could not easily afford to take time off to see their children participate in school events or other activities. Late in the century, poor fathers who did not reside with their children but were supposed to pay child support sometimes had reduced contact with children even though they wanted to see them, because the children's mothers refused to let them until they paid back child support. Sometimes children in low-income families had to be employed at relatively young ages, which reduced time for children and fathers to interact.

Cultural beliefs about fathers as breadwinners. One consistent cultural expectation throughout the century was that fathers were to be the main wage earners in their families; their primary familial duty was to provide. Consequently, men holding these cultural beliefs sometimes found it hard to be involved as fathers when they were not employed because they saw themselves as failures. Although this cultural ideology affected poor fathers more than upper-income men, even some wealthy fathers and fathers in two-earner families were periodically absent from their children's lives because they were too busy earning money to have time for childrearing.

An interesting aspect of fathering and fatherhood in the 20th century was the durability of the breadwinning ideology. Despite periodic changes in how fathers were expected to relate to their children (e.g., masculine domesticity and companionate families, fathers as role models, new fathers, responsible fathers), a constant expectation across the century was that the primary duty of men in families was to earn money. This ideology or cultural expectation was so strong that many men considered themselves good fathers if they were able to feed, house, and clothe their children; hanging out with their children or teaching them skills or helping with homework were unnecessary for men to have fulfilled their obligations. This belief persisted even when wives and mothers entered the work force in large numbers. For instance, 23 percent of married mothers with children under age 6 and 28 percent of married mothers with children between ages 6 and 17 worked for wages in 1950; by the mid-1980s, the percentages of married mothers who were working were 54 percent and 70 percent, respectively, and these percentages continued to climb. In the 1990s, almost 25 percent of married women earned more than their husbands, but still men considered themselves to be the primary breadwinners. Given the persistence of this role expectation, it is not surprising perhaps that, for some fathers, there is little to the fatherhood role beyond breadwinning.

Gender socialization and fathers' beliefs about parenting. Male socialization in the 20th century did not place fathering at the center of roles for which boys were prepared. In contrast to little girls, who often included "mommy" in response to questions about what they wanted to be when they grew up, boys rarely included "daddy" as a future role—not because they did not expect to be parents but because job and career roles were much more important to males' identities. Little boys were discouraged from playing with dolls (at least by most parents for much of the century), and in many ways gender socialization of boys was not conducive to becoming actively engaged fathers, whether married or not. For most of the century, their own fathers were little boys' models for fatherhood; and, for most boys, fathers were totally absent or worked long hours and were functionally absent or distant emotionally. Despite advice of childrearing experts encouraging fathers to interact with their children in warm and loving ways, gender socialization did not match this advice, and most boys were not raised to be "new fathers." Although paternal identity in the 20th century involved several roles, foremost among them was breadwinner, just as it had been in previous centuries. As a result, when men became fathers they usually were undersocialized for the job.

Studies of fathers in the 1980s and 1990s indicated that many would like to be more involved in raising their children—in a 1990 poll, 39 percent of fathers said they would quit their jobs if they could to be with their children more. In another poll, 48 percent of men between the ages of 18 and 24 said they would like to stay home with their children someday. The actions of fathers, however, did not match these surveyed attitudes. In a study of middle-class men, 71 percent had *no responsibility* for any child care tasks, and 22 percent were responsible for only one task, with the remainder of tasks being done by their wives. In the Middletown longitudinal study of the late 1970s, 77 percent of the fathers and 89 percent of the mothers reported that mothers performed virtually all of the child care, while 80 percent of the fathers earned all or most of the family income; the study authors concluded that parental roles had changed little since 1924 (Caplow et al., 1982).

Fathers' self-confidence and parenting skills. Given the gender socialization experienced by most U.S. fathers, it should not be surprising that most men in the 20th century did not feel comfortable engaging in child care activities with infants and young children. Until the last quarter of the century, few fathers were expected to be active parents, and there were few supports for them to do so. What efforts that existed in society consistently were addressed to middle-class fathers.

Interpersonal constraining factors. What fathers did with their children usually was limited by whatever their children's mothers let them do. Known by social scientists as *gatekeeping,* mothers controlled how much contact fathers had and what they would do with children. In some extreme cases following separation or divorce, mothers did not allow fathers to see their children or to have contact.

Institutional policies and practices. Corporations, factories, and businesses of all kinds for most of the century made no allowances for fathers to take time off to participate in childrearing activities. Few companies had policies that allowed fathers and mothers to take time off for family needs. In a 1989 survey, 1 percent of the employees of private large and medium-sized employers had access to paid paternity leave; 37 percent of Fortune 500 companies provided unpaid paternity leave, and, of those companies, 90 percent made little effort to let employees know that such leaves were available. Even when corporations had flexible scheduling— as some did in the 1980s and 1990s—informal and implicit norms penalized men who took advantage of policies that allowed them to take time off to watch their children perform in sporting events or school activities, to care for sick children at home, or to take children to doctor's appointments. Many such fathers were seen as less committed to work-related success than other men, and they feared being passed over for promotions if they used family leave or took time off from work to spend with their families. It was not until 1993 that the United States created a law, the Family and Medical Leave Act, that allowed parents to take up to 12 work weeks per year to take care of sick children or to bond with newborns and newly adopted children without fear of penalty from their employers. This law did not apply to all work settings or to all employees, but it was a step toward removing some institutional barriers for fathers (and mothers).

Technology and Father-Child Connections   Toward the very end of the century, rapid technology advancements facilitated contacts between nonresidential fathers and their children. Cell phones and e-mail access allowed fathers to contact their children more frequently than before, but these options typically were available only to fathers and children who could afford cell phones and who had ready access to computers. However, these technologies were growing in familiarity and becoming cheaper, so they appeared to be increasing in use by long-distance dads and their children.

STEPFATHERS

A lot of the men helping to raise children in the 20th century were not genetically or legally related to the children. A sizeable proportion of U.S. children, as many as 15 percent at any point in time, were raised by stepfathers. For the first 70 years of the 20th century, the vast majority of stepfathers were men who "stepped in" and married a mother whose husband had died. In these situations, stepfathers generally acted as the fathers of their stepchildren—they were breadwinners, disciplinarians, advisors, and role models—whatever roles fathers were expected to fulfill, stepfathers also were expected to meet.

The expectation that stepfathers would replace or substitute for deceased fathers was based on prevailing cultural beliefs about families and the roles of men and women in families. For much of the century—at least among middle-class and upper-class families—most people believed that the only natural, normal family was a nuclear family (i.e., mother, father, and their children in a single household). This model of family life was the standard to which remarried individuals aspired, and, in this model, the role of stepfather replaced the role of father.

This meant that many stepfathers interacted with stepchildren as if they were their own offspring, or at least that was the expectation. In some stepfamilies, children took their stepfather's last name and called him "dad." Stepfathers operating from the reconstituted nuclear family model presented themselves to outsiders (e.g., school teachers, clergy, and neighbors) as their stepchildren's fathers. These were unofficial adoptions—for all intents and purposes, these stepfamilies hid their status and presented themselves as first-marriage nuclear families.

Although many stepfathers assumed they would relate to their stepchildren as fathers, how they enacted these roles varied, depending on their views of fatherhood. Some were as actively involved with their stepchildren as any fathers would be; others were relatively uninvolved and left childrearing to their wives; and others were involved only as disciplinarians of their stepchildren, a role they saw as the main duty of a father. Anecdotal evidence suggests that the reaction of remarried mothers and stepchildren to stepfathers' attempts to discipline generally ranged from active support and acceptance of the stepfather to passive resistance and resentment to outright rebellion (by children, at least).

Stepfathers as Fathers to Their Stepchildren

Stepfathers' assumption of the breadwinner role received more general acceptance than any other fatherhood role. Widowed mothers often remarried for financial security—for most of the 20th century, it was extremely hard for a single woman with dependent children to survive. There were social and sometimes legal restrictions against women's employment, wages for women were lower than men's earnings for comparable work, and in rural areas there were usually few jobs for women. Most widowed mothers found themselves mired in abject poverty with no prospects of improving their status; remarriage to a man with a farm or a business might bring rapid relief from their struggle to take care of themselves and their children. Although money became less of a motivation to remarry for middle- and upper-class mothers in the final quarter of the century, financial incentives to remarry loomed large for most single mothers throughout the century. Remarriage tended to be the quickest way out of poverty for single mothers.

Stepfathers as Friends, Quasi-Kin, and Nonparents

Lack of widely held beliefs about stepfathers' roles in postdivorce stepfamilies led to diversity in how they related to stepchildren in the last two decades of the 20th century. A role enacted by perhaps as many as one-third of stepfathers was that of friend to their stepchildren. This role was adopted most frequently by men who remarried mothers whose children were grown—it made sense in most families for older stepfathers and adult stepchildren to be friends rather than to try to recreate any type of parent-child bonds. Some stepfathers of minor-age stepchildren also assumed the role of friend—rather than tell the stepchildren what to do, these men developed bonds based on common interests.

A relatively small proportion of stepfathers held an almost-kinship status, called quasi-kin by family scholars. Some stepfathers described this as acting like they were fathers most of the time, but not assuming quite as much parental control or responsibility in childrearing. Finally, a substantial proportion of stepfathers were relatively disengaged from their stepchildren. They showed little affection toward them and engaged in relatively little supervision.

By the final decades of the 20th century, stepfathers were as numerous as at the beginning of the century, but their relationships with stepchildren were more diverse. Late 20th-century stepfathers typically shared some childrearing duties with both of their stepchildren's biological parents, and there were more part-time residential stepchildren than ever before as children went back and forth between their parents' households. Relationships between stepfathers and stepchildren were increasingly defined by the emotional quality of the bonds between them—some stepfathers were replacements for absent fathers; some were close friends or quasi-kin with parental responsibilities that varied with the emotional closeness; and some were relative strangers, with no real family connections.

Stepfathers were stigmatized throughout the century, although less so than stepmothers. A series of slasher horror movies in the last two decades of the century were based on tales of horrible stepfathers (i.e., *The Stepfather, Stepfather II*). Paradoxically, although stepfathers were expected to replace fathers in many ways, there was also a cultural expectation throughout the century that they would not be able to completely, or even adequately, substitute for deceased or divorced fathers. For this reason, and because it was familiar, acting like and thinking of themselves as a reconstituted nuclear family unit worked for some stepfathers and their families. This appeared to work most effectively when: (a) the nonresidential father and his family had no contact with children in the stepfamily household; (b) the children were young when they acquired a stepfather so they did not remember much about prior family life; and (c) all stepfamily members wanted to recreate the nuclear family and agreed, implicitly or explicitly, to do so.

SUMMARY: FATHERS AT CENTURY'S END

Throughout the 20th century, fathers were seen as important figures in their children's lives, but experts worried that children might not get enough fathering. Part of this concern was due to fathers' absences—leaving the family household for work, for war, and to escape family and marital pressures via divorce. Fathers for most of the century were seen as necessary counterweights to mothers' strong influences. During the last quarter of the century, when mothers were more likely to work outside the home, fathering advocates advised men to become "new" fathers—men who shared nurturing and childrearing duties with mothers.

The century ended with scholars and observers of family life debating whether the new fathers ideal was more hype than reality. Some conservative critics saw new fatherhood as a threat to children, in that fathers who adopted stereotypical mothering behaviors could confuse appropriate gender role development, resulting in children with poorly formed gender identities. Other critics contended that fathers' greater involvement with children was more cosmetic than substantive. They contended that even fathers who were spending more time with children were not necessarily fully engaged with them. Some simply put in time to appease wives or to be seen by others as good fathers—they were technically present but functionally absent. These were dads who watched the children when wives worked, ran errands with their children, or took them along when they worked out at the gym—but they were not necessarily interacting with their children while performing these tasks.

In some ways, fathering at the end of the century was extremely variable—at the same time that some fathers were actively engaged in childrearing and involved equally with mothers in raising their children, a growing number of children had little or no contact with their fathers. In between were men who were not substantively different in their interactions with children than their own fathers and grandfathers had been. Moreover, for many children, the man in their life was a stepfather.

One dimension of fatherhood that was not variable over the course of the century was the role of breadwinner. A constant expectation—and one that cut across social classes, regions of the country, and racial and ethnic groups—was that fathers' main duty was to earn money for their families. There were differing views in society about fathers' other responsibilities, but there was widespread agreement that fathers needed to bring home the bacon.

7

Children and
Adolescents in Families

Every culture defines childhood in its own way, determining what it means to be a child, how children should look, and how they should behave. In the United States, the conception of childhood has changed dramatically over time. Long ago, children were thought of as miniature adults; they dressed in similar clothing styles as adults and participated in the same work and leisure activities. Children were valued primarily for what they could add to family sustenance and, thus, family survival. Children were put to work as soon as they were able, and older children in large families often had full responsibility for the caretaking of younger children and babies. Because there was little or no birth control, many children were unwanted, and children too young to work were sometimes seen as a burden to parents. Many children died from disease and accidents, and probably from various kinds of neglect as well.

During the 19th-century Victorian era, childhood became recognized as a stage of life distinct from adulthood, and children came to be viewed as having their own unique thoughts and views about the world. They began to be seen as vulnerable beings needing careful nurturance and constant support to grow healthily. Childrearing became more exclusively the province of mothers because they were seen as more innately equipped to foster children's tender emotional needs. Gradually, it was believed that children needed protection from the adult world and time to be free from adult concerns. This view dominated much of 20th-century thinking about children and childrearing.

Swedish author Ellen Key argued in a 1909 book that the 20th century should be "the century of the child." She pleaded for parents to take a more active role in their children's lives, suggesting that children should be the center of family life. Her plea became prophesy. Over time, views of children as useful economic assets for families shifted to perceptions of them as fragile and in need of sheltering from life's hardships by parents and others. In many ways, the 20th century was indeed the century of the child.

THE PROGRESSIVE ERA

The turn of the century was the Progressive Era, a period of immense social and economic changes for American children. Their lives were greatly affected by the shift from a rural to an industrial economy and the resulting migration of families from rural areas to urban settings. Children also were affected by the rapid influx of new immigrants, rising family incomes, and smaller family sizes. Social reformers of all kinds were attempting to alter societal institutions for the betterment of all, and many of their efforts were focused on children's well-being—their health and mortality, their education, and their character.

In 1900, Americans were having fewer children than before. For example, among white Americans, in 1830 there were 128 children for every 100 adults, but by 1920 there were 66 children for every 100 adults. This declining fertility rate among native-born white Americans was of great concern to some, particularly in the North, where children of immigrants predominated—half of the children in Boston, Cleveland, St. Louis, Milwaukee, and San Francisco were immigrants in 1920. President Theodore Roosevelt went so far as to say that native-born white Americans were committing "race suicide," and eugenicists declared that "inappropriate" people were having too many children. These concerns were ill-founded, however; fertility among immigrant women nationwide was less than 5 percent higher than among white native women. Furthermore, in 1910 more than half of the white children were born to women who already had five or more children.

Infant and Child Mortality For centuries, infancy and childhood were considered perilous times of life. Vulnerable to childhood illnesses and diseases, many children did not survive to their first birthday. In fact, for most of history, parents were reluctant to become attached to infants and young children because mortality was so high; some parents waited until children were seven or eight, when they were more likely to survive into adulthood, to emotionally invest in them. After scientists in the late 19th century identified the microorganisms, or germs, responsible for many fatal childhood illnesses, mortality rates declined, but they were still high in 1900. More than half of all child mortalities occurred in the first year of a child's life, and most

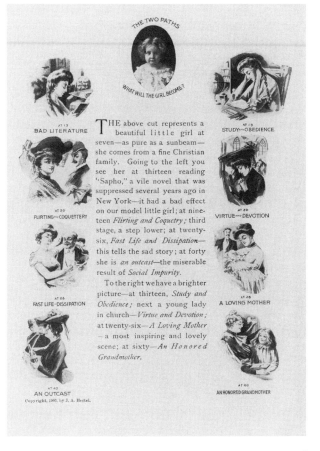

The two paths—What will the girl become? (Courtesy of the Library of Congress.)

of the rest occurred before they reached their fifth birthday. At the start of the century, 20 percent of American children died before they reached age five. Most deadly were gastrointestinal, respiratory, and infectious diseases. One of the most devastating diseases was diphtheria, which took thousands of young children's lives each year.

In the early 1900s, most women breast-fed their babies. If they were unable to breast-feed or chose not to, they used wet nurses, fed their babies animal milk, or fed them pap—a mixture of water, flour, and rice. The alternatives to breast-feeding significantly reduced infants' chances of survival—the milk and water supplies in cities were sources of typhoid, dysentery, and diarrhea. One estimate was that during the first month of life, the mortality rate for infants fed only artificial milk was 55 percent, the mortality rate was 36 percent for those provided with a combination of breast milk and formula, and 17 percent for infants fed breast milk only.

Women living on farms tended to breast-feed longer, which seemed to protect their children from disease. They also shared table food with their infants at younger ages than recommended, but the end result was positive for the health of most rural babies. Because working mothers were more likely to use formula, their infants were more likely to die. Breast-feeding was also less common among black mothers, resulting in a higher infant mortality rate for their infants. Despite these findings, most physicians in the first three decades of the century recommended that women shift away from breast-feeding to formula, because it was deemed to be a more scientific way to feed infants.

Early in the century, class differences and geographic location shaped children's diets. Low-income children, especially those in urban areas, were fed diets high in starch and low in dairy, which placed them at risk for rickets and pellagra. Children on farms tended to have far better diets regardless of income because they were more likely to eat fresh fruits and vegetables as well as meat and diary products. Urban children typically had little access to fresh foods until food distribution was available via the railroads.

By 1910, vitamins had been identified as necessary for good health, and nutrition researchers began emphasizing the importance of good nutrition for children. Early in the century, the milk consumption of children had been low, but milk producers capitalized on Americans' new fascination with vitamins and began recommending that children drink at least a quart of milk a day. Only middle-class families were able to afford that much milk.

As was true throughout the century, poverty—particularly urban poverty—was related to higher rates of infant and childhood death. Poor children were likely to be underweight because they got neither enough food nor the right kind of food to stay healthy, or they were overweight due to eating more starches and animal fats, which were cheap. Although the Depression further worsened the diets of millions of Americans, many children were poorly fed simply because their parents did not know how to feed them properly.

Urban children also often lived in crowded, unsanitary conditions that increased their exposure to infection. It was generally much safer to grow up in rural than in densely populated urban areas. Their relative isolation protected children from others' germs. Mortality for children was also related to race and ethnicity—death rates for black and Native American children were significantly higher than for whites, even in rural areas. Overall, black and Native American children were poorer than white Americans and could not pay for good health care or healthy living environments.

Educational programs on home sanitation and nutrition eventually helped lower child mortality rates. Physicians in the 19th century had discovered an association between impure milk and infant death rates, so, by the start of the 20th century, there were many efforts to instruct new mothers about the importance of clean milk. In 1908, Chicago became the first city in the world to require pasteurization of milk to reduce infant mortality. By 1910, well-baby clinics and home visits by public health nurses designed to educate mothers about sanitation and infant nutrition were established programs in many urban areas. Child deaths from diarrhea—a cause of many fatalities at the time—had declined rapidly by 1920, in part due to healthier diets and cleaner homes.

Concerns about Children's Welfare: The "Child Savers"

As children became more likely to survive childhood and as families became smaller, parents had more time, money, and energy to spend on each child. The ideal of intensive parenting, prolonged economic dependence of children, and the need for longer periods of time spent in education made having fewer children more practical—at least for urban middle-class parents. This goal was not attainable for all families, however, because children in many immigrant, working-class, and farm families needed to work and contribute to their families' income.

As the view of children needing to be nurtured and protected grew more popular, so did the notion that the care of children should not be the sole responsibility of parents. The "child saving" movement grew out of concerns for the well-being of poor and immigrant children, and the notion that parents might not always be able to raise their children properly. In 1912, the federal government established the Children's Bureau, a research office that distributed pamphlets and booklets about baby and child care. The underlying assumption of these publications was that proper protection and socialization would better equip all children to carry the nation into the future. Most immigrant and middle-class mothers welcomed the information. The Children's Bureau was based on the philosophy that every child had a right to be safe from abuse and free from poverty, exploitation from adults, and ill health. The Bureau's advocates fought for a juvenile court system, federal support for programs designed to enhance infants' and children's health, and aid to poor families with dependent children.

Protection from cruelty. U.S. society has shown interest in child abuse erratically over the years. The reformers of the late 19th century expressed some interest, and by 1908 there were 55 organizations designed to protect children from cruelty and abuse. Unlike modern child abuse groups, these organizations did not question parents' rights to physically punish and beat their children. Their attention was placed almost solely on neglect by poor immigrant parents, single mothers, and unemployed parents. Many times, parents themselves brought their children to these organizations because they were unable to feed or care for them.

Orphanages, adoption, and foster care. Early in the century, many children were on their own, living in the streets and sleeping in alleyways in cities across the country. They were homeless for various reasons—some were runaways, others were abandoned by their parents, orphaned, or had become separated from their parents for other reasons. Historians estimate that as many as 30,000 homeless children lived in New York City at the turn of the century, mostly the children of German and Irish immigrants.

It was not unusual for children to find themselves without parental support; life spans were short, so children's parents tended to die at an early age. In 1900, 20 percent to 30 percent of all minor children had experienced the death of at least one parent. When fathers died, children often found themselves in dire straits, even when their mothers were alive—women were usually not employed outside the home, and when they did work it was for extremely low wages that were inadequate for raising children. Some older children went to work in such cases, and some left home to ease their family's burdens. Some parents had to give their children up for adoption because they either could not afford to feed them or they could not look after them and also work. Although day nurseries and playgrounds were established in cities so that working parents could leave their children during the day while they made a living, most parents did not like to leave their children at these centers because the quality of care was low.

Some children lived in almshouses (or poorhouses) with people of all ages, and many were placed in orphanages. Few children were true orphans, however; that is, seldom were both parents dead. In 1910, there were approximately 150,000 children living in about 1,150 orphanages across the country. Children in orphanages tended to receive harsh treatment and little warmth and affection and sometimes were forced to work at strenuous and exhausting jobs to help pay for their keep. Food was generally of poor quality and insufficient amounts. As awful as conditions in orphanages were, many poor parents placed their children there because the alternative was slow starvation.

Other alternative living arrangements for homeless children were temporary foster families or permanent adoptive families. During the 1909 White House Conference on the Care of Dependent Children, attendees agreed that children should live with their mothers when possible, and that foster homes were the next best option. Permanent adoption was the goal for many religious and charitable organizations, as well as some state agencies. "Orphan trains"—an adoption experiment that began in the mid-19th century—were the brainchild of Charles Loring Brace, founder of the Children's Aid Society, who believed that children would be happy to work in exchange for a place to live. Homeless or displaced children in the Northeast were sent by railroad to live, work, and perhaps be adopted by families in the Midwest. Although many reformers thought it was better to place children with foster families in their home states, between 1853 and 1929, orphan trains resulted in about 200,000 children being placed with families in other states. Many children were formally adopted, but some were treated as slave labor. Younger children generally adapted well, but many older children became homesick and eventually headed back east. Others ran away and became homeless rather than work as slaves for cruel foster parents.

Many retarded or mentally ill children were institutionalized because their parents could not manage them and handle the demands of making a living. Given concerns about the inheritability of insanity and retardation, thousands of children and young adults were placed in sexually segregated institutions and sterilized. This practice was upheld in a 1927 U.S. Supreme Court decision and continued well into the 1960s.

Given the low level of care and sometimes cruel treatments suffered by children in orphanages and other institutionalized care arrangements, a major goal of child welfare reformers of this era was to end the practice of institutionalizing dependent children. In 1911, the state of Illinois enacted a law allotting widows a pension so they could care for their children in their homes. By 1919, 39 states and two territories had adopted mothers' pensions. However, eligibility for these pensions was narrow—blacks were excluded in most states, as were divorced women, never-married mothers, and women who engaged in what was seen as immoral behavior—smoking, drinking alcohol, and not attending church. In addition, these pensions were generally so small that widowed mothers still had to find work to feed their children. Nonetheless, this was the first recognition that the public had an obligation to provide support for dependent children. In 1929, the Children's Bureau sponsored a conference in Washington, DC, to address the adequacy of child welfare. Participants decided that state governments should be more active in providing welfare programs, and they argued that social casework should be available for families of at-risk children. Later that year, however, the country entered the Depression, which prevented these dreams from becoming reality.

Child labor. One of the main thrusts of the child reform movement was children's employment. The belief that all children, even those from working-class families, deserved a childhood devoted to play and education was a driving force for the child welfare reformers. Child labor reformers did not include farm work, however, because this type of work was thought to build character; nor did they target service jobs such as newsboys, soda jerks, and store clerks.

Labor organizations joined the reformers in supporting laws curtailing child labor because they wanted to protect jobs for their members, but there was a great deal of opposition to laws and policies that would limit child employment. Most poor parents opposed these reforms because they needed the incomes from their children. A survey of Polish immigrants in 1911 found that children of unskilled workers contributed 46 percent of their family's income; the children of skilled workers contributed 35 percent. The Catholic Church opposed child labor laws because of concerns about government intrusion into family life and because poor parents, many of whom were Catholics, needed the money. Industry leaders who employed large numbers of poorly paid children in mining jobs, canneries, and textile factories also opposed laws limiting child labor. Given the widespread opposition, child labor reforms were slow in becoming laws. The first federal child labor bill was proposed and defeated in 1906; and the first one that passed (in 1916) was declared unconstitutional by the Supreme Court in 1918. Although several states had some restrictions on child labor, it was not until the Depression years that the federal government responded with laws of its own.

The "Invention" of Adolescence

In 1904, G. Stanley Hall's book, *Adolescence,* based on years of scientific study of children, significantly influenced how youth were thought about and treated. Hall was instrumental in what was known as the child study movement, which began late in the 19th century and had as its aim the scientific study of children and their development. Hall's writings about adolescence contributed significantly toward establishing adolescence as a qualitatively different period of life from what preceded or followed—characterized by intense emotions, conflicts with parents, and exploratory behaviors. At a time when youngsters, as adolescents were known at the time, had been expected to act like adults at a relatively young age, Hall suggested it was important to overlook their misbehavior and quirks because these behaviors and attitudes were part of growing up. Although the concept of adolescence as a period of life was not new, Hall was the first to give this age group a label and describe it as a stage distinct from childhood and adulthood. Prior to Hall, educators had emphasized continuity between childhood and adulthood, but to Hall adolescence was a time of developmental crisis. He argued that, during this developmentally chaotic time, adolescents needed to be protected from the challenges of adulthood and separated as much as possible from the world of adults, except for receiving guidance from caring adults who would help them reach adulthood safely.

Hall and other child study movement researchers, along with many lay people, proposed that radical changes occurred when children reached adolescence, and some physicians suggested to parents that feeble-minded and otherwise unfortunate children would be all right once they reached puberty. Hall's work influenced generations of scholars' thinking about the nature of adolescence, and this body of scholarly work affected how society would treat adolescents for much of the century.

Several factors contributed to the "discovery" or "invention" of adolescence. The U.S. economy was expanding, so the need for child workers diminished, making it more acceptable to consider adolescence as an extension of childhood rather than as immature adulthood. Children spent longer periods of time in formal schooling, which meant that adolescence began to be seen as the age when children were in high school.

The greater number of years in which middle- and upper-class children remained dependent on their parents was reflected in changes in many social institutions. New types of courts were established, public education became more age graded

Children, Adolescents, and Societal Institutions

and was expanded to reach more children and youth, and organizations were started whose goals were to help build character and good citizenship among young people.

Juvenile courts. As adolescence came to be viewed as a unique stage, child advocates fought for children to be tried in their own system and protected from adult expectations and adult penalties. Juvenile court advocates argued that adolescents lacked the wisdom and decision-making abilities of adults and were still being shaped as people—thus, juvenile courts were designed to try to help rehabilitate young people before they entered a life of crime. Instead of jailing them, juvenile courts used probation officers much like social workers to assess a young person's home environment and help propose treatments that would change their lives.

The first juvenile court was established in Chicago in 1899. Ten states had juvenile court laws by 1905; this increased to 46 states by 1915 (Macleod, 1998). In the end, however, many juvenile courts denied children some legal protections, and they also made it possible for young people to be removed from their homes or punished for acts that would be considered lesser crimes or not crimes at all, if committed by adults. For instance, juveniles were arrested in New York in 1913 for playing with water pistols, throwing snowballs and stones, and shooting craps in the street. Critics accused the juvenile courts of prejudicial judgments against blacks—during the 1920s, black young people in New York City were twice as likely as whites to be arraigned in juvenile court, and, following arraignment, blacks received fewer services and were less likely than white youths to be placed on probation.

Education. At the beginning of the century, education was becoming one of the most common, unifying experiences for American children and adolescents. More and more parents, particularly those in the middle class, believed education was critical for their children to prepare for adulthood. In 1870, about 6.8 million children and adolescents attended school. By 1900, this number had grown to about 15.5 million, or 72 percent of the children between the ages of 5 and 17. However, most children dropped out of school after completing just a few years, and only about 8 percent of youth between ages 14 and 17 were enrolled in 1900.

Many children who were enrolled in school attended irregularly. School attendance varied by geographic region, with children in the South and

Southwest less likely to attend than children in other parts of the country. Attendance also depended on whether children lived in rural or urban areas, with urban children more likely than those from rural settings to be in school. Many families, especially rural ones, could not afford to have their children regularly attend school; they were needed to help with housework, farm work, and to contribute to their families' incomes. It was common for parents on farms and ranches to keep their children at home for weeks at a time to help plant, care for, and harvest crops. A lack of schools also contributed to lower attendance rates in rural areas. Although one-room schools containing grades one through eight and children ages 5 to 17 were usually within walking distance, many children from farms had to travel great distances to attend high school. Because of this, some farm children rode horses to school and stabled them during the day; others boarded with families in town during the week.

As society and the economy became increasingly complex, young people and their parents gradually recognized they could not compete for jobs without an education. Additionally, job opportunities for young people had diminished, as social reformers had somewhat discouraged factory owners from hiring children and teenagers. These combined factors contributed to rising school enrollments, but there were age group differences because dropout rates were high. By 1918, all states had enacted compulsory attendance laws; seven states required attendance until age 15, 31 states required attendance until age 16. As a result, high school enrollments doubled nearly every decade between 1890 and 1920, from 7 percent in 1890 to 22 percent in 1920. Only one in six adolescents, however, finished high school in 1920.

Quality of education. At the turn of the century, schools ranged from drafty shacks to modern buildings, and some had antiquated textbooks while others had the newest equipment and educational aids available. In many urban schools, children sat together in cramped rooms, interacted little with one another, and engaged in large-group instruction or in solitary "busy work." Although many rural one-room schoolhouses were dilapidated, they had the advantage of being less crowded than urban schools, resulting in more one-on-one time with the teachers. Older children in one-room schools helped teach younger children, which reinforced learning for both age groups.

Most reformers of the era, however, believed that urban schools were superior to rural ones, so they sought to upgrade them following strategies used in cities—centralization, close supervision of children by teachers and other adults, age-grading of instruction, and large-group instruction. In 1908, President Theodore Roosevelt appointed a Country Life Commission to investigate rural deficiencies. The commission criticized the relevancy of instruction in many rural one-room schools and argued that teachers were training farmers' children for white collar jobs in urban areas rather than preparing them for farm work and domestic tasks. Farm parents countered that they could teach their children about agriculture and household tasks; they preferred their children's education to focus on reading, writing, and math. In 1920, 195,000 one-room schools still existed nationwide, and, despite criticisms of the inadequacies of the one-room school, only 10,000 rural schools had consolidated by 1920, and many of those had only two rooms.

During the 1910s and 1920s, larger schools began offering extracurricular activities (e.g., athletics, debate teams, drama clubs, musical groups, and other clubs); smaller schools generally sponsored few activities. To educators, high school focused the attention of youth on a healthy social life. However, educators increasingly found that school-sponsored activities had to compete with commercial entertainment (e.g., movie theaters, dance halls), and, although they were able to control some activities within schools, they could not prevent the creation of independent sororities and fraternities in about half of larger high schools by 1904. Educators saw these groups as fostering drinking and smoking, encouraging lewd behaviors, and interfering with academic achievement.

Despite their emphasis on preparing young people for adulthood, many educators also conferred on youth a more childlike status. The Cardinal Principles of Secondary Education report, published in 1918 for the National Education Association, recommended schools follow a specific set of objectives: (1) health, (2) command of fundamental processes, (3) worthy home-membership, (4) vocation, (5) citizenship, (6) worthy use of leisure, and (7) ethical character. Thus, the implicit belief was that young people were still children and must be told exactly what to believe and do. All youth were instructed to meet society's expectations for adulthood, with girls learning how to efficiently run their homes and boys learning to provide for their families.

Socializing immigrants. Many social reformers saw schools as a way to help Americanize immigrant children, as well as those from poor and working-class families. They were especially concerned about the immigrants who had begun arriving during the late 19th century and the first two decades of the 20th century. Whereas earlier immigrants hailed from northern and western Europe, many new immigrants came from southern and eastern Europe, spoke little English, and most were Catholic or Jewish, which was seen as a threat to the Protestant majority in the United States. Partly out of fear of these new immigrants and their practices and behaviors, many teachers used harsh discipline and public humiliation to control immigrant children's behaviors. Most schools were taught in English only, so some immigrants who were unable or unwilling to learn English left school.

School teachers typically emphasized American experience with little consideration for other cultural practices or needs. In home economics classes, teachers emphasized middle-class standards for domestic tasks that placed some immigrant girls at odds with their mothers' ways. For instance, girls learned recipes that mixed meat and dairy products, which violated kosher practices of Orthodox Jews. Vocational classes frequently taught lower-class boys skills that limited them to entry-level positions. It eventually became clear to school leaders that these approaches would not benefit U.S. society and were not effective in socializing immigrants. Schools gradually established classes and services to cater to immigrants' needs, including special English classes.

Black students. Race was a factor in schooling; black children attended at lower rates than whites, and they quit at younger ages on average than did whites. This was mostly due to economic necessity—most rural black children needed to work and add to family incomes. In 1896, in *Plessy v. Ferguson,* the Supreme Court ruled that schools and other public facilities that were "separate but equal" did not violate the Constitution; therefore, in most of the United States, but especially the South, education was segregated by race.

Segregation limited the number of high schools available to black youth. In 1916, there were 67 high schools for black youth in the South, and in 1928 this number had increased to 1,860. Funding for black classrooms and teachers was far less than that provided for white schools. In the South, governments spent more than twice as much on schools for white students as they did for black students. The school year also was much shorter for black children, in part due to lack of funding, but also so that black students could help in the fields. Many white landowners saw no need for young blacks to be educated because they believed that they would never live an independent life. Discrimination and prejudicial practices discouraged black students and their parents from having high ambitions—blacks were told repeatedly that their opportunities for social class advancement would be limited by their skin color, regardless of educational attainment or talents. In 1930 in the rural South, only 11 percent of black teenagers were enrolled in high school.

Native Americans. For many, the term *boarding school* evokes thoughts of exclusive schools for the wealthy elite, but for Native Americans, boarding schools represented something very different. Beginning late in the 19th century, the Bureau of Indian Affairs was charged with establishing schools away from Indian reservations to assimilate Native American children into white American culture. In 1889, as part of the Indian Homestead Act, officially known as the Dawes Act, the government allocated parcels of reservation land to individual Native American families and sold the remaining land to white Americans. Funds from the sales were used to establish Indian schools where students could be immersed in white culture and taught to become more like mainstream Americans. In 1900, 5,000 Native American children attended public schools, and another 17,000 were sent to one of 150 boarding schools that were hundreds or thousands of miles away from their families. In the 1920s, at the peak of the Indian boarding school movement, more than 30,000 children were enrolled.

Many parents who were approached about sending their children to Indian schools were reluctant. Sending children away went against Native American cultural norms that valued strong family cohesion (Szasz, 1985), but many did so anyway. Some parents were willing to have their children attend the schools because they wanted them to be educated, but others were given no choice—they were threatened with having their food supplies cut off unless they gave their children to the boarding schools.

The schools varied greatly from reservation life. Indian children faced actions intended to strip them of their tribal and cultural identities; many were given short haircuts, and their traditional clothing was taken away. They were also given English names that bore little resemblance to their given names. (European immigrant children's names were also changed to sound more American, but their new names usually resembled their old names.) Many children were so homesick that they ran away despite being thousands of miles from home. Those caught running away were likely to face harsh, military-like punishments when they were returned to the schools. Children also were punished for speaking their native language at school.

Many Indian schools lacked funds to adequately clothe and feed the children so some administrators, unable to afford paid help, used student labor to keep their schools running. Girls were taught to cook, sew, and clean house, and boys were taught carpentry, blacksmithing, and farming. These skills were then put to use to maintain the schools.

By the 1920s, the schools had numerous critics who recognized that they were not in the best interest of Indian children. Secretary of the Interior Hubert Work commissioned a study on federal Indian policy; the 1928 report heavily criticized the harsh treatment children endured, the poor education they received, and the condition of school buildings. Embarrassed by the report, U.S. President Herbert Hoover increased funds to the schools, but most of the money went to increasing the food allocations to help schools meet nutrition minimum requirements rather than improving the quality of education. Indian schools, including boarding schools, were still in operation at the end of the century, but they were located near Indian reservations and students attended the schools voluntarily.

In cities at the turn of the century, children were increasingly spending time away from home where they were influenced more by peers than parents. Many adults believed that children should spend their free time doing something useful. As concerns grew about what unsupervised children were doing, several organizations were established to provide boys and girls with character-building information and experiences and to prepare

Youth Organizations

them for adult roles as husbands, wives, and community members. Reformers were initially mostly concerned about boys, because they left school earlier, and in 1912, 20 times more programs served boys than girls (Macleod, 1998). All of these organizations served a fairly narrow range of young people—mostly white, middle-class children and adolescents. The leaders came from the ranks of the middle class, and their children and friends of their children were the participants. Boys and girls usually were in separate organizations with different goals; when they were together— such as in 4-H clubs—activities often were divided along gender lines (e.g., cake decorating and fashion shows for girls, firearm safety for boys). Even the mottos of two of the leading organizations indicated different gender expectations—Boy Scouts were asked to "be prepared," and Girl Scouts were expected to "be happy."

One of the most successful organizations was the Boy Scouts of America, founded by a British general, Robert S. S. Baden-Powell in 1907, and established in the United States around 1910. In 1914, there were more than 100,000 Boy Scouts, and there were 430,000 by the mid-1920s. In 1999, 3.4 million boys were members of almost 124,000 scout units. Scouting helped allay some adults' fears about how boys were possibly being influenced by social changes. Scout leaders believed that scouting helped adults shape boys' character by instilling traditional values and morals. *Boys' Life,* the official magazine for the Boy Scouts of America, offered information about moneymaking strategies to help boys learn how to make a good living and support their families. One of the motivations for the American Boy Scout movement was to toughen up generations of young boys that some critics saw as less masculine and less manly than their fathers and grandfathers had been as boys. Although leaders hoped to prolong preadolescent boyhood, scouting appealed primarily to younger boys and most quit around puberty.

Girls' organizations emphasized skills girls needed to fulfill domestic roles in adulthood. They needed to learn about music, art, and theater so they would be able to provide their children with a rich introduction to life, and they also needed to learn skills such as housework, cooking, shopping, and nursing. One of the most popular organizations for girls was the Girl Scouts, well known for their cookie sales. In 1912, Girl Scouts founder Juliette Low organized a group of 18 girls in Atlanta, Georgia. In addition to encouraging girls to be proficient as homemakers, Low's other concern was to bring girls out of the isolation of their homes so they could enjoy outdoor activities in the fresh air. By 1920, there were 50,000 members nationwide; membership numbered over 3.5 million at the end of the century. Another girls' organization, Camp Fire Girls, was founded in 1910 by Luther and Charlotte Vetter Gulick, who hoped to reiterate "the first grand division of labor" when "the woman stayed at home and kept the fires burning" (Macleod, 1998, p. 148). By 1917, total membership numbered about 94,000. Boys were invited to join in 1975, and the organization was renamed Camp Fire Boys and Girls; in 1999, boys comprised about 45 percent of the membership of 667,000.

4-H started around 1902 as a way to bring science and technology from land grant universities and the United States Department of Agriculture to young people across the country. Boys and girls participated in clubs specializing in activities such as canning tomatoes, growing vegetables, and raising livestock. By 1912, nearly 73,000 boys and 23,000 girls were 4-H members. After the Smith-Lever Act established federal and state cooperation in land grant university extension programs in 1914, extension became the primary sponsor of 4-H, and the program flourished, especially after World War I. Children participated in individual projects, such as raising livestock or growing vegetables, that were separate from families' overall farming operations, and they competed for blue ribbons at county and state fairs. Originally, boys and girls participated together, but by 1919, club leaders encouraged girls to participate in cooking, sewing, and other gendered activities to help them prepare for their adult roles. Separate 4-H clubs and activities were established for black children; by 1923, more than 55,000 were in 4-H. In 1943, 4-H enrolled 1.6 million participants, ages 10 to 20, and members could choose from over 30 projects, including the traditional livestock and crops as well as food preservation, clothing, arts and crafts, and junior leadership. In 1974, 4-H reached a membership of 7 million children and adolescents, and by the end of the century, millions remained involved in both rural and urban area clubs.

Although the Progressive Era started the "century of the child," for many children and their families not much changed, or at least changes were extremely gradual. For instance, children from farming families likely did not notice that their **Children at Home** parents became more child-centered, nor did they find their adolescent years to be a moratorium from adult work and concerns. Instead, they continued to work alongside their parents as farmers. Some may have attended a few years more of school than they would have in earlier times, but rural life was probably almost as busy and demanding of long hours from all family members as it was in the decades prior to the 20th century. Family lives of working-class children and immigrants also probably were not generally affected by the advice of childrearing experts and the child study movement to be more child-focused—social institutions that were in contact with children from these families interacted with them in different ways than in the past, but family life, and parent-child relations in particular, were not drastically different than they were before. Changes in children and their families were occurring, but not all American families experienced the same changes at the same pace.

Leisure time. Gradually, as the economy grew and efforts to limit child workers in factories and mines began to prevail, even working-class children found that they had more leisure time than previously. Certainly, middle-class children had more time to play. In 1918, an international conference on childhood promoted a New Bill of Rights of Childhood, including "a right to play." Spurred on by the advice of childrearing experts, parents increasingly recognized the importance of children's play to development so they found ways to make it constructive.

At the turn of the century, most young children in cities played on the sidewalks and streets. For many, the streets represented a place where they could act as they chose. Boys began creating societies for themselves, spending time with others who shared common interests. The advent of automobiles made this practice dangerous, and children's deaths in traffic accidents nationwide nearly doubled between 1915 and 1920 (Macleod, 1998).

Concerned about children's safety and looking for a way to curb juvenile delinquency, progressive reformers set out to develop areas where children could play safely in crowded urban neighborhoods. In 1906, Joseph Lee joined Henry Curtis, director of playgrounds in Washington, DC, and Luther Gulick, director of physical education for New York City public schools, to develop the Playground Association of America. The three men firmly believed in the importance of play as a natural part of development and thought that play and work should go hand in hand. They believed, however, that play time should be regulated in adult-supervised games with rules. Although public playgrounds soon were built in cities across the country, many children still preferred street play.

The rise of adolescence saw an increase in commercial enterprises designed to help them spend their free time away from parents. Amusement parks, movie theaters, and ice cream parlors grew in abundance because urban and suburban adolescents had time and money to spend. Although they had less discretionary money to spend than later adolescents would, they had enough—and they had sufficient free time for businesses to begin marketing their products specifically to them.

Toys. Toy manufacturers introduced many new toy designs at the turn of the century. Prior to the Progressive Era, most toys were intended to be enjoyed by several children at once—kites, marbles, jump ropes, balls of all kinds—but many of the new toys were aimed at solitary players. Among the most popular were cast-iron mechanical banks in the shape of familiar scenes and characters. Many children loved these banks because of the movements they made when change was inserted. Adults liked them because they helped children learn to save money. Other playthings, such as Crayola crayons, first made in 1903, encouraged children's creativity and imagination. There were several varieties of construction toys aimed for boys, including Erector Sets (1913) and Lincoln Logs (1916). Lincoln Logs provided children a nostalgic image of earlier times, and Erector Sets gave children an opportunity to imagine the future.

Toys for girls were designed to socialize them for motherhood and domestic life—tea sets, doll houses, and, of course, dolls were favorite gifts for parents to give their daughters. Prior to the 20th century, most dolls were handmade. Beginning around 1900, dolls that had small

Children's game at the turn of the century. (Courtesy of the Library of Congress.)

straight eyes, high cheeks, and an adult body were replaced with baby dolls that had large, round, wide-open eyes, chubby cheeks, and a more child-like body. Dolls provided parents the opportunity to teach nurturing behaviors and to instill domestic values in their daughters.

In the 1920s, manufacturers began advertising directly to children, creating consumer interests that parents would have to satisfy. These advertising efforts were effective, resulting in yo-yos becoming the first toy fad (in 1928). By the end of the 1920s, celebrities and cartoons were used to sell toys, much as they were later in the century. Mickey Mouse watches, Shirley Temple dolls, and other movie tie-ins helped fuel the demand for manufactured playthings.

Clothing. As early as the 16th century, customs required that children have clothing unique from adult clothing. At the turn of the 20th century, it was not uncommon for infants from wealthy families to wear gowns up to a yard and a half long. Beginning at six months, they were dressed in gowns that ended just above the ankle. Although babies' clothes had become simpler by 1920, flannel petticoats and stiff linen binders were still considered necessary for most babies.

Most older children continued to wear fancy clothing. It was considered inappropriate for older girls to wear pants, so they were expected to wear skirts and dresses. Young boys wore knickers with knee socks until around age 12 to 15, when they began wearing long pants. As late as 1910,

Boy in knickers. (Courtesy of the authors.)

however, very young children's clothing was androgynous—both boys and girls wore gowns up to age six, and there were no gender distinctions in colors. However, feminization of the home and young boys' concerns about being mistaken for girls led to style updates. It also became less common for young boys to be dressed in gowns. The notion that pink is for girls and blue is for boys was not well established until the 1930s.

THE DEPRESSION YEARS

Infants and Breast-Feeding

During the 1930s, more than 70 percent of firstborn children were breast-fed. The propensity to breast-feed probably had more to do with the cost of formula than recognition of breast-feeding's benefits. Commercially prepared powder formulas that imitated human milk were available as early as the late 1800s, but they were expensive and seldom used. By 1930, there had been improvements in the handling of milk, and most families had iceboxes that could be used for storing milk. Vitamin supplements, glass bottles, and rubber nipples that could be sterilized became available, and L. Emmett Holt (1894) a leading child expert of the era, recommended that mothers use modified cow's milk to provide their infants with adequate nutrition. Formula feeding was only moderately successful, however. Some formula-fed infants were not getting enough fatty acids, and many suffered from iron deficiency (commercially prepared, iron-fortified formulas were not introduced until 1959). Despite poor outcomes, as the economic burdens of the Depression lifted, the number of mothers who breast-fed dropped to 50 percent and continued to decline until the mid-1970s.

The Depression was a frightening time for children. In 1932, at the height of the Depression, 28 percent of America's households did not have a single employed person living in them. Economic burdens meant that for many children life was full of stress, tension, and constant insecurity about the future. Many families were forced from their homes because they could not pay rent or taxes, and some children and families became homeless. An estimated half million children were homeless during the winter of 1931, and the worst of the Depression was not until 1932. Some children found shelter with extended family members, but not all were so fortunate. In some families, children were separated from their parents or siblings—parents placed their children with whoever would take them. Many fathers left their families to find work, and some parents had to give up their children to orphanages because they were unable to provide adequate food and clothing. Other parents placed their children in temporary foster homes, and many families volunteered to be foster families to take advantage of the free labor that foster children represented.

Family Life for Children and Adolescents

With parents devoted to finding ways to earn a living, children were left with increasing household responsibilities, and many older children and adolescents were required to find ways to contribute to family income. This was more difficult than it had been in prior decades because high rates of unemployment accomplished what years of child labor reformers could not—children and adolescents were fired from factories, mines, and businesses. Just as pressure was put on women to give up jobs so men could work, young workers were dismissed to make room for men, if there were any jobs to be had at all.

Greatest generation. The stress of family and community life during the Depression may have forged an unusual degree of toughness in the children and adolescents who grew up in those bleak years. Later called the greatest generation in U.S. history, these youngsters had to deal with higher than usual amounts of family conflict, father absence, household migration in the search for work, and family deterioration, all while dealing with real and ever-present questions about getting enough food to eat and finding a place to live. Almost overnight, poor families became destitute, working-class and middle-class families became poor, and solutions to the economic hardships facing individuals and families seemed beyond individual or even local government solutions. Against this backdrop, many American children learned to cope with challenges, take care of themselves when necessary, and contribute when they could.

Children's clothing changed during the 1930s to reflect the need for durability. Most families could not afford many clothes, so boys began to wear blue jeans because they were easy to wash and extremely durable. Boys' causal wear increasingly consisted of blue jeans, T-shirts, and sneakers, a style that continued to be popular throughout the rest of the century. Clothing also became more androgynous, perhaps so that hand-me-downs could be used regardless of the sex of the younger children. Girls also wore jeans, T-shirts, and sneakers, at least when playing.

As might be expected, games that children played during the Depression seldom involved expensive toys or equipment. Among boys, the most popular choices were baseball, basketball, marbles, jacks, and catching-fleeing games (e.g., blind man's bluff, king of the hill, drop the handkerchief); baseball was the most popular activity by far. Girls were more likely than boys to enjoy singing games (e.g., London Bridge, Here we go round the mulberry bush) and jumping-hopping games (e.g., hopscotch, jumping rope). The most popular game among girls was jacks. Younger girls enjoyed playing school and house.

When children lacked the proper equipment for games, homemade substitutes usually were easily found—an old broomstick became a bat, a taped-up ball of cloth became a baseball, a hollyhock bloom became a doll. Depression-era children had to be creative and resourceful—parents were too concerned with trying to find work or holding on to jobs to spend as much time monitoring and watching after children as they had in previous decades.

Not surprisingly, given the stress and strife that families faced, one societal problem during the 1930s was the high number of transient, or runaway, youth. With lack of parental control and supervision, adults worried that the rise in disaffected youths spelled serious problems for society. These youth were born at a time when living the American dream was a reality for many, but by the time they reached adolescence, the Depression had created an economic outlook in which they had little hope for a prosperous future. According to social workers, many youth described themselves as "discouraged, disgusted, sullen, and bitter" (Palladino, 1996, p. 38). In 1936, Maxine Davis wrote,

This generation does not think. While the level of intelligence is high, it is atrophied with inactivity. These young men and women do not think for themselves.

They take what they like of what they hear, and reject by instinct rather than by reason. . . . They are utterly lacking in any sense of responsibility toward the conduct of this nation . . . This generation is straying aimlessly toward middle age. Soon it [the generation of youth] may be altogether lost. Then we as a nation will face a future dominated by a defeated citizenry. . . . These boys and girls are *ours.* Under prompt, competent handling, they may yet be transmuted into normal, busy, productive men and women. (pp. 369–371)

To address the problem of out-of-school and transient youth, the federal government established the National Youth Administration (NYA), which provided job training, apprenticeships, and education. Boys were trained in farming and mechanics while girls learned domestic skills. The NYA was also a character-building program, designed to help disadvantaged youth learn middle-class values. Although the NYA helped out-of-school youth learn new skills, it did not provide them with a high school diploma, so they were not competitive in an already tight job market. The NYA was successful, however, in discouraging other youth from dropping out of school by funding jobs for high school students over age 16 whose families were struggling to make ends meet. Participants were generally pleased with the program. It helped diminish their concerns about their families' financial problems, and they had enough money to buy the same supplies as their classmates and to look and dress like them.

Education In the early 1930s, despite mandatory attendance laws in many states, the U.S. Bureau of Education estimated that more than 25 percent of school-aged children were not in school. Previously, high school had been primarily reserved for the wealthy elite and the middle class, but as the Depression progressed, more teenagers were moved out of the workplace and into school so that adult men could be employed. By 1936, 65 percent of teenagers were high school students; 75 percent were in high school by 1939; and, by 1940, half of the country's 17-year-olds were high school graduates— twice as many as there were just before the Depression began in 1929 (Palladino, 1996).

Ironically, as school enrollments increased, many communities slashed their school budgets in response to taxpayers' complaints. Taxpayers wanted school boards to cut out the frills and the fads, such as kindergartens, music classes, school lunches, classes for children with learning impairments, and vocational training. Citizens had to tighten their belts at home, and they expected schools to do the same. Many citizens resented and considered unnecessary classes such as music and art that had not been available in the past. One person said, "I never got farther than the fifth grade. . . . Just tell me how a course in French is any good to a boy who is going to be a bank teller or a carpenter?" (Davis, 1936, p. 63).

The years 1933 and 1934 were the worst for the nation's schools. Because they were funded by property taxes, schools were hit hard by the Depression. Expenditures for students dropped nationwide, many schools were open only half as long as they should have been, and 700 schools across the country closed. In the mid-1930s, the National Education Association collected data from half the states and discovered that more than 700,000 school children were attending schools that were condemned for being unsafe or unsanitary. Staff reductions led to classroom overcrowding—sometimes 80 children attended classes in rooms intended for 30 (Davis, 1936). Textbooks were outdated, and some children studied from history books that made no mention of World War I.

Indian boarding schools. Like most other families, Native American families were severely affected by the Depression. Many parents who previously had been able to prevent the Bureau of Indian Affairs from taking their children to boarding schools now found it necessary to send their children because they lacked the means to provide adequate care. Ironically, the government began closing many of the schools because of the costs of running them, and those that remained open usually were filled beyond capacity. By 1941, there were 49 schools with an enrollment of 14,000, compared to 21,000 enrolled in 77 schools in 1928 (Hawes, 1997).

Another irony of Indian boarding schools was that many failed to prepare Native American children for their adult roles. After being educated for life in urban, white America, most students returned to reservations, where they had little in common with family and tribe members. Some lacked the skills necessary to work on the reservation and had forgotten their own languages. They also were different in appearance and had new values and beliefs. Gradually, educators began to realize that the children should be trained for life on the reservation instead of being prepared to work in the cities; therefore, during the 1930s, many schools stressed preparation for rural living. Some introduced classes in Indian history and arts, and some students were allowed to return home to celebrate religious holidays. Most schools also used less military-style discipline. Despite changes, however, an emphasis on white American culture remained.

With the arrival of Word War II, many Indian schools were forced to close. About 24,000 Indians served in the armed forces, and another 40,000 were employed in war-related positions. After the war, many American Indians, especially war veterans, moved to urban areas to find jobs. With this shift came a renewed interest in teaching about urban life in the remaining Indian schools, including offering urban-oriented courses for returning veterans.

Federal Aid to Families

During the Depression, the federal government introduced a number of plans to help Americans. Many programs, such as the Works Progress Administration, helped families by creating work for family breadwinners. One plan designed to provide support for children was Aid to

Dependent Children, which later became Aid to Families with Dependent Children. Through this system, part of the Social Security Act of 1935, federal funds were distributed to states, and states were required to create agencies to distribute aid to eligible families based on federal guidelines. The program was controversial from its inception, and it took a decade for all states to establish the necessary agencies to run the program.

The expansion of high school enrollments during the Depression helped solidify the notion that adolescence was a distinct life stage. Although the word *teenager* was **Youth Culture** not used until 1941, the concept of teenagers was alive and well by the late 1930s. Movies helped foster an image of what the teen years should be like, with Mickey Rooney's *Andy Hardy* films and movies starring Lana Turner and Judy Garland presenting images of "Kleen Teens" and the *Little Rascals,* the *Dead End Kids,* and later the *Bowery Boys* portraying gangs of impoverished, rough-talking juvenile delinquents. Comic books full of the exploits of superheroes such as *Superman* and *Batman* were aimed at this growing youth culture.

As youth became increasingly enamored by commercial culture, listening to swing music on the radio and going to dance halls, they developed their own language and way of dressing, and they organized fan clubs. Parents sought ways to control their teens' behaviors, but they also became increasingly aware that there were limits to what they could do. Some parents believed that part of the problem with youth was that they knew too much, and they believed that ignorance about matters such as sex would protect them from harm. However, these strategies often backfired. For example, teenagers were curious but ill-informed about reproduction, and many of them obtained information about sex from friends who knew little more than they did.

Adults also grew concerned about gangster movies and violent radio shows for children. One author compared watching movies to using drugs. Reform efforts were not terribly successful—when the entire nation sought escape from daily problems through movies and music, it was not likely that efforts to crack down on adolescents' favorite entertainments would be vigorous.

WORLD WAR II

Just as the Depression dominated family life and the lives of children and adolescents in the 1930s, so too did World War II dominate the experiences of children in the 1940s. Once again, young children found themselves frequently on their own, as fathers and mothers became engaged in the war effort. Children lived in fear, were unsure about their futures, and worried about older brothers, uncles, and fathers fighting in the war. Adolescents resented the war for taking away their youthful independence, just as their counterparts during the Depression resented the economic crisis that limited their options. Gas shortages meant that teenagers could not go on dates in cars, and working mothers and fathers who were away at war meant that adolescents had more household responsibilities than they might have wanted. In addition, the war meant that families sometimes had to move to new cities or states to follow work opportunities, which gave children a sense of impermanence.

Latchkey children. For perhaps the first time on such a large scale, America had a problem with child care for toddlers and young children. With fathers waging war and mothers employed outside of the home in large numbers, the question of what to do with dependent children during the day became an issue. Unlike England, the United States had no provision for affordable quality day care services for working parents. The federal government set up a few day care centers for workers employed in industries essential to the war, but they generally were expensive, of low quality, and inconvenient for parents to use. Older siblings and neighbors did a lot of baby-sitting, as did grandmothers when they were close enough geographically. Many children were left alone and were referred to as latchkey children because they kept their house keys attached to ribbons or chains around their necks. The majority of the federal child care programs ended after the war because the government did not want the responsibility.

The transformation in teenagers that started at the beginning of the Depression continued through the 1940s. Although the war limited adolescents in many ways, they had more job opportunities, and with jobs came a degree of independence and financial freedom that they used to have fun and, inadvertently, to create a youth culture. Businesses quickly found ways to exploit this culture for economic gain, marketing movies, records, clothing, magazines, and leisure activities exclusively to adolescents. Instead of appealing to parents to buy things for their children, commercial enterprises appealed directly to teenagers, who now had their own money to spend. Helped along by these entrepreneurs, American adolescents developed several distinct subcultures with their own clothing styles, hairstyles, dances, and language. Values that were distinguishable from those of adults also became more obvious.

Bobby-soxers. Teenage girls who attended concerts of popular singers such as Frank Sinatra and frequented dance halls became known as *bobby-soxers* because of their distinctive socks, which were an integral part of their look. Middle-class teenage boys wore jeans and penny loafers, wore their hair neatly trimmed, and hung out in groups, feeding nickels into the juke box at the local malt shop so that they could hear the latest tunes from their favorites. Magazines such as *Seventeen,* printed first in 1944, instructed teens on how they should dress and act.

Some nonwhite racial and ethnic groups had alternative youth cultures to the bobby-soxers and the boys hanging out at the malt shops. Many Mexican American boys (*pachucos*) wore zoot suits (long coats, baggy pants, and watch chains), wide-brimmed hats, and duck-tailed haircuts patterned after jazz musicians; many Mexican American girls (*pachuqui-tas*) wore tight skirts, dark red lipstick, and dark mascara, purposefully rebelling against the middle-class values of a white America that they felt discriminated against them. Most of these pachucos did not want to fit in with other teenagers; half dropped out of high school, and few educators paid much attention to them. Some pachucos formed gangs, but most stayed away from delinquent activities. The white majority society, however, only paid attention to those who broke the law, so it was widely assumed that all pachucos were troublemakers. The rise of this youth culture did not go unnoticed. Many adults expressed concerns that peer and popular culture influenced adolescents more than did their parents, and there was a perception that teenage lawbreakers were a growing problem.

Mark McCloskey, recreation director for the Office of Community War Services, blamed delinquency on the lack of teenage recreation facilities, which communities had cut back on during World War II to save money and materials (Palladino, 1996). McCloskey believed that teenagers should design their own centers that reflected their tastes. By 1944, over 3,000 teenage canteens, modeled after recreation centers available for the military during the war, were established across the country. Most of them featured game rooms, lounges, dance floors, and snack bars. To ensure community support, all canteens had adult sponsors, but teenagers selected the activities and decided how to spend their time. For the most part, these canteens were organized within neighborhoods, so there was little mixing between different cultural and ethnic groups. Until the end of the war, teen canteens helped allay adults' fears about juvenile delinquency, but after the war there was no concerted effort to increase canteens or other recreational opportunities for teenagers.

The term *juvenile delinquency* was coined prior to 1940, but it became a common phrase during the 1940s and 1950s. The perceived rise in juvenile delinquency during the war worried some, but most attributed it to mothers working and fathers being overseas. Teenagers generally were granted freedom and independence during the war years that previous generations never had, and, although juvenile crime did rise, it rose less than Americans feared it would. In fact, the increase in juvenile crime may have been more perceptual than real—a perception stemming from growing frustrations that adults were becoming less able to control teenagers' behaviors.

World War II changed American families in many ways. The war was won in 1945, but some families felt the aftermath for years. At least 183,000 children lost fathers to the war, and their families were forever altered. Millions more **Aftermath of the War** children and adolescents knew someone who died in the war. It would be difficult to imagine a person who grew up during World War II who was not affected by a sense of loss and sacrifice. Children had an enormous sense of generational and cultural pride, and they believed they had been a part of a cause greater than themselves.

Many families struggled with how to welcome fathers back into their lives and households. Returning soldiers were often changed by war experiences, and their children had grown older, often in surprising ways. Some men returned with alcohol problems and psychological troubles, and all of them had to get reacquainted with their families. Given the losses experienced by American families, it is not surprising that children and adolescents from the 1940s tended to grow up appreciating their families. In the postwar years, Americans placed a strong emphasis on relationships and family life.

THE BABY BOOM

The end of World War II ushered in a return to economic prosperity. Inflation was low and earning power increased rapidly as the country shifted into a peacetime economy. A generation of young adults who had endured first a decade of economic hardships and then a world war were eager to marry, settle down in their own homes, and raise children. Following the war, there was a sharp drop in the age at first marriage, and women began having more children than had past generations. The year 1946 marked the beginning of what would later be referred to as the baby boom. Between 1946 and 1964, more than 75 million children were born—150 percent more than had been born in the previous 19-year period. The average number of children per family peaked at about 3.7 in 1957, nearly double the birth rate in the 1930s.

The years after the war represented a child-centered period in the United States. There were a lot of children, and, for the last time in the United States in the 20th century, many mothers were stay-at-home moms whose main job, as they saw it, was to raise those children. Although some Americans look back on this era as the standard by which all subsequent periods should be compared, the fact that so many working-class and middle-class families could afford to live well on one wage earner's salary was a historical anomaly.

Grandparents and parents spent more money on children in this child-centered period than ever before. Children were sent to summer camps, music and dance lessons were common, and children had more toys than ever. The huge numbers of young children growing up in this era provided many opportunities for toymakers to profit. Toys such as Silly Putty (1950), Mr. Potato Head (1952), and Barbie dolls (1959) were immensely popular. Children of the baby boom generation were prone to fads, starting with coonskin caps made popular by the 1955 television show, *The Adventures of Davy Crockett*, followed by hula hoops (1958), Slinkys (first marketed in 1946, but achieving fad status later), and other must-have playthings. Given the size of the youth market and parents eager to fulfill their children's wants and wishes, the baby boom generation had a lot of buying clout. Although businesses had previously focused their marketing efforts directly to children, the onset of television in the late 1940s and early 1950s allowed toymakers to advertise on a scale never before seen. Product placement became a common part of some programming, and soon commercials were geared toward children, too. Toys and games based on popular television shows became available, and Disney and other entertainment corporations refined the product tie-in; the Mickey Mouse Club was both a show and a way to sell products such as watches, toys, and the Disneyland experience.

Television was first marketed to parents as a way to educate their children with the implicit threat that families who **Television** did not have a TV would be compromising their children's educational competitiveness. This era produced numerous shows for children (*Romper Room School* [1953–1994], *Captain Kangaroo* [1955–1984]), and many were free of commercials. Corporations had convinced families to pay for a medium (buy a television set) that would soon be used to promote products. Not until near the end of the century, when corporations convinced youth to pay for clothing that prominently displayed the manufacturers' names and turned them into walking billboards was such a commercial plan again as successful.

Although television sets quickly populated U.S. households, everyone was not convinced of television's positive contributions. Educators, clergy, and citizen groups raised concerns about its influence on children, particularly on children's attention in school. Despite concerns, television began to exert a greater and greater influence on children's household behavior, including everything from eating and sleeping to homework and household chores.

Educators, child psychologists, psychiatrists, and broadcasters provided parents with tips on controlling children's television viewing. Among the top concerns was protecting innocent children from secrets of the adult world. One critic, Robert Lewis Shayon, said in 1951, "Television is the shortest cut yet devised, the most accessible backdoor to the grownup world" (Spigel, 1992, p. 198). In 1950, Phyllis Cerf, wife of the *Parents Magazine* publisher, said, "Television, like candy, is wonderful provided you don't have too much of it" (Spigel, 1992, p. 198). Many critics worried that television undermined parents' influence over their children because it was difficult to monitor what their children heard or saw when viewing television. Child specialists began advising parents to establish viewing schedules to limit the amount of television children watched, and also suggested that parents supervise their viewing and point out problem behaviors portrayed on shows.

Burt Tillstrom was the first children's entertainer on TV—he broadcast a live show from the 1939 World's Fair, but few people saw it because television sets were rare. The first shows for children (*Animal Clinic,* featuring live animals, and *Acrobat Ranch,* a show with a circus theme) were aired by the American Broadcasting Company on August 19, 1950. CBS began showing animated cartoons in 1955. The advent of children's shows lessened parents' concerns about the content of programs, but not about how much children watched. Popular shows for young children included *The Lone Ranger* (1949–1957), *Howdy Doody* (1947–1960), and *Captain Kangaroo* (started in 1955). Preteens enjoyed shows like *The Mickey Mouse Club* (1955–1958). Beginning in the early 1960s, networks aired cartoons on weekend mornings when adults were less likely to watch, and, by the end of the decade, watching cartoons had become a Saturday morning ritual in many homes. The Saturday morning cartoons also marked the beginning of advertising directed specifically to children.

Congressional hearings in the early 1950s raised concerns about violence in children's programs, including cartoon violence. Experts at *Parents Magazine* and several psychologists, however, assured parents that their children would not reenact violence. Experts incorrectly assured parents that viewing violence would help children displace their aggression. Still, parents were advised to encourage children to engage in outdoor play rather than watch too much television.

Despite experts' advice, children spent more and more time inside watching television. In fact, television influenced children's pretend play even when they were not watching TV. Historically, preschool-aged children had pretended to be people they were close to and desired to model, such as parents, firemen, nurses, and community workers. Around age seven, children began engaging in more combative and adventure fantasies, playing games such as cops and robbers, cowboys and Indians, and army. As television became more common, preschool-aged children began to prefer fantasy heroes rather than people they knew, and, by the mid-1970s, they engaged in much more superhero play than children had in the past. Increased availability of superhero action figures and television shows featuring superheroes was given as the reason for the increase. Compared to the superheroes of the 1940s, 1970s superheroes engaged in more violence and used more destructive weapons. The shift away from preschoolers modeling people they knew concerned some social critics because it could mean that young children were becoming less likely to engage in play that would help them negotiate future relationships and practice adult roles.

A Child-Centered Society

The 1950s seemed to be especially child-focused, but this may have been partially due to the large numbers of new children demanding attention. For instance, schools were overcrowded, and construction of school buildings to accommodate baby boomers continued for nearly two decades. When the oldest baby boomers reached their senior year of high school in 1964, one out of every four people in the country was enrolled in public schools. In 1965, there were 12.9 million high school students, an 80 percent increase over 1955 (West, 1996).

After-school activities such as scouts and 4-H remained popular in the 1950s. Enrollment in Cub Scouts increased 325 percent from 1949 to 1959, and enrollment in Brownies and Girl Scouts increased over 200 percent during the same time period. Little League baseball, which started in Williamsport, Pennsylvania, in 1939, had spread to 300 communities across the nation by 1950 and continued to grow throughout the decade. Pop Warner football, the little league counterpart for gridiron enthusiasts, started in Philadelphia in 1929 and went national in the late 1950s. Thousands of boys participated in this tackle football program. Because many families with young children had moved to the suburbs after the war, parents (usually mothers) had to transport children to their various activities; distances made it impractical for children to walk or ride their bikes.

The postwar era also witnessed medical advances that positively impacted children's health, further decreasing mortality rates. One of the most significant discoveries happened during the war—the 1942 development of antibiotics. As a result, children became less vulnerable to common childhood diseases and infections. Prior to World War II, the infant mortality rate was 47 deaths for every 1,000 births, compared to 26 deaths per 1,000 births by the 1960s. Early in the 1950s, Jonas Salk invented a vaccine for the deadly and crippling disease, polio—a breakthrough that convinced many Americans that science held the solutions to many of the world's threats. Prior to Salk's vaccine, swimming pools closed and children were kept at home at the slightest hint of an outbreak of polio.

Although there were important improvements in children's health, fewer and fewer mothers were breast-feeding their infants. By 1960, convenience had won out over cost considerations and the vast majority of parents were purchasing powdered formula for their infants. An additional reason, other than convenience, for the low incidences of breast-feeding was a lack of public support. Although no states had laws against breast-feeding in public, many people considered it indecent exposure.

The socialization of middle-class children in the 1950s was focused on assuring that boys and girls grew up with gendered interests. Boys were encouraged to play sports and to engage in rough outdoor play activities. Playing soldier and cowboys and Indians were popular pastimes, which was not surprising because boys were exposed to many movies celebrating the Allies' victory in World War II, and many top television shows were westerns. Girls played indoors more often with dolls and miniature household appliances (the Easy Bake Oven, which could cook real food, first appeared in 1963). Many parents were worried that their sons would not be manly enough, so a great deal of attention was paid to how sons and daughters were raised.

Teen Culture   The 20 years following World War II saw the culmination of the creation of a youth culture that had its roots at the start of the century. Public high schools were a breeding ground for the new teen culture because most teens, for the first time in U.S. history, shared a common experience in high school. Adolescents also had more discretionary income than ever before and more free time to spend with each other, so there were ample opportunities for the teen culture to develop. Teen culture took on great significance because most young people could expect to have achieved many of the status indicators of adulthood within a few years of completing high school. Expectations were that adolescents would be married, have a job, and be parents by their early 20s, and, therefore, dating and peer friendships in high school took on special importance. Dating was taken quite seriously in the 1950s; it was truly courtship for marriage for many teens.

The teen culture was heavily influenced by a new musical form that adolescents listened to and their parents did not—rock and roll. Rock and roll music hitting the airwaves and dance halls seemed to correspond with parents losing much of their control over teenagers. Critics suggested that rock and roll was the expression of a delinquent street culture and worried about lower-class youth influencing the styles and behaviors of youth in the middle class. Many critics also believed that there was a direct link between juvenile delinquency and rock and roll music. Beginning with Bill Haley's *Rock Around the Clock* in 1954, credited with being the first universally acknowledged rock and roll record, and later with Elvis Presley's rockabilly music and hip-shaking moves, mainstream adolescents found their route into a teenage culture that had a strong flavor of rebellion. Rock and roll music quickly established a huge teenage fan base, and there was little adults could do to stop it. When Dick Clark's *American Bandstand* was introduced on network television in 1957, it became an instant hit. Clark eventually helped to allay some adults' fears about the negative influence of the music by ensuring that teenagers on his show set a good image for the show's fans.

Middle-class youth began to assert more independence from their parents as they sought more control over their lives—adolescents expected a voice in family decision making and they wanted a private social life. The consumer culture enveloped teenagers as the postwar ushered in prosperity, and popularity with peers and an active social life became their main goals to a degree not seen before. They had insatiable appetites for fads and fashions, popular music, and movies. Greater family affluence than before the Second World War gave adolescents more access to cars than previous generations of youth—teenagers were said to drive "as fast as their little cars could carry them" (Palladino, 1996, p. 52). Movies, books, magazine articles, social critics, and politicians all began warning that teenagers were behaving in disturbing ways. Youth misconduct became a frequent topic of discussion in women's clubs, PTA meetings, and community groups.

Partly in response to the strangeness of the youth culture, with its slang, fashions, new music, and dance steps, American adults became increasingly concerned about juvenile misconduct. Social critics worried about **Concerns about Delinquency** juvenile delinquency because it was no longer limited to the lower classes. Historically, delinquent behaviors had been blamed on lower-class life, so it was generally ignored by middle-class adults. When it became evident that middle-class youth also were engaging in delinquent activities, concerns began to be expressed about finding solutions.

Youth misbehavior was blamed on a number of factors, including immoral families, comic books, the swing music craze, and the media. Many adults believed that teenagers had too much money, more leisure time than they needed, and they had been coddled too much. The Children's Bureau suggested much of the blame could be placed on public schools where lower- and middle-class teenagers mingled in the same classes. Clean-cut adolescents from well-to-do families walked the high school halls alongside tough-looking teenagers from working-class and poor families. In response, many high schools established dress codes that prohibited tight blue jeans and excessive makeup, but most of these codes backfired because adolescents resented being told what to do and how to dress.

In many ways, middle-class teenagers were fortunate compared to previous generations of adolescents. Postwar prosperity made television, clothes, automobiles, and rock and roll music easily accessible. Youth were able to take life relatively easy, spending afternoons working on their cars, playing tennis, or swimming with friends, and evenings going cruising. Many of those who dropped out of school were guaranteed work in factory positions. Teenagers during the 1950s knew fewer financial and educational boundaries than earlier cohorts of adolescents and were better able to take personal identity and individual choice for granted.

The long-distance view of the 1950s as heyday for families tells only part of the story. Although the booming economy improved the financial situation of many, some families still **Families at the Margins in the 1950s** struggled to achieve the American dream. The 1950s were hard for most black and Latin American families, who faced racial discrimination in jobs, housing, and education. In the mid-1950s, racial segregation of schools was legally required in 17 states and the District of Columbia, and it also was common in other states. This all began to change, however, when the black father of a four-year-old girl filed suit against the Topeka, Kansas, school board to allow his daughter to attend a neighborhood school with white children instead of one farther away for blacks only. In the 1954 landmark case, *Brown v. Topeka Board of Education,* the U.S. Supreme Court ruled unanimously that separate facilities were inherently unequal. Despite the court's ruling, it would take decades for states to comply. White parents were concerned that their children's education would be compromised by integration of black students into their classrooms. Because black schools lagged behind historically, they worried that their children's progress would be slowed while teachers helped black students catch up. Desegregation efforts met with resistance across the country, but reactions were especially virulent in Little Rock, Arkansas, where nine African American students enrolled in Central High School in 1957. Crowds shouted racial slurs as these youth approached the school, and a riot broke out. President Dwight Eisenhower called in paratroopers from the 101st Airborne Division to help state and local police bring the situation under control.

Poor families of all racial and ethnic backgrounds struggled in the 1950s, and as many as one-third of all children lived below the poverty line. Unlike during the Depression, not everyone was impoverished and struggling together. In the 1950s, many poor children were constantly exposed to commercial appeals to purchase products they could not afford, and there were frequent reminders that other children were enjoying the goods of a booming economy while they did without. Separate schools, separate water fountains, sitting at the back of the public bus— daily examples of blatant discrimination based on race—and more subtle discriminations based on ability to pay were reminders that not everyone enjoyed the 1950s.

1960s Era   The 1960s that remains in the minds of most people—the period of social unrest, of protests against the Vietnam War, racism, sexism, heterosexism, and other types of discrimination, the period of race riots and challenges to many social institutions— did not really start until sometime in the mid-1960s, and it extended to the mid-1970s and the United States' military withdrawal from Vietnam. The first few years of the 1960s were more similar socially and historically with the 1950s than with the remainder of the decade.

The 1960s was a period of enormous change in U.S. society. The unrest of the era was not only based on politics and worries about social injustices; many of the changes directly involved American families and their children. Family relationships and family structures were a focus of individual and collective unease—divorce rates soared in the 1960s, cohabitation rates increased 600 percent, and many young adults delayed marriage, raising the average age at marriage by several years in a short time. Black young people began turning away from marriage, and about 25 percent of black children born in the 1960s were born to unmarried mothers. Women openly expressed doubts about equality in marriage, and a few young men began questioning whether the breadwinner role was right for them.

Demographic changes in the decade also contributed to social unrest in ways that affected children and their families. First and foremost, the oldest cohort of baby boomers reached college age and adulthood. Just as they had strained the resources of communities when they were younger, colleges scrambled to build dorms and classrooms for them—the college student population increased by 400 percent from 1946 to 1970. These students also strained their parents' budgets, because many parents had several children to educate. Second, the migration of rural Southern black Americans to cities in the north accelerated after World War II. They wanted access to the same quality of schools as whites, and they were vocal in their advocacy for their children's educations. The movement of blacks into cities spurned many whites to rapidly move out of the cities and inner-ring suburbs to newer suburbs farther from city centers.

Political activity also affected children and their families. The Civil Rights movement led by black Americans helped increase white Americans' awareness that the United States was a multiracial society. Political pressure by black parents and black activists led to busing (in 1968) as a way to address the de facto racial segregation of schools created by the residential migration to the suburbs by whites. President Lyndon Johnson's Great Society program focused much attention on poor children and their parents, and programs such as Head Start, which began in 1965, were federal efforts to help parents rise out of poverty and to level the educational playing field for poor children. The problem of sexism was partially addressed when Title IX of the Educational Amendments of 1972 prohibited gender discrimination in any school activity, which led to sweeping changes in school sports. Prior to the 1970s, girls were discouraged from competing in sports, and many high schools did not have athletic teams for girls. Up to this time, many people believed that active physical exercise might hamper girls' ability to bear children; others thought it unladylike for girls to publicly engage in sports; and still others thought girls were biologically incapable of excelling at sports so providing them with teams wasted school funds.

Youth Culture in the 1960s Era

Much has been written trying to explain how the relatively stable, quiet family life of the 1950s could spawn such a rebellious generation of adolescents and young adults. Social critics blamed permissive parents and a child-centered culture—a reverse of parenting philosophy in the 1950s. Indulgent parenting, it was argued, resulted in spoiled youth who wanted only to consume what they wanted and to do what they wanted, when they wanted. Other social observers proposed alternative explanations— Kenneth Keniston (1960) blamed families with distant fathers and frustrated mothers who were overly involved in their children's lives. In reaction, he asserted, morally sensitive young people rejected their parents' goals in favor of less acquisitive and more socially responsible ones. Other social critics blamed a materialistic society that trained children to be primarily consumers, an emotionally empty existence that fostered rebellion in favor of more authentic living. Another case was made that the conformity of the prior decade was so stifling that minority groups of all types—racial, ethnic, life-style—could no longer tolerate being marginalized and ignored. The debates about the influences on this decade and the generation that came of age in the 1960s still have not been settled.

Historians do agree, however, that the youth culture of the 1960s helped change society and led consumer culture in fashion, media, and entertainment in unprecedented ways. In 1964, there were 22 million teenagers, making up a significant proportion of U.S. consumers. Their purchasing power influenced national trends, a fact that would have been appalling to most adults in the past. Mini-skirts, Nehru jackets, bouffant hairstyles, Beatle boots, granny dresses, Afros, tie-dyed clothing—the list of fashion trends started and dominated by the young could go on and on. As a *Time* magazine article (1967) described them,

The young have already staked out their own mini society, a congruent culture that has both alarmed their elders and, stylistically at least, left an irresistible impression on them. No Western metropolis today lacks a discotheque or espresso joint, a Mod boutique or a Carnaby shop. No transistor is immune from rock 'n' roll, no highway spared the stutter of Hondas. There are few Main Streets in the world that do not echo to the clop of granny boots, and many are the "grannies" who now wear them. What started out as distinctively youthful sartorial revolt—drainpipe-trousered men, pants-suited or net-stockinged women, long hair on male and female alike—has been accepted by adults the world over.

Adolescents and young adults were trendsetters, but they also went to different movies than their parents, and listened to rock and roll, soul music, and rhythm and blues, all of which their parents avoided. For seemingly the first time in history, parents looked at their offspring as if they had arrived from another planet, and children viewed their parents as being increasingly irrelevant and out of touch with their needs and wishes. By the mid-1960s, teenagers had become more likely to defy their parents and to talk back to their elders. Many adults attempted to shape teenage culture; some magazines ran advice columns to remind them that they were not equal to adults. As the decade wore on, it became increasingly obvious to many adults that middle-class children were no longer passively willing to allow adults to shape their behaviors. As the 1967 *Time* article put it, "The young seem curiously unappreciative of the society that supports them. 'Don't trust anyone over 30,' is one of their rallying cries. Another, 'Tell it like it is,' conveys an abiding mistrust of what they consider adult deviousness."

Thus, the *generation gap* was born, a term invented to describe the rift between baby boomers and their parents. Most social scientists who studied intergenerational relationships in the 1960s did not find support for such a gap, but for many parents and their offspring who found themselves on opposite sides of disputes about dress and hair lengths, the war in Vietnam, or civil rights, the gap was real.

Most baby boomers seemed to go out of their way to distinguish themselves from prior generations. Some ways that youth distinguished themselves were on the surface—boys signaled their independence from convention by wearing their hair long, growing beards and moustaches, and girls flaunted custom by letting their hair grow straight and not wearing bras. African Americans of both genders wore their hair long in Afros and dressed in dashikis (loose, brightly colored African shirts) to symbolize pride in their African heritage. Young people of all races and both genders wore love beads and bell bottoms as generational symbols.

The youth culture in the 1960s also had more serious aspects to it. The invention of the birth control pill helped create an atmosphere of more sexual freedom early on, and a counterculture hippie movement promoted "free love." The hippies also promoted a less materialistic lifestyle and attempted to live more "authentic" lives than their parents had. A drug subculture also grew among young people—illegal drugs had always been present in U.S. society, but the use of drugs such as marijuana, hashish, cocaine, and heroin had been the province of marginal elements of society—jazz musicians, criminals, and, sometimes, upper-class society members. The counterculture in the 1960s expanded the use of these drugs to middle-class youth. Marijuana, in particular, was popular because it was cheap and readily available. Many parents were dismayed at the appearance of their children, but they were even more concerned about the dangers of drugs, which most parents knew nothing about.

The Vietnam War served to further fragment teenagers and adults. The Selective Service had existed for 25 years, and teenage boys understood that it was their duty to serve in the military, if drafted. However, many youth saw little reason for the war. As President Johnson increased the number of troops serving in Vietnam, high school students' support for the draft diminished. In 1960, about 60 percent of high school boys surveyed liked the idea of being drafted; by 1969, 14 percent of boys responded similarly. Although most older Americans saw military service as honorable, teenagers became more likely to see military service as an unnecessary sacrifice for young men to make. By the late 1960s, college students became antiwar activists, and violent protests were common on college campuses across the country.

Many of the protests and social unease in the 1960s were not generational disputes of young versus old, but young people seemed to be at the forefront of many of these movements, although not always as leaders. Sit-ins and protest rallies opposing racial discrimination against Latin Americans and African Americans, gay rights marches, and war protests sometimes made it appear that the youth of the 1960s were forging new ways of relating in society. Alternative family forms seemed to flourish, and many progressive social scientists in the late 1960s and early 1970s predicted that the

United States was about to enter a new age of open, creative, and enriching relationships, both within and outside of family boundaries.

CHILDHOOD IN THE FINAL QUARTER OF THE CENTURY

America did not, however, enter a new period of open and authentic relationships. Those who predicted that Americans would continue to explore and expand how childrearing and family living were defined and lived had not anticipated changes in society that would affect the rest of the century. For instance, there were sharp increases in the divorce rate; higher rates of children were born to adolescent and unwed mothers; more mothers were employed outside the home; and more children lived with single parents, stepparents, grandparents, and other relatives. All of these changes reduced the amount of time children and parents were together. Also, an influx of immigrants from Asia, the Middle East, and Latin America brought with them family customs and beliefs that sometimes were at odds with mainstream U.S. culture. Accompanying all this were changes in how parents, and society as a whole, thought about childrearing. Changes in family formation worried social conservatives, and there was general public concern about such social problems as juvenile crime, teenage pregnancy, illicit drug use, child abductions, child abuse, and children's academic performance. These widespread concerns led to new social policies designed to address these problems.

Living Arrangements of Children Although American families have always been diverse, from the mid-1970s to the end of the century the pace of change in family households accelerated. Between 1940 and 1980, the average percentage of children who were not living in two-parent first marriage homes increased from 30 percent to 50 percent; for white children, the increase was from 25 percent to 40 percent; for black children, 55 percent to 75 percent (Hernandez, 1993). At the end of the century, about 60 percent of the 72 million children in the United States lived in two-parent households with both of their biological parents.

In 1960, about 1 of every 10 American children lived in single-parent households; by the early 1990s, nearly 1 in 4 did so. Most of this was due to parental divorce—in 1992, 61 percent of all children who lived in single-parent homes had parents who were divorced or separated, 34 percent lived with a never-married parent. Black children were much more likely to be raised by single parents than children of other races; 20 percent of black children lived in single-parent households in 1960, by 1991 the percentage had increased to 58 percent. At the end of the century, researchers estimated that about half of all American children born in the 1990s would spend some time living in a single-parent home before reaching age 18.

Many people fretted about the supposed disappearance of traditional two-parent nuclear families because they were concerned about children's well-being, and they considered two-parent biological families ideal settings for raising children. Numerous problems, such as higher rates of delinquency, sexual activity, teen pregnancy, and drug and alcohol abuse were blamed on living in non-nuclear families.

Although rates of childbearing among adolescents peaked in 1957, it was in the last quarter of the century that many parents, educators, and policymakers became alarmed at what was thought to be an epidemic of teenage pregnancy. There was cause for alarm. Researchers consistently found **Children of Unmarried Adolescent Parents** that children born to unmarried adolescents were more likely to have a variety of physical and cognitive problems. In contrast to earlier times, when teenagers who found themselves with an unplanned pregnancy either got married or gave their babies up for adoption, unmarried teenage mothers in the final quarter of the century were more likely to raise their babies alone. Even though some teenage mothers received support from the fathers of their children and their extended family, they tended to remain mired in poverty, as did their children.

Babies born to teenage mothers had a greater risk of being born prematurely, having developmental delays, and being abused and neglected. In the long term, children of adolescents had higher likelihoods of depression and anxiety, delinquency, incarceration (among boys), dropping out of school, teen parenthood, poverty, and unemployment. Despite these greater risks, not all children of adolescent parents were negatively affected; many grew up to be productive citizens. Researchers in the 1990s suggested that low socioeconomic status and poverty had more significant influences on children's outcomes than their parents' ages.

Not all children born to unwed mothers were necessarily raised in single-parent homes. About one in eight children whose mothers were unmarried when they were born lived **Children of Cohabiting Parents** with both of their biological parents. Although their households were structurally similar to two-parent, first marriage homes, children in cohabiting households were more likely to have exhibited behavioral and emotional problems, and to have done worse in school, than children with married parents. These differences were accounted for partly by parental differences between the two types of households. In general, cohabiting couples made less money than their married counterparts, stayed together less frequently, and led less stable lives (e.g., they moved more often than married couples, changed jobs more often).

Of all of the non-nuclear family types, families headed by divorced parents received some of the harshest criticisms. **Children of Divorced Parents** Many religious conservatives considered divorce to be a sin, and critics suggested that divorcing parents gave up on their marriages too easily, much to the detriment of their children. Parents were encouraged to stay together for the sake of their children. Some of the earliest research on children's well-being following divorce suggested that the children would have behavioral, emotional, and academic problems. For example, psychologists Judith Wallerstein and Joan Kelly (1980) reported that one-third of the 131 children they studied were adjusting well five years after divorce. Another one-third were said to be clinically depressed, experiencing trouble in school, and having problems maintaining friendships. These early findings influenced the way many people viewed children's experiences following parental divorce.

Although many people believed that children would suffer long-term harm as a result of their parents' divorce, most studies indicated that 75 percent to 80 percent of children experienced only short-term emotional adjustments. In 1991, sociologists Paul Amato and Bruce Keith examined the findings of dozens of studies on children's well-being following divorce and found that, compared to children whose parents were continuously married, children of divorced parents were slightly more likely to have poorer academic achievement, more conduct problems, poorer peer relations, and lower self-esteem and psychological well-being. Average differences between children of married and divorced parents were fairly small, and about as many children's well-being improved as got worse after parents' divorce. More significant influences appeared to be the loss of parental support and supervision after divorce, economic hardships, conflict between parents, and a lack of community resources to help divorced parents and their children adjust to family changes.

Although conservative social critics pointed to divorce as the social problem that most affected children in the final quarter of the century, many social scientists contended that differences between children of divorced and married parents were explained by circumstances prior to, during, and following divorce. Longitudinal studies in which researchers followed families for several years indicated that some negative child behaviors that were attributed to parental divorce had been noticeable years before the parents divorced. According to several researchers, parental conflict—whether within marriage, during the divorce process, or within the postdivorce coparenting relationship—was the major source of children's problems rather than the divorce per se. Following divorce, children had to adapt to numerous changes that might include living on a smaller income, moving to a new residence, enrolling in a new school, and establishing new friendships. In addition, diminished contact with the noncustodial parent was potentially harmful to children. Children's reactions to parental divorce varied widely, even within the same family. Researchers found that children's outcomes were dependent on a number of factors, including age, temperament, quality of the relationship with each parent, parental conflict prior to and following divorce, socioeconomic status, and how much time elapsed since the divorce. By the end of the century, it was not clear to researchers or to policymakers what the effects were of this rapidly increasing phenomenon on children's well-being.

At the end of the century, it was estimated that about one in six children were stepchildren. About 11 percent of children lived with a half-sibling (i.e., they shared one biological parent), and 3 percent lived with a stepsibling **Children in Stepfamilies** (i.e., children who are not biologically related). Children have lived in stepfamilies throughout history, but during the 1970s parental separation replaced mortality as the precursor to stepfamily formation, resulting in children sometimes having three or four adults in parental roles (e.g., a mother and stepfather and a father and stepmother).

Stepfamily living was complex for children. Not only did they have multiple adults in their lives, but they often belonged to two households, with varying numbers of siblings, half-siblings, and stepsiblings in each one. Stepfamily members lacked norms for how their postdivorce families should function, and clinicians reported that children who experienced a parent's death often felt loyalty conflicts if they liked spending time with a stepparent—they felt disloyal to the memory of their parent. Children in postdivorce stepfamilies had an even more complex situation, and loyalty conflicts were often more pronounced for them. The quality of stepparent-stepchild relationships varied widely.

When parents remarried or moved in with a partner, children experienced a new set of changes, some of which (e.g., moving, adapting to having other people in the household, and adjusting to new routines) increased their stress. Researchers who studied children in stepfamilies reported that their academic achievement, psychological adjustment and emotional well-being, behavior problems, and interpersonal relationships were more similar to children of divorced parents than to children of married parents. The differences from children of married parents, however, were generally modest. One positive change of parental remarriage was usually an increase in the children's standard of living.

Being a stepchild in the 20th century generally was a stigmatized status. The word stepchild was used throughout the century to denote something that was neglected or ignored (e.g., "the national park service is the stepchild of the federal government"). The largest number of adoptions late in the century was of stepparents adopting their stepchildren, typically to remove stigma. Children whose parents divorced and remarried several times had lives that contained many transitions, and researchers indicated that these children experienced more stress than other children, and their adjustments were less successful.

Social critics decried the negative effects of parental remarriage on children, and policymakers tended to ignore stepfamilies, even when advocates tried to lobby for legislation that would give stepparents and stepchildren some legal protections and rights and responsibilities for each other. The complexity of stepfamilies and the fact that most parents had been divorced, made stepfamilies seem unhealthy to many conservative social critics.

Children and Grandparents

By the end of the century, having a grandparent was the norm. There were nearly 90 million grandparents in 2000; about 75 percent of those 65 and over were grandparents, and nearly half would become great-grandparents. Because women lived longer than men, children were more likely to have grandmothers and great-grandmothers than grandfathers and great-grandfathers.

More grandparents. Over the course of the 20th century, the number of years in which children had a grandparent increased dramatically, due to longer life spans. In 1900, 4 percent of the population was over 65, with an average life expectancy of 48 years for men and 47 years for women. Given these life spans, many grandchildren never knew their grandparents. Less than 25 percent of infants born in 1900 had four living grandparents when they were born; most of these grandparents were not still alive when the grandchild reached adulthood. Few children had great-grandparents (Uhlenberg & Kirby, 1998). In contrast, the expected life span in 2000 was 76 years for men and 80 years for women, so 98 percent of the infants in 2000 had at least one grandparent living when they were born, and 70 percent could expect to have at least one grandparent alive when they reached adulthood. In 2000, two-thirds of children had four grandparents throughout their entire childhood.

Grandparent health. Grandparents gradually became more active and healthier during the 20th century. At the end of the century, the majority of grandmothers were between the ages of 49 and 53 when their first grandchild was born, although some became grandmothers sooner. Most grandmothers worked and had many years until retirement age. These women were physically active and much healthier than earlier cohorts of grandmothers and they could expect to live 20 to 25 years after retirement. Grandfathers also were more vigorous and had more time for grandchildren. In 1900, it was rare for a man to have many years left after retiring. From an average of 4 years of retirement in 1900, the number of retirement years rose to 15 late in the century. Although a sizeable proportion of retired grandfathers after World War II worked part-time to make ends meet, these grandfathers still had more time to spend with grandchildren than had previous generations. Social security benefits and retirement pensions also meant that life for older adults was more economically secure after World War II, which freed up time for leisure activities, including time with grandchildren.

Making contact. Technological innovations made it easier than ever for grandparents and grandchildren to be in touch. Prior to World War II, half of American homes had a telephone, a percentage that rose to nearly 75 percent by the end of the 1950s and to nearly 100 percent (not counting cell phones) by the end of the century. The telephone allowed grandparents and grandchildren to talk occasionally, even though they may have lived miles apart. E-mail, cell phones, and computer video also enhanced grandparent-grandchild contacts in the last decade of the century.

Although there were more grandparents and great-grandparents at the end of the century than there were at the start, families had fewer children on average at the end of the century than at the beginning, which meant that grandparents in 2000 had fewer grandchildren than their counterparts had in 1900. For instance, women ages 60 to 64 had an estimated average of 12 grandchildren in 1900, but fewer than 6 at the end of the century (Uhlenberg & Kirby, 1998).

Grandparent-grandchild relationships. It is likely that the increased number of shared years together, improvements in health of older adults, improvements in communication technology and transportation, and the reduced numbers of grandchildren resulted in more emotionally close relationships between grandparents and their grandchildren in the latter half of the century than before. Evidence from personal diaries and interviews in the 1980s and 1990s indicated that some grandparents were influential individuals in grandchildren's lives.

The grandparent role for most of the century was whatever a particular grandparent and his or her extended family members wanted it to be. Many grandparents did as much or as little as they wanted with grandchildren. For most grandparents this meant fewer childrearing

Modern grandparent-grandchild interaction. (© Royalty-Free/Corbis)

responsibilities and more fun with grandchildren than they had raising their children. Older grandparents, especially those in poor health, were more emotionally remote and more formal in their interactions with grandchildren; younger grandparents were more likely to be fun-loving.

Race, ethnicity, and grandparenthood. Race, ethnicity, and cultural influences played a factor in how grandparents interacted with grandchildren. For the first half of the century, white grandfathers were mostly seen by their grandchildren as distant, but respected, authority figures. They were not expected to take care of grandchildren. White grandmothers often served nurturing roles, baby-sitting for children when mothers were shopping or ill.

White grandfathers' roles began changing when the baby boomers became grandfathers. Younger, healthier, and with fewer grandchildren than previous generations of grandfathers, many of these men had the money and leisure to spend quality time with grandchildren, taking them on trips, going fishing and hunting with them, playing sports, and otherwise being a pal. Because they had more years to share together, grandfathers and grandchildren typically got to know each other better and were emotionally closer than previous generations. There was also a change in societal expectations, and many of these grandfathers wanted to be involved with grandchildren as friends. White grandmothers' roles also changed late in the century, as more of them were employed. Consequently, some grandmothers were less available for baby-sitting and child care. In many ways, the roles of white grandmothers converged with those of grandfathers, as they became more like pals and playmates with grandchildren, taking them on trips, going to movies, and having fun with them.

Most black grandparents were more involved with their grandchildren throughout the 20th century than were white grandparents. Black grandparents helped instruct their grandsons and granddaughters on ways to cope when they encountered racism and discrimination. They helped their children discipline grandchildren, and they shared their resources (e.g., money, housing, advice).

Older family members in Asian families are revered. The Confucian concept of filial piety—honoring and being responsible for elders—meant adult children and grandchildren were obligated to do whatever necessary to meet the needs of grandparents. This concept is part of all Asian cultures. Asian American grandfathers were considered to be the heads of their extended families by virtue of age and gender, so they maintained decision-making authority over children and grandchildren even when they were quite old and frail.

Because laws limited the immigration of Asians, there were few grandparents in Asian American families in the United States until the last decades of the century. This meant that most Asian grandparents had been born and raised in their traditional cultures, whereas their grandchildren were raised in the United States. The differences in cultural backgrounds sometimes led to intrafamily strife because grandparents held traditional values about filial piety or filial responsibility, and their grandchildren held more Americanized values about intergenerational ties. This sometimes led to Asian grandparents feeling neglected or disrespected by their acculturated younger kin.

One aspect of filial piety that was honored in Asian American households was the expectation that older adults would live with their children and grandchildren, and multigenerational households were more common among Asian Americans than among other ethnic groups in the last quarter of the century. These households often contained older, foreign-born grandparents who spoke little or no English living with their child and grandchildren, some of whom spoke English only. Asian grandparents tended not to be emotionally involved with grandchildren, nor were they involved in most areas of childrearing. Their main function as grandparents tended to be that of family historian. More acculturated grandparents probably functioned more like other American grandparents and were more emotionally involved with their grandchildren.

Latin American grandparents also represented a diverse group of cultural backgrounds from Central and South America and the Caribbean. These cultures share an ethic known as *familismo,* which holds that family well-being is a high value and that the welfare of the family takes precedence over individuals' needs. For some, familismo meant that grandfathers' and grandmothers' needs were unconditionally provided by adult children and grandchildren, and their wishes were respected and followed as well. There were indications that familismo was less adhered to by Latin American families who were acculturated into mainstream U.S. society. For example, many Latin American grandparents had roles similar to white grandparents—they were friends and playmates of their grandchildren—while others functioned more like black grandparents, providing a variety of support and assistance to the younger generations in their families, and sometimes sharing a residence with them.

Some Latin American families had resided in the United States for many generations, while others were recent immigrants, both legal and undocumented. For recent Latin American immigrants, grandparent-grandchild ties were usually long-distance relationships because most grandparents remained in their home countries while younger family members sought jobs in the United States. Visits with these long-distance grandparents were irregular and infrequent, due to cost and distance.

Stepgrandparents. Stepgrandparents were not prevalent for most for the 20th century. In addition to the factors that contributed to the increase in grandparents (e.g., greater longevity), the increase in the divorce rate boosted the number of stepgrandparents. Late in the century, approximately 39 percent of families contained stepgrandparents (Szinovacz, 1998). Adults became stepgrandparents by marrying a person who was a grandparent, having a son or daughter marry someone with children, or having their grown stepchildren reproduce. It is likely that these different pathways to stepgrandparenthood led to quite different relationships between generations, but, despite the large numbers, little was known about the relationship between stepgrandparents and stepgrandchildren. Stepgrandparenthood is perhaps an even more voluntary status than grandparenthood.

Working Mothers From the early 1960s to the end of the century, mothers were increasingly employed outside the home. Between 1960 and 1990, the percentage of children under age six whose mothers were in the labor force doubled from 30 percent to 60 percent. During the last quarter of the century, for the first time, many U.S. households were empty during work-week days; everyone was at work or school. Some children came home to empty households, and, when mothers and fathers arrived, there usually was little time for anything but preparing and eating dinner (unless someone had stopped by a fast food restaurant or take-out had been ordered), homework for the children, and a little TV before bedtime. Although the employment of mothers was not the only reason for the hurried pace of American family life, social critics often blamed it on mothers' working. In fact, working mothers got blamed for several social ills; foremost among them were the lack of parental socialization and the reduced monitoring of children and teenagers. Working mothers' concerns, however, tended to be pragmatic, such as finding adequate child care for their children while they earned a living.

Child care and preschools. Since the 1920s, some Americans had shown interest in early childhood education for children too young to attend school. This interest expanded dramatically during World War II and again during the 1960s as mothers' labor force participation necessitated nonparental child care. By the end of the century, early and extensive child care enrollment was the norm for families in the United States. In fact, one study in the early 1990s found that preschool-aged children spent 1,102 hours with their parents each year versus 1,715 hours in child care or with babysitters (West, 1996). The 1999 National Household Education Survey reported that over 61 percent of children under age four were in child care on a regular basis. Most were over age two, but 44 percent were younger than a year old; by age six months, some children were spending an average of 30 hours a week in child care (U.S. Census Bureau, 2000); 45 percent were in center-based care; and the rest were cared for by their parents or other relatives. Child care participation rates varied by race and ethnicity. Latin American children were less likely to receive nonparental care than their white and black counterparts—about 46 percent of Latin American children were in the care of others in 1995, compared to 62 percent of white and 66 percent of black children.

Until the 1960s, most children in preschools were from middle-class families who were able to afford to send their children there. In 1962, the

Social Security Act was amended to provide funds for numerous children's programs, including providing subsidies for low-income families needing child care. In 1990, Congress authorized $2.5 billion over three years to help pay for child care as well as before- and after-school programs for children of low-income parents.

One of the best known preschool programs was the Office of Economic Opportunity's Project Head Start, which originated in 1965 as an eight-week summer program designed to help provide a firm, comprehensive educational foundation for children whose families lived below the poverty line. By 1999, more than 850,000 children were enrolled in Head Start, which by then operated year round and also offered health screenings, social services, and parent education. There have been mixed findings regarding the program's long-term impact, although higher-quality programs were found to have benefits.

Dramatic increases in the number of children in child care were accompanied by greater public acceptance of nonparental child care, but many critics remained. The biggest concerns were that mothers and children would not develop secure attachments to one another or that children's cognitive or social-emotional development would be negatively affected by spending time in child care. Numerous studies, however, provided

Head Start, a Great Society program, began in the 1960s. (Associated Press)

evidence that the quality of child care settings was much more important than the quantity of time children spent there, and high-quality child care had a positive influence on developmental outcomes of children living at or near the poverty line. Unfortunately, many children of the working poor were at the greatest risk of receiving low-quality care. Their family incomes were too high for Head Start eligibility and too low to afford higher-quality facilities. As a result, many low-income children were in child care settings that had the potential to harm them physically, emotionally, socially, and cognitively.

At the end of the century, there were no systems in place to ensure quality control of America's child care programs. Existing controls applied primarily to health and safety issues, and church-operated day care and preschools were exempt from those regulations in some states. The general belief remained—society should not be responsible for the care of young children until they reach age five or six and are ready to enter school systems. Rather than supervise and regulate the plethora of programs in operation, federal and state governments for the most part ignored them.

Latchkey kids. By the mid-1990s, the U.S. Census Bureau estimated that about 1.6 million children (8 percent) between the ages of 5 and 14 were caring for themselves part of the time. Most were over age 11 (about 5 percent of 5- to 11-year-olds cared for themselves), but by age 14 about one in five children spent time alone while their parents worked. The very poor were less likely than those in the middle class to leave their children home alone, primarily because they were more likely to live in unsafe neighborhoods. As the number of latchkey children grew, educators began developing programs to help parents prepare their children for self-care. Many schools, libraries, and community centers established before- and after-school programs as well.

During the 1980s, researchers' conclusions on the effects of self-care varied greatly. Some compared latchkey children to supervised children and found little or no difference in school achievement, self-esteem, and social skills. Others, however, found that latchkey children had more social and academic problems, greater susceptibility to peer pressure, and a higher incidence of alcohol use. Later research generally supported the latter findings; unsupervised children were more likely to drink alcohol and smoke cigarettes and marijuana, they were more likely to engage in delinquent activities, and they were more likely to be the victims of crimes.

Other Changes in Children's Lives

Breast-feeding. In the mid-1970s, researchers began to discover more information about the long-term benefits of breast-feeding for mothers and children, and, by the early 1980s, the number of infants who were breast-fed had increased to around 65 percent. Although many people still equated breast-feeding with indecent exposure, at the end of the century, public attitudes were growing more positive toward breast-feeding in public. More workplaces permitted breast-feeding mothers to take pumping breaks and provided storage for breast milk, and laws were passed making public breast-feeding legal. In 1984, for example, New York became the first state to exempt breast-feeding from its criminal statute on indecent exposure, and, in 1993, Florida passed the first law that protected the right to breast-feed in public. Despite the laws, however, some breast-feeding mothers were asked to leave public places because of complaints. Additionally, although in the 1990s pediatricians strongly advocated that mothers breast-feed for one year, most quit after a few months. Black and Latina mothers were less likely than white mothers to breast-feed their infants.

Toilet training. Advice from experts about developmental milestones such as toilet training changed in the final decades of the century. T. Berry Brazelton had introduced child-oriented toilet training in 1962, and this method remained standard practice for the next 40 years. It was also the method advocated by the American Academy of Pediatrics. Children were given opportunities to experiment and to gradually become comfortable with toilet training. In contrast, structured-behavioral approaches similar to those of earlier experts such as L. Emmett Holt and John B. Watson also reemerged during the 1960s and 1970s; these techniques informed parents how to toilet train their children in a short period of time. Parents were advised to increase children's fluid intake, establish scheduled toilet times, and give children a great deal of positive reinforcement when they were successful.

At the end of the century, psychologist and child care expert John Rosemond suggested that Brazelton's advice was resulting in toilet training problems. Brazelton reacted by ascribing the problems with toilet training to dual career parents' unwillingness to be patient and child care facilities' insistence that children be toilet trained by age three (many facilities would not accept children who were not toilet trained). According to the American Academy of Pediatrics, in 1961, 90 percent of two-and-a-half-year-olds were toilet trained compared to only 22 percent in 1997. As toilet training took longer, disposable diaper manufacturers introduced larger diapers and training pants, as well as disposable underpants for children with bedwetting problems. The increased use of disposable diapers glutted landfills and raised concerns of environmentalists, but few parents were willing to return to using cloth diapers.

Other changes. Families were smaller than in the past, so there were more children growing up as only children or with only one sibling. Fewer children in families and larger houses meant that children were more likely to have their own rooms, and as families became more affluent it was not unusual for children to have televisions in their rooms and, in the 1990s, personal computers. Many children lived farther from their schools than in the past, which meant that they probably had fewer classmates nearby to play with, so they spent more time playing video games, surfing the Internet, and watching TV alone than had previous generations. Gradually, children became more sedentary, and less exercise, combined with frequent fast food meals of fatty and sugar-laden foods, meant that children became heavier and less physically fit than previous generations. Although concerns about children's health and rising obesity rates had been raised, by the end of the century, vending machines containing candy, chips, and soft drinks were widely available in most schools, and school cafeterias offered calorie-laden, high-fat foods such as pizza, that children liked. Along with eating more fast food meals and larger servings of food in restaurants, high-calorie cafeteria food contributed to one out of six children being overweight or obese at century's end.

Consumption had become a primary activity of many children, and American children in the last decades of the century had more toys, clothes, and other entertainment goods (e.g., electronic gear, movies, music) than any group of children in the world. Grandparents lived longer than in the past, and there were more gift-giving elders per child than there had ever been, so children received more goods and money than ever in history. In two-income families, parents' guilt about spending less time with their children sometimes resulted in them making sure their children got whatever they wanted. In 1993, total toy sales surpassed $23 billion, compared to $15 billion just two years earlier.

Most middle-class children expected to obtain driver's licenses at age 16, and many of them received cars of their own. More adolescents worked part-time than ever before, in part to pay for car-related expenses and in part to have their own discretionary money to purchase entertainment and leisure goods. Some adolescents worked as much as 40 hours per week, and teachers raised concerns that these students were falling asleep in classes and not completing their homework. Unlike children at the beginning of the century who worked to help their families maintain a basic level of subsistence, adolescents at the end of the century worked to provide themselves with items that many people would consider luxuries—such as concert tickets, movies, electronic gadgets, and expensive clothing. By the end of the century, 44 percent of 17-year-old boys and 42 percent of 17-year-old girls worked part-time, compared to 29 percent and 18 percent, respectively, who worked in 1953.

At the same time that middle-class and upper-class children were becoming skilled consumers, more children lived in poverty than ever before. In the late 1990s, an average of 15 percent of all U.S. children lived below the poverty line (the averages were 30 percent of black children and 28 percent of Latin American children). Less than half of those growing up in inner cities had ever had a job by the age of 25 because opportunities for gainful legal employment in their neighborhoods usually were few. Many poor children at the end of the 20th century grew up with no realistic life goals—despair and drugs were serious impediments to them seeing a future for themselves.

Families were changing, and family life in the last quarter of the century seemed to most Americans to be qualitatively different from what had gone before. Many Americans agreed that changes in families were linked to at least some of the major problems facing

Changes in Attitudes about Childrearing

society, but they disagreed on whether the changes in families were the causes of social problems or their consequences. These differing perspectives led to sometimes contentious policy and political debates, but what was less debatable as the century ended was that raising children had changed because attitudes about families and children had altered. There were two concurrent themes in the last quarter of the 20th century pertaining to childrearing : (1) the world was a dangerous place and children needed to be protected, and (2) children needed to be prepared for the adult world as early as possible. These two themes were not often compatible, or at least not easily so. For instance, it was hard for parents to facilitate the development of their children's technological skills by buying them computers and paying for Internet access, while at the same time protecting them from objectionable material and predators on the Internet that might do their children harm. Nonetheless, parents simultaneously became increasingly protective and preparation-focused.

Many parents were concerned about raising their children in a world they viewed as dangerous and full of temptations and hazards. Social problems such as rising juvenile crime, adolescent sexuality that could lead to pregnancy and

Protective Parenting

sexually transmitted diseases, child abductions, and drug use frightened parents a great deal.

The media facilitated this sense of ever-present danger. Around-the-clock news channels often focused on crimes against children, especially middle-class children. Hours, and sometimes days, of television time was given to gruesome but rather isolated events, which nonetheless panicked parents. For instance, the kidnap and murder of six-year-old Adam Walsh in 1981 contributed to a nationwide panic about child abduction. Reports were widely circulated that every year as many as 50,000 children were murdered and half a million kidnapped by strangers. Billboards and milk cartons had pictures of abducted children, and the U.S. government established a Center for Missing and Exploited Children. In 1988, Adam's father created a successful television show, *America's Most Wanted*, which kept alive the idea that child abduction was at epidemic levels. The truth was somewhat different from this popular portrayal. A federal study revealed that about 500 to 600 children were abducted by strangers each year, and about 50 were murdered. Most of the abductions were by non-residential parents, and some were children running away from home and were not abductions at all. Children were far more likely to be killed by a parent than a stranger, but public perceptions, fueled by the media, remained quite different. As a result of fear, fewer children were allowed to play outside without adult supervision, fewer children were allowed to walk to school, and children were taught at young ages to be suspicious of any person they did not know.

The relative safety enjoyed by American children did not stop policy-makers from contributing to parents' sense of danger. After a 12-year-old California girl was abducted from a slumber party and murdered in 1993 by a prison parolee, states quickly passed "three strikes" bills that mandated long sentences or life in prison for repeat offenders. In 1996, the state of Texas created Amber Alerts (named after Amber Hagerman, a nine-year-old girl who was abducted and murdered)—a quick-response system using mass media to alert communities when a child has been kidnapped. Within a few years, every state had an Amber Alert system in place.

Supervised play. Most middle-class parents made sure that children were monitored when they played, which meant that play times had to be arranged for times when an adult could be present. Given parents' busy schedules, this resulted in less outdoor play for children. Children's play was protected in other ways, too. Helmets for children riding tricycles and bicycles were a common sight, and playground equipment was designed to protect children from injury.

Inner-city parents also monitored their children to keep them safe from gangs and drug dealers. Poor children in dangerous inner-city neighborhoods were sometimes kept indoors by anxious parents. Black parents engaged in more physical punishment of their children than did white parents. Although they also expressed more warmth, black parents tended to be stricter than whites with their sons in particular, in part because the stakes for misbehavior were perceived to be much higher for black children than white children. Some black parents reasoned that their sons were potential targets not only of gang members and lawbreakers in their communities, but also they could be targets of racist police officers if they broke the law or if they appeared to do so—African American parents wanted their children to be above suspicion to avoid dangerous situations.

Neil Postman (1994) suggested that children's games had become an endangered species at the end of the 20th century. At the beginning of the century, children played for the sake of play—boys played spontane-ous games of baseball in the streets, and girls jumped rope and played hopscotch on the sidewalks. By the end of the century, these games had largely disappeared. When children did play games, they were often accompanied by adults who helped enforce rules, and winning became the purpose of much play. Postman and other media critics warned par-ents that frequent participation in structured, adult-supervised activities left little room for children to engage in unstructured, imaginative play, which behavioral scientists had found to be one of the most important activities for children's cognitive and emotional growth. Many parents, however, were motivated by safety concerns and the desire to help prepare their children for what they believed would be a competitive environment when the children became adults.

Youth violence. One area of concern about safety had to do with what was perceived to be a rising tide of youth violence. To be sure, gang violence in inner cities was a major problem in the 1980s and early 1990s, and crimes committed by adolescents and children of all races seemed to most Americans to be more ruthless and cruel than in the past. As a result, by the end of the century, the country had witnessed a growing criminalization of youth. According to the National Center for Juvenile Justice, between 1987 and 1996, juvenile arrests increased 35 percent, and, although youth violence occurred at about the same rate in 1996 as it had in the mid-1980s, the consequences of these crimes were much greater because firearms became the weapon of choice. Most adults no longer thought it was appropriate to treat youthful offenders with leniency, and by the end of the century all 50 states had passed laws making it easier to prosecute juveniles in adult criminal court. Some states had no minimum age at which children could be tried as adults. These laws reversed Progressive Era reformers' attempts to protect youth from being treated like adults.

Stimuli for these changing laws were school shootings that made news headlines late in the century. Most notable, perhaps, was on April 20, 1999, when Dylan Klebold and Eric Harris shot and killed 12 students and one teacher before killing themselves at Columbine High School in Littleton, Colorado. That event and other random public school attacks by white middle-class suburban boys who killed or attempted to kill their classmates and teachers, encouraged some parents to enroll their children in private schools, believing their children would be safer. Other parents home schooled their children to protect them from dangers and unacceptable outside influences. Although there were other reasons for the rise of private schools and home schooling, fear was a factor.

Youth drug use. The 1960s were popularly perceived as the drug decade, but drug abuse actually increased in the decades following the 1960s. Many children were home alone after school, and drug use was easy to engage in and hard to detect by parents. Baby boomers had rebelled against their parents by using recreational drugs such as marijuana, and they tended to be somewhat ambivalent about their children's use of alcohol and drugs, although most parents opposed it. By the mid-1980s, amidst a sense that America was losing the war on drugs proclaimed by President Ronald Reagan, parents, police officers, and school systems joined together in an antidrug program called D.A.R.E. (drug abuse resistance education) that encouraged children to "just say no" to drug use of all kinds. Although controlled studies did not find the D.A.R.E. program to effectively reduce drug use, the program was still widely offered at the end of the century. Educational programs to prevent smoking tobacco were more successful, and, by 2000, the smoking rate among adolescents was half of what it was in 1974.

Sexuality. Another grave concern of many parents was juvenile sexuality. Parents were concerned about pregnancy, sexually transmitted diseases, and AIDS. As society became more sexualized in music, television, advertising, and movies, children's sophistication about sexual matters grew, and both boys and girls were becoming sexually active at younger ages; by the end of the 1980s, nearly as many girls as boys had become sexually active. In 1973, about 35 percent of high school seniors were not virgins; by 1990 70 percent of seniors and 40 percent of high school freshmen were not. This increase was due, in part, to the amount of unsupervised time adolescents spent after school, some as many as five hours a day. Children in the final decades of the 20th century grew up faster than earlier cohorts of children. The prevalence of cable television, movies, and the Internet had exposed children to more overt sexual images at earlier ages, and in many ways they appeared to know more at younger ages than their less-worldly parents. Although they were more sexually active, adolescent rates of pregnancy and abortions dropped in the 1990s.

Adolescent sexuality was one arena in which the culture war was fought. Parents and educators were concerned about adolescent sexuality and possible problems that could befall those who were sexually active, but there was no consensus on how to prevent problems. Some advocated sex education in public schools; others insisted that it was the job of parents to provide such information to their children. Even those who agreed that sex education might be useful disagreed on what should be taught to children and by whom. Those who advocated abstinence grew in power in the 1990s—2 percent of high school sex education programs taught abstinence only in 1988; by 1999 nearly 25 percent were abstinence-only programs. Despite research indicating that abstinence-only programs were unsuccessful in reducing adolescent sexual activity, the programs continued to grow in number.

Preparing Children for the Unknowns Ahead

By the late 1980s, experts cautioned parents not to overschedule their children. Despite these warnings, it was not uncommon for children to take music lessons, dance lessons, participate in two or more team sports, attend church groups, and be involved in scouting and other activities. From a very young age, some children were enrolled in academically challenging preschools to help them outpace their peers and eventually get into the best colleges.

In a best-selling book, *The Hurried Child,* childrearing expert and psychologist David Elkind (1981) warned parents about the dangers of raising children who were overextended and whose time was too highly scheduled. Elkind said children felt pressured to perform, and they risked burnout and disillusionment when they got older. For many children, the result of overscheduling and abundant adult-supervised activities was less time to do homework and play with other children. They were also missing out on one-on-one time with their parents, talking, playing games, and relaxing. The end result was that many children and parents felt hurried and stressed, and increasing numbers of both were taking antidepressants. Some parents also felt guilty that they could not give their children everything they wanted or everything that other children had, and many felt guilty that work prevented them from spending a lot of time together.

Despite warnings about children growing up too fast, ambitious parents wanted their children to have every advantage in life, and they made great efforts to provide it—physical development (e.g., sports camps, developmental teams to build skills in specific sports), intellectual (e.g., camps for all areas of academic specialties, special magnet schools for gifted children), emotional (e.g., parents did not hesitate to put children in counseling or take them to psychiatrists at early signs of distress), and social (e.g., parents sponsored parties for their children, enrolled them in cotillions). Children with specific interests or abilities, such as musical talent, were encouraged by their parents to enroll in summer camps, take private lessons, and practice, practice, practice. Even children whose "talents" were their good looks were pressed by their parents to excel. Beauty pageants for little girls, which began in the 1960s, were very popular, especially in the South. By the end of the century, childhood beauty pageants were estimated to be a billion-dollar industry; more than 100,000 American children under age 12, including infants, competed annually in some 500 contests.

At the end of the century, adolescents thought growing up was harder for them than it was for earlier generations, and they believed they faced more serious problems. Some observers noted that they were the first "to live so well and complain so bitterly about it" (Palladino, 1996, p. 257). Although many had their own cars, telephones, televisions, computers, and other amenities, adolescents tended to believe that they were worse off than their parents had been when they were adolescents. Some adults argued, however, that the reason teenagers struggled was because they had unrealistic expectations and sought immediate gratification.

SUMMARY

The "century of the child" was characterized by contradictory notions of children's roles in the family and in society. As the century opened, children were vulnerable to disease and death, were expected to work to help support their families, and received very little formal education. By the end of the century, more children died from accidents than from disease; many adolescents (and almost no younger children) worked, but only for their own monetary benefit; and time spent in formal education had lengthened considerably, extending into adulthood, at least for the middle class. At the beginning of the century, families tended to be large and parents had little time to invest in each individual child. At the end of the century, families tended to be smaller, but shared parent-child time together, especially leisure time, was at a premium for a variety of reasons.

Most parents did their best to protect their children from becoming mature too fast. However, social forces often worked against them, pulling children toward adulthood—children and adults were beginning to look and act more alike, children's clothing bore a strong resemblance to adults' clothing, they watched many of the same television shows and movies, played the same games, used the same language, and ate the same foods. These trends became more pronounced during the last two decades of the century. In many ways, the quality of children's well-being was mixed; what children gained in one area of their lives, they often lost in another.

8

Family Abuse and Neglect: The Dark Side of Families

Most Americans associate positive connotations with the concept *family* and think that family life is generally characterized by supporting, caring relationships, working together for common goals, and looking out for each other's welfare. These widely held positive images of family life that have dominated the media (in entertainment programming and advertising) for the last 100 years reflect idealized views of what transpires in U.S. families more than the reality of all, or even most, families. Such idealized perceptions can make it easy to overlook the fact that families also may have dark sides, that family members sometimes hurt, neglect, and even kill each other. Although family violence was "discovered" by social scientists and the media as a new phenomenon in the 1960s, violence among family members has been prevalent since the beginning of time.

Public awareness and societal concerns about abuse and neglect in families have varied enormously over the course of U.S. history. There have been times, for instance, when social reformers have attempted to increase public awareness of domestic violence and have proposed interventions and policies to help victims of family abuse and neglect. These periods of reform generally were short-lived, and proposed solutions were not very effective. For instance, among the first laws in the world prohibiting wife beating and cruelty to children were those enacted by the Puritans of the Massachusetts Bay Colony between 1640 and 1680. Few men were arrested for committing abusive acts, however—only 12 cases of wife abuse were prosecuted in the colony between 1633 and 1802 (Pleck, 1987). It is unlikely that these laws were such effective deterrents that there averaged only one case of wife abuse every 14 years; it is far more probable the laws were ignored and rarely enforced.

Nearly 200 years passed before there was another period of public concern about family violence. Between 1870 and the end of the 19th century, women activists became interested in crimes against women, including wife abuse. They also were concerned about children's welfare, and societies for the prevention of cruelty to children (SPCCs) were founded. These societies originated because of a famous case of child abuse and neglect that shocked the nation. In 1874, the sufferings of a 10-year-old girl named Mary Ellen marked the beginning of a worldwide campaign against child cruelty. Born in New York City, Mary Ellen endured years of abuse at the hands of a woman with whom she was placed at age two. After tiring of hearing the young girl's screams, concerned neighbors contacted a charity worker who visited the home and found a bruised, scarred, and malnourished little girl. Despite a New York law permitting authorities to remove children from homes of abusive caregivers, the charity worker was reluctant to intervene, finally contacting several local asylums in an attempt to have Mary Ellen removed from her home. When these attempts failed, the charity worker appealed to the American Society for the Prevention of Cruelty to Animals (ASPCA) for help. An ASPCA investigator posing as a census worker went to the home the following day, and within 24 hours Mary Ellen was removed from the household and placed in an orphanage. She was later adopted. This case received widespread publicity, shocking many Americans that it was easier to protect an abused dog or cat than a child. Consequently, later that year, the New York Society for the Prevention of Cruelty to Children (NYSPCC) was founded, becoming the first organization in the world dedicated to protecting children from cruelty. By the end of the first decade of the 20th century, there were nearly 500 such organizations.

Thus the 20th century opened with social reform movements in place against wife battering and cruelty to children, but these movements were short-lived. When cases of family violence were identified by outside authorities, the abuse often was blamed on poverty, mental disturbances, and other family problems. As a result, law enforcement was gradually replaced by social casework as the preferred method of intervention, and the public focus of the social reformers shifted to other political issues such as women's right to vote. Soon the problem of family violence was all but forgotten.

Public awareness of family violence as a social problem remained underground for decades and did not again receive much public recognition as a large-scale problem until the 1960s, when awareness of parental violence against children and wife abuse reemerged. Recognition of other forms of family maltreatment soon followed, including violence perpetrated by wives against husbands, child neglect, violence between brothers and sisters, the abuse and neglect of elderly family members, and physically hurtful behavior against gay and lesbian partners.

In a break with historical trends, the public awareness about domestic violence and child neglect raised in the 1960s did not fade away. Instead, the last four decades of the 20th century saw an increase in research on the causes and effects, and social policies and therapeutic interventions were designed to prevent family violence and neglect and to treat those who had been either victims or perpetrators. Unlike the prior 400 years of American history, in the last decades of the 20th century, the country began to take a long hard look at this serious family and societal problem.

BARRIERS TO RECOGNIZING FAMILY VIOLENCE AND NEGLECT

For most of the 20th century, there was little public recognition of the extent of family violence and neglect, and efforts to prevent or to stop violence and neglect within families occurred relatively late in the century. Social observers have speculated that American social norms and cultural beliefs explain why the dismal and violent side of families was ignored.

In particular, it has been argued that Americans historically have shown a fairly high tolerance for violent behavior, regardless of its context. According to this perspective, a certain amount of violence or aggression has been seen as an acceptable way to resolve interpersonal disagreements and problems, at least by many Americans. Some popular movies, television shows, and literature celebrate the use of violence as a solution to problems, and when aggressive action becomes normative in those settings, it is hypothesized that family life becomes another context in which violence is seen to occur naturally. Consequently, the argument goes, a certain amount of violence is accepted as being within the norm for family behaviors. For some Americans, husbands are within their rights to hit, kick, or otherwise physically harm or threaten to harm their wives to control them or to assert their proper role as head of the household and family. For most of America's history, men have been seen as having the right to dominate their wives, and, although most Americans of any historical period would have objected to husbands severely beating or battering their wives, they also probably would have agreed that it was appropriate for a husband to punish a wife as he saw fit if she was shirking her household responsibilities or acting in an insubordinate manner. Similarly, many Americans consider the physical punishment of children as acceptable parental behavior. Although few Americans would defend a parent for viciously beating their child, for many families, physical punishment has been a normal part of child discipline.

Another possible explanation for the lack of awareness of family maltreatment is that Americans have long believed that family activities should be private; it is not anyone else's business how parents discipline their children, how a couple resolves their disagreements, or how an adult child treats an older mother or father. The cultural norm of family privacy means that what goes on behind closed doors is for family members only. This emphasis on family privacy and the sanctity of the home has historically been a barrier to domestic violence reform efforts, and despite the fact that many acts of violence committed in homes would be considered serious crimes if committed in public, law enforcement officers generally have considered domestic fights to be private matters, and they were reluctant to interfere. As a result, even though domestic violence laws existed, they were seldom enforced until toward the end of the century.

Finally, another barrier has been the belief held by some that marriages and families should be preserved at all costs—that it was preferable that incidents of domestic violence or neglect be ignored or downplayed if the alternative meant that couples would be divorced or families would be separated. Given these cultural beliefs, it is not surprising that awareness of family violence and neglect and public standards for what constituted family maltreatment varied greatly over the course of the century. At different periods of time, there were differences in how abuse and neglect cases were identified and reported to authorities, and probably most cases were not reported.

By the last part of the century, however, it was widely known that millions of people were injured or killed by close family members each year. Individuals were more likely to be hit or fatally injured by family members in their own homes than by anyone else (e.g., friends, strangers) in any other location. Additionally, many children and adults who were not the victims of violence witnessed acts of violence in their homes. Although they may not have suffered direct physical consequences, they were likely harmed psychologically and emotionally by witnessing such events. Despite continuing differences in how family violence and neglect were defined, most Americans perceived family violence as a major social problem as the century concluded.

What had changed perceptions of family violence and neglect? The feminist movement made abuse of women by their intimate partners a major part of its political agenda and refused to let the matter be ignored. Social scientists began studying family violence and neglect, and they shared startling statistics about the incidence of abuse and neglect. Although these topics were extremely challenging to study, given that such behaviors were illegal and many people considered them immoral and repulsive, some social scientists became quite persistent in attempting to document the extent of these problems. Abused wives who felt supported by a cultural atmosphere and determined reform movements began to tell their stories publicly, and some of these stories became books and movies (e.g., *The Burning Bed*, 1984 [based on McNulty, 1980]; *Bastard out of Carolina*, 1996 [based on Allison, 1992]; *The Color Purple*, 1985 [based on Walker, 1983]). As the cultural environment shifted, men, children, and others who had been victims or who had witnessed family abuse also spoke out, and policymakers had little choice but to revise the laws about family abuse and neglect. The law enforcement and therapeutic communities also began to examine their practices and change to be more effective.

Given the unevenness with which Americans have been willing to face the issue of family violence and neglect, it should not be surprising to find that historical evidence of such behaviors varies tremendously, with much of what we know coming in the last 40 years of the 20th century. Reliable statistics about the extent of abuse and neglect were lacking until late in the century, and even then there were questions about their validity. Family members were often reluctant to report each other to authorities. Shame and worry about what people would think and fear prohibited families from coming forward, and children often did not know how to report being victimized by older family members. Even when no data showed the prevalence of certain behaviors, it should be kept in mind that physical violence against family members and neglect of dependents has been an enduring aspect of family life.

CHILD ABUSE AND NEGLECT

Reforming the problem of family violence was a goal that fit with the Progressive Era movements of improving U.S. society, and child abuse and wife beating received attention from women activists early in the century. The Societies for the Prevention of Cruelty to Children formed after the shocking 1874 case of Mary Ellen sometimes removed children from their homes for their safety, which was a controversial solution, and there also were concerns about what happened to children once they were removed from their violent homes.

Child Abuse

Foster care, a general term used to describe a variety of arrangements in which children lived with people other than their parents, was often underfunded and inadequate. Some abused and neglected children were placed temporarily in homes where they had to work to pay for their keep, some went into private homes for varying lengths of time, some were placed in orphanages, and others were put up for adoption. None of these foster care arrangements were considered to be satisfactory practices by many, but soon after the formation of SPCCs, public interest in anticruelty societies began to wane. Social reformers of the Progressive Era assumed that curing social ills such as poverty would ultimately end family violence, so many members of anticruelty societies shifted their focus to the elimination of poverty and other concerns. This shift in focus ultimately led to the demise of the SPCCs, and child abuse intervention was left to be handled by social workers. A general unwillingness to treat child abuse as a crime left beating children as a social or psychological problem rather than a legal one. Law enforcement officials were generally pleased to be out of the business of arresting abusive parents and willingly let social workers and other helping professionals handle such cases.

At the beginning of the Depression, agency funding for investigating child abuse complaints was drastically reduced. Government funds were scarce, philanthropies were overwhelmed with the number of requests from people needing help, and the 1933 White House Conference on Children reported that the more severe forms of child cruelty were no longer as prevalent, and the problem was on its way to being solved. This inattention continued through the 1940s, although at least one medical researcher took note of the problem. X-ray technology, developed in the 1940s, helped reveal injuries that previously had remained hidden from view. Pediatrician and radiologist John Caffey became concerned after investigating six cases in which infants suffered subdural hematomas and long bone fractures. Unable to link these injuries to skeletal diseases or other physiological causes, he determined that the injuries were the result of traumatic forces—physical abuse. Although he noted that these unexplained injuries to children were a problem, his reports received little attention.

It was another 20 years before C. Henry Kempe and his colleagues published *The Battered-Child Syndrome* (1962). From a survey, 302 children in 88 hospitals were identified and labeled by Kempe as *battered.* Battered-child syndrome was described as a clinical condition in young children who had suffered nonaccidental, unjustifiable violence or injury committed by a trusted adult, usually a parent. Kempe and his colleagues noted that battering could occur at any age, but most child victims were under age three (Kempe, Silverman, Steele, Droegemueller, & Silver, 1962). The report provided graphic accounts of brutality committed against young children. Kempe identified battered-child syndrome as a significant cause of disability and death among children, and, unlike the earlier work of Caffey, Kempe's findings received widespread public attention. Other medical and helping professionals, government, charities, and the news media helped further increase public awareness about child abuse.

Among the outcomes of Kempe's report were appeals for mandatory child abuse reporting to ensure that cases would be reported even if there were only suspicions that children were being battered. Kempe had found that some physicians chose not to report cases of battered children to the proper authorities for two reasons. First, they were hesitant to point blame at parents, and, second, some doctors had difficulties believing that parents would harm their children. Kempe warned that children placed back home following hospitalization could be at risk for additional abuse; therefore, he advised that children be temporarily placed with other family members or in a foster home.

When *The Battered-Child Syndrome* was published, there were no effective U.S. laws regarding child abuse reporting, but by 1968 all 50 states had passed legislation regulating child abuse, including mandatory reporting by health care professionals who suspected maltreatment. Nonetheless, the American Humane Association estimated there were about 10,000 child maltreatment cases each year during the 1960s, and many went unreported.

In the 1970s, among several significant events related to increasing awareness of child maltreatment was Senator Walter Mondale's introduction of the Child Abuse Prevention and Treatment Act of 1973 (CAPTA), the first federal investigation of child maltreatment. The act established the National Center on Child Abuse and Neglect, which was created to support local, state, and national efforts to address abuse (Demos, 1986). Child abuse and neglect were defined to include physical, mental, or sexual abuse, negligent treatment, or other maltreatment of children under age 18. When the act was renewed in 1978, it was expanded to include child abduction, sodomy, and incest, as well as expanded mandatory reporting requirements.

There was a rapid increase in reports of child abuse between the mid-1970s and late 1980s. Greater public awareness may have been one explanation for the increase, but also revised definitions of child abuse and neglect meant that some disciplinary techniques once considered appropriate punishments were now being defined as child abuse and had to be reported by physicians. By 1986, nearly every state required that neglect—defined as the withholding of dependent family members' basic needs (e.g., food, water, shelter, affection)—be reported to child abuse investigators. Forty-one states had statutes that explicitly mentioned that emotional or psychological abuse of children also should be reported. Initially, mandated reporting was limited to physicians, but this was eventually expanded to include teachers, nurses, counselors, and the general public.

Beginning in the mid-1980s, American parents were bombarded with messages about the dangerous world in which their children lived. The world seemed to be a frightening place for most parents and their children. This atmosphere of ever-present child danger contributed to the public awareness of child abuse and to parents' fears that their children could be abused. Most media attention was aimed at potential harm from family outsiders. Families still were reluctant to admit abuse internally, and tended to protect abusers who were family members. Individuals also were reluctant to admit to illegal behaviors that were considered abhorrent by most members of society. The exception to this was following separation and divorce—then, accusations of abuse increased, sometimes as part of the physical custody wrangling between parents and sometimes out of vengeance. Given heightened awareness of the prevalence of child abuse and neglect, legal authorities took allegations of child abuse or neglect between former spouses (or divorcing or separating partners) very seriously. In part because of the increase in such accusations, one goal of no-fault divorce legislation—to reduce legal costs due to extended conflicts between divorcing spouses—was not fully realized.

In 1990, the U.S. Advisory Board on Child Abuse and Neglect declared a national emergency in the child protection system. By then, nearly 3 million cases were reported annually to law enforcement and county and state social services. This was a stark contrast to Kempe's 1962 survey that estimated about 750 cases of child abuse annually. The situation was described as an emergency because prevention and treatment were not being addressed. State social service agencies did little other than investigate cases in which children were found to have been maltreated; rarely were any services provided. Because of this sense of emergency, throughout the 1990s, considerable attention was placed on prevention policies and programs designed to reduce the incidence of child abuse and neglect. Educational and support programs were created for new parents, and public awareness campaigns were expanded. By 2000, however, child abuse remained a serious problem; more than 1,000 children died annually from child abuse and neglect.

One problem throughout the century was that child abuse in general was a family phenomenon that was hard to identify. Consequently, researchers late in the century tried many ways to assess its prevalence, mainly relying on court records and legal documents, surveys of abused women and children in social service agencies who had sought help, and, less often, general population surveys. None of these ways of assessing the extent of child abuse was ideal, but the composite picture presented was that child abuse was a widespread social problem that affected many children and families.

Sexual Abuse and Incest

Sexual abuse of children, like physical abuse, is a timeless social problem that did not start in the 20th century. Sexual exploitation of children by family members and others is a problem that often eludes legal authorities and the helping community. Incest—defined as sexual relations between a parent or grandparent and child or between siblings—is banned in most cultures, and is illegal in all 50 states. Incest is also known as sexual abuse, which has been generally defined as sexual acts committed by an adult who is responsible for a child's care. Sexual acts committed by someone else (a neighbor, for instance), has been defined as sexual assault. By the last decade of the 20th century, experts had agreed on several ways to distinguish sexual abuse: (1) an age difference of five or more years between the victim and offender; (2) specific sexual behavior, including kissing, fondling, penetration, and photography; and (3) sexual intent, wherein the purpose of the abuse was the sexual gratification of the adult. Although age differences and specific types of behavior were easily identified by authorities, the intent of the adult has been less clear, which has made the determination of sexual abuse and incest difficult at times. For instance, in the United States, some groups believed that sexual activity between adults and young family members, particularly between fathers and daughters, was a healthy way to teach children and adolescents about sex.

A pioneer investigator of the prevalence of sexual abuse of children was Alfred Kinsey (between 1938 and 1949), who collected data from 4,441 women, most born between 1900 and 1929. Nearly 25 percent of these women indicated that they had had sexual contact with adult men, usually family members, before they were 13 years old. Kinsey's findings shocked Americans, and many, including most psychologists and sociologists, denounced his data as inaccurate. People could not imagine so many children being sexually exploited by adults, so they gave Kinsey's study little credibility. As a result, concern about child sexual abuse drifted off the societal horizon.

It was not until many years later that a study of sexual abuse again received attention. In 1986, Diana Russell studied adult women to learn the extent of childhood sexual abuse. Her results suggested that child sexual abuse was far more prevalent than indicated in Kinsey's disputed study. Perhaps greater societal recognition of child abuse in the 1970s made it easier for women to discuss sexual abuse than it was decades earlier, or it may have been because, unlike Kinsey, Russell used female interviewers.

Although sexual abuse of children by adults had gained widespread public attention by the late 1970s, it remained unclear for the rest of the century whether the general public was aware that sexual abuse of children was as prevalent as physical abuse. Although sexual abuse leaves deep emotional wounds, unlike physical abuse, it leaves no physical signs—making it difficult to detect. Many experts suspected that sexual abuse was the most underreported form of child maltreatment of the century because child victims tended to remain silent for years, often well into adulthood. There were many reasons given for this silence. Children may have felt guilty or embarrassed about engaging in sexual relationships with parents or grandparents, and many feared that speaking out would result in more serious abuse or other forms of retribution from the abuser. In addition, they may have feared being removed from their parent's or caregiver's home or that their disclosure would be destructive for their family. Some feared that no one would believe them.

Girls were about twice as likely as boys to be victims of sexual abuse. Research in the mid-1980s indicated that the prevalence ranged from 6 percent to 62 percent for girls and from 3 percent to 31 percent of all boys. The large discrepancies were accounted for by variations in how studies were done, but even at the lowest estimated rates, significant numbers of children were sexually abused. The variation in estimates presented problems for policymakers and professionals, however, because they tended to make people think the incidence in most studies was overestimated or given too much attention.

Research suggested that child sexual abuse in the United States tended to occur in families that were socially isolated and structured along traditional gender lines. That is, men tended to be highly controlling heads of their households, and wives and children were expected to be submissive and follow husbands' dictates. Male dominance and control, as well as cultural attitudes that family matters are private issues, contributed to the veil of secrecy in these families.

Researchers estimated that sibling incest was five times more frequent than parent-child incest. Victims of sibling sexual exploitation tended to keep the abuse secret, and, even when informed, many parents were unwilling to report it to authorities. In a 1980 college survey, 15 percent of women and 10 percent of men reported some sexual interaction with a sibling. In a 1997 study, 66 percent of respondents who were abused by siblings reported being sexually abused. Compared to other juvenile sexual offenders, sibling incest offenders began at a younger age, were more likely to have younger siblings, and more likely to have been victims of sexual abuse themselves.

The Third National Incidence Study of Child Abuse and Neglect (U.S. Department of Health and Human Services, 1996) estimated that more than 300,000 children in the United States were sexually abused in 1993 alone, and in 1999, one of seven substantiated child abuse and neglect cases involved sexual abuse. Sexual abuse reported to child protective services showed the largest reported increase of any form of abuse or neglect during the last two decades of the century.

Emotional Abuse   Emotional abuse of children generally was not discussed until the last two decades of the century. The idea that children could have their feelings hurt by their parents was known, of course, but most Americans would not have considered psychological or emotional abuse of children by their parents as a possibility. Parents were expected to criticize children as a way of helping them grow up to be good citizens; if some parents went overboard yelling at their children or calling them names, for most of the century such behaviors were seen as sometimes necessary to get children's attention. If children were upset by these efforts, it was more often seen as a character deficiency of the child ("she is so sensitive") rather than as abusive parental behavior.

The National Incidence Study estimated that 532,200 children were emotionally abused in 1996—a 183 percent increase over the 1986 estimate. However, in the 1997 *Child Maltreatment* national report, emotional maltreatment was reported in only about 6 percent of the 817,665 child abuse reports received from 43 states. This report likely greatly underestimated the actual number of children who were the targets of emotionally abusive behaviors.

Emotional abuse includes negative verbal interactions, such as belittling, put-downs, name calling, and humiliation, as well as psychologically damaging discipline. Researchers in the 1990s found that emotional abuse of all kinds had devastating effects on children's emotional and psychological development and often resulted in serious emotional and behavioral problems for children—including lack of emotional attachment to a parent or caregiver, depression, impaired cognitive ability, low academic achievement, and poor social skills. Despite these negative outcomes, many states had no laws against emotional abuse, even as late as the 1990s, after child abuse and neglect were widely recognized as serious social problems. Physical injury was often necessary before the authorities would intervene on behalf of children who were emotionally abused. Emotional maltreatment often accompanied other forms of child maltreatment; it rarely occurred in isolation. This made it challenging for researchers to separate the outcomes of emotional abuse from other types of abuse. Emotional abuse was the most difficult to detect and measure, which may be why it was the least studied and least recognized of all types of child abuse. At the end of the century, researchers were still struggling to adequately define emotional abuse.

Early in the century, social reformers had difficulty recognizing when parents were neglecting children. By **Child Neglect** modern standards, many impoverished children in the early decades of the century suffered from neglect. It would not have been unusual for immigrant children or other poor children to have been hungry frequently, inadequately clothed at times, left to fend for themselves during the day, and to have not received preventive medical care or any dental care. These conditions would not have been seen as neglect, however, so it is difficult, in retrospect, to make judgments about the extent of child neglect early in the century.

The concept of neglect was introduced during the initial White House Conference on Children and Youth in 1909. Prior to that, children were sometimes removed from their homes, not because of abuse or neglect, but solely because their families were poor. This practice came under fire during the 1909 conference when child experts made the assertions that children should stay in their homes except in extraordinary circumstances, and when it was pointed out how costly it was to society to remove children from their homes. There were far more poor families with children than there were resources to house them and meet their needs.

The Great Depression of the 1930s saw an upsurge of families living in poverty, which likely resulted in an upsurge in child neglect—if neglect is defined as parents not providing enough to eat, not providing adequate shelter, and being too distracted to supervise children as much as they normally would have. Some child protection agencies in the 1930s considered maternal employment to be a form of child neglect, a judgment that fit with public sentiment at the time about women working. Because jobs were scarce, it was widely believed that women should be fired or voluntarily resign from their jobs so that more men could be employed. By equating maternal employment with child neglect, more pressure was placed on working mothers to resign their jobs. During World War II, women's working to support the war effort helped relieve some of the blame placed on working mothers for neglecting their children, but they were still frequently accused of neglecting their children.

In 1954, John DeFrancis, lawyer and former director of the NYSPCC, became the head of the Children's Division of the American Humane Association and conducted the first national survey exploring the extent of child abuse, neglect, and exploitation. The publicly distributed findings revealed that many child welfare departments lacked specialized agencies to deal with abuse and neglect. DeFrancis believed that social casework to help address the problem of neglectful parents was preferable to going to court or having children placed in out-of-home care. In 1957, the Children's Bureau issued a report recommending that each state examine the extent of child abuse, neglect, and abandonment in its state, and either provide social services when problems were found or ensure that police were contacted. This mid-century report was the federal government's first acknowledgment of child maltreatment as a national public policy concern.

During the early 1960s, removing children from their homes was no longer considered necessary or good practice, so parents rather than children became the focus of social casework efforts. Children were typically removed from their homes only when it was determined that social services alone would not prevent further harm. The key principle that guided decisions about children's welfare was "the best interests of the child." At the end of the century, child welfare workers generally agreed that it was in the best interests of most children to remain with their parents, but over half a million children were in the foster care system. About 144,000 victims of child maltreatment entered foster care in 1998 alone. Most were removed from their homes as a result of substantiated child abuse or neglect. By the end of the century, it was estimated that more than 2.5 million were abused or neglected each year, and 1,000 to 2,000 of those children died as a result of abuse or neglect (U.S. Department of Health and Human Services, 1999).

Stepchildren   Although most stepmothers and stepfathers throughout the century were kind and supportive of their stepchildren, there were also stepparents who were mean, neglectful, and abusive. Regardless of how stepparents treated stepchildren, however, widespread perceptions were that stepparents generally were quicker than parents to punish children, and that sometimes these punishments resulted in physical abuse. The perceived differences between parents' and stepparents' use of physical aggression against children was first documented in 1971 by David Gil, a researcher who reported that stepfathers or men who were functioning as father substitutes (e.g., mothers' boyfriends) were responsible for one-third of reported child abuse cases. Ten years later, David Finkelhor and colleagues (1983) published research indicating that sexual abuse of children was four to five times more likely in stepfamilies then in first marriage nuclear families.

Several other studies were published in the latter two decades of the century that found that children living in a household with an adult who was not their parent were at greater risk of abuse than if they lived with both of their parents. It remained unclear to the end of the century, however, how much more likely stepchildren were at risk for being physically abused.

Identifying the extent of child abuse generally was difficult, but in the case of stepchildren's abuse, an additional complication was marked inconsistencies in how researchers identified stepparents, especially stepfathers. Some researchers included legally remarried stepfathers only in their studies; others included mothers' boyfriends; and still others grouped together siblings, uncles, grandfathers, mothers' boyfriends, other unrelated men, and stepfathers. Another complicating factor in determining the extent of abuse of stepchildren compared to children in first marriage families was that stepchildren may have been less hesitant to report sexual and physical abuse by stepfathers or mothers' boyfriends than by biological fathers. Additionally, because of cultural stereotypes about stepfamilies, medical personnel may have been more likely to attribute children's injuries to abuse in stepfamilies than in other families.

Despite problems in gathering data about the extent of stepchildren's risk compared to children with both parents, researchers were confident that stepfamilies experienced some greater degree of domestic violence against children than first marriage nuclear families. A number of reasons for this were proposed in the 1990s. According to some researchers, child abuse in stepfamilies was related to the higher levels of stress experienced by stepparents. Stepfamilies late in the 20th century were formed after multiple family transitions (e.g., parental divorce, perhaps followed by cohabitation, then remarriage of one or both parents, sometimes followed by another divorce); the cumulative stress accompanying these transitions was thought to increase the risk of abuse. Perhaps the most controversial and widely known of the proposed explanations was *evolutionary theory,* which asserted that physical abuse of stepchildren was more likely because stepparents had a lesser investment in children who did not carry their genes. Just as some animals attack and kill the offspring of others so their own offspring have a better chance of survival, it was suggested that stepparents might abuse children who are not the product of their reproductive efforts. Evolutionary theory also suggested that stepchildren were at risk for sexual abuse, because incest taboos did not apply to them. Margo Wilson and Martin Daly (1987) argued that

children's extreme dislike of discord between their natural parents and their alarm at the prospect of parental remarriage reflect a remarkably astute assessment of their own best interests, and may even be adaptive emotional responses that have been specifically favored in our natural selective history. (p. 227)

However, other scholars pointed out that evolutionary explanations did not account for the prevalence of physical and sexual abuse of children by their biological parents; nor did it explain the vast majority of stepparents who helped raise and care for their stepchildren. For example, not all studies found less involvement and investment in stepchildren by stepparents, although some evolutionary theorists suggested that stepparents' investment in their stepchildren does indeed fit the theory—when stepfathers invest in their stepchildren, they enhance the likelihood that the mothers of their stepchildren will reproduce with them. Although the evolutionary arguments do not entirely explain the disconfirming evidence and do not account for low rates of abuse among adopted children, at the end of the century this was the most prevalent theory used to explain stepchild abuse and neglect. Sociologist David Popenoe (1994), convinced by the evolutionary argument, went so far as to suggest in the mid-1990s that parents who remarried were committing child abuse by putting their children at risk of abuse by the stepparent.

Foster Children   America's foster care system was developed to provide shelter and protection for children requiring out-of-home placement. The first foster child in America was in 1636 in the Jamestown Colony, but the first system of paid foster care started in 1853 in New York City. Charles Loring Brace, disturbed by the large numbers of immigrant children sleeping on the streets of New York, funded the New York Children's Aid Society, which provided funds to families willing to take in homeless children too young to be indentured servants. During the early 1900s, social service agencies began supervising these foster parents.

Before 1945, foster care referred to various arrangements of care for children who needed placement outside their own home, and fostering essentially meant noninstitutional care (such as orphanages or poor houses). Foster parents were sometimes paid to take in children, and sometimes they were not. Usually these placements were with nonrelatives, but many children were placed with other relatives in kinship care. Foster care was intended to be temporary, with the goal to either return children to their families as soon as feasible or locate suitable adoptive homes. However, many children spent several years in foster care. Often after returning to live with their parents, children moved back into foster care following additional abuse. The research on attachment that became widely known after World War II convinced social workers that adoption was the best solution for abused and neglected children.

The movement to get children out of institutions was relatively successful by 1950, which was the first time that children in foster care outnumbered institutionalized children. By 1960, twice as many children were in foster care as were institutionalized, and there was growing awareness of child abuse and neglect that led to public financial support for foster care. Increased understanding of abuse and neglect had greatly increased both reporting of abuse and the need for foster placements.

By the 1980s, state policies (through federal funding incentives) included making a reasonable effort to keep children with their families—a policy known as family preservation—and efforts were made to avoid foster family care, shorten a child's time in foster care if avoidance was impossible, or facilitate adoption in some cases. Family preservation policies changed somewhat when too many instances of continued abuse and death were reported when children were allowed to stay in or were returned to their homes.

Children who have been maltreated experience developmental delays and behavioral disorders, factors that can put them at risk for further abuse. A small portion of children who were placed in foster care experienced additional trauma and abuse from foster parents or other foster children. General Accounting Office data indicated that the median percentage of children who were abused and neglected in foster care in 1999 was about 1 in 200 children. Kinship care was not the solution to this problem, because children in kinship care were more likely to have unsupervised visits with their biological parents, placing them at greater risk for reabuse. When children were abused in foster care, it undermined the rationale for state intervention, and the relatively high incidence of reported abuse and neglect in foster placements led some at the end of the century to question whether out-of-home placement was in the best interests of children.

By the end of the century, more than half a million children lived in foster care at any given time. For children who were not safe in the care

Child abuse victim. (© Royalty-Free/Corbis)

of family members, the focus late in the century changed from foster care to rapid adoption. In 1999, 36,000 children were adopted nationwide and 64 percent were adopted by their foster parents, who then dropped out of the system, contributing to the shortage of appropriate foster care homes. This shortage also was made worse by the number of dual-earner households (foster care was less lucrative than most other paid positions—in fact, payment seldom covered the cost of the child's care) and the aging of current foster parents. Foster parents dropped out of the system for many reasons: fatigue and stress (especially when caring for special needs children), lack of training, minimal support, and poor relationships with social workers and social service agencies.

Who Abused Children? For the first seven decades of the century, the American public and most helping professionals believed that parents who abused and neglected their children were either mentally ill or were low-income, uneducated individuals who did not know any better and had few skills for resolving conflicts and raising their children. More recent researchers, however, provided a more complete picture of child abusers.

First, researchers found that child abuse occurred in all socioeconomic groups; abusive parents could be well-educated professionals as well as poorly educated, unskilled workers. This shocked many Americans because it did not fit the prevailing stereotype of abusive parents. Although abuse was most common or at least more often reported within poor or disadvantaged households, middle- and upper-class families with educated parents were not immune to child abuse and neglect.

Both mothers and fathers were possible abusers, which also disturbed people and violated widely held assumptions about mothers. They were thought to be less capable of abuse than fathers; however, mothers and fathers abused their children at similar rates. In fact, some research suggested that, when young children were physically abused, mothers were more likely than fathers to have committed the acts. One explanation was that mothers spent more time with their children; therefore, they had more opportunities to be abusive.

In addition, researchers indicated that parents who were abused as children were more likely to abuse their own children—often referred to as the cycle of violence. Although child guidance workers first suggested a cycle of violence during the 1920s, they were unable to establish a clear connection between being abused as a child and becoming abusers as adults. The connection was made again during congressional hearings for CAPTA in the 1970s, when expert witnesses emphasized that children must be protected to interrupt the cycle of violence that could one day lead them to become juvenile delinquents and batterers themselves.

By the 1990s, it was known that parents who abused their children often used authoritarian, neglectful, and verbally abusive parenting techniques, and they were more likely to use physical punishment to discipline their children. They also tended to have unrealistically high expectations for children, and they were more likely than nonabusive parents to believe that a child who made a mistake had misbehaved intentionally. For example, researchers found that abusers were more likely than other parents to expect very young children to follow difficult directions or to be toilet trained at an unreasonably early age. They also were more likely to become enraged when young children cried or had a toileting accident, because they assumed that the child was doing this on purpose. Abusers also attributed children's misbehaviors to fixed and unchangeable characteristics of the child; nonabusers, on the other hand, attributed children's misbehaviors to factors that could be changed with guidance from them.

Abusive parents lived stressful lives and were overrepresented among the young; the unmarried; those with low levels of education, poor self-esteem, and higher rates of depression; those who had been abused as a child; and those who had alcohol or drug abuse problems. The prevailing view of child abuse at the end of the century was that, when parents experienced great stress, frustration would build and sometimes explode into violence directed against children. Moreover, parents who abused their children were often socially isolated and had little or no contact with relatives and friends. Interventions were designed to address each of the components.

Throughout the century, it was not unusual for children to be in the same room during violent outbursts by other family members; nor was it uncommon for them to hear screaming in another room or to see bruises on their mothers the day

Children Who Witnessed Domestic Violence

after a beating. For most of the century, households were small enough that physical violence between parents could be easily heard by all household dwellers. In fact, it was probably rare when children of parents who abused each other (or, more frequently, when fathers abused mothers) did not witness at least occasional incidents of violence.

Given the blind eye that the nation turned toward child abuse in general, it is not surprising that, for most of the century, helping professionals, policymakers, clergy, and legal professionals showed little awareness of the possible harm to children of seeing physical violence in their households. It was not until toward the end of the century that social workers and other helping professionals became aware that, each year, millions of children witnessed one of their parents, usually their mother, being abused by the other parent or by an intimate partner. Experts on children's development argued that, for some children, repeatedly witnessing domestic violence could have long-term negative consequences—particularly when the abuse they witnessed was frequent and severe and when the child was emotionally close to the victim. Some children required intensive therapy to help them overcome the experience

Girl witnessing domestic conflict. (© Royalty-Free/
Corbis)

of seeing a parent being abused physically. Many times the physical safety
of children who observed domestic violence was in jeopardy as well. For
example, some children were unintentionally hit by thrown objects, while
others were physically assaulted when they tried to intervene to protect
their parent. In the long term, these children were at greater risk of using
physical violence to resolve their own conflicts. Children who had witnessed or experienced abuse were significantly more likely as adults to
abuse their own children than were those who had never experienced or
seen domestic violence as a child.

Despite growing awareness that exposure to domestic violence could
be emotionally and psychologically damaging to children, by the end of
the century, witnessing domestic violence was not considered a type of
child abuse subject to mandatory reporting—although a handful of states

enacted legislation making committing domestic violence in the presence of children a crime. Many policy advocates for children considered this action a step in the right direction, but critics of these laws raised concerns about potential negative outcomes. Under such laws, children would be more likely to be asked to testify against offenders, which could put them at risk of future abuse and negatively affect the quality of their relationship with a parent if he or she was the perpetrator. Additionally, critics argued that it placed the adult victim at risk of being charged for not protecting the child from witnessing the violence or for acting in self-defense in the child's presence.

ABUSE AGAINST PARTNERS AND SPOUSES

For most of America's history, men and women were not considered equals, either within the family household or in society as a whole. Some people regarded wives as the **Wife Abuse** property of their husbands, just as children were considered their fathers' property during much of American history prior to the 20th century. Given their status as subordinates, and the general acceptability of using force to maintain their dominance, physical violence was a way that some men kept women in their place. Old adages reveal how women have been viewed historically, such as the French proverb "Women, like walnut trees, should be beaten every day," and an English proverb, "A woman, a horse, and a hickory tree; the more you beat 'em, the better they be." It has been said that in English common law a husband had the right to physically reprimand his wife with a stick as long as the stick he used was no bigger than his thumb, supposedly the origin of the saying "rule of thumb."

Throughout the 20th century, just as with child abuse, there was variability in public awareness about the extent to which wives were physically attacked by their husbands. Some people accepted that husbands would, on occasion, slap, hit, punch, kick, throw things at, or otherwise physically harm their wives. For these Americans, domestic violence was a normal part of marriage and was not a social or relational problem unless a man seriously injured the woman. Privacy norms and the right of a man to run his house as he deemed necessary were enough for most Americans to look the other way and ignore domestic violence.

Early in the century, social reformers worked on behalf of women who were victims of violent crimes, including those who were beaten by husbands. However, some of the reformers' efforts on behalf of women were controversial. For example, some activists encouraged women to divorce abusive or drunken husbands, advice that was widely considered inappropriate. Women were expected to sacrifice themselves and their personal happiness to look after their children. Because it was believed that husbands who beat their wives were more fearful of public disgrace

than of being fined or spending time in jail, several states proposed
legislation that punished physically abusive husbands with the public
whipping post or pillory. Most of these laws, if passed, were rarely
enforced. When they were, punishments were enacted disproportionately
against men from racial minority groups and the poor.

During the Progressive Era, domestic violence was thought to be a
problem primarily of immigrant and lower-income families. Some wives
were struck or kicked for protecting their children when the children were
being beaten by their husbands, and some were attacked if husbands
thought they were being too lenient with children. Although women
defended their children against mistreatment, they typically did not protect themselves, and only a few reported their husbands' assaults to police
or social workers.

For most women who had been attacked severely enough to come
to the attention of law enforcement authorities, leaving their abusive
husbands was not a realistic option. Motherhood was their primary role,
and they feared losing their children if they escaped abusive husbands.
Women were discouraged by helping professionals, extended family, and
friends from filing for divorce because it was believed that divorce was
not in the best interest of children. Rather than divorce, a few abused
wives filed for legal separations in which they also asked the judge to
order their husbands to pay a weekly sum to support their families.
The amount of this support was rarely enough for women and children
to live on, so most women returned to their abusive husbands (Pleck,
1987). Considering that most women were not able to financially support themselves and their children, reconciliation with the abuser generally was thought to be the best alternative for them, their children, and
for society at large (so the women and their children would not become
dependents of the government). Laws and public policies thus had the
effect of encouraging battered wives to remain with their abusive husbands, which likely made them more rather than less susceptible to being
beaten and abused.

The legal system did not seem to enjoy dealing with wife-beating
cases. When such cases did go before the courts, judges typically advised
women to withdraw their complaints and told both spouses to forget they
had ever been in court. In the Progressive Era, men and women were considered to be equally responsible when husbands were accused of beating
their wives. Men were blamed for losing their tempers and for not knowing how to handle their women, and women were accused of being bad
wives or poor housekeepers, giving their husbands reasons to be upset
with them. Several days after a woman filed charges with the court, a
caseworker would visit her home to investigate her housekeeping abilities and to assess how much she was contributing to her own physical
abuse. Judges' main advice to battered women usually was to keep their
homes and children clean in order to gain their husbands' respect (and

presumably eliminate any reason to get angry and hit her). Husbands were told to try to keep their tempers in check.

With the arrival of the Depression, the country's families became focused on dealing with economic hardships. Although there are no firm statistics to prove that violence between spouses was greater during the 1930s than it had been in previous decades, marital disputes and marital separations increased as husbands and wives struggled with each other while facing the demands of trying to provide for their families under conditions of extreme economic distress. It is highly probable, therefore, that domestic violence increased during the Depression.

There was great public sympathy for unemployed husbands during the Depression, and, as a result, women were held accountable for marital violence perpetrated against them. Wives were encouraged to overlook their husbands' physical and verbal abuse and were reminded of the strains their unemployed or underemployed husbands were experiencing. Some social workers discouraged abused women from leaving their husbands because they could not manage economically on their own and they would be removing a male role model from their sons. Concerns about the absence of male role models were far greater than concerns about the effects of violent male role models on boys.

Public awareness of domestic violence between spouses during the 1940s and 1950s remained low. Individual psychiatric problems were pinpointed as the causes of violence rather than family or environmental factors, and abused wives continued to be blamed for violent acts committed by their husbands. During the 1950s, wife battering was not considered a crime, and, when women came forward to complain about abuse, it was often assumed that they had somehow provoked their husbands' behavior. Wives were rarely allowed to obtain restraining orders against their husbands unless they simultaneously filed for divorce.

During the 1960s, feminism, which had waned after the 1920s, made a comeback. The National Organization for Women (NOW, a nonradical feminist organization whose members were mostly middle- and upper-class women) was created in 1966, but during its early years wife abuse was not an organizational emphasis, possibly because such violence was believed to occur mostly among the lower classes. The women's movement, however, gradually helped facilitate awareness among the American public that all middle-class marriages were not peaceful. It was radical feminists, however, not the more moderate NOW members, who were most critical of traditional marriages and who were responsible for bringing wife battering to the forefront of public recognition.

In the 1970s, NOW shifted its focus to marital abuse in addition to the causes they originally championed (workplace discrimination, publicly funded child care, and legalized abortion). Some of this shift was due to the efforts of Nancy Kirk-Gomez, who, after enduring 10 years of beatings by her husband, established a self-help group for battered women.

As a member of NOW, she noted that the organization addressed many issues of importance to women, but not abuse. Her self-help group eventually led to the founding of the Pennsylvania Task Force on Household Violence (Pleck, 1987). Among the task force goals were emphasizing divorce as a long-term solution, prosecution of abusers, allowing self-defense pleas, and reforming law enforcement practices. At its 1975 conference, NOW declared that wife abuse was a major issue and established the National Task Force on Battered Women/Household Violence. A year later, the National Task Force held a massive media campaign, and in March of that year, 2,000 women from 33 countries met in Belgium for the International Tribunal on Crimes Against Women. Following this event, the U.S. news media could no longer ignore issues related to battered women and children.

The women's movement continued to pressure police, social service agencies, and the government to address the problem of wife beating, and it raised awareness of the lack of sanctions against wife abuse and the absence of protections for victims. Within the criminal justice system, marital violence had been viewed as a pervasive and persistent problem that created dangerous situations for police officers, and these cases were difficult for courts to resolve. Because police officers who made arrests at scenes of domestic violence were at risk of injury or death, they frequently favored reconciliation and referral to counseling over arrest of an abusive husband—officers believed that arrests increased the rate of injuries to officers, so they were seen as a last resort. Some police used a "stitch rule" whereby husbands were arrested only if their wives' injuries required a certain number of stitches. Because police were not willing to remove abusive husbands from their homes, many abused women went into hiding with their children while their husbands remained free.

In 1971, the world's first shelter for battered women was founded by Erin Pizzey in London, England. This shelter was initially established as a child care center and shelter for homeless women, but Pizzey soon learned that many of the abused women sought refuge there because they were unable to get necessary help from the police, physicians, or social workers, so she expanded the range of services. Women from throughout the United Kingdom sought refuge at the shelter, and soon women's groups opened similar shelters across Great Britain.

By 1974, the women's shelter movement had spread to the United States. These shelters provided women a place to stay while deciding whether to return to their husbands. Many offered schooling, job counseling, information about welfare and food stamps, legal information, and other social services. Some offered rape crisis centers and rape hotlines. In 1976, there were 20 shelters for abused women in the United States, but state and federal funding helped establish women's shelters across the country, and there were about 2,000 of them at the end of the century. Despite this progress, Rep. Barbara Boxer (D-CA) testified in 1990 before

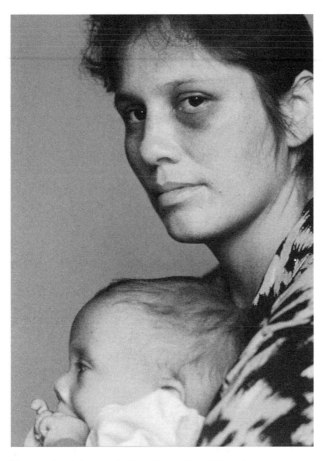

Domestic violence victim. (Associated Press)

the Subcommittee on Crime and Criminal Justice during the Senate Judiciary Hearings for the Violence Against Women Act that there were three animal shelters for every one shelter for battered women.

It was not until the last three decades of the 20th century that progress was made in the legal protection of victims of domestic violence. Until then, the same violent behaviors that would get a man arrested and charged with a felony crime if directed at a stranger were only enough for a misdemeanor charge if the victim was the man's wife. During the late 1970s, several states passed legislation that served as prototypes for the rest of the country. In 1976, Pennsylvania became the first state to offer orders of protection against wife abusers. An order of protection meant that the courts could order a man accused of beating his wife to stay away from her. The following year, Oregon became the first state to enact legislation mandating arrest of the abuser in domestic violence cases, and its

Family Abuse Prevention Act served as a model for other states. For the first time, a woman could get a restraining order regardless of whether her abuser was prosecuted. By 1980, 44 states had enacted similar laws (Pleck, 1987). In 1978, Minnesota became the first state to allow arrests when there was probable cause, regardless of the presence of an order of protection. By 1982, about 48 states had coalitions that provided services for battered women. Reports of violence against wives rose dramatically during the 1970s and 1980s, but it is likely that this increase reflected a rise in public awareness and willingness to report rather than an increase in the number of cases.

The federal government's response to the war on violence against women was formally recognized in 1978 when hearings were held before the U.S. Civil Rights Commission. One year later, President Jimmy Carter established the Office of Domestic Violence in the U.S. Department of Health and Human Services. Its purpose was to be a national clearinghouse of information, grants, research, and prevention materials. This political focus on domestic violence was short-lived.

By 1980, the New Right, a coalition of conservative religious fundamentalists, began emphasizing the importance of strengthening families. They viewed the domestic violence legislation of the late 1970s as a feminist attack on the family values they favored, and they opposed what they saw as invasions of family privacy. The New Right was also uneasy because the shelters took mothers out of their homes. President Ronald Reagan closed the Office of Domestic Violence two years after it was established. Some of its staff were reassigned to the National Center on Child Abuse and Neglect, and seven years after its initial introduction, domestic violence legislation was attached to the Child Abuse Prevention Treatment Act Amendments of 1984 as the Family Violence Act of 1984.

Attention to domestic violence diminished for a few years until the passage of the Violence Against Women Act (VAWA) was signed into law by President Clinton in 1994. Until then, all 50 states had enacted some legislation against domestic violence, but consistent policies were lacking. VAWA provided a specific set of standards for states to follow, including warrantless arrests; mandatory arrests; stalking laws; orders of protection; and required training for law enforcement, prosecutors, and judges. VAWA also provided funding for shelters, counseling, domestic violence hotlines, and other programs designed to reduce violence against women and children.

A significant event in the same year that VAWA became law helped shed more light on the problem of domestic violence than any legislative act could. On June 12, Nicole Brown Simpson, estranged wife of retired football star O.J. Simpson, and her friend Ronald Goldman were murdered. Soon the media began reporting about her tumultuous marriage to Simpson, and for months this case brought the issue of domestic violence into homes across America and sparked public interest in domestic violence. Millions of Americans watched the televised trial at which Simpson was ultimately acquitted of the murders—a verdict that many considered controversial.

Marital rape. One type of wife abuse that was rarely talked about was marital rape, defined as using threats and aggression to force a wife to engage in sexual activities against her will. For most of the century, there was no such phenomenon as marital rape, because it was thought that sexual intercourse was a marital right, making it impossible for a man to legally rape his wife. As a result, for decades women who were coerced into unwanted sexual relations with their husbands rarely defined their experiences as rape. This changed as definitions of abuse were broadened in the 1970s and 1980s, however, and by the end of the century, all 50 states had laws stating that husbands could be prosecuted for marital rape. Nonetheless, many prosecutors were hesitant to charge husbands, and jurors were less likely to find husbands guilty of rape than they were strangers. It was estimated in the late 1990s that between 10 percent and 14 percent of married women had been victims of marital rape (Langhinrichsen-Rohling & Monson, 1998).

By the end of the century, domestic violence against wives continued to be a major social problem. Domestic violence was the leading cause of injury among women, and studies suggested that as many as 5.3 million women age 18 and over were abused by a spouse or partner each year (Campbell & Soeken, 1998). Women were still reluctant to report being beaten or threatened by their husbands or boyfriends, however, so most domestic violence cases were still not reported to the police at the end of the century. It was estimated that one in four women in the United States would be abused by a partner during her lifetime, but, according to one national survey, only 25 percent of physical assaults against women by intimate partners were reported to police.

Those women who lived with more violent, dangerous batterers tended to be the least likely to leave their situations due to fear, and many faced questions from family and friends about the decision to stay. Ironically, at the beginning of the 20th century, battered women who left their husbands were criticized for abandoning family obligations; by the end of the century, battered women were criticized for not leaving their abusive partners and husbands.

Research on domestic violence. Domestic violence against women seldom consisted of a single incident; it was instead more like a continual state of victimization. Instances of intimate partner violence were often not identified until they escalated, and relatives and neighbors sometimes were surprised to learn of serious injuries resulting from domestic violence. Although family outsiders may have been unaware of previous abuse, many serious acts of violence were the culmination of years of abuse. People who abused their partners tended to use a number of methods to maintain power and control, including physical violence, threats and intimidation, emotional abuse, and isolation. Violent acts ran the gamut from threats and slaps to severe beatings and murder. When confronted about abuse, perpetrators tended to assert their rights and make excuses about how their past or their partners' behaviors caused the violent episode. Abusive husbands sometimes were able to convince their wives that it was their nagging or unrealistic expectations of him that caused the violence. Victims rarely reported abuse because they were ashamed or because they accepted fault for the violence. Victims also did not report abuse because they feared more serious injury when their spouse or partner returned home. Additionally, husbands tended to apologize elaborately for their abusive behavior and make promises that they would never do it again—these promises were almost never kept unless the man received therapy. During the last two decades of the century, laws shifted to recognize domestic violence as a crime rather than a family issue, and, in many locations, the arrest of batterers became mandatory.

Researchers could not identify a single factor for the cause of domestic violence. Rather, multiple risk factors led to violence between intimate partners. Victims and perpetrators came from all types of backgrounds—all ages, races, ethnicities, educational levels, socioeconomic statuses, sexual orientations (gay and lesbian couples also reported domestic violence), and religions. The vast majority of domestic violence victims were women. In addition, although domestic violence occurred in all socioeconomic groups, evidence suggested it was more common among lower socioeconomic groups. This was particularly true when husbands were employed in unskilled positions or were unemployed. It may be that those in lower social status positions experienced stress that put them at greater risk of being violent. It may be, however, that partner violence was kept secret among middle- and upper-class families. Some of the most common features of abusive relationships reported in studies included being abused or witnessing abuse as a child, low self-esteem, alcohol or other drug abuse, poor conflict resolution skills, and low relationship satisfaction.

Abuse against Husbands and Male Intimate Partners Although male abuse of their female partners was the most common form of domestic violence throughout the century, a few men were the victims of aggressive behavior directed at them by their wives or girlfriends. It is not known how many were abused, nor do we know much about the history of partner violence against men, because rarely would men admit to being the victims of assaults by their spouses or intimate partners. Men were supposed to be the masters of their households and the dominant partners in their marriages; to be hit, beaten, or threatened with violence by the supposedly weaker sex was a source of embarrassment, shame, and humiliation. Consequently, men rarely went to legal authorities to complain, and, even in confidential research investigations, men usually denied being abused by their wives and female partners. It was not until late in the century that the issue of domestic violence against men was raised.

A 1975 survey led some researchers to conclude that women were more violent than men in marriages. The initial source of this debate was a questionnaire in which respondents were asked how many times women had hit their partners. Results indicated that a lot of women had hit their partners. Whereas men were found to be severely violent in 38 out of every 1,000 families, women were found to be severely violent in 46 out of every 1,000 families. This led to the startling conclusion that women showed more violent aggression against their partners than did men. What the survey could not determine, however, was how many women struck their husbands while acting in self-defense; nor was it clear how much force was exerted (for example, in response to the survey questions, throwing a pillow was equivalent to throwing a knife). Another problem some critics cited was that the study did not take into account differences in strength between men and women—even if there were an equal number of hits, men's blows did more damage typically because they were bigger and stronger than women. Despite the problems with this measure of women's aggression, the reports of women being physically aggressive against men became a source of debate among academics.

In 1995, Michael Johnson, a Penn State researcher, distinguished two types of domestic violence. One he called *patriarchal terrorism*—defined as violence, threats, and other actions that resulted from women being subordinate to men. Such acts were usually initiated by men and typically involved more than one violent act per week with increasing intensity over time. Johnson suggested that patriarchal terrorism should be differentiated from a second type, which he called *common couple violence*—a term he used to describe arguments between couples that occasionally led to physical attacks, which he argued applied to most domestic disputes. Unlike patriarchal terrorism, common couple violence rarely escalated in intensity and frequency, and it was just as likely to be initiated by the woman as the man. He described common couple violence as a response to either partner's attempts to control a specific situation. In contrast, he described patriarchal terrorism as a man's desire to control his female partner over time, or to be in charge of the relationship as a whole. Johnson's typology helped dispel much of the disagreement among academics; among the U.S. public, there always had been less controversy about this issue, because most people believed that men aggressed against their partners more than women. What was not in dispute was the fact that men's aggression resulted in more harm than did women's; for instance, in 1994, 39,000 men were treated in emergency rooms because of domestic violence, compared with 204,000 women (DeMaris, 2001).

The issue of husband abuse never received the public attention or concern of wife abuse. Even when there was social science evidence from studies, people seemed generally unconcerned about this as a social problem. Just as wives had been blamed for being the victims of domestic violence in the past, husbands also seemed to be blamed for letting a woman punch or kick them. There were no cultural norms that fit men who were battered. Husbands who always did what their wives wanted them to do and were submissive were ridiculed in cartoons and in entertainments as being henpecked—women punching or kicking their usually larger husbands were often portrayed in movies and television shows in a humorous way—no wonder few men sought help from outsiders when this situation happened in their daily lives.

SIBLING ABUSE

Sibling relationships are the longest lasting relationships that many people experience during their lives. For some individuals, they are also among the most violent. Sibling abuse includes physical, emotional, and sexual abuse against a brother or sister or against stepsiblings. Although some family violence experts estimated that sibling abuse was the most common form of family violence in the 20th century, it was one of the most underreported and received little attention. In the late 1980s, experts estimated that as many as 36 million acts of sibling violence occurred every year, and 3 of every 100 children were seriously violent toward a sibling (Gelles & Strauss, 1988). Historically, people have tended to expect arguments and fights among siblings, and unusual violence between siblings often was overlooked until a child was seriously injured. Child protective services, clinicians, law enforcement officials, and families made little distinction between normal power relationships among siblings and sibling assaults. Child welfare workers were bound by state laws to investigate only acts of violence against children that were committed by adults in the home. Therefore, unless sibling abuse escalated to the point of causing serious injuries, it usually did not receive attention from the police or court system.

ELDER ABUSE

For most of the century, the abuse of elders was not a major problem because there were relatively few older adults. As the life expectancy for American men and women increased from 47.3 years in 1900 to 77 years in 2000 (U.S. Census Bureau, 2000), and the proportion of Americans over the age of 65 grew from 4 percent in 1900 to 12.5 percent by 2000, the number of vulnerable older citizens multiplied, and their risk of abuse increased. As U.S. society aged, more families had elderly family members who needed help to manage the activities of daily living.

Prior to the social welfare movement early in the 20th century, the health and well-being of elderly individuals received little public recognition. The relatively few older adults usually lived near or with children or other family members, and most Americans viewed the needs of dependent elderly as family problems. The older adults without family nearby and those who lived alone typically had to struggle on their own to survive, unless they were wealthy and could hire assistance. It was not until the Depression that government on any level turned attention to the plight of older Americans. The federal Social Security Act of 1935 helped ensure financial provisions for the elderly. Title I of the act required states to provide social support and financial assistance for frail elderly, but it did nothing to ensure their safety from abuse and exploitation.

Elder abuse began to be noticed in the 1970s, about the time that many elders were calling on their adult children and other younger kin to help them remain in their homes as independent adults. Better health care and more effective medicines that prolonged the life of the elderly meant that older Americans lived more years in a frail and weakened condition and they were not always able to do all of the things they did when they were younger (e.g., shopping, cooking, cleaning, home maintenance, dressing themselves). Their children, many of whom were raising their own children and were employed, found that they were increasingly called upon to take care of their older parents. Gerontologists called these middle-aged, middle generation adults the *sandwich generation,* because they were stuck between dependent elders and dependent children.

By no means were caregiving and elder abuse synonymous—most caregivers were unselfish and loving—but some, including the spouses of dependent elders, did not manage the demands of their situations well and they abused their charges. Both men and women were reported to be abusive to older family members.

Although it had been previously noticed, maltreatment of the elderly was not identified as a serious social problem until the mid-1970s, when health care professionals and social workers started to see a growing number of abused elderly when they made home visits to check on homebound older adults. First called granny battering or granny bashing, it did not take the U.S. Congress long to investigate the extent of the problem. Led by Rep. Claude Pepper from Florida, Congress held hearings on the so-called hidden problem of elder abuse, and, in 1980, the Joint Congressional Hearings on Elder Abuse recommended the passage of laws protecting the elderly, including laws requiring mandatory reporting. These hearings led many states to require reporting of elder abuse. By 1985, 46 states had agencies dealing with the issue, and, by the end of the century, all 50 states had passed some form of elder maltreatment prevention laws and had reporting systems in place. A lack of funding for increased services, however, prevented many states from fully implementing the laws.

The federal Older Americans Act of 1987 initiated a national program to address elder abuse that required Area Agencies on Aging to determine the need for elder abuse prevention services and to learn whether others were already providing these services. In 1988, the U.S. Administration on Aging funded the first national resource center to help raise public awareness of elder abuse, and, in 1992, Congress passed Title VII, the Vulnerable Elder Rights Protection Title, established as an amendment to the Older Americans Act. This legislation developed advocacy programs, including the Programs for the Prevention of Abuse, Neglect and Exploitation. It also required the development of the National Center on Elder Abuse.

By the end of the century, it was estimated that 2.1 million older Americans were victims of physical, psychological, or other forms of abuse and neglect every year. However, these numbers may not paint the true picture. As with other types of family abuse and neglect, the majority of cases probably were not reported. Frail older adults, the most likely to be abused or neglected, usually were homebound and could not report transgressions against them because they lacked access to ways to contact authorities, some were cognitively confused, and they typically had no other options but to go into nursing homes if their caregivers got into trouble for abusing or neglecting them. Some older adults were ashamed to report that they were victims of abuse at the hands of loved ones, and some elders may have believed they were at fault. Others feared future repercussions from the aggressor for reporting an abusive spouse or child.

Older women reported being abused more often than men, perhaps because there were more of them, perhaps because women were more likely to report abuse than were men, or it may have been that women were attacked or neglected more than men. Individuals over age 80 were at the greatest risk for abuse, mostly because they had the most need of constant care and were most likely to depend on family for help and support. Elderly who lived alone were less likely to be abused than were those who lived with immediate relatives, including their spouse or child. A 1996 study indicated that adult children comprised more than 47 percent of perpetrators in substantiated elder abuse cases compared to 19 percent of spouse perpetrators. Some studies of adult children pointed to stress as one factor that led to abuse or neglect. Because the decision to move an elderly family member to an adult child's home was sometimes made when family emotions were strained, some adult children perceived that the decision was forced upon them. Others were unsure how to properly care for their parents and consequently felt overwhelmed and helpless, unaware of available sources of support. As a result, they resorted to using physical force in response to the frustration or resentment they felt. Caring for elderly relatives with major mental or physical impairments heightened the risk of elder abuse or neglect. Although young parents had a wide variety of books, magazines, and other resources for information about raising their young children, there were few informative resources available to adult children trying to care for their parents. In some cases, family members may not have known how to appropriately care for their aging family member. The parent's dependency, and potential power conflicts as parents and children exchanged roles, may have increased the potential for violence.

Unresolved parent-child conflicts were another factor that placed additional pressure on some parent-child relationships. For example, elderly fathers who governed their households with an iron fist may have found it difficult to relinquish power to their adult children. Similarly, their children may have found it difficult to try to tell their elderly fathers what to do. As more adult children had surviving parents, stepparents, and in-laws, they faced growing pressures and strains. The financial and emotional costs, as well as the stress of caring for the individual, may have resulted in abuse or neglect.

Several other factors were identified as contributing to a higher likelihood of elder abuse. Alcoholism, drug addiction, and mental illness of caregivers contributed to high numbers of abused elderly, because each of these disorders can make some individuals more abusive. Intergenerational violence was also used to explain elder abuse, meaning that abusers may have learned to be violent while growing up. Finally, many cases of elder abuse came about as a result of the caregiver being dependent on the abused individual for housing and financial assistance.

Although older adults were subject to being hit, kicked, or otherwise physically abused by children, grandchildren, or other family members, **Types of Maltreatment** the most common form of elder abuse was neglect; over half of elder abuse cases reported by the end of the century were cases of neglect. Some of this neglect involved the intentional failure of younger kin to provide the basic physical needs of an elderly individual. In cases of active neglect, family members purposefully withheld food or water, or they refused to help bedridden elders go to the bathroom or change their soiled clothing if they had an accident. Some older adults were victims of passive neglect, which occurred as a result of a caregiver's ignorance, with no intent to cause harm. This type of neglect occurred when younger kin failed to look in on older adults who were living alone. Psychological or emotional abuse, including actions that resulted in fear or mental anguish, was a form of maltreatment that was usually difficult to prove due to a lack of concrete evidence and cognitive impairment of some elderly persons. Financial exploitation was the least likely type of elder abuse to be reported and the most difficult to identify because signs of this were not always immediately evident. Financial abuse included forgery, illegal money or property transfers, and credit card fraud. Financial neglect was also common—caregivers did not use available funds to buy necessities for their elderly relative, perhaps out of a desire to protect their inheritance.

Since the early 1990s, elder maltreatment came to be viewed as a medical and social problem, and many efforts to prevent it and methods of ensuring protection from it developed. Underreporting of incidents and problems in detecting abuse and neglect against the elderly, however, hampered efforts to reduce this problem.

SUMMARY

Throughout the 20th century, there were periods of heightened social and political awareness of family violence characterized by sincere, but usually short-lived, attempts to reduce the negative effects of abuse and neglect on individuals and families. It was not until the last few decades of the century that the country witnessed an era of widespread and enduring awareness. Unlike reform attempts at the turn of the century, in the 1960s, health care professionals, feminists, social scientists, social workers, child welfare advocates, policymakers, and law enforcement officials began to work together more than ever before. The media contributed to enhancing public awareness, and researchers, practitioners, and policymakers were vocal about the results of their investigations. Unlike earlier times, these messages and messengers did not fade away. In fact, in the 1990s, many universities created courses on family violence, and several professional scholarly journals were dedicated to publishing research on family abuse and neglect. The century ended with a much greater understanding of the nature and scope of family violence than it had had before. Damage caused by family violence was known to be associated with numerous physical, emotional, and psychological costs and to have far-reaching costs for society as a whole.

An understanding of the root causes and consequences of family violence was still lacking. Early in the century, it was thought that only mentally ill people and those in impoverished families committed acts of abuse and neglect. Over time it became clear, however, that family violence occurred across all social and economic categories. Some groups were at greater risk—urban families, poor families, people with a little education—characteristics that may have placed individuals and families at higher risk for experiencing stress, which may have contributed to family violence.

For much of the century, there were minimal efforts to assist victims of abuse; nor were their treatment programs for abusers. By 2000, treatment programs had been established across the country, but many were implemented only after abuse or neglect occurred. Prevention programs to stop domestic violence before it could begin existed, but they were few in number.

Efforts to support victims of abuse evolved differently depending on the type of abuse experienced. Helping professionals played a key role in drawing attention to and soliciting funds to help support advocacy against child abuse; they were less successful in efforts regarding spousal abuse, although health professionals, teachers, and others were legally mandated to report suspected abuse.

By the century's close, conservative estimates were that one in four children and adults in the United States would be affected by family violence during their lives. Norms about family privacy and tolerance for violence within families were barriers to awareness, prevention, and treatment of family abuse and neglect throughout the century.

9

Alternative Family Forms

This chapter describes several alternative family forms that existed in the 20th century. These alternatives ranged from new ways of defining families and family membership to attempts to modify family life in ways that differed from the stereotypically conventional two-parent, one-marriage family with the proverbial 1.5 children.

MARRIAGE ALTERNATIVES

Among the alternatives to conventional marriage in the 20th century were so-called swinging, polygamy, open marriages, group marriages, and voluntarily childfree marriages. Although all of these alternative life-styles existed to some degree throughout the century, the heyday of marital alternatives in the United States occurred in the mid-1960s and early 1970s. During this era there was a great deal of social experimentation with sexual and emotional relationships by young and middle-aged adults. Some experimenting was more sexual than relationship-focused (e.g., swinging), some alternative life-styles focused more on enhancing the quality of relationships than on sex (e.g., open marriage), and still others tried to focus on both sexual and relational issues such as power (e.g., group marriage communes). Although none of these marital alternatives were invented in the 20th century, they were new alternatives to most Americans.

Swinging
Given that group sexual activities—sex engaged in by more than two people at a time—were illegal in every state the entire century, it is not surprising that little is known about the extent of it in the first half of the 20th century. People who engaged in such practices had to be extremely discrete to avoid legal problems and social disapproval. Given the hidden nature of group sex activities, it is probable that prior to 1950 this life-style was practiced only by the avant garde—artists, bohemians, and other nonconformists. The personal and public costs of being caught engaging in group sexual activity were too great for most ordinary people to risk, and the opportunities to participate in such activities in small towns and close-knit urban neighborhoods were extremely rare before World War II.

The first public mention of swinging was in 1956 in a men's magazine called *Mr.*, so it is safe to assume the practice of swinging existed in the mid-1950s, and probably before. Swinging, or comarital sex, included married couples exchanging partners with another couple or couples participating in group sex, usually as part of a large social gathering arranged for that purpose. Sometimes called "wife swapping" in the late 1950s, this term fell out of favor in the late 1960s because it implied that husbands traded their wives, which was not the case. Instead, swinging was seen by its practitioners as an egalitarian arrangement in which every person had the right to participate or not, with whomever they chose, and in whatever way they saw fit. At so-called key parties, men put their car keys in a hat or bowl and at the end of the party the women would reach in and pull out a set of keys. They would then spend the night with the owner of the keys. In reality, some wives were coerced into swinging by their husbands, but trading spouses was never part of the swingers' credo.

It is impossible to know accurately the extent of this phenomenon because swingers were secretive and difficult to study. It was not until the end of the 1960s that social scientists published a few studies of the swinging subculture, partly because swingers were unwilling to participate in research out of concern about what would happen to them if their friends, coworkers, neighbors, and children knew about this activity. Researchers estimated that about 1 percent of the population, or about 2 million people in the late 1960s, participated in swinging at least once.

Studies of swinging couples revealed them to be ordinary men and women—they were predominately middle-class, white, lived either in suburbs or in cities, held conventional beliefs about marriage, and were politically conservative. They did not, however, belong to civic organizations nor have many hobbies or outside interests. In fact, one early study reported that the *only* interests married swingers had were watching television and swinging. Although most had grown up in religious homes, they were not particularly religious as adults and seldom attended religious services. About the only way that swingers differed from the mainstream was in their attitudes about sex. Despite advertising themselves in publications for swingers that sprung up in the 1960s and 1970s as individuals who engaged in many interesting activities, the truth was that most swingers led staid, nondescript lives.

In some ways, the sexual activities of swingers were more conventional and less free-spirited than the notion of mate swapping suggests. Instead of wild, hedonistic parties with no limits to inventive sexual behaviors, there tended to be rather strict rules of conduct at swinging parties, and there were fairly well-known norms regulating behaviors when couples exchanged partners. Drinking was acceptable, but drugs, including marijuana, were not. Homosexual activities generally were forbidden for men, but in some groups women were encouraged to engage in sex with other women. There also were rules about who could initiate sexual activity and who could refuse. In addition to intercourse, oral but not anal sex was acceptable. Rules of conduct were enforced by expulsion of individuals or couples from future activities.

One rule that swingers closely followed was keeping their life-style secret from their children. Swingers went to great efforts to make sure children were not around during house parties, and parents tried to make sure that evidence of their swinging (e.g., phone messages from other couples arranging dates, copies of swingers' magazines) were not found by their children. For most couples, swinging seemed almost a hobby, a way to enrich their marriages without changing any other aspect of their lives. They were not trying to create a new type of marriage as practitioners of open marriages were, nor did they expect their sexual liaisons to lead to long-term relationships. Swinging was more about sex and leisure and less about emotional fulfillment or relationship development.

Almost from the start of swinging, dozens of magazines were published that contained ads by swingers looking for other couples. An ad placed by a swinging couple might read:

Lexington, Kentucky marrieds. Attractive, college, white, want to hear from other attractive marrieds, but will consider extremely attractive single girls and men. She, 37–27–35, 5'6", 135. He, 40, 6'2", 190. Photo and phone a must. Discretion. Box #

Ads in swingers' magazines and personal contacts were the primary ways swingers met new people until the 1990s, when the widespread availability of the Internet quickly made it the preferred medium for contacting other couples. The Internet also probably helped make swinging more widely available than before because it made it easier for people to discretely locate potential partners in their geographic area. Swinging started in urban and suburban areas on the coasts, and, although it was never limited geographically to specific parts of the country, swinging as a life-style was more challenging in less populated regions because exposure was more likely. The Internet made it easier to practice swinging with a degree of anonymity.

Clubs for swingers began in the 1960s, and early ones, such as New York City's Plato's Retreat, achieved some degree of national fame. Most swingers' clubs were quite discrete, however, and were known only to avowed swingers. House parties continued throughout the rest of the century to be a popular venue for swinging.

Most studies reported that people engaged in swinging for a few years. Wives were more likely than husbands to end the activity, for reasons such as jealousy, guilt, and concern that sexual activities with extramarital partners were threatening the marriage. Swinging was supposed to be recreational—not a way to find another partner—so becoming emotionally involved with another swinger sometimes led to the end of swinging for a couple and sometimes led to divorce or separation. Finally, some couples quit because they were bored or found swinging to be disappointing.

In the 1980s and 1990s, the fear of AIDS scared some people away from engaging in sex with strangers, but it did not eliminate swinging. Because strong antihomosexual rules were enforced by swinging groups, many people believed they were protected from being infected with AIDS. Swinging clubs also imposed other rules designed to protect the members' health (requiring the use of condoms, for instance). The increased prevalence of divorce in the 1970s and early 1980s meant that there were fewer married couples to participate in swinging activities; thus, single people began to disguise themselves as married couples so that they could engage in swinging, and some couples were willing to swing with single adults. In the last decade of the 20th century, the number of swingers apparently increased. Swinging magazines were thriving, annual conventions held by national swingers' organizations were usually attended by several hundred couples, and hundreds of swingers' clubs existed across the United States, most with their own Web sites.

Multiple-Partner Marriages and Intimate Relationships Polyamory (a label abbreviated to *poly* by practitioners of the life-style) is the practice of being involved in more than one long-term, emotionally intimate, and, often, sexual loving relationship at the same time, with the full knowledge and consent of all partners involved. The term *polyamory* was coined in 1990, but committed relationships between multiple partners existed well before then. Like swinging, this life-style became increasingly visible in the 1960s. Although often perceived by outsiders and the media as identical to swinging, it was different. In contrast to swingers, who saw development and maintenance of ongoing relationships as unnecessary or even inappropriate, polyamorists expected the relationships to be both ongoing and meaningful, regardless of whether sex was involved. Swinging was more accurately called *group sex,* and polyamory was sometimes known in the 1960s as *group marriage.*

Polyamory encompassed a wide range of relationships. Polyamorists could have one primary (i.e., close emotional and/or sexual partner) and one or more secondary partners to whom they were faithful (called *polyfi-delity*). They also could have multiple partners to whom they were committed but remained open to forming new relationships (sexual or emotional), or they could have multiple primary partners (everybody was equally involved and committed to everyone else). In addition, polyamorists could be either unmarried or legally married (to one person only, according to the laws of the United States), and they could be heterosexual, homosexual, or bisexual (some polyamory relationships contained individuals of all three sexual orientations). The number of individuals in a polyamorous union could vary, but there had to be at least three people in the relationship. What linked this disparate collection of multiple-person relationships was the notion that all of the relationships were to be taken seriously; polyamory partners were not just casual sexual partners and one-night stands.

The polyamorists' group marriages formed in the 1960s and 1970s were seen by their practitioners as a viable alternative to conventional marriage, and interest in them was stimulated by popular late 1960s novels (e.g., *Proposition 31* [Rimmer, 1969] and *The Harrad Experiment* [Rimmer, 1967]) and by movies (e.g., *Bob and Carol and Ted and Alice*, [1969]) that portrayed group marriages in a favorable light. Because most group marriages were communal arrangements in which several adults and their children lived together, they are discussed in more detail later in this chapter as one form of communal living.

Marriage, even marriage involving several partners operating under different norms and practices than conventional marriages, was not the goal of all polyamorists. Instead, they generally sought to form other types of multiple-person intimate bonds that were not easily seen as marriages—in fact, some wanted to stay married but add close emotional ties with other individuals, as they saw fit. Polyamorists in the 1980s and 1990s, for instance, increasingly did not live in the same household with all of their relationship partners. The notion of how to function in one of these multiple partner relationships became more fluid, with polyamorous unions crossing household boundaries and other restrictions (e.g., sexual orientation).

Multiple-person primary relationships probably increased slightly from 1970 until the end of the century, although there is no way to know for certain. In the latter part of the century, it became relatively easy for individuals to use the Internet to make contacts with like-minded people to form polyamorous relationships, and burgeoning Web pages with polyamorous themes made it appear that this was a booming movement. It is likely, however, that the number of people engaging in multiple personal relationships was still small.

Open marriage. This term was coined by George and Nena O'Neill in 1972. The main focus of an open marriage was the personal growth of each spouse. They wrote:

Open marriage means an honest and open relationship between two people, based on the equal freedom and identity of both partners. Open marriage involves a verbal, intellectual, and emotional commitment to provide each other with the right to grow as an individual within the marriage. (O'Neill & O'Neill, 1972, pp. 39–40)

They saw open marriage as a new kind of marriage between equals and believed that it was unrealistic and, in fact, unhealthy to expect spouses to fulfill all of each other's needs. Instead, marriage should be open so that husbands and wives could freely explore opportunities for personal development in whatever ways they saw fit. These open marriages placed a premium on trust and communication.

Although sexual openness to intimate relationships outside of marriage was a minor part of the O'Neills' notion of open marriage, it received the most attention from the media and general public. Most of their best-selling book focused on ways that spouses could facilitate each other's personal growth and improve the quality of their relationships through "open and honest" communication, but many readers and some practitioners of open marriages were attracted not only to the ideas about personal growth and interpersonal flexibility, but to the notion that open marriages need not be sexually exclusive. Sexual partners of husbands and wives in open marriages were called *intimate friends*—they resembled traditional friendships, with the exception that sexual intimacy between the friends was considered appropriate.

Studies of open marriages in the 1970s indicated that spouses in these relationships were similar psychologically to the population in general, although they were more idealistic about relationships and more willing to take risks to achieve relational goals. Open marriage appealed to college-educated, white, middle-class Americans more than to other demographic groups.

Many concepts of the open marriage ideology grew in popularity late in the century. Although few couples ascribed to the idea of having intimate friends, many middle- and upper-class Americans tried to incorporate at least some aspects of the open marriage ideal into their marriages (e.g., openness, egalitarianism). This was true even of individuals who had never heard of open marriage or the O'Neills. For instance, single young adults who had not yet been born in the 1970s enjoyed "friends with benefits" in the 1990s—opposite-sex friends with whom they shared an occasional sexual experience. These friends with benefits were simply an updated version of intimate friends, appropriated by single adults.

The principle of having an open, sharing, egalitarian relationship was extremely well received in the last decades of the century. During this period, egalitarian relationships grew in number, egalitarian spouses encouraged each other to develop as independent people (e.g., learning new skills, exploring new opportunities), and there was a general emphasis on open and honest communication between marital partners.

Of course, married polyamorists in the 1990s intentionally adopted all aspects of the O'Neills' vision for an open marriage, including sexual and emotional openness and lack of marital exclusivity.

Polygamy. Polygamy, the marriage of one man to more than one woman, is illegal in every state, and thus polygamists generally hide their status to avoid legal problems and social disapproval. It is difficult to study them for these reasons. Polygamy once was, but no longer is, an approved practice of the Church of Jesus Christ of the Latter Day Saints (Mormons). Based on the Biblical story of Sarah and Abraham, and Sarah's willingness to let Abraham take another wife so that he could have offspring, the original purpose of polygamy was to encourage childbearing. Mormon law changed in 1890, however, to no longer support polygamy by church doctrine. Despite this ban, polygamy continued to exist, mostly among renegade Mormons who generally lived reclusive life-styles residing in sparsely populated rural areas of the western United States. There is no way of knowing how many polygamous families there were, but they continued to exist in small numbers throughout the century.

Polygamous families sometimes lived as a kind of extended family, often with separate dwellings for each wife and her children on the same property. Husbands were the family heads, and usually wives' power was based on entry into the family (that is, first wives had more power than later wives; second wives had more power than all but the first wife). Economically, polygamous families resembled some communes in that incomes were pooled and wealth was shared. Unlike most communes, however, polygamous fathers were the primary financial decision makers.

Voluntary Childlessness or Childfree Marriages

America has long been a pronatalist society, and some observers have claimed that Americans are obsessed with reproduction and fertility. Early in the century, not having children was considered unpatriotic. In 1903, President Theodore Roosevelt in an address to Congress made the accusation that "willful sterility is, from the standpoint of the nation, from the standpoint of the human race, the one sin for which the penalty is national death, race death; a sin for which there is no atonement. . . . No man, no woman, can shirk the primary duties of life"—one of which was having many proverbially good American children.

Normative expectations throughout the 20th century were that every married couple would bear children. Consequently, childless couples received pressure from family and friends to reproduce soon after marriage. Infertile couples who could not conceive but wanted children were often pitied for their barren state and were encouraged to adopt.

For most Americans, children were seen as gifts from God, personal blessings, or national resources, and the general sentiment was that something was wrong with anyone who avoided parenthood. Voluntarily childless couples were stigmatized as deviant and studies done in the last four decades of the century consistently found that most Americans perceived voluntarily childless individuals to be selfish and emotionally immature.

Research on the causes of childlessness did not begin until the 1930s, but, given cultural expectations regarding having children, it is probable that most childless couples were involuntarily in that state, at least until the 1970s. Late in the century, medical technologies made it possible for infertile couples to have children who could not have done so ever before in history. Other medical breakthroughs allowed individuals who wished to avoid becoming parents greater ease than ever before in preventing or terminating pregnancy. So, even though the percentage of Americans that finished their childbearing years without becoming parents was relatively steady over the century (about 20 percent), it is likely that a greater proportion of these individuals in the last quarter of the 20th century had chosen this status and were not infertile and childless against their preferences.

Men and women who chose the childfree life-style in the last three decades of the 20th century did so because they enjoyed their freedom (e.g., to pursue careers, to travel) and the opportunities they had for personal fulfillment. Some couples did not want to risk jeopardizing the quality of their marriages by adding the stress of childrearing; research late in the 20th century indicated that voluntarily childless couples had happier marriages than did couples who were parents. Childfree couples also tended to have more egalitarian relationships than those with children, and some couples did not want to upset this balance.

Others chose to not have children because they did not want to detract from the pursuit of their careers. Many considered themselves to have meaningful careers, and they had decided that trying to achieve in demanding occupations would be unfair to children. They were unwilling to either raise children or work at professions on part-time bases. For them, it made sense to forgo childrearing in pursuit of career goals.

Dislike of children was another reason to forgo childrearing, for men primarily, although a few women admitted to this as well. Voluntarily childfree adults toward the end of the century were more likely than parents to have been the only child in their families, so they may have had little contact with other children except as classmates in school.

For women, the decision to be childfree was sometimes based on their concerns about being good parents, the state of the world and society, and their not having had good models of parenting. Women who felt this way may have been reacting to the myths of motherhood with which they had been socialized. Some social commentators and social scientists contended late in the century that childfree women were reacting to unrealistically high expectations for women to be supermothers—to successfully juggle work, childrearing, and marriage. Women reacted to this myth in a variety of ways, and some chose to reject the motherhood mandate entirely. In short, if they could not be perfect or at least excellent mothers and meet their other life demands with equal skill, then they would not pursue motherhood at all.

As the century ended, the number of involuntarily childless couples was lower, and the number of voluntarily childfree couples was larger than ever before. Most Americans still planned to have children, however, and did so. General cultural stigma about being childless had diminished as the century came to a close, but certain subgroups, such as conservative religious faiths, continued to see childless individuals as deviant.

ALTERNATIVES TO CONVENTIONAL NUCLEAR FAMILIES

Communes Communes existed in the United States well before the start of the 20th century. In fact, one of the most famous and successful alternative family communes was the Oneida Community in the mid-19th century. The Oneida Community rejected monogamy and practiced *pantagamy*—every man was considered to be the husband of every woman, and every woman was the wife of every man. Couples who wished to have a child together had to get approval from a ruling board of elders, and there was considerable grousing that the elders only allowed the most desirable women to reproduce with them. Despite reported significant amounts of sexual activity of Oneidans with multiple partners over time, childbearing was low due to rigid adherence to certain contraceptive practices, mainly male withdrawal before ejaculation. Children in the Oneida Community lived together in a Children's House and were taken care of by trained child care experts rather than their parents. Although financially successful, this community dissolved after several decades, in part because younger members rejected complex marriage and the politics surrounding it in favor of monogamous marriages and nuclear families. Descendents of the communal ruling elders still served on the board of directors of Oneida Incorporated, a famous silverware company, in 2000.

Hundreds of other communes existed in the United States before 1900. Many of these were utopian communities based on religious or philosophical principles, such as the Shakers (who dissolved eventually, partially because celibacy was one of their main principles and—not being able to convert sufficient numbers of others to join their ranks—they eventually ran out of members) and the Amana Colonies (which lasted for decades until economic setbacks and widespread discontent with rigid rules governing commune members' behavior led to a vote to change their utopian commune into a joint-stock corporation in 1932). Few of the communes attempted to become alternative families in the manner that the Oneida Community did, although they often tried to control marriage, sexual behavior between adults, and childbearing and childrearing.

The heyday of communal living in the United States was in the mid-1960s through the mid-1970s. Events such as Woodstock, a large 1969 outdoor concert staged on Max Yasgur's farm in upstate New York, stimulated the creation of communes, and musical groups such as the Grateful Dead and others of that era not only lived communally, but were seen by their fans as role models for living together in intentional communities. It is estimated that there were as many as 30,000 rural communes at the peak of this movement in the early 1970s, and there were probably close to 100,000 communes in urban areas. Educated guesses of the number of communal dwellers ranged from 10,000 to 750,000 (Miller, 1999).

Communal living declined from the late 1970s throughout the rest of the century. By the mid-1990s, researchers estimated that there were between 3,000 and 4,000 communes, most of them containing fewer than 50 members. New communes were still being created in the 1990s, however, and a few of the earlier communities had been in existence for two decades or more. At the end of the century, it could be said that the communal movement was alive, but not especially thriving.

The numbers of communes as well as the numbers of members are approximations because some intentional communities were short-lived, and turnover of members was high. Commune membership was extremely fluid, and, for some, the membership changed daily. Tallying the number of communes also was hard because some were mobile. Many refused to divulge information to outsiders or they deliberately communicated inaccurate information, and smaller communes sometimes tried to make themselves invisible to outsiders to avoid hostility from neighbors who might not welcome a group of counterculture young people and assorted children and pets moving in next door.

Communes varied in many ways—some were extremely open to outsiders, and others subjected potential members to rigorous scrutiny. For instance, in some communes membership consisted of showing up and moving in; others scrutinized prospective members carefully to see whether they would fit into the culture of the group by requiring them to attend several communal meetings and to share meals and work tasks.

Communes also varied in the degree to which they were organized around a clear set of principles and guidelines. On one extreme were communes in which members had to follow group rules and adhere to certain shared principles or risk being asked to leave. Other communes were less ideologically driven and more casual and laissez-faire in how they functioned.

A few communes were economically self-sufficient and others were extremely poor, relying on handouts from wealthy benefactors (often parents or other individuals sympathetic to their cause). Rural communes generally tried some types of farming operations or cottage industry (e.g., growing food, making baked goods to sell at farmer's markets, weaving baskets, making furniture, growing flowers to sell, raising livestock) to make ends meet, while urban communes generally either worked together in a joint business activity (e.g., running a natural foods store) or members worked outside of the commune. For instance, Kerista, one of the most long-running communes in the 1970s and 1980s, operated a successful communal computer business in San Francisco.

Communes also varied in how they lived physically. Some shared a single dwelling. For instance, a large group marriage commune, The Family, had 50 adult and child members who resided in Taos, New Mexico, in a two-bedroom house and a school bus. Commune members slept on the floors, turning them into wall-to-wall beds every night. Urban communes were smaller than rural communes (generally 5 to 20 people), and members usually lived together in rented or purchased houses. In some rural communes, members lived in separate housing but on shared acreage. Still others had multiple dwellings for sleeping, but ate, held meetings, and generally lived in shared space such as a meeting room or dining hall. At The Ranch in rural California, approximately 24 adults and their children lived in their own dwellings on 140 acres. There was a communal dining room and a communal outhouse. They lived rather primitively in many ways—no electricity or telephones, kerosene for light, and wood for heating fuel. In some of the more established and still existing rural communes, such as Twin Oaks in Virginia and The Farm in Tennessee, residents live in separate housing as individuals, couples, or families, but spend time together in communal buildings (for dining, health care, schooling of children, community meetings, work). By the end of the century, these communes had more creature comforts than when they began in the early 1970s, but the residents of both lived far more simply than most of their contemporary Americans.

Despite diversity, communes generally shared several characteristics— property and goods were owned by the group instead of individuals, membership was voluntary, and the members shared a belief system or ideology. The creation of communes was inspired by several different purposes: (1) to put into practice shared political beliefs (there were several self-proclaimed anarchist communes, for instance); (2) to practice philosophical principles (e.g., Twin Oaks, based on noted Harvard psychologist B.F. Skinner's ideas about egalitarian communal living) or religious values (there were 200 Christian communes, known as "Jesus" communes, in California in the early 1970s); (3) to create supportive environments in which to withdraw from (or "drop out" of) society; and (4) to create opportunities to explore alternative life-styles (e.g., vegetarianism, nudism, gender egalitarianism, environmentalism). Most alternative family communes were environmentalists of some sort.

Most communes were not established as alternatives to conventional nuclear families, and, in fact, most did not consider themselves families, although they may have contained nuclear families or married couples within their memberships. Commune members often used the language of families to describe themselves ("we are all brothers and sisters here at Daystar") and may have functioned similarly to extended families, even when they did not use family language and did not purposefully try to create a family atmosphere. Some communes, however, did attempt to function as families.

Communes as families. Many utopian communities in the 1960s and 1970s formed specifically to explore alternative ways of relating and living as families of chosen kin. A communitarian historian wrote that

American communes are looked to by their members for the fulfillment of familial functions without the restrictions of the family structure (e.g., sexual and child-rearing functions [are performed] without [the limitations imposed by traditional] marital and intergenerational responsibilities). . . . The communes use voluntaristic structure to create family without nuclear dependence. (Zablocki, 1980, p. 52)

Some of these alternative family communes operated on the assumption that all of the adults were married (group marriages in function, if not always in name). The majority of alternative family communes were not group marriages, however, but rather collections of nuclear families, couples, single parents and their children, and single individuals that functioned as an extended kinship group. Communes were particularly attractive to some single mothers, who turned to them for help with childrearing, physical protection, and economic support.

The majority of commune members had grown up in conventional nuclear families. Their parents had not divorced, and their childhoods were rooted in what many would consider standard American families. They sought communal living as an alternative family form for many reasons. Most of them shared a belief that conventional families did not work—they were not good places to raise mentally healthy children; they were not conducive to satisfying male-female relationships; and they were not systems that developed creative, open, happy individuals. In response to such beliefs, communards attempted to choose their family members from among like-minded individuals.

As one commune member, Marty Jezer, described this desire for an alternative family:

The idea that we are a family is important to the people on the farm. This sense of the family wouldn't be so much a part of our present awareness if we didn't carry within us memories of what our family life was in the past; where it broke down and ceased being meaningful and how, now, it can be reconstructed to that end. . . . We seemed to be running not as much from our families but in search of family, looking for the sense of community and family life we . . . found lacking at home. (Miller, 1999, p. 156)

Men and women in communes. Many alternative family communes structured themselves around egalitarian beliefs that men and women should share power and responsibility, and they organized themselves so that all adults equally shared in decision making, the burden of earning a living or growing food, child care, and household duties. Implementing these ideals was challenging, and some communes made purposeful strides toward equality by having women fix the cars and other machinery and assigning men the responsibility for child care and cooking. Other communes mandated that everybody had to do *every* task, regardless of skill levels or aptitudes—but some of these communes, particularly those on farms and in rural areas, found that this plan did not work well.

Men and women were seen as sexual equals in most alternative family communes, and women were encouraged to express their sexuality and initiate sexual activities if they wished. Some of communes in the 1960s and 1970s practiced polyamory, discussed earlier in this chapter, and considered themselves married to each other (although state laws did not). Partners in group marriages generally saw themselves as equal decision makers, and there was a concerted effort to live their lives as free from gender stereotypes as possible. Exchanging sexual partners was a norm among many communes—living in close physical proximity to each other and away from conventional rules about sexual behavior facilitated, for many people, opportunities for sexual exploration and multiple (sequential or concurrent) partners.

Not all communes were sexually open, however; some of them, particularly those based on religious principles, prohibited sexual relations between unmarried members. For many communes, long work days that involved heavy physical labor limited the energy and reduced somewhat the opportunities for sexual liaisons. Some communards, at least those that were shy, reported that living in housing that offered little privacy reduced their opportunities for sexual intimacy.

Children in communes. Most alternative family communes contained children. Childrearing responsibility was generally shared among all of the adults, although, for the most part, parents had final say and primary responsibility for their children. Compared to children raised in conventional family settings, children in communes were exposed to more adults, more experiences, and more ideas. Commune dwellers generally viewed their life-style as an advantage for the children, which led to the children being more sophisticated about interpersonal relationships and more capable of interacting with a variety of people than were other children. Several studies of communal childrearing in the 1960s found that children enjoyed living communally, and they benefited from it socially and intellectually. Follow-up studies reported that adults who grew up in 1960s-era communes had fond memories of their experiences, and many had successful careers and led accomplished, if conventional, lives.

On the negative side, there were occasional reports of child abuse or neglect among children living in communes, but no more or less of this than in other family types. Children in communes also were exposed to

Child of an Ozarks commune, 1970s. (Courtesy of the authors.)

more adult behaviors, including drug use and sex, and were sometimes not carefully monitored, which resulted in the children engaging in what most people would call adult activities at younger ages than most children. In some communes, children were thought of as small adults, and they were allowed to participate as if they were adults in decision making, working, engaging in sexual intimacy, drinking alcohol, and smoking marijuana. The issue of schooling for children also created problems, in rural communes in particular (urban children usually went to local schools). Home schooling was a popular option, but many communes found this challenging, given the wide age range of children in the communes and sometimes few adults with the appropriate backgrounds and skills to teach.

Stability of communes. Communal families proved even more fragile than conventional nuclear families. Jealousy, hurt feelings, and anger were common problems. There was some sexual exploitation of women, despite rules designed to limit its possibility. People found it much harder to manage emotions and interpersonal problems in group unions than they had expected, which led to high rates of attrition. Group marriages were hard to sustain over time, and most had fairly short life spans. One sociologist estimated that half of legal marriages ended within a year of joining a commune; if a marriage was weak or shaky when the couple joined, the stresses of communal living and readily available replacement companions sometimes proved too much for marital survival.

Another problem contributing to relationship fragility was a tendency for commune members to gradually revert to conventional gender role behaviors and attitudes. Even when they sought to create egalitarian communities, it was hard for men to give up control over resources and the right to make decisions, and in some communes men refused to engage in "women's work," such as taking care of children, cooking, and cleaning. In general, female commune members were more willing than were men to alter gender roles. The failure of men, and sometimes women, to live the egalitarian philosophy they admired led many to drop out. Some unhappy women created women's communes in reaction to the failure, as they saw it, of men to make their espoused egalitarian communal ideals work.

Members of communes found it harder to function in multiple-adult units than they had anticipated. Everything—decision making, the discipline of children, and day-to-day activities—was more complex because there were more people having input into what was going on. Many commune members found it hard to maintain intimate relationships in the presence of others. Couples who predated the formation of the commune resented the intrusion of others into their relationship and found it challenging to maintain boundaries around their relationships. Some couples broke up as a result of these pressures. Commune members sometimes found themselves in a series of romantic relationships—not vastly different from individuals in the rest of contemporary society, except that they might continue to live with their former partner as well as a current partner.

Parents sometimes found it stressful to yield discipline and control of their children to other commune members. Although not having sole responsibility to monitor and nurture children was usually considered an advantage, it became challenging when parents disagreed with the punishments being meted out to their children by others or when their children seemed to enjoy being with other adults more than with them. As one mother told researchers,

I'm trying to loosen possessive feelings around a kid, giving up some of that. Letting other people parent her, the decision to give up my total investment in her creation, was hard. I can no longer project myself and invest in making her my ideal. It's risky in a way, to give up some control. (Kanter et al., 1975, p. 444)

Other costs of group upbringing that parents noted were that multiple rule makers and rule enforcers for children might create inconsistency and contradictions in how rules were applied, resulting in ambiguity and confusion on the part of children, and that they found less time for intimacy with their children: "There are times when communes seem to leave out extreme love and tight relationships . . . [my daughter and I] have gained a great deal, but we have lost a little too" (a single father, in Kanter et al., 1975, p. 447).

GAY AND LESBIAN FAMILIES

Cultural reactions to same-sex relationships are not universal. Some cultures have embraced homosexuality, others have tolerated it, and others have stigmatized and persecuted individuals who admit to being homosexuals. For the most part, American culture in the 20th century fits into this latter category—homosexuality was at best a stigmatized status and, in most parts of the country and during most of the century, it was a dangerous label to have attached to oneself. Men were beaten and killed for being gay, women lost their children because judges would not accept the idea that lesbians could be good parents, and both homosexual men and women faced job loss, housing discrimination, and other types of public censure by "coming out." There were private costs for being homosexual as well; extended family members and friends were known to shun lesbians and gay men, sometimes to the extent of severing ties with them.

For most of the century, the prudent course of action for homosexual men and women was to hide their sexual orientation. Some individuals "passed" in society by marrying a heterosexual person and raising children and having same-sex affairs when they could manage it. Others hid their sexual orientation by cross-dressing and presenting themselves in public as members of the other gender. This strategy worked better if their voices, facial features, and body builds were such that people would be fooled. Another strategy was to live quietly as a single man or woman, sometimes with a roommate or alone, but sophisticated Americans knew that phrases such as "confirmed bachelor" and "spinster" were sometimes code terms for homosexuality. These three strategies were available to gays and lesbians who wanted to avoid social stigma and possible physical harm to themselves and their loved ones—living in a sham marriage, physically passing as the other gender, or living as quietly as possible as a lifelong single person. Consequently, for most of the century, gay men and lesbians were not able to openly form intimate adult relationships (at least outside of a few urban areas) or openly reside in family households with their children. Although gay and lesbian long-term relationships existed throughout the century, as did gay and lesbian parents, the stigmatized status of homosexuality generally meant that they did not make themselves available for scrutiny by researchers and other scholars until late in the century.

Gay men and lesbians began to be more visible in U.S. society after a 1969 riot at the Stonewall bar in New York City. This fight between lesbians, gay men, and police officers became a symbol to homosexuals that they could stand up for themselves. The final three decades of the century witnessed a growing movement among gay and lesbian activists to assert their rights to exist in society without harassment. Organizations such as Queer Nation and Act-Up were created to serve as educational and advocacy/awareness groups. Gradually, gay and lesbian individuals began to speak out and identify themselves as homosexuals, and some dared to live openly as couples and families. Although there were counter movements in response to gay activism, and political backlash to restrict their rights, in the last quarter of the 20th century, the visibility of homosexuals and their families increased greatly.

Affectional preferences and sexual experiences that are socially acceptable during one point in time may be thought of as sick, dangerous, or antisocial during another period of history. For

Gay Men and Lesbians from 1900 to 1969

example, in the late 19th century and in the early years of the 20th century, women could experience *romantic friendships* with each other. These romantic friendships were accompanied by many behaviors characteristic of romantic cross-sex relationships but were generally assumed not to be sexual in nature. That is, there could be declarations of love and devotion between women; they might share a bed for weeks, months, or even years; they sent each other gifts, notes, and flowers; and, at women's colleges in the East, they went to dances together and went out on dates. It was common knowledge that female college students had crushes (also known as smashes or spoons) on each other.

Some of these romantic friendships were called *Boston marriages*, because there were so many of them in that city in the late 19th and early 20th centuries. Boston marriages were households containing two never-married women, usually professionals or career women, who lived together in long-term relationships. Were they always lesbian couples? Probably not, but nobody asked. In the early part of the 20th century, having advanced education and a profession was a legitimate way for a woman to remain single; it took her out of the mainstream and allowed her more latitude within which to live and create a life-style for herself without answering to others—in particular, without answering to men. A college-educated woman in 1900 was five times more likely to be single than women in general. So for women across the country, regardless of whether sexually involved with each other, a Boston marriage was a way for women to gain personal independence that was otherwise unavailable to them, and yet enjoy the security and satisfactions of having their own households.

Affectionate relationships between men also were seen as appropriate and normal in the late 19th and early 20th centuries, although there was not the equivalent of Boston marriages for men. Men were expected to settle down with a wife and children once they could afford to do so, although it was certainly acceptable for men to publicly express warm feelings to each other and to spend a great deal of time together engaged in manly pursuits such as playing sports, gambling, and hunting.

Early in the 20th century, however, public perceptions of same-sex relationships began to change drastically, mostly because an influential group of European and American physicians, who called themselves sexologists, declared same-sex romantic friendships to be sexual perversions. Women who loved women were called "congenital inverts" and were portrayed by the sexologists as abnormal, masculine women who had enormous sex drives. Men who wanted to have sex with other men and who exhibited "feminine" characteristics also were called inverts (or fairies), and were portrayed as neurotic and emotionally immature. The sexologists invented the term homosexual in 1892 as a way to label what they thought to be unhealthy interests in same-sex relationships (they also coined the term heterosexual, a term originally used for other types of sexual neuroses). Homosexuality was declared an inborn condition; that is, individuals who had sexual relations with other individuals of their same gender were sick and could not help themselves.

By the end of World War I, public tolerance of romantic friendships for women had ended. Instead of encouraging young women to pursue higher education and careers if they so desired, women were urged to find personal fulfillment in companionate marriages and to forgo school-girl crushes and careers altogether. Subsequent generations of women who loved other women therefore had little choice but to consider themselves lesbians (or to spend a lot of energy denying their feelings). Women began to hide their affection for other women, and even those who were living together and presumed to be couples denied their status and even sided publicly with the sexologists' views. For example, the female president of Mount Holyoke College and a woman professor lived together for 55 years, yet Professor Jeannette Marks wrote an essay in 1908 denouncing "unwise college friendships" as a sickness; she contended that only through an intimate relationship with a man could a woman be fulfilled. Even women who admitted to intimate relationships with other women distinguished themselves from the sexual inverts described by the sexologists by defining their relationships as love affairs that were not just sexual, but of a "higher type" than that of working-class lesbians, who were thought to be driven by sexual desire only, and not love.

For men, being identified as a homosexual was a problem mostly among those who showed culturally defined feminine characteristics (e.g., acting in effeminate ways, being interested in the arts, not being interested in or being poor at playing physical sports). Masculine-acting gay men generally passed as heterosexual bachelors.

In the early decades of the 20th century, some working-class women passed as men by cutting their hair and wearing men's clothes. Passing was relatively easy then because women did not wear pants. Most women who wore a hat and men's pants did not get second looks because it was assumed that pants-wearers were men. The primary motivation to do this was economic—a lower- or working-class woman on her own could barely survive, even if she worked very hard. As a man, she got paid more, had a wider array of available jobs, and had the freedom to travel about on her own. Some of these women were interested in having sex with other women, but not all of them, and probably not even most. In fact, historian Lillian Faderman (1991) speculated that some women turned to homosexuality *after* they began cross-dressing. The few men who cross-dressed were generally prostitutes who lived in the largest cities of the country. There was much less motivation for gay men to cross-dress than there was for women.

In the 1920s, outside of a few lesbian and gay communities in San Francisco, New York City (i.e., Harlem, Greenwich Village), and other large cities, gay men and lesbians usually lived by themselves, passing as bachelors or spinsters. In Harlem, however, bisexuality was tolerated. Harlem became a destination for upper-class individuals who went there for exotic entertainment, such as watching men dance with men, observing live sex shows, and listening to blues singers celebrate being gay and lesbian. Lesbians were tolerated in Harlem to the extent that some held wedding ceremonies. A few of these couples applied for real marriage licenses, using initials to replace feminine names, having male friends pick up the applications, and filing them with the Marriage Bureau. Many blacks living in Harlem did not approve of homosexuality, but they tolerated it because they understood and empathized with what it was like to be marginalized in society. Gay men and lesbians also generally could live quietly as couples in places such as Greenwich Village, where there were large populations of artists, writers, and other creative people who tolerated diverse life-styles.

The economic crisis of the 1930s, coupled with increasingly negative public opinions about homosexuality, was particularly hard for lesbians. They were caught in an antifeminist backlash—employed women were seen by some people as taking jobs that rightfully should go to unemployed men who might have children and a wife to support. Working women became the scapegoat for an economy in which 25 percent of the labor force was out of work. One commentator suggested that there were 10 million women in the labor force and 10 million people out of work so the simple solution was to fire all of the women—an instant cure for the Depression. Women were encouraged for the public good to give up employment and find their satisfaction in marriage and childbearing. As a result, many lesbians married men, partly for financial reasons and partly to avoid public disapproval of being single and, possibly, gay. It was simpler for lesbians to marry than be vilified as perverts who were stealing jobs from husbands and fathers. As Faderman (1991) put it,

Lesbians were . . . considered monstrosities in the 1930s—an era in which America needed fewer workers and more women who would seek contentment making individual men happy so that social anger could be personally mitigated instead of spilling over into social revolt. In this context, the lesbian (who needed to work and had no interest in making a man happy) was an anti-social being. (p. 119)

Because a greater proportion of women were marrying, including lesbians, it was clearer (in hindsight) in the 1930s than ever before that some married women conducted long-term affairs with women (Eleanor Roosevelt, for instance). These relationships had to be extremely discrete because the costs were great if they were caught. Some husbands, however, simply looked the other way and others were obtuse to the possibility of such a liaison. Although some married gay men conducted short-term sexual relationships with other men, it was relatively rare for them to have long-term affairs with other gay men.

During World War II, gay men and lesbians generally were left undisturbed, ignored, or even tolerated (at least in the military), because the nation was at war and men and women, regardless of their choice of sexual partners and love interests, were needed to fight the enemy and keep the country running. Although lesbians and gay men were still stigmatized and seen as perverts, Americans during war time were pragmatic. If gay men and lesbians were discrete, most other Americans would look the other way. For instance, General Dwight Eisenhower rescinded an order to a female sergeant to find out who were lesbians in the Women's Army Corps in order to purge the troops of them when he was told,

If the General pleases, I will be happy to do this investigation. . . . My name is going to head the list. . . . You should also be aware that you're going to have to replace all of the file clerks, the section heads, most of the commanders, and the motor pool. (Faderman, 1991, p. 118)

Ironically, the social structures that emerged in both military and civilian life during World War II served to segregate men and women by gender, which some believe led to more men and women coming out of the closet. For instance, men in male-only military units provided many opportunities for men to become close to each other, sometimes in tense life-or-death situations. Many intense relationships were formed in military service, and some of them probably had sexual components. Similarly, many women found themselves in female-only or female-dominated social systems at work and in the community. Besides volunteering for military duty in the Women's Army Corps, women returned to the labor force in large numbers, working in factories, offices, and other locations. These settings provided opportunities for women to meet lesbians, make judgments about their own sexual orientations, and, for some, decide that maybe they did not need a man to fulfill them. Surrounded by strong and independent women, some women who had assumed they were heterosexual or who had given their sexuality little thought found themselves attracted to women. Moreover, some women during the war years discovered that they could fend for themselves without men, which opened up many possibilities, including intimate relationships with women.

When the war ended and the GIs returned, however, popular sentiment returned to demonizing homosexuals and encouraging heterosexuality. Psychoanalytic therapists wrote about the "illness of homosexuality" during the late 1940s and throughout the 1950s, as they had between the world wars, once again sending lesbians and gay men underground. In society as a whole, the prevailing view was that a woman's place was in the home. Therefore, women were encouraged to marry and to fulfill themselves through running their households and taking care of their families. The returning soldiers, airmen, and sailors were hailed as heroes, and society wanted to help these young men make up for lost time by finding them jobs, wives, and places to live to start (or resume) their families. There was little room in postwar America for sexual diversity—marrying and bearing children were normative expectations, and there was little support or tolerance for alternatives.

After World War II, however, more women than before identified themselves as lesbians, and a lesbian subculture emerged. For gay men, who had had an urban singles subculture for decades, the end of the war meant more jobs in the cities, as factories and businesses geared up to help Europe and Japan rebuild. Urban areas were easier places than rural areas or small towns for gay men and lesbians to find each other and locate gathering places (usually bars, but restaurants and rooming houses as well). The rise of gay and lesbian subcultures was in part a response to being stigmatized and persecuted by society as a whole, and partly the result of the need to be with people who had similar worldviews and life experiences.

The political and social turmoil of the 1960s affected gay men and lesbians, just as it did everyone else. Sexual experimentation in the 1960s—especially changes in sexual attitudes and behaviors led by the counterculture movement—helped create an atmosphere that fostered gay men and lesbians gradually becoming more open about their lives, at least in selected urban centers of the country.

For many gay men, the primary issue post-Stonewall riot was about civil rights. In gay pride parades they shouted, "We're here, we're queer, get used to it!" Within a decade, AIDS brought disparate groups of gay men together in a common cause, one that united them in grief over the losses of friends and loved ones. Many lesbians and some straight men and women also rallied around gay men because of AIDS—it was a force that brought people together in the 1980s and 1990s.

From the start of the century to nearly the end of the 1960s, the history of gay men and lesbians in the United States was about individual men and women. The notion that there are families headed by gay and lesbian individuals is a fairly recent historical

The Rise of Gay and Lesbian Family Households

phenomenon. To be sure, there were gay men and lesbians who were parents, and there were same-sex couples who were in committed, long-term relationships; however, there was little concept of same-sex marriage or gay/lesbian families, even among members of the gay and lesbian communities, and certainly not among the larger U.S. culture. Most gay and lesbian parents functioned in relative isolation, and most long-term same-sex couples lived quietly, thankful that they could manage to do so without harassment and persecution.

Creating gay and lesbian family households. Nobody knows how many children were raised in gay and lesbian family households throughout the century. In the 1990 census, 21.7 percent of partnered lesbians had children in the home, and 5.2 percent of the partnered gay men did. In the 2000 census, 594,000 households were headed by same-sex couples, and children lived in 27 percent of these households. Although it is not known exactly how many children lived in those households, at least 160,000 children did.

The most common way that gay and lesbian couples created family households in the last two decades of the century was for one or both adults to have reproduced or adopted children in earlier heterosexual relationships—in one study, approximately three-fourths of the children of both lesbians and gay men were offspring from a previous heterosexual marriage. In the 1990 census, about 30 percent of gay men and 46 percent of lesbians had been married previously. These families were in many ways like heterosexual stepfamilies—children generally were connected emotionally more to their parent than to the other adult in the household, and, in some of these families, the children had frequent or episodic contact with their nonresidential parent. The mother's lesbian partner or the gay father's partner was, in effect, a stepparent. Because mothers generally were granted physical custody of children after divorce, gay couples rarely had children with them all or most of the time, whereas lesbians more likely had the children with them all of the time or shared physical custody with the children's fathers.

The second way in which gay and lesbian couples formed families was via donor insemination. This was more practical for lesbians than it was for gay men; changes in reproductive technologies made it simpler than ever for lesbians to become pregnant. For gay men, donor insemination meant finding a surrogate mother to bear the child (a difficult task, and usually expensive because the mother typically had to be paid and provided health care), so this option was seldom explored.

Although costly, motherhood via donor insemination grew in popularity. In the last 15 years of the century, about one out of seven lesbians who became pregnant did so through donor insemination. Sometimes women asked brothers of their lesbian partners to donate sperm so there would be a genetic connection to both the birth mother and the co-mother. Occasionally, gay friends were asked to donate sperm, but most lesbian mothers-to-be used donations from sperm banks and clinics, which reduced the chance of having to share parenting with the child's father.

Adoption of a child by a gay or lesbian individual, regardless of whether he or she was in a committed relationship, was a third way of forming a gay or lesbian family, although this was relatively uncommon due to barriers to adoption for openly gay and lesbian individuals. Adoptions of an unrelated child were limited in most states to either one adult or a married couple. Because gays and lesbians could not legally marry, they could adopt only as a single person, which meant that only one of the partners in a gay and lesbian relationship could be legally connected to the child. Some states explicitly prohibited gay and lesbian individuals from adopting, and even if they didn't, social service agencies typically would not recommend them as fit parents for adoption because of their sexual orientation.

Gay and lesbian couples who acquired a child via donor insemination or through one of them adopting a child usually functioned as if they were a nuclear family, but with two mommies (or two daddies) instead of a mother and father. Structurally, they were similar to heterosexual (first marriage) nuclear families in that the couple relationships existed prior to the addition of children, so that children had no recall of a time when both co-parents were not present in their lives. Most of these lesbian families (and the few gay family households) generally functioned differently than lesbian (or gay) families formed after either or both partners had been in heterosexual unions that produced children; those functioned more like stepfamilies. For instance, when children were born after the lesbian or gay couple had formed, there was no nonresidential parent to deal with, children did not recall living in any other family household, and children typically had strong emotional ties to both co-parents.

Parenting. Most of what is known about gay and lesbian parents is based on studies focused on lesbian parents. These studies indicated that lesbian mothers were as skilled as heterosexual mothers at raising children. Given that some lesbian mothers **Family Dynamics in Gay and Lesbian Families** and their co-parents may have felt under attack by the mainstream society (and by some other lesbians), it is not surprising that they reported themselves to be committed to their children and heavily invested in being good parents. A person does not generally risk what these women risk unless he or she is determined to be a good parent.

Although lesbian genetic mothers shared childrearing duties and decision making with their co-parents more frequently than did mothers in heterosexual families, lesbian genetic mothers and straight mothers assumed the lion's share of responsibility for their children. Lesbian co-mothers tended to teach feminist values to both sons and daughters, and most tried hard to teach their children to be open-minded and accepting.

Studies in the last decade of the 20th century consistently found that children of gay and lesbian individuals fared as well academically, socially, emotionally, and physically as their counterparts raised by

Lesbian co-mothers celebrate parenthood, 2000. (Courtesy of the authors.)

heterosexual parents. They were not more likely to be gay or lesbian than were children of heterosexual parents, and they did not have any more problems. They tended to be more tolerant than other children, not just of sexual orientation, but of differences between people in general.

Protecting children from stigma and discrimination. One important factor that distinguished gay and lesbian parenting was their fear that their children would be harmed as a result of the parents' sexual orientations. Gay and lesbian parents sometimes were reluctant to come out to their children, not because they were afraid of rejection—although this was perhaps a plausible fear for some—but because they did not want to put pressure on their children to have to hide their parents' sexual orientation from outsiders. Many also worried that if the children were not discrete, other children would tease or bully them and teachers and parents of the children's friends would discriminate against the children. Consequently, lesbian and gay parents tended to be overprotective of their children, and they tried to shield their children from the negative attitudes of outsiders.

One way that gay and lesbian parents sheltered their children was by creating extended "families of choice"—social support networks of other gays and lesbians, straight friends, and family members. These became networks of aid and emotional support. For example, lesbians with sons sometimes "adopted" gay men and straight male friends to serve as role models.

In 1970, Jack Baker, a law student at the University of Minnesota, and Mike McConnell, a librarian, attempted to obtain a marriage license in Hennepin County, Minnesota, and were rebuffed. Both men were gay rights **Marriages and Civil Unions** activists, and they had invited reporters to witness their attempt to get a marriage license as part of an effort to raise awareness among the general public of gay rights issues. Although they were unsuccessful in their quest to be married—and suffered social rejections and economic hardships as a result (Mike lost his job)—they launched the beginning of a long battle by gay men and lesbians for the right to legally marry. Indeed, although some gay men and lesbians were critical of conventional marriage and thought that they were better off as single adults, by the end of the 20th century, a sizeable segment of gay men and lesbians were advocating for their rights to be legally married and to form families recognized by laws and social policy.

After a series of mid-1970s legal court decisions in Minnesota, Washington, and Kentucky that essentially ruled out marriage between same-sex couples, this issue appeared to be dead as a legal issue until the late 1980s. Throughout the 1980s, the Metropolitan Community Church, a denomination founded in 1968, held hundreds of wedding ceremonies for its members, which were not legally recognized as marriage but satisfied the needs of gay and lesbian couples to make public affirmations of commitment. In 1987, over 1,000 same-sex couples joined in marriage at the National Cathedral as part of the second gay rights march on Washington; increasingly, the right to marry was becoming a critical part of the fight for civil rights for gays and lesbians.

Several state courts were asked to make judgments about same-sex marriage in the 1990s. In 1993, the Hawaii Supreme Court ruled that limiting marriage to heterosexual couples might be discrimination and ordered the state to make its case why same-sex marriages should not be legal. The state argued that legalizing same-sex couples would encourage childrearing by those couples, which would be bad for their children. The state lost this argument in 1996, and, in 1997, the Hawaii legislature approved a constitutional amendment to be presented to voters that would ban same-sex marriages. At the same time, the legislature passed the Reciprocal Beneficiaries Act, which allowed same-sex couples many of the same rights as married couples (such as inheriting property from a deceased partner without a will and some employer-provided health benefits). The Hawaii Supreme Court ruling of 1993 galvanized conservative opposition across the country, and, in state after state, legal rulings rejected arguments in favor of same-sex marriages.

This opposition culminated in the 1996 federal Defense of Marriage Act (DOMA), which was overwhelmingly supported by both houses of

Congress and signed into law by President Clinton. DOMA ruled that no state would be required to recognize same-sex marriages from other states and stated that, for federal purposes, the terms *marriage* and *spouse* would apply only to heterosexual unions. DOMA was followed by state legislatures either amending state constitutions or making laws that similarly explicitly defined marriage as reserved for only a man and a woman.

Marriage lite. Concurrent with the movement to legalize same-sex marriage were efforts to legally recognize gay and lesbian couples as domestic partnerships or civil unions—relationships that would hold many of the legal benefits of marriage without being called marriages. The opponents to such relationships sometimes called them "marriage lite." In the 1980s and 1990s, some cities in California (Berkeley, San Francisco, and West Hollywood) and many academic communities began to recognize same-sex and heterosexual cohabiting couples as domestic partnerships. In addition to Hawaii's Reciprocal Beneficiaries Act, Vermont passed a civil union bill in 1999 that applied to same-sex unions. Large corporations, such as Disney, also began to allow same-sex couples and cohabiting heterosexual couples to obtain health insurance and other benefits previously reserved for married couples.

As the 20th century ended, gay marriage was one of the most divisive social and political issues in the United States. Opponents were well organized and highly motivated, while many proponents and gay rights activities were more vocally in favor of marriage as a right than ever before.

Gay and Lesbian Parents and Legal Issues

Over the last 30 years of the 20th century, a number of legal issues surrounding gay and lesbian parenting received scrutiny from the public and from the courts: adoption of children by same-sex couples, the right to reproduction technology, custody after divorce, and protecting the nonbiological lesbian parents' relationship with a child after the union with the mother ends. In general, public opinion opposed homosexual parenting, and legal decisions reflected this sentiment.

Adoption by gay men and lesbians. Homosexuals generally could adopt as single parents if they were closeted, but same-sex couples had difficulties in most states being seen as acceptable adoptive parents. Because of this obstacle, most adoptions were done by only one of the partners. In the 1990s, a few states (New York, Vermont, Massachusetts) began to allow second parent adoptions to the partner who was not the biological parent of their partners' children from a prior heterosexual relationship. Most states did not allow such second parent adoptions, however, which meant that when same-sex couples split (mostly lesbians, because mothers were more likely to have physical custody of children than gay fathers were), the lesbian co-parent usually lost contact with the former partners' children and had no legal recourse to seek visitation. Many biological fathers of children born to lesbians via artificial insemination also sought visitation rights, with more success.

Custody of children. If a divorced parent revealed his or her homosexuality openly, such as by having a same-sex partner, there was an excellent chance that he or she would lose physical custody of children from heterosexual unions and would be denied anything but supervised visitations. Starting in the early 1970s, lesbian mothers formed political action groups to help mothers who lost access to their children after divorce. These groups generally were not effective in changing laws—in state after state, lesbian mothers lost court decisions to keep their children; although some states (e.g., California, Washington, Ohio) did overturn restrictions on visitation rights in the late 1980s.

The backlash to gay and lesbian parents was ferocious in intensity. Led by fundamental religious groups such as Focus on the Family and the Family Research Council and political conservatives, the attack on gay and lesbian parents' rights was organized and widespread. "Save our children" was the battle cry of Anita Bryant, entertainer and spokesperson for Florida orange juice, who spearheaded a successful and well-publicized drive to repeal a Dade County, Florida, gay rights ordinance. This motto was picked up by many who opposed homosexuality as sinful and damaging to children. States and courts worked to clearly define parenthood with the intention of denying parental claims of all but biological mothers and fathers, and heterosexual men and women as adoptive parents. The 1990s saw the battle between gay rights advocates and gay rights opponents heat up—at the same time that the American Psychological Association was issuing a monograph entitled *Lesbian and Gay Parenting: A Resource for Psychologists* (Patterson, 1995)—in which a review of 43 studies showed no indication that children of gay and lesbian parents were disadvantaged in comparison to children raised by heterosexual parents—politicians were passing DOMA and other legislation designed to define marriages and families narrowly enough that gay and lesbian families were excluded. The end of the century saw both more openness by gay and lesbian parents *and* more attacks against them.

GRANDCHILDREN LIVING WITH GRANDPARENTS

Throughout history, grandparents have been active in raising their grandchildren, many shared households with their children and grandchildren, and others provided child care for those who resided nearby. Late in the 20th century, however, many grandparents experienced a shift in their role—becoming primary caregivers of their grandchildren, responsible for meeting children's basic needs including housing, food, clothing, education, discipline, socialization, and emotional nurturing. Their reasons for assuming this responsibility were numerous and might include a parent's substance abuse, incarceration, single parenthood, child abuse or neglect, mental illness, HIV/AIDS or other serious illness, unwillingness to raise the child, or death.

Researchers suggested that children living with grandparents were generally healthier than children in single-parent or stepfamilies—they had fewer behavioral problems and were better adapted socially. However, many did have problems that started before they moved in with their grandparents, including abuse, neglect, prenatal exposure to drugs and alcohol, and loss of parents (e.g., death, abandonment, and incarceration). Furthermore, the majority of children living in grandmother-only households lived in poverty.

Since 1940, Census Bureau statistics indicated that the percentage of children living with grandparents only (with no parents in the household) remained fairly steady during the last 60 years of the century, as did the percentage of children living in the same household as a grandparent and other adults. These statistics, however, obscure the amount of childrearing done by grandparents because, although the incidence of living together changed very little over time, the reason for sharing a residence changed. At the end of the century, in about 75 percent of the households containing three or more generations, grandparents had taken in their children and grandchildren to live with them. Grandparents usually functioned as parental figures when their grandchildren moved in with them, and, in the mid-1990s, an estimated 10 percent of grandparents were primary caregivers for a grandchild for at least six months before the child reached age 18. In 2000, about 2.4 million grandparents were raising their grandchildren without the children's parents present. More than 60 percent of these households were headed by grandmothers. Although the majority of grandparents raising grandchildren were white, proportionately more grandparent-headed households occurred among African Americans than in other racial and ethnic groups.

Earlier in the century, when grandparents took responsibility for raising their grandchildren, it was usually because the children's parents were seriously ill and incapable of taking care of children, the children's parents had died an untimely death, or the parents had to move elsewhere to find work. Toward the end of the century, however, reasons for assuming the primary caregiver role became more varied, and grandparents spent longer periods of time in the roles of parent-substitutes. Among the reasons that grandparents assumed the childrearing responsibilities for their grandchildren in the final quarter of the century were imprisonment or drug and alcohol addiction by the grandchildren's parents, parental divorce, the inability of parents to handle crises on a short-term basis, child abuse or neglect, parents' mental illness, chronic illnesses of parents (particularly HIV/AIDS), or death of the parents. Very often grandparents were thrust into childrearing duties with little warning.

Raising grandchildren was hard work for most grandparents. Although most willingly took their grandchildren into their homes and cared for them, grandparents who were taking care of their grandchildren had more health problems than other grandparents—grandmothers raising grandchildren alone were particularly susceptible to having health problems. Having adolescent grandchildren and having several grandchildren were associated with greater health risks for grandparents. In contrast, some research indicated that having one younger, well-behaved grandchild had a positive influence on grandmothers' health.

Multigenerational coresidence was more likely in poor families than in middle-class and wealthy families, and many grandparents raising grandchildren struggled financially. Some were retired and on fixed incomes, so adding household members strained their budgets. Many grandparents who were working when they assumed responsibility for their grandchildren gave up their jobs, thus lowering their incomes and losing benefits. In general, the grandchildren's parents were unable to financially assist them. Although grandparents with grandchildren to raise were more likely to be on welfare than grandparents not raising their grandchildren, in some states, grandparents were not eligible to receive welfare unless they were the legal guardians of their grandchildren, a step that some families were reluctant to take because it involved the legal system and altered the rights of the grandchildren's parents.

Many grandparents raising grandchildren also faced social as well as financial costs. For instance, many grandparents who had childrearing responsibilities found they had less time to spend with their friends, and so their social and recreational activities were reduced.

Although raising grandchildren resulted in negative outcomes for some grandparents, many grandparents benefited from the experience. Caring for grandchildren gave some grandparents a sense of accomplishment and pride when children did well in school or had successes directly associated with the care the grandparents had provided.

Grandparent caregivers had few legal rights at the end of the century. Traditionally, biological and adoptive parents had almost exclusive legal authority over their children; laws ensured that children could not be taken away from their parents unless they were in danger. Without parental consent, grandparents were not able to enroll grandchildren in school or to seek nonemergency medical care on grandchildren's behalf. Those living in subsidized housing for older adults often had to move if their units did not allow children to reside there on a permanent basis. Many grandparents were hesitant to seek primary custody or to pursue adoption due to concerns that their adult children would refuse consent or feelings of disloyalty. In addition, custody battles were time consuming, costly, and emotionally draining processes.

SUMMARY

American families were diverse throughout the 20th century, but a sea change of public attitudes toward gender roles and the meanings of marriage and family life occurred in the final four decades of the century that led to explorations of alternative marriage and family forms. Consequently, there were more variations in family households in the final decade of the century than in the first. First marriage nuclear families remained the norm and the standard by which other families were compared, but other types of families were increasingly recognized and tolerated. As the century ended, there were huge debates about these alternatives—were they solutions to problems in conventional families and society or were they problems that threatened the viability of conventional families and society? The 21st century will likely be a time when this question receives even greater scrutiny than it has. It is likely that alternative family forms will be the topic of much more debate and discussion in the future.

References

Action Agenda: Existing Federal Policy. (2006). *Alliance for Healthy Homes*. Retrieved January 11, 2007, from http://www.afhh.org/aa/aa_existing _policy.htm.

Alan Guttmacher Institute. (1976). *11 million teenagers: What can be done about the epidemic of adolescent pregnancies in the United States.* New York: Planned Parenthood Federation of America.

Allison, D. (1992). *Bastard out of Carolina.* New York: Dutton.

Amato, P. R. (2004). To have and have not: Marriage and divorce in the United States. In M. Coleman & L. Ganong (Eds.), *Handbook of contemporary families* (pp. 265–281). Thousand Oaks, CA: Sage.

Amato, P. R., & Keith, B. (1991). Parental divorce and the well-being of children: A meta-analysis. *Psychological Bulletin, 110,* 26–46.

Arendell, T. (2000). Conceiving and investigating motherhood: The decade's scholarship. *Journal of Marriage and Family, 62,* 1192–1207.

Bachu, A. (1999). Trends in premarital childbearing: 1930 to 1994. *Current Population Reports,* Series P23-197. Washington, DC: U.S. Government Printing Office.

Bailey, B. L. (1989). *From front porch to back seat.* Baltimore: Johns Hopkins University Press.

Baum, L. F. (1900). *The wizard of Oz.* Chicago: George Hill.

Bell, R. R., & Chaskes, J. B. (1970). Premarital sexual experience among coeds. *Journal of Marriage and the Family, 32,* 81–85.

Boonstra, H. (2002). Teen pregnancy: Trends and lessons learned. *Guttmacher Report on Public Policy, 5,* 7–10.

Braden, D. R. (1988). *Leisure and entertainment in America*. Dearborn, MI: Henry Ford Museum and Greenfield Village.

Brazelton, T. B. (1969). *Infants and mothers*. New York: Dell.

Calkins, E. E. (1934). *Care and feeding of hobby horses*. York, PA: Maple.

Campbell, J. C., & Soeken, K. (1998). Women's responses to battering over time: An analysis of change. *Advances in Nursing Science, 21*, 1–15.

Cantave, C., & Harrison, R. (2003). Marriage and African Americans. *Joint Center DataBank*. Retrieved August 15, 2006, from: http://jointcenter.org/DB/factsheet/marital.htm.

Caplow, T., Bahr, H. M., Chadwick, B. A., Hill, R., & Williamson, M. H. (1982). *Middletown families*. Minneapolis: University of Minnesota Press.

Chafe, W. H. (1991). *The paradox of change*. New York: Oxford University Press.

Cherlin, A. (1978). Remarriage as an incomplete institution. *American Journal of Sociology, 84*, 634–650.

Chesler, P. (1988). *Sacred bond*. New York: Crown.

Clark, C. E., Jr. (1986). *The American family home, 1800–1960*. Chapel Hill: University of North Carolina Press.

Coley, R. L., & Chase-Lansdale, P. L. (1998). Adolescent pregnancy and parenthood: Recent evidence and future directions. *American Psychologist, 53*, 152–166.

Collins, G. (2003). *American women*. New York: HarperCollins.

Coltrane, S. (1988). Father-child relationships and the status of women: A cross-cultural study. *American Journal of Sociology, 93*, 1060–1095.

Coontz, S. (2005). *Marriage, a history*. New York: Viking.

Cowan, R. S. (1983). *More work for mother*. New York: Basic Books.

Crittenden, A. (2001). *The price of motherhood*. New York: Henry Holt.

Davis, M. (1936). *The lost generation*. New York: Macmillan.

Degler, C. N. (1980). *At odds*. New York: Oxford University Press.

DeMaris, A. (2001). The influence of intimate violence on transitions out of cohabitation. *Journal of Marriage and Family, 63*, 235–246.

Demos, J. (1986). The changing faces of fatherhood. In J. Demos (Ed.), *Past, present, and personal* (pp. 41–68). New York: Oxford University.

Doan, M. C. (1997). *American housing production, 1800–2000*. Lanham, MD: University Press of America.

East, P. L., & Felice, M. E. (1996). *Adolescent pregnancy and parenting*. Mahwah, NJ: Erlbaum.

Elkind, D. (1981). *The hurried child*. Reading, MA: Addison-Wesley.

Faderman, L. (1991). *Odd girls and twilight lovers*. New York: Columbia University Press.

Farmer, F. M. (1918). *Fannie Farmer cookbook*. Boston: Little, Brown.

Fields, J., & Casper, L. M. (2001). America's families and living arrangements: March 2000. *Current Population Reports*, P20-537. Washington, DC: U.S. Government Printing Office.

Finkelhor, D., Gelles, R. J., Hotaling, G. T., & Straus, M. A. (Eds.). (1983). *The dark side of families.* Beverly Hills, CA: Sage.

Freeman, L. (2006). *There goes the 'hood.* Philadelphia: Temple University Press.

Friedan, B. (1963). *The feminine mystique.* New York: Norton.

Garey, A. (1995). Constructing motherhood on the night shift: Working mothers as stay-at-home moms. *Qualitative Sociology, 18,* 415–437.

Garey, A. I., & Arendell, T. (2001). Children, work, and family: Some thoughts on "mother blame." In R. Hertz & N. Marshall (Eds.), *Working families* (pp. 293–303). Berkeley: University of California Press.

Gauer, J. (2004). *The new American dream.* New York: Monacelli.

Gelles, R. J., & Straus, M. A. (1988). *Intimate violence.* New York: Simon & Schuster.

Gesell, A. (1925). *The mental growth of the pre-school child.* New York: Macmillan.

Gil, D. G. (1971). Violence against children. *Journal of Marriage and the Family, 33,* 637–648.

Gillis, J. R. (1996). *A world of their own making.* Cambridge, MA: Harvard University Press.

Good wife's guide. (1955, 13 May). *Housekeeping Monthly*

Goode, W. J. (1963). *World revolution and family patterns.* New York: Free Press.

Hall, G. S. (1904). *Adolescence.* New York: Appleton.

Hareven, T. (2000). *Families, history and social change.* Boulder, CO: Westview Press.

Hareven, T. K., & Uhlenberg, P. (1995). Transition to widowhood and family support systems in the twentieth century, northeast U.S. In D. Kertzer & P. Laslett (Eds.), *Aging in the past* (pp. 273–299). Berkeley: University of California Press.

Hawes, J. M. (1997). *Children between the wars.* New York: Twayne.

Hernandez, D. (1993). *America's children: Resources from family, government, and the economy.* New York: Russell Sage Foundation.

Hite, S. (1976). *The Hite report.* New York: Macmillan.

Hochschild, A. R. (1997). *The time bind.* New York: Metropolitan.

Holt, L. E. (1894). *The care and feeding of children.* New York: Appleton-Century-Crofts.

Huang, C., & Pouncy, H. (2005). Why doesn't she have a child support order? Personal choice or objective constraint. *Family Relations, 54,* 547–557.

Hulbert, A. (2003). *Raising America.* New York: Knopf.

Imber-Black, E., & Roberts, J. (1998). *Rituals for our times.* New York: HarperCollins.

Johnson, M. P. (1995). Patriarchal terrorism and common couple violence: Two forms of violence against women. *Journal of Marriage and the Family, 57,* 283–294.

Kain, E. L. (1990). *The myth of family decline.* Lexington, MA: Lexington Books.

Kanof, N. M., & Smart, M. S. (Eds.). (1965). *Mother's encyclopedia.* New York: Parents' Institute.

Kanter, R. M., Jaffe, D., & Weisberg, K. (1975). *Coupling, parenting, and the presence of others: Intimate relationships in communal households.* New York: Harper & Row.

Kempe, C. H., Silverman, F. N., Steele, B. F., Droegemueller, W., & Silver, H. K. (1962). The battered-child syndrome. *Journal of the American Medical Association, 181,* 105–112.

Keniston, K. (1960). *The uncommitted.* New York: Harcourt, Brace & World.

Key, E. (1909). *The century of the child.* New York: Putnam.

Kohn, M., & Carroll, E. E. (1960). Social class and the allocation of parental responsibility. *Sociometry, 23,* 378–392.

Kubler-Ross, E. (1969). *On death and dying.* New York: Macmillan.

Langhinrichsen-Rohling, J., & Monson, C. M. (1998). Marital rape: Is the crime taken seriously without co-occurring physical abuse? *Journal of Family Violence, 13,* 433–443.

LaRossa, R. (1997). *The modernization of fatherhood.* Chicago: University of Chicago Press.

Leon, K., & Angst, E. (2005). Portrayals of stepfamilies in film: Using media images in remarriage education. *Family Relations, 54,* 676–682.

Lerman, R. I. (2002). *How do marriage, cohabitation, and single parenthood affect the material hardships of families with children?* Washington, DC: Urban Institute. Retrieved August 10, 2006, from http://aspe.hhs.gov/hsp/marriage-well-being03/SippPaper.pdf.

Lewis, J. J. (2006). Jacqueline Kennedy Onassis quotes. *About women's history.* Retrieved August 29, 2006, from http://womenshistory.about.com/od/quotes/a/jackie_kennedy.htm.

Lovegren, S. (1995). *Fashionable food.* New York: Macmillan.

Lynd, R. S., & Lynd, H. M. (1929). *Middletown.* New York: Harcourt, Brace & World.

MacLachlan, P. (1985). *Sarah plain and tall.* New York: HarperCollins.

Macleod, D. I. (1998). *The age of the child.* New York: Twayne.

Marsh, M. (1990). *Suburban lives.* New Brunswick, NJ: Rutgers University Press.

Martin J. A., & Park, M. M. (1999). Trends in twin and triplet births: 1980–97. *National Vital Statistics Reports, 47.* Hyattsville, MD: National Center for Health Statistics.

May, E. (1994). *Pushing the limits.* New York: Oxford University Press.

May, E. (1999). *Homeward bound.* New York: Basic Books.

McAlester, V., & McAlester, L. (1984). *A field guide to American houses.* New York: Knopf.

McKenzie, E. (2005). Constructing the Pomerium in Las Vegas: A case study of emerging trends in American gated communities. *Housing Studies, 20,* 187–203.

McNulty, F. (1980). *The burning bed.* New York: Harcourt.

Mechling, J. (1975). Advice to historians on advice to mothers. *Social History, 9,* 44–63.

Miller, T. (1999). *The 60s communes.* Syracuse, NY: Syracuse University Press.

Mintz, S. (2004). *Huck's raft.* Cambridge, MA: Belknap Press of Harvard University Press.

Mintz, S., & Kellogg, S. (1988). *Domestic revolutions.* New York: Free Press.

Moynihan, D. P. (1965). *The Negro family: The case for national action.* Washington, DC: Office of Policy Planning Research, U.S. Department of Labor.

Myrdal, G. (1944). *An American dilemma.* New York: Harper and Brothers.

O'Neill, N., & O'Neill, G. (1972). *Open marriage.* New York: Evans.

Ooms, T. (2002). Strengthening couples and marriage in low-income communities. In A. J. Hawkins, L. D. Wardle, & D. O. Coolidge (Eds.), *Revitalizing the institution of marriage in the 21st century* (pp. 79–100). Westport, CT: Greenwood Press.

Padavic, I., & Reskin, B. F. (1990). Men's behavior and women's interest in blue collar jobs. *Social Problems, 37,* 613–629.

Palladino, G. (1996). *Teenagers.* New York: Basic Books.

Patterson, C. J. (1995). *Lesbian and gay parenting: A resource for psychologists.* Washington, DC: American Psychological Association.

Peterson, K. S. (2000, 27 September). Wooing the past: Courtship flirts with a comeback. *USA Today,* 9D.

Pleck, E. (1987). *Domestic tyranny.* New York: Oxford University Press.

Pleck, E. H. (2000). *Celebrating the family.* Cambridge, MA: Harvard University Press.

Popenoe, D. (1994). The evolution of marriage and the problem of stepfamilies: A biosocial perspective. In A. Booth & J. Dunn (Eds.), *Stepfamilies: Who benefits? Who does not?* (pp. 3–29). Hillsdale, NJ: Erlbaum.

Post, E. (1922). *Etiquette.* New York: Funk and Wagnalls.

Postman, N. (1994). *The disappearance of childhood.* New York: Vintage.

Reese, E. (2005). *Backlash against welfare mothers.* Berkeley: University of California Press.

Reskin, B. F., & Padavic, I. (1990). *Women and men at work.* Thousand Oaks, CA: Pine Forge.

Reynolds, M. (1962). "Little Boxes." Schroder Music Co.

Richards, E. (1882). *The chemistry of cooking and cleaning.* Boston: Estes & Lauriat.

Rimmer, R. (1967). *The Harrad experiment.* New York: Bantam.

Rimmer, R. (1969). *Proposition 31.* New York: Signet.

Robinson, I. E., & Jedlicka, D. (1982). Change in sexual attitudes and behavior of college students from 1965 to 1980: A research note. *Journal of Marriage and the Family, 44,* 237–240.

Roosevelt, T. (1905). *On motherhood.* The National Center for Public Policy Research. Retrieved January 11, 2007, from http://www.national center.org/TRooseveltMotherhood.html.

Rosenberg, R. (1992). *Divided lives.* New York: Hill and Wang.

Rothman, E. K. (1984). *Hands and hearts.* New York: Basic Books.

Ruddick, S. (1980). Maternal thinking. *Feminist Studies, 6,* 342–367.

Russell, D.E.H. (1986). *The secret trauma.* New York: Basic Books.

Schenone, L. (2003). *A thousand years over a hot stove.* New York: Norton.

Schor, J. (1991). *The overworked American.* New York: Basic Books.

Shapiro, L. (2001). *Perfection salad.* New York: Modern Library.

Shea, V. (1994). *Netiquette.* San Francisco: Albion.

Sorensen, E., & Halpern, A. (1999). *Child support enforcement is working better than we think.* Washington, DC: Urban Institute.

Spigel, L. (1992). *Make room for TV.* Chicago: University of Chicago Press.

Spock, B. (1946). *The common sense book of baby and child care.* New York: Duell, Sloan, & Pearce.

Spock, B., & Rothenberg, M. B. (1992). *Dr. Spock's baby and child care.* New York: Pocket.

Steinbeck, J. (1939). *The grapes of wrath.* New York: Viking.

Stranger, J. D., & Gridina, N. (1999). *Media in the home.* Philadelphia: University of Pennsylvania Press.

Szasz, M. C. (1985). Native American children. In J. M. Hawes & R. Hiner (Eds.), *American childhood: A research guide and historical handbook* (pp. 311–342). Westport, CT: Greenwood Press.

Szinovacz, M. E. (Ed.). (1998). *Handbook on grandparenthood.* Westport, CT: Greenwood Press.

Time. (1967, 6 January). *The generation gap.* Retrieved September 4, 2006, from http://www.colorado.edu/AmStudies/lewis/film/gap.htm.

Uhlenberg, P. (1980). Death and the family. *Journal of Family History, 5,* 313–320.

Uhlenberg, P. R. (1996). Divorce. In L. A. Vitt & J. K. Siegenthaler (Eds.), *Encyclopedia of financial gerontology* (pp. 137–140). Westport, CT: Greenwood Press.

Uhlenberg, P. R., & Kirby, J. B. (1998). Grandparenthood over time: Historical and demographic trends. In M. Szinovacz (Ed.), *Handbook of grandparenthood* (pp. 23–39). Westport, CT: Greenwood Press.

U.S. Census Bureau. (2000). *Population profile of the United States: 2000 (Internet release).* Chapter 4. Motherhood: The fertility of American women, 2000. Retrieved March 18, 2006, from http://www.census.gov/population/pop-profile/2000/chap04.pdf.

U.S. Department of Health and Human Services, National Center on Child Abuse and Neglect. (1996). *Third national incidence study of child abuse and neglect*. Washington, DC: U.S. Government Printing Office.

U.S. Department of Health and Human Services, National Center on Child Abuse and Neglect. (1999). *Child maltreatment 1997: Reports from the states to the national child abuse and neglect data system*. Washington, DC: U.S. Government Printing Office.

Van Horn, S. H. (1988). *Women, work, and fertility, 1900–1986*. New York: New York University Press.

Van Vliet, W. (Ed.). (1998). *The encyclopedia of housing*. Thousand Oaks, CA: Sage.

Walker, A. (1983). *The color purple*. New York: Washington Square.

Wallen, J. (2002). *Balancing work and family*. Boston: Allyn and Bacon.

Wallerstein, J. S., & Kelly, J. B. (1980). *Surviving the breakup*. New York: Basic Books.

Watson, J. B. (1924). *Behaviorism*. New York: Norton.

Welty, E. (1942). *The robber bridegroom*. Garden City, NJ: Doubleday, Doran.

West, E. (1996). *Growing up in twentieth century America*. Westport, CT: Greenwood Press.

Whyte, W. H. (1956). *The organization man*. New York: Doubleday.

Wilson, M. I., & Daly, M. (1987). Risk of maltreatment of children living with stepparents. In R. J. Gelles & J. B. Lancaster (Eds.), *Child abuse and neglect: Biosocial dimensions* (pp. 215–232). New York: Aldine de Gruyter.

Wilson, S. (1955). *The man in the grey flannel suit*. New York: Simon & Schuster.

Wind, R. (2003). *After three decades of legal abortion, new research documents declines in rates, numbers and access to abortion services* [news release]. Retrieved June 23, 2006, from http://www.guttmacher.org/media/nr/2003/01/15/nr_011003.html.

Wolfe, T. (1929). *Look homeward, angel*. New York: Scribner.

Wolfe, T. (1940). *You can't go home again*. New York: Harper.

Wylie, P. G. (1942). *Generation of vipers*. New York: Ferrar and Rinehart.

Zablocki, B. (1980). *Alienation and charisma*. New York: Free Press.

Zelizer, V. A. (1985). *Pricing the priceless child*. New York: Basic Books.

FOR FURTHER READING

Apple, R. D. (2006). *Perfect motherhood*. Brunswick, NJ: Rutgers University Press.

Apple, R. D., & Gordon, J. (1997). *Mothers and motherhood*. Columbus: Ohio State University Press.

Bailey, B. (1999). *Sex in the heartland.* Cambridge, MA: Harvard University Press.

Braverman, L. (1989). Beyond the myth of motherhood. In M. McGoldrick, C. M. Anderson, & F. Walsh (Eds.), *Women in families* (pp. 227–243). New York: Norton.

Coontz, S. (1992). *The way we never were.* New York: Basic Books.

Coontz, S. (1997). *The way we really are.* New York: Basic Books.

Cox, C. B. (Ed.). (1999). *To grandmother's house we go and stay.* New York: Springer.

Cross, G. (2004). *The cute and the cool.* New York: Oxford University Press.

Demos, J. (1986). *Past, present, and personal.* New York: Oxford University Press.

Ehrenreich, B., & English, D. (2005). *For her own good.* New York: Anchor.

Friedman, A., & Drawitz, D. (2002). *Peeking through the keyhole.* Montreal: McGill-Queen's University Press.

Gordon, L. (1988). *Heroes of their own lives.* New York: Viking.

Hayden, D. (1984). *Redesigning the American dream.* New York: Norton.

Hays, S. (1996). *The cultural contradictions of motherhood.* New Haven, CT: Yale University Press.

Hochschild, A., & Machung, A. (1989). *The second shift.* New York: Viking-Penguin.

Lynd, R. S., & Lynd, H. M. (1937). *Middletown in transition.* New York: Harcourt, Brace.

Mitford, J. (1963). *The American way of death.* New York: Simon & Schuster.

Moore, C. W., Smith, K., & Becker, P. (1983). *Home sweet home.* New York: Rizzoli.

Pizzey, E. (1977). *Scream quietly or the neighbors will hear.* Short Hills, NJ: Ridley Enslow.

Rossi, A., Kagan, J., & Hareven, T. (Eds.). (1978). *The family.* New York: Norton.

Index

About the Authors

MARILYN COLEMAN is Director of Graduate Studies and Curators' Professor in Human Development and Family Studies at the University of Missouri. She has co-authored with Larry Ganong *Stepfamily Relationships: Developments, Dynamics and Intervention* (2004), *Handbook of Contemporary Families: Considering the Past, Contemplating the Future* (2003), *Changing Families, Changing Responsibilities: Family Obligations Following Divorce and Remarriage* (1999) and *Remarried Family Relationships* (1994).

LAWRENCE H. GANONG is Professor in Human Development and Family Studies and the School of Nursing at the University of Missouri. He has co-authored with Marilyn Coleman *Stepfamily Relationships: Developments, Dynamics, and Intervention* (2004), *Handbook of Contemporary Families: Considering the Past, Contemplating the Future* (2003), *Changing Families, Changing Responsibilities: Family Obligations following Divorce and Remarriage* (1999), and *Remarried Family Relationships* (1994).

KELLY WARZINIK obtained her MS in Human Development and Family Studies from the University of Missouri. She previously worked as a family living educator for the University of Wisconsin-Extension.